INSTRUCTOR'S MANUAL AND TEST BANK

FOR

FUNDAMENTALS OF BUSINESS LAW

INSTRUCTOR'S MANUAL AND TEST BANK

FOR

FUNDAMENTALS OF BUSINESS LAW

Rate A. Howell
The Ohio State University

John R. Allison
University of Texas, Austin

N. T. Henley
Georgia State University

THE DRYDEN PRESS
Chicago   New York   Philadelphia
San Francisco   Montreal   Toronto
London   Sydney   Tokyo   Mexico City
Rio de Janeiro   Madrid

© 1984 CBS College Publishing
All rights reserved

Address orders to:
383 Madison Avenue
New York, New York 10017

Address editorial correspondence to:
One Salt Creek Lane
Hinsdale, Illinois 60521

ISBN 0-03-063628-0
Printed in the United States of America
456-066-987654321

CBS College Publishing
The Dryden Press
Holt, Rinehart and Winston
Saunders College Publishing

TABLE OF CONTENTS

PAGE

PART ONE: INTRODUCTION TO THE LEGAL SYSTEM

Chapter 1.   The American Legal System   1
Chapter 2.   Major Bodies of Law   4

PART TWO: PRINCIPLES OF CONTRACT LAW

Chapter 3.   Nature and Classification of Contracts   9
Chapter 4.   The Agreement   14
Chapter 5.   Consideration   20
Chapter 6.   Contractual Capacity   26
Chapter 7.   Illegality   30
Chapter 8.   Reality of Consent   35
Chapter 9.   Contracts in Writing   39
Chapter 10.   Rights of Third Parties   42
Chapter 11.   Discharge of Contracts   45

PART THREE: COMMERCIAL TRANSACTIONS

Chapter 12.   Sales/Introduction to the Law of Sales   50
Chapter 13.   Sales/Formation and Interpretation of the Sales Contract   54
Chapter 14.   Sales/Title, Risk of Loss, and Insurable Interest   58
Chapter 15.   Sales/Warranties   62
Chapter 16.   Sales/Performance and Remedies   67
Chapter 17.   Commercial Paper/Types, Parties, and Basic Concepts   71
Chapter 18.   Commercial Paper/Negotiability   73
Chapter 19.   Commercial Paper/Transfer and Negotiation   78
Chapter 20.   Commercial Paper/Holders in Due Course   82
Chapter 21.   Commercial Paper/Defenses   86
Chapter 22.   Commercial Paper/Liability of the Parties   89
Chapter 23.   Commercial Paper/Checks and the Bank-Depositor Relationship 94
Chapter 24.   Secured Transactions   97
Chapter 25.   Bankruptcy   102

PART FOUR: AGENCY

Chapter 26.   Agency/Nature, Creation, Duties, and Termination   106
Chapter 27.   Agency/Liability of the Parties   109

PART FIVE: BUSINESS ORGANIZATIONS

Chapter 28.   Forms of Business Organizations   114
Chapter 29.   Partnerships/Nature, Formation, and Property   116
Chapter 30.   Partnerships/Operating the Business   120
Chapter 31.   Partnerships/Termination   124
Chapter 32.   Corporations/Nature and Formation   128
Chapter 33.   Corporations/Corporate Powers and Management   132
Chapter 34.   Corporations/Rights and Liabilities of Shareholders and 136
               Managers
Chapter 35.   Corporations/Merger, Consolidation, and Termination   140

PART SIX: PROPERTY AND BAILMENTS

Chapter 36.   Real Property   144
Chapter 37.   Personal Property   148
Chapter 38.   Wills, Trusts, and Estates   152
Chapter 39.   Bailments   156

TEST BANK   163

INSTRUCTOR'S MANUAL AND TEST BANK

FOR

FUNDAMENTALS OF BUSINESS LAW

PART ONE: INTRODUCTION TO THE LEGAL SYSTEM

CHAPTER 1

THE AMERICAN LEGAL SYSTEM

AUTHORS' SUGGESTIONS:

1. The idea should be stressed that the term "law" is so broad and multi-faceted in scope that no single definition is necessarily right or wrong. That is why it can properly be said (under the traditional view) that law consists of rules, and also (under the environmental view) that law consists of legal processes.

2. The term "civil law" sometimes raises a problem because it has several different menaings. It is, for example, often used to refer to that system of jurisprudence administered in the Roman Empire (based on rules set forth in a code), as distinguished from the common law of England. As used in this chapter, however, "civil law" refers to that body of law which determines private rights and liabilities, as distinguished from "criminal law."

3. The requirement that the plaintiff must be asking for more than $10,000 in order to bring an action in the federal courts is applicable only to actions based on diversity of citizenship. Suits that present federal questions, in other words, can be initiated in the federal courts without having to meet the $10,000 requirement.

4. In the case of United States v. Douglas Aircraft Company, we are told that the court instructed the jury, among other things, on the subject of "unavoidable or inevitable accidents." While this is not as important a matter as those of negligence and contributory negligence, the meaning may come up in class. Accordingly, such an accident is defined as "one which could not have been foreseen and prevented by using ordinary diligence, and resulting without fault on the part (of either party)." U.S. v. Kansas City Southern Ry. Co., 189 F. 471.

CASE BRIEFS:

Schultz v. Cheney School District

Facts: Vicki Schultz, passenger on a school bus, was injured when the bus driver lost control of the vehicle after being stung by a bee. She brought this action against the school district, alleging that the driver was guilty of negligence. The trial court was asked by plaintiff to rule that the driver was guilty of negligence as a <u>matter of law</u>. The trial court refused this request and submitted the question of negligence to the jury. Verdict and judgment for defendant school district.

<u>Holding</u>: Judgment for defendant affirmed. Under the facts presented, it was possible for a jury to find either that the driver was guilty of negligence, or was not guilty of negligence. Thus the trial court was correct in refusing to rule as a matter of law that the driver was guilty of negligence. (It was also held that the trial court did not commit error in giving an instruction on "unavoidable accident.")

United States v. Douglas Aircraft Company

<u>Facts</u>: A Douglas plane, while taxiing on a runway, collided with an immobilized government plane. The U.S. brought this action for damages, alleging that the Douglas pilot was guilty of negligence. The government asked the trial court to rule <u>as a matter of law</u> that (a) the Douglas pilot was negligent, and (b) that the government was not guilty of contributory negligence. The court refused this request and submitted both questions to the jury. Verdict and judgment for defendant in trial court.

<u>Holding</u>: Judgment for defendant affirmed. Under the facts adduced at the trial, reasonable men could differ as to whether or not the Douglas pilot was negligent. Therefore, the trial court was correct in submitting both questions to the jury.

ANSWERS TO QUESTIONS AND PROBLEMS:

1. This first question is presented largely because it offers a good class-discussion issue -- one on which most students have an opinion. Obviously it has no right or wrong answer, because the members of the Texas legislature that voted for the statute obviously felt that it was proper for the state to sharply limit the conditions under which abortions could be performed, while the members of the U.S. Supreme Court did not. (In the cited case, <u>Roe v. Wade</u>, the U.S. Supreme Court held that the statute violated the Due Process clause of the federal constitution, thereby ruling -- in effect -- that a pregnant woman has an absolute right to an abortion during the first trimester of pregnancy.)

2. Breach of contract is not a crime simply because the laws of the various states do not impose criminal penalties -- such as a fine or imprisonment -- upon one who breaches his contract. Thus, if X breaches his contract with Y, X's only legal liability is to pay damages to Y (a sum of money to compensate Y for the loss he has incurred) if Y brings a <u>civil suit</u> requesting such relief.

3. The requirement of "certainty" brings about a basic stability in the law. This in turn permits persons to make contracts (and other decisions) knowing that the legal rights which they have acquired through such transactions will not substantially change or be eroded in the future.

4. (a) The requirement of "certainty" would cause the court to be reluctant to effect a change in the law. If existing rules are changed frequently, the law loses its vital quality of stability.

(b) The requirements of "flexibility" and "reasonableness" would certainly permit the court to consider a change in the existing law. If, for example, that rule of law was adopted at an early time when the financial condition of most non-profit institutions was precarious, and if in more recent years such institutions were, in fact, financially sound, then the protection afforded such institutions by the earlier rule would no longer be necessary.

5. Judge-made law continues to govern in those areas of law where the legislatures have chosen not to pass all-encompassing statutes. In the areas of contract law, torts, and agency, especially, the legislatures apparently continue to feel that the common-law rules are bringing about satisfactory results, and that the enactment of legislation in these areas is therefore unnecessary.

6. The district court held that the fact that Hennepin Broadcasting was subject to the rules and regulations of the Federal Communications Commission did not raise any real federal questions, and therefore, the federal district court did not have jurisdiction over the case. The plaintiff did not seek relief under the laws or the Constitution of the United States, but merely asserted a tort action alleging that Hennepin unlawfully interfered with his contract with Arrow. No federal question is in any sense alleged to be an essential part of the plaintiff's suit, and collateral (secondary) federal issues raised in defense are not grounds for removal to federal court.

7. Jackson's request will not be granted. Because the suit was based on diversity of citizenship alone, the plaintiff (Rate) has the sole choice of bringing the suit in a state trial court in Florida or in a U.S. District Court in Florida. (If, on the other hand, the suit were based on a federal statute, Jackson's request to have the suit removed to a federal court would be granted.)

8. There was substantial evidence that Scott, the pilot of the Douglas plane, was actually exercising due care at the time of the collision. Such evidence consisted of (a) the fact that Scott was zig-zagging his plane down the runway in order to have better vision than he would ordinarily have, and (b) the fact that the government plane was camouflaged, which might very well convince the jury that Scott's failure to see it was not the result of carelessness on his part. In the light of such evidence, a judge could not rule, as a matter of law, that Scott was guilty of negligence.

The second ruling of the trial court was also correct. Where there was evidence that the plaintiff, the United States, may have been guilty of negligence in failing to move its aircraft from the runway within a reasonable time, after it had landed, a court could not rule, as a matter of law, that the government was <u>not</u> guilty of negligence.

CHAPTER 2

MAJOR BODIES OF LAW

AUTHORS' SUGGESTIONS:

1. While common-law principles still control several important areas of law, it should be emphasized that most of our law today is statutory (and that the trend in this direction continues).

2. Because two or three cases involving the claim of "negligence" have been encountered in Chapter 1, no case involving the basic elements of this tort (duty owed, breach, damage or injury, proximate cause) appears in this chapter. However, for an additional case for class discussion the class might be asked to read Jasko v. F.W. Woolworth Co., used as Item 10 in the Questions and Problems at the end of this chapter. (A brief for the instructor is found in the Answers at the end of this chapter.)

3. On the subject of statutory interpretation: the term "circumstantial context" perhaps should be given more visibility. The term refers to an examination of the conditions (or problem) that caused the legislature to pass the particular statute in the first place. In the Holy Trinity Church case, for example, the circumstantial context of the statute was the fact that the law was passed to prohibit the importation of manual laborers rather than ministers.

4. Most Supreme Court decisions do not stir up enough popular dissatisfaction to spawn serious efforts to have the decisions nullified by the enactment of constitutional amendments. At least three decisions briefly referred to in the text, however, have produced such efforts (although they have not been successful to date): (1) Engel v. Vitale (school prayer); (2) Brown v. Board of Education (school desegregation); and (3) Roe v. Wade (abortion).

5. The importance of administrative law cannot be over-emphasized. Very few of us are ever involved with the judicial system; in a class of 30 or so students no more than two or three have ever been a party to a lawsuit. Yet each of us is touched daily by the rules and regulations of the administrative agencies.

CASE BRIEFS:

MacPherson v. Buick Motor Company

Facts: Action by MacPherson against the Buick Company alleging that it was guilty of negligence in failing to inspect wheels (which it purchased from a supplier) before putting its automobiles into the stream of commerce, and further alleging that this negligence caused MacPherson to be injured. Buick's defense was based on the argument that under New York case law a negligence action could not be successful since there was no privity of contract between plaintiff and it (i.e., plaintiff did not buy the car directly from Buick). The trial court held for plaintiff, ruling that privity of contract was not necessary.

Holding: Judgment for plaintiff affirmed. The court noted that under New York cases privity was not necessary if the defendant's negligence was of such a nature as to put human life "in imminent danger." It then ruled that a defectively manufactured automobile (like a mislabeled poison) was "reasonably certain to place life and limb in danger."

George v. Breisig

Facts: The owner of a car left it at Breisig's garage for repairs. When the repairs were completed, Breisig left the car on his parking lot with the keys in it so the owner could pick it up that evening. The car was stolen from the lot and the next day a friend of the thief, while driving negligently, struck plaintiff, George. George brought this action alleging that Breisig's act of leaving the keys in the car was negligence, and that this negligence was the proximate cause of his injuries. The trial court rejected this contention, and directed a verdict in favor of defendant Breisig.

Holding: Judgment affirmed. While Breisig owed the car owner the duty to use reasonable care to prevent the theft, he did not owe George such a duty. In other words, the breach of Breisig's duty owed to the car owner did not constitute a breach of any duty owed to George. The proximate cause of George's injuries, therefore, was the negligent driving on the part of the thief's friend, not Breisig's act of leaving the keys in the car.

Holy Trinity Church v. United States

Facts: The United States brought this criminal action against the church, claiming that its employment of an English minister violated a federal statute forbidding the importation of foreigners "to perform labor or service of any kind" in this country. The trial court found the church guilty.

Holding: The U.S. Supreme Court reversed the judgment, ruling that although the church's act was literally a violation of the statute, the real meaning of the statute depended upon its interpretation. After examining the statute's title, circumstantial context, and legislative history, the court concluded that Congress meant only to prohibit the importation of foreign manual laborers, not ministers, and the church did not therefore violate the statute.

Hicklin v. Orbeck

Facts: An Alaskan statute provided that certain employers in the state had to hire qualified Alaskan residents in preference to nonresidents. The law was challenged on the ground that it violated the Privileges and Immunities clause of the U.S. Constitution.

Holding: The U.S. Supreme Court ruled the statute to be unconstitutional. The court conceded that the Privileges and Immunities clause did not prevent a state from treating nonresidents differently from residents if the state had a strong legitimate purpose for doing so. However, the court said (a) that it had not been constitutionally established that the alleviation of unemployment is a sufficient legitimate purpose for the enactment of a special law, and (b) even if the purpose were legitimate, in this case the Alaska Hire Law is still unconstitutional because it was drafted too broadly (i.e., it granted preference to employed as well as unemployed).

ANSWERS TO QUESTIONS AND PROBLEMS:

1. The Supreme Court of Michigan held that the injured persons could recover from the drivers even though it was impossible to determine which injuries were caused by which defendants. The court reasoned that "when we impose upon an injured plaintiff the necessity of proving which impact did which harm in a chain collision situation, what we are actually expressing is a judicial policy that it is better that a plaintiff, injured through no fault of his own, take nothing, than that a tortfeasor pay more than his theoretical share of the damages which his wrong has helped to create." It is obviously unfair to place the burden of proving the specific shares of harm done by each on the injured party.

The better rule might be taken from Cooley on Torts: "Where the negligence of two or more persons concur in producing a single indivisible injury, then such persons are _jointly and severally_ liable, although there was no common duty, common design, or concert action." (Note: "severally liable" means individually liable. Thus in the instant case it means that the one driver who was within the jurisdiction of the court was fully liable for Mrs. Maddux's injuries.)

2. The Supreme Court of New Jersey ruled that lack of privity of contract was not a bar to recovery under the theory of breach of implied warranty of merchantability. While Mrs. Henningson was not a party to any respective warranties, she was a person who, in the reasonable contemplation of the parties to the warranty, might be expected to become a user of the automobile. The implied warranty of merchantability extends to the purchaser of the car, members of his family and to other persons occupying or using it with his consent.

3. The U.S. District Court rejected the state's defense, and found the statute to be unconstitutional. The court ruled that that part of the statute which prohibited the coercion of new-car dealers by automobile manufacturers was valid, because "coercion" normally refers to the use of threats or to some other unlawful pressure. However, the court said, there is nothing inherently bad or unlawful in a manufacturer's attempting to induce new-car dealers to purchase cars, and for that reason the Colorado legislature did not have the power to substantially burden interstate commerce for the particular purpose. In fact, the court said, if a state were permitted to prohibit sellers of goods from inducing buyers to buy, such a prohibition would virtually eliminate all of the salesmanship and the marketing of new products that are so essential to "the American way of life." The court also noted that while a state might _regulate_ inducement, this statute absolutely _prohibited_ it.

4. The U.S. Supreme Court, in reversing the convictions, ruled that the ordinance in question violated the due process clause.

The court said, in part, "We are relegated . . . to the words of the ordinance. If three or more people meet together on a sidewalk or street corner, they must conduct themselves so as not to annoy any police officer or other person who should happen by. In our opinion, the ordinance is unconstitutionally vague because it subjects the exercise of the right of free assembly to an unascertained standard. . . Conduct that annoys some people does not annoy others. Thus, the ordinance is vague not only in the sense that it requires a person to conform his conduct to an imprecise normative standard, but rather in the sense that no standard of conduct is specified at all. As a result, 'men of common intelligence must necessarily guess at its meaning.' "

5. Two interpretative points are at least arguable: (1) that a hang glider is not an "aircraft," and (2) that the occupant of a hang glider does not have sufficient control to be "piloting" it. Additionally it may be argued that the federal government has "pre-empted the field" in this area of law -- i.e., that the control of airspace is essentially in the hands of the federal government, rather than in the states.

6. The Supreme Court agreed with the State of Montana that the regulation was constitutional -- i.e., did not violate the privileges and immunities clause. The court first agreed with the state that the protection of wildlife in Montana was a legitimate matter of state regulation. Secondly, and perhaps more importantly, the court said that the privileges and immunities clause applies only to nonresidents' rights that are basic to the maintenance or well-being of the Union, and it held that "access by nonresidents to recreational big-game hunting in Montana" did not fall in this category. In other words, the court said that the right which Baldwin sought protection of was simply too inconsequential in nature to merit constitutional protection.

7. The U.S. Supreme Court held that the statute constituted discriminatory treatment against those who were unable to pay a fine and court costs. An indigent may not be confined under the Equal Protection Clause beyond the maximum term specified by statute simply because of his failure to pay fines and court costs.

8. The U.S. Supreme Court upheld the appellant's contention. On a question such as this, the court said, the test is whether or not "the mayor's situation is one which would offer a possible temptation to the average man as a judge to forget the burden of proof required to convict the defendant."

(Note: In its decision, the court took pains to point out that it was not invalidating convictions in *all* mayors' courts in Ohio. It said, for example, that it would continue to uphold convictions occurring in such courts in those cases where it was shown that the mayors possessed very limited executive powers -- such as might be the case, for example, where a City Manager and/or a Commission had the responsibility for financial affairs, rather than the Mayor.)

9. The employer might challenge the fine on grounds that the statute creating OSHA lacked "standards and guidelines" and was therefore an unconstitutional delegation of power by Congress.

   The employer could seek judicial review of the fine levied by OSHA claiming that the agency had acted arbitrarily or capriciously or had abused its discretion.

10. The Supreme Court of Colorado held the store's practice of selling slices of pizza on wax paper to customers who consumed them while standing in aisles created a reasonable possibility of danger to customers. Because this danger resulted directly from Woolworth's operating methods, and because this dangerous condition was a continuous one and easily foreseeable, the company's employment of a worker to sweep up the area was not a sufficiently effective way to deal with the danger. Accordingly, Woolworth was found to be guilty of negligence and liable in damages to Mrs. Jasko.

PART TWO: PRINCIPLES OF CONTRACT LAW

CHAPTER 3

NATURE AND CLASSIFICATION OF CONTRACTS

AUTHORS' SUGGESTIONS:

1. It is probable that students are generally aware of the important role that contract law plays in their daily lives. However, if additional emphasis is needed by way of introduction to the subject, the statement of a judge on an Ohio court of appeals may be cited. His observation: "In my opinion, half of the legal disputes that reach my court (excluding criminal cases) would never have arisen if the parties had had even a rudimentary knowledge of the principles of contract law."

2. Of the various classifications of contracts appearing in this chapter, the express/implied/quasi-contract classification is probably the most useful to the student. In that regard, this major distinction should be underlined: while express and implied contracts arise only as a result of a real or apparent <u>agreement</u> between the parties, quasi-contracts are found to exist by the courts (in limited situations) <u>without</u> <u>regard</u> to whether any kind of agreement had actually been entered into between the parties.

3. A further example of a situation in which a quasi-contractual obligation was imposed is the case of <u>Sommers v. Board of Education</u>, 148 N.E. 682 (1925). There an Ohio school board had a legal obligation under state law to transport all children to school who lived more than four miles from the nearest high school. When the board refused Sommers' request to transport his children, he drove them to school and back for an entire school year. He then brought an action against the board to recover his expenses in so doing, and to recover the value of his services. The Supreme Court of Ohio required the board to reimburse Sommers under the quasi-contract theory. (Obviously, neither an express or implied contract had been made.) The court said that if reimbursement were not ordered, the board would have been unjustly enriched (i.e., it would have received the services of Sommers for nothing, where he was performing a duty which the board by law was obligated to perform).

CASE BRIEFS:

Judd Realty, Inc. v. Tedesco

Facts: Tedesco signed a listing contract under which he agreed to pay a real estate firm (Judd Realty) a commission of 8% if it found a "purchaser" willing to pay $25,000 for a lot he wanted to sell. The firm produced a qualified buyer, but Tedesco refused the buyer's offer to purchase. When Judd Realty sued for its commission, Tedesco contended that there was no "purchaser" in this case in view of the fact that no sale of the land ever took place. The trial court agreed with this contention and dismissed the action. Judd Realty appealed.

Holding: Judgment reversed. A listing contract is a unilateral offer which is accepted by the performance of an *act* by the real estate firm --- i.e., the production of a buyer able and willing to buy the property on the listed terms. Thus a contract between Tedesco and Judd Realty was formed the moment that the firm produced a qualified buyer. Judd Realty at that time produced a "purchaser," obligating Tedesco to pay it its commission; it is irrelevant whether or not Tedesco actually sold the land to such purchaser.

Rockwell & Bond, Inc. v. Flying Dutchman

Facts: Rockwell & Bond (RB), a contracting firm, began remodeling work for the Flying Dutchman Restaurant (FD). The drawings at this time were tentative, and RB "estimated" that the cost would be about $55,000-$60,000. Work continued for a period of time, with the president of FD present almost every day (and making numerous changes in the original plans as work progressed). Later, when RB billed FD for $100,000 for the job, FD contended that an *express* contract existed between the parties, under which the maximum cost was to be $60,000. The trial court ruled that no express contract was formed, but, on the contrary, an *implied* contract existed under which RB was entitled to the $100,000. FD appealed.

Holding: Judgment affirmed. No express contract existed because the "terms" --- drawings and estimate --- were too vague. An implied contract, however, *was* formed. When the president of FD made the continuous requests for the work, he thereby *impliedly* promised (offered) to pay RB a reasonable sum for all of the work rendered in response to these requests. When RB performed the requested work, it thereby accepted this offer, which resulted in the formation of an *implied contract* between the parties. RB is thus entitled to the larger sum.

Deskovick v. Porzio

Facts: The Deskovicks, brothers, paid their father's hospital bills under the impression that he was not financially able to do so. After their father's death it was discovered that his estate was adequate to pay all of such bills, whereupon the brothers brought this action against the estate to recover the payments made. In the trial court the plaintiffs sought recovery on the theory that an implied contract had been entered into between them and their father while he was in the hospital. The trial court ruled as a matter of law that no implied contract was formed. Plaintiffs appealed, contending now that they should recover on the quasi-contract principle.

Holding: The higher court made two points. (a) No implied contract was formed since the father did not know that the payments were being made; thus he could not give his implied consent to repay the sons. (b) However, the court agreed that if the facts were as the plaintiffs alleged them to be, then this was a situation where recovery should be allowed on the basis of quasi-contract, for if no recovery were allowed the sons, then the estate would be unjustly enriched. (The reason why the case was remanded to the trial court, instead of granting judgment outright to the plaintiffs, was so that a true determination of facts could be made; this was not done by the trial court since it ruled the estate was not liable as a matter of law even if plaintiffs' version of facts was correct.)

ANSWERS TO QUESTIONS AND PROBLEMS:

1. The Appellate Court of Illinois held that an express unilateral contract existed, which bound the corporation to pay Redd (the subcontractor) for his time and materials. It was clear, the court said, that no express bilateral contract, oral or written, was ever formed. However, it ruled that the corporation's promise to Redd was a unilateral offer, and that this offer was accepted when Redd performed the requested act --- the construction of the barn.

2. The Supreme Court of Ohio held that the father could recover money reimbursement under a quasi-contract theory. In order to recover, the father had to prove the following elements: (1) the obligation was of such a nature that actual and prompt performance is of grave public concern; (2) the School Board must have failed or refused to perform the service with knowledge of the facts to perform the obligation; and (3) the father, who intervened, must, under the circumstances, be a proper person to perform the duty.

All of these elements, the court said, were present in this case. The performance of the board's legal obligation (the transporting of the child) was obviously a benefit to the School Board because it saved them from the necessity of performing the duty themselves. If the board were permitted to retain this benefit without charge, it would obviously be unjustly enriched; thus the imposition of quasi-contractual liability was proper.

3. The primary reason why no _implied_ contract existed between Deskovick and his sons was the fact that Deskovick did not know that his sons were paying his hospital expenses and doctor bills. Without this knowledge, it was not possible for Deskovick to indicate, in any way, that he would repay the sons for their expenditures.

4. The Superior Court of New Jersey held that Oakwood Homes was _not_ liable on the quasi-contract theory.

The court said that a "common thread" running through the cases (in which recovery on this theory was allowed) was a showing by the plaintiff that he reasonably expected remuneration _from the defendant_ at the time the benefit was conferred. The court also said, "It is further noted that the quasi-contract cases involve either some _direct_ relationship between the parties or a mistake on the part of the person conferring the benefit."

In this case, there was _no direct relationship_ between Callano and Oakwood Homes, and no mistake on Callano's part. Therefore, while Callano's work did "enrich" the value of the property, the court held that it would not, under the circumstances, be "unjust" to permit Oakwood Homes to recover the improved property without liability to Callano. In other words, Oakwood Homes was blameless in this situation. (As a result, the court said, Callano's only cause of action was against Pendergast's estate to enforce the express contract he had made with Pendergast prior to his death.)

5. The Supreme Court of Wisconsin held that the contractor could not recover the reasonable value of the wall under the quasi-contract theory. The evidence showed that Mrs. Gilligan, the landowner, did _not_ unjustly retain the benefit of the breakwater in these particular circumstances. First, the court noted, the breakwater was built when Mrs. Gilligan was absent from the premises; she had never contemplated that particular kind of structure being built, and never indicated a desire to obtain the breakwater after it was built. (In fact, she demanded that it be removed.) Under these circumstances, the quasi-contract theory is inapplicable. (I.e., Mrs. Gilligan was no way at fault, and was not _willfully_ retaining the benefit of the wall.)

6. S' contention is not correct. While it is the general rule that a decree of specific performance will not be granted unless the plaintiff can show that the subject matter of the contract is unique, a major exception to the rule exists in regard to contracts calling for the sale of real property (i.e., land and buildings). Thus, the buyer of a particular parcel of land is entitled to receive the very parcel which he has agreed to buy, the courts taking the view that every parcel of land is unique _as a matter of law_.

7. The Second Circuit ruled that an injunction was a proper remedy. Whether

an injunction shall be issued under such circumstances rests in the sound discretion of the court. The District Court found that the defendant's services in this case _were_ unique and extraordinary. A negative covenant in a contract for such personal services is enforceable by injunction where the damages for a breach are incapable of ascertainment.

CHAPTER 4

THE AGREEMENT

AUTHORS' SUGGESTIONS:

1. This chapter deals essentially with the rules that determine whether a contract has been formed as a result of the exchange of communications, with each party perhaps bargaining with the other in order to get the most favorable contract possible. However, it is well to point out in class that many other contracts come into existence everyday with little or no bargaining; that is, one person presents a detailed proposal (offer) to the other on a take-it-or-leave-it basis. (One example is the landlord who presents a tenant with a standard lease form to sign; another is the retailer selling goods on credit who requires the buyer to sign a standard security agreement.) Contracts formed in this way are called <u>contracts of adhesion</u>, with the one asked to sign having little or no bargaining power insofar as his ability to make changes in the proposal is concerned. Such contracts are generally lawful unless their terms are so extremely one-sided as to be considered by the courts to be "unconscionable."

2. In regard to the <u>Richards</u> case, it can be noted that while the trial court reached the right result (no contract), it did so on the wrong grounds. The trial court ruled that Flowers was not liable for the reason that, although there was an offer and acceptance insofar as ordinary contract law was concerned, the written terms of Mrs. Richards' acceptance were not complete enough to satisfy a California statute requiring land contracts to be in writing. The appellate court, on the other hand, ruled that no contract was ever formed for the reason that Flowers' response to Mrs. Richards' inquiry was <u>not an offer</u> in the first place. Thus Mrs. Richards' "acceptance" of Flowers' response could not result in the formation of a contract.

3. One point in the <u>Lucier</u> case ties in with a subject discussed in an earlier chapter, the subject of quasi-contracts. The trial court, after ruling that no express contract was formed between Lucier and the town for the reason that there was merely an offer and a counter-offer, nevertheless required the town to pay him $35 for one day he actually drove the bus. The

imposition of this liability was based on the quasi-contract principle; if liability were not imposed, the town would have been unjustly enriched.

4. On the subject of <u>indirect revocations</u>, please see answer to Question Six in "Answers to Questions and Problems" at the end of this chapter.

CASE BRIEFS:

Richards v. Flowers et. al.

<u>Facts</u>: Mrs. Richards inquired if Flowers would be interested in selling a piece of ground he owned. Flowers replied, "Considering what I paid for the lot, and the taxes which I have paid, I expect to receive $4,500 for this property." Mrs. Richards then wired her "acceptance" of Flowers' terms. When Flowers later refused to convey the property, Mrs. Richards sued him for damages for breach of contract, contending that Flowers' reply to her inquiry <u>constituted an offer to sell</u>, and that her wire was an acceptance of that offer. The trial court ruled that there <u>was</u> an offer and an acceptance, but it further ruled that the contract was invalid because its terms were not sufficiently in writing (and thus did not meet the requirements of a special California statute applicable to land contracts). Mrs. Richards appealed.

<u>Holding</u>: Judgment for Flowers affirmed. The court ruled that the response did not **constitute** a definite offer to sell the land from a legal standpoint, but, rather, was merely a preliminary negotiation; thus Mrs. Richards' wire could not constitute an acceptance, and no contract was ever formed. Flowers' letter failed to qualify as a definite offer to sell for two reasons: (1) the language "I expect to receive $4,500 . . . " did not indicate an unequivocal intent to sell, and (2) this was particularly true where he was merely responding to a suggestion or inquiry of a tentative nature which was initiated by Mrs. Richards.

Rivers v. Beadle

<u>Facts</u>: A real estate agent, Ms. Rivers, entered into a written agreement with the Beadles. Under the terms of the agreement, the Beadles were to build a "speculative home" on each of three lots, and Ms. Rivers was to have the exclusive right to sell the homes at a set commission. The homes were never built, and Ms. Rivers brought this action for damages for breach of contract. The Beadles defended on the ground that the terms of the agreement were too vague to constitute a contract. The trial court rejected this defense and entered judgment for Ms. Rivers.

<u>Holding</u>: Affirmed. The appellate court held that, under the circumstances surrounding the formation of the agreement, the term "speculative home" was

reasonably definite; that it meant a home "of the type and price of homes being then generally built and sold in the area." Accordingly, the agreement constituted a contract and the Beadles were liable for damages arising out of their breach of the contract.

Green's Executors v. Smith

Facts: Smith, owner of a garage, brought this action to hold Mrs. Green liable on an alleged contract. Smith's contention was that he legally communicated the terms of an offer (appearing in a note in a folder mailed to Mrs. Green), and that she accepted the offer by continuing to have her car garaged at his establishment. Mrs. Green, who did not read the note, claimed that the note was not legally communicated to her under the circumstances, and that she was thus not bound by its provisions. The trial court ruled that the note was legally communicated to Mrs. Green, and judgment was thus granted to plaintiff, Smith.

Holding: Judgment reversed. Where the language on the cover of the folder merely indicated that new service rates were contained inside, with nothing to indicate that there was a substantial change of patrons' liability also included inside (arising out of the note contained therein), the terms of the note inside were not legally communicated to Mrs. Green. She did not, therefore, have a legal duty to examine the inside terms and conditions to see if any provisions in addition to the new service rates were included. Accordingly, the terms of the note were not incorporated into the new agreement, and Smith's action to recover from her a sum of money which he had paid to an injured third person thus fails.

Lucier v. Town of Norfolk

Facts: Lucier offered to drive a school bus at "$175 per week" for the 1920-21 school year. The town school board, after receiving the bid, voted to award him the contract "at $35 per day." Later Lucier contended that a contract had been formed at $175 per week, and the board contended that a contract had been formed at $35 per day. The trial court, ruling that there was merely an offer by Lucier and a counter-offer by the board, held that no contract was entered into and that the board was thus not liable for damages arising out of its refusal to employ Lucier.

Holding: Judgment affirmed. Under Lucier's offer he would be entitled to $175 for every school week, even those weeks in which a holiday fell. Under the board's action, however, Lucier would be entitled only to $35 for each day he actually drove during a week. Thus the trial court was correct in ruling that an offer and a counter-offer were made, which did not result in the formation of a contract. (The court also ruled that the statements made by the board member, Stevens, were of no legal consequence insofar as Lucier's argument was concerned. First, Stevens was not authorized by the board to legally convey its action to Lucier, and, secondly, even if authority existed, Stevens could not legally vary the actual terms of the board's resolution, which were $175 per week.)

Cushing v. Thomson

Facts: An officer of the New Hampshire National Guard sent a letter to the Clamshell Alliance, offering to rent its armory to the alliance for a given night at a specified sum. Cushing (a member of the alliance) accepted the proposal by signing it. He then put proposal in the "outbox" in the alliance's office, but there was no evidence when the acceptance actually reached the U.S. mails. On the evening of the next day, while the acceptance was in the mail, the officer called Cushing to say he was revoking the offer. In subsequent litigation, the question was whether a valid acceptance had occurred prior to the attempted revocation. The trial court ruled that such an acceptance _had_ occurred, and the national guard appealed.

Holding: Judgment affirmed. Where the offer was sent by mail, the acceptance is valid when placed in the U.S. mails. Since there was evidence that mail in the outbox was picked up daily for delivery to the U.S. mails, the trial court was correct in ruling that the acceptance was presumably in the U.S. mails prior to the time of the attempted telephonic revocation. Result: a contract existed between the parties.

ANSWERS TO QUESTIONS AND PROBLEMS:

1. The Supreme Court of Arizona held that no contract was formed, because there was such a lack of specified material terms that "the parties cannot be said to have shown a mutual assent to incur contractual obligations." The court pointed out that in most construction contracts there are certain provisions that are ordinarily felt by the parties to be essential; e.g., provisions relating to manner of payment, time for completion, penalties in the event of late performance, and bonding. In this case, all of these elements were absent; only the price and the work involved were agreed upon. The court concluded by saying that "courts cannot be contract makers" for parties who themselves have not made a contract.

2. The Court of Appeals of Maryland ruled that no contract was ever created. The resolution authorizing the sale of the stock was clearly not in itself an offer, since it required the president subsequently to determine which employees would be entitled to buy the stock. And, the court said, the statement of the president at a salesmen's meeting was too general to constitute an offer, and thus failed to manifest an intent to contract. As a result, when McGinn later told the president he wanted some of the stock, McGinn's statement was _not_ an acceptance of an offer, but rather merely an offer to purchase that was never accepted by the corporation.

3. A contract does not exist. The New York Supreme Court held that the letter of the Nelson's "cannot be regarded as an offer. On its 'face', it expresses the price at which Nelson would _not_ sell, rather than the price at which he _would_ sell. They were words of negation, and although they may have _invited_ _an_ _offer_ (from Blakeslee), they clearly constituted no offer (in and of themselves)."

(_Note_: For class discussion purposes, this question may be put: "If the Nelsons, after receiving Blakeslee's original letter, had written back saying that they were _accepting_ his offer of $49,000 for their property, would a contract at $49,000 now exist between the parties?" The answer is quite clearly no, for the reason that Blakeslee's letter is merely an _inquiry_, rather than an offer to purchase.)

4. While there may be cases to the contrary, the court would probably rule in favor of the company. In the instant case, the Supreme Court of Wisconsin entered judgment for the Pilgrim Village.

The court first cited Section 32 of the _Restatement of Contracts_, reciting the familiar view that an offer must be definite, and then quoted "comment b" to that section as follows: "Promises may be indefinite in time or in place, or in the work or things to be given in exchange for the promise. In dealing with such cases the law endeavors to give a sufficiently clear meaning to offers and promises where the parties intended to enter into a bargain, but _in_ _some_ _cases_ _this_ _is_ _impossible_." (Emphasis added.)

The court then ruled that Pilgrim Village's promise to pay "a share of the profits" was too indefinite to constitute an offer, in view of the fact that "the parties never came to any agreement as to what that percentage of the profits was to be."

5. The court felt that there were at least two reasons why the note was not legally communicated to Mrs. Green. First, the title of the folder did not in any way call to her attention the fact that there was a proposal on the inside page which, if accepted by her, would very substantially enlarge her liability to Smith if an accident occurred while her car was being driven between her home and his garage. Secondly, the enclosure of the folder with her regular monthly bill did not give adequate visibility to the terms of the folder. That is, the attention of any patron receiving the envelope was primarily concerned with the regular bill, not with any additional printed matter that also happened to be enclosed. (The main purpose of the letter, in other words, was only to notify the patron of the amount owing.)

6. The issue is whether or not an _indirect_ _revocation_ had occurred in this fact-pattern. While the text does not mention this topic, an indirect revocation is effective if the offeree has received "reliable information" that the offeror has changed his mind --- i.e., the offeree has received the information via some person or agency other than the offeror himself. In

this particular case, where the radio station merely indicated that the sale of the land to a third party had "purportedly" occurred, it is probable that this information is <u>not</u> sufficiently reliable or definite to effect a legal termination of the offer. Thus the subsequent mailing of the acceptance by the offeree probably resulted in the formation of a contract.

7. The Cator Company is not correct. Under the UCC section referred to, the Sooner Company's response to the Gator Company's offer <u>constitutes an acceptance</u> despite the fact that it contains a term that was not embodied in the offer. In other words, while the Sooner Company's response is probably a counter-offer under contract law because of the new term, it is an <u>acceptance</u> under Sec. 2-207 of the UCC. (Whether the new term also became a part of the contract is a different question. Probably it did not, because it appears that it "materially alters" the term of the offer.)

8. A contract was formed on December 21, when Tayloe deposited his acceptance in the mail.

In this early case, one of the relatively few involving contract law to reach the U.S. Supreme Court, that court affirmed the general rule that an acceptance of an offer made by mail was effective the moment it was placed in the mail.

Where the parties are communicating by mail, the court said, "it is obviously impossible . . . to perfect a contract by correspondence if a <u>knowledge</u> of both parties at the (precise) moment they become bound is an essential element in making out the obligation. * * * It therefore seems to us more consistent with the acts and declarations of the parties to consider it (the contract) complete on the transmission of the acceptance of the offer in the way they themselves contemplated, instead of postponing its completion till notice of such acceptance has been received by the (offeror)."

CHAPTER 5

CONSIDERATION

AUTHORS' SUGGESTIONS:

1. As a practical matter, the subject of consideration is probably not as important as the subject of offer and acceptance (treated in the prior chapter), and the subjects covered in the chapters that follow. Accordingly, if the instructor wishes to emphasize only the broad aspects of consideration in class, they would be these: (a) the general concept (legal detriment); (b) application of the general rules to three "real life" situations (i.e., modification of contracts, requirements contracts, and debt settlement agreements); and (c) the type of situation in which a substitute for consideration --- promissory estoppel --- is accepted by the courts.

2. As an introduction to the general concept of consideration, the following illustration has been found to be helpful in class. X, a long-time employee of the Y Corporation, decided to retire. Thereafter, on X's last day of work, X was given a letter signed by the board of directors of the corporation which was, in essence, a promise by the corporation that it would pay X $100 a month as long as he should live. When the corporation stopped making payments after the first three months of his retirement, X brought suit to recover damages for breach of contract (i.e., X sought to hold the corporation liable on its promise). Result? The corporation is not liable on its promise, since X (the promisee) did nothing in return for the promise. That is, consideration on the promisee's part was lacking, making the promise unenforceable.

3. Probably the two most important points regarding the subject of promissory estoppel are these: (a) the rationale underlying the concept (i.e., the prevention of injustice to promisees in certain situations where, because of the absence of consideration on their parts, they would normally be given no recovery against the promisors), and (b) the fact that the concept does not repeal or supersede the requirement that, in general, consideration must be present (i.e., the situations to which the concept is applicable are exceptional).

CASE BRIEFS:

Hamer v. Sidway

Facts: Story promised to pay his nephew $5,000 if he refrained from drinking, using tobacco, swearing, and playing cards and billiards for money until he became 21. The nephew refrained from these activities, but the administrator of the uncle's estate refused payment on the ground that the nephew's conduct did not constitute consideration. More specifically, the administrator argued that the nephew (promisee), by refraining from the specified activities, did not incur a detriment but, rather, received a benefit. The trial court accepted this argument and thus ruled the promise of the uncle was unenforceable because of this lack of consideration.

Holding: Judgment for the estate was reversed. Since the nephew had a legal right to engage in the specified activities, by refraining from those activities he gave up a legal right (i.e., incurred a legal detriment) regardless of whether or not he may have been physically benefitted. Thus, the nephew did give consideration, with the result that the uncle's estate is liable on the promise to pay the $5,000. (Note: in case the nephew did not have the legal right to engage in some of those activities under New York law, he still would have given consideration as long as he had a legal right under the law to engage in at least one of the specified activities.)

Lampley v. Celebrity Homes, Inc.

Facts: Action by an employee of Celebrity Homes, Linda Lampley, to enforce a profit-sharing plan under which all employees were to receive bonuses if a specified "profit goal" were reached by the end of the 1975 fiscal year. The company defended on the ground that there was no consideration on Lampley's part to support the company's promise to pay the bonus. (More specifically, the company's argument was that Lampley was already an employee when the profit sharing plan went into effect, and that she was not asked to do anything extra in order to receive the bonus.)

Holding: The trial court was correct in rejecting the company's defense. Institution of the profit-sharing plan resulted in the company's receiving a benefit --- increased productivity, a higher quality operation, and better performance for its customers. Additionally, Lampley presumably incurred a detriment by staying in the company's employ (in order to get the bonus) longer than would otherwise have been the case. Thus, under either the "benefit to the promisor" or the "detriment to the promisee" tests, the company's promise was supported by consideration (and is thus binding upon it).

Quarture v. Allegheny County et. al.

Facts: Sniderman, a lawyer, contracted to represent Quarture in a lawsuit against Allegheny County to recover damages incurred as a result of the county taking some of Quarture's land for highway purposes. Quarture, in return, was to pay Sniderman 10% of the sum received from the county. The contract also provided that Sniderman would handle the case "to final determination" for this fee. When Quarture was awarded only $1,650 he made a new contract under which he promised to pay Sniderman 33-1/3% of any sum recovered if Sniderman would handle the case on appeal. Sniderman did so, with the result that Quarture was awarded $2,961. When Sniderman asked the court for one-third of that sum, Quarture contended that his promise to pay the one-third was not supported by consideration on Sniderman's part. The trial court rejected that contention and awarded Sniderman one-third of the $2,961.

Holding: Judgment for Sniderman reversed. Under the original contract, Sniderman promised not only to try the case initially for 10% of what was recovered, but also to handle any appeal for the same percentage. (This was so because under the original contract Sniderman agreed to handle the case "to final determination" if necessary, for the 10% fee.) Since Sniderman thus had a pre-existing obligation under the first contract to handle the appeal, his actual work in appealing the case did _not_ constitute the giving of consideration. Result: Quarture's promise to pay the higher percentage was not supported by consideration, and he is thus not liable on that promise.

Laclede Gas Company v. Amoco Oil Company

Facts: Amoco contracted to deliver quantities of propane gas to Laclede Gas Co. for a minimum period of one year. The contract gave Laclede the right to cancel the contract after one year, by giving 30 day notice to Amoco, but did not **give** Amoco a right to cancel. When Amoco refused to carry out its obligations under the contract several months later, Laclede sued it for damages. Amoco contended that the contract was not binding on it from the start, for the reason that there was no consideration on Laclede's part (as a result of Laclede's right to cancel).

Holding: Judgment for plaintiff, Laclede. _If_ the contract had given Laclede the _unrestricted_ right to cancel the contract at any time, then there would have been no consideration on its part and Amoco's contention would have been correct. However, in this case Laclede's right to cancel was limited --- i.e., it could not cancel during the first year, and only then after giving 30-days notice. Thus, there was consideration on Laclede's part, and Amoco is accordingly liable for damages for breach of contract.

Hoffman v. Red Owl Stores, Inc.

Facts: A Red Owl representative advised Hoffman that if he would sell his grocery store in Wautoma, Wisconsin, he would be given a Red Owl franchise within a few months. After selling the store, Hoffman was told that he must also sell a building he owned in Wautoma in order to finance the anticipated franchise. Hoffman sold the building, but Red Owl never did build the new store which it had indicated would be built, and it never did grant him a franchise. When Hoffman brought this action to recover damages for breach of contract, Red Owl claimed that its promises were not supported by consideration on his part. The trial court agreed that there was no consideration on Hoffman's part, but it nonetheless entered judgment for him on the theory that Red Owl was liable under the doctrine of promissory estoppel. The company appealed.

Holding: Judgment affirmed. The court said that Hoffman's acts of selling his business and building were not only substantial in nature, but also were, under the circumstances, made in reasonable reliance upon Red Owl's assurances. Since a failure to hold Red Owl liable on its assurances would thus cause substantial injustice to Hoffman, the court held that the doctrine of promissory estoppel was properly applied by the trial court (thus causing Red Owl to be liable for breach of its promises).

ANSWERS TO QUESTIONS AND PROBLEMS:

1. The Supreme Court of Washington ruled that Browning's promise to pay the $40,000 was supported by consideration. Browning bargained for Johnson's act of giving up the contract of sale (i.e., giving up his rights to receive Browning's practice), and Johnson, by giving up the contract, clearly incurred a detriment.

2. Grombach's contention was rejected. In April of 1953, when Oerlikon asked for Grombach's promise to extend its right of cancellation to June 30, Oerlikon had the right to cancel the contract immediately. When Grombach then made the requested promise to Oerlikon, there was consideration given by Oerlikon because it thereby gave up its right to cancel the contract immediately. Grombach's promise, therefore, was an enforceable one, with the result that Oerlikon did have the right to cancel the contract at the later date (June 24).

3. Under the usual rule, Leggett is not bound by his promise to pay the additional sum.

The Supreme Court of Mississippi, in denying a recovery by Vinson beyond the $3,950, said: "The great weight of authority seems to establish as the general rule the proposition that a promise to do what a party is already legally bound to do is not a sufficient consideration to support a promise by the other party to the contract to give the former additional compensation, . . . and such a promise cannot be legally enforced although the other party has completed his contract in reliance upon it. Mere inadequacy of the contract price which is the result of an error of judgment on the part of the contractor is insufficient, and nothing more is made in this case. The contractor (as a result of the owner's promise to pay the amount over the contract price of $3,950) assumed no obligations or burdens other than those already imposed."

4. This promise is not binding on the Hy-Test Company. On the limited facts presented, the promise is clearly not supported by consideration on the part of the promisee, Lang. Lang did nothing in return for this promise, nor was he asked to do any act in return for the promise.

5. The Supreme Court of New Mexico held that the dealer's promise to hold the car for the balance due was not supported by consideration on Knoebel's part. In order to constitute consideration for a creditor's extension of time for payment of a debt, there must be a benefit received by the creditor/promisor, or a detriment incurred by the debtor/promisee. In this case the creditor did not receive from Knoebel anything that he (the dealer) could not otherwise demand under the original contract, nor did the debtor (Knoebel) obligate himself to do something that he was not already otherwise bound to do under the original contract. Thus, the dealer's promise to hold the car was a naked promise, and he was, accordingly, not bound by it. Result: Knoebel's suit was dismissed.

6. The Court of Appeals of New York held that the father's **argument** ("lack of consideration on the part of his daughter and her fiance") was not valid. Accordingly, he was held liable for damages for breach of contract. The court conceded that the daughter and her fiance were legally bound to marry each other as a result of their engagement contract --- i.e., neither had the right, alone, to cancel the agreement. However, the court observed, the parties to an executory (unperformed) contract always have the right to mutually cancel the contract. Thus, when the father made his promise and subsequently the parties did actually marry, the parties thereby gave up the right to mutually cancel the contract, and thus they both incurred a detriment --- that is, gave consideration. (Had the father's promise been to pay one of the parties alone, however, there would not have been consideration, since one party alone does not have the right to cancel a contract.)

7. Walquist is bound by his promise to release, and he will thus be unable to recover any additional damages from Christensen. This is so because, as explained below, the payment of $500 by Christensen --- the promisee --- constituted consideration under the circumstances.

The importance of this case: whenever one person has an alleged claim against another, the validity of which has not been judicially determined, the "unliquidated debt" rule is applicable. In a claim arising out of an alleged tort, then, the person against whom the claim is asserted has a legal right to have his liability --- if any --- determined by a court. Therefore, when such person makes a payment to the claimant in return for the latter's promise to release, the person making the payment --- in this case, Christensen --- has thereby given up the legal right to contest the claim in court. It is the waiver of this right by Christensen which constitutes consideration and which causes Walquist's release to be binding.

8. There was no true consideration on Mrs. Harmon's part, since her act of retirement was not requested by the company as a condition of payment. However, the company *is* liable on the principle of promissory estoppel. Under the facts of this case, the company's president should have realized that the promise would induce --- and did induce --- Mrs. Harmon to retire immediately.

CHAPTER 6

CONTRACTUAL CAPACITY

AUTHORS' SUGGESTIONS:

1. It is helpful at the outset to explain, procedurally, the two different ways in which disaffirmance problems may arise. The first situation occurs where the minor pays <u>cash</u> at the time of making the contract, and then later wishes to disaffirm. In that situation, the minor is the plaintiff, attempting to recover the purchase price. In the second situation, the minor purchases goods <u>on</u> <u>credit</u>, and then, after deciding to disaffirm, simply refuses to make any payment. In that case, the minor is ordinarily the defendant, being sued for the purchase price by the competent party. Regardless of how the cases arise, however, the basic issues remain the same --- e.g., was the person seeking to disaffirm actually a minor when making the contract; did a ratification take place prior to the disaffirmance; was the article purchased by the minor a necessity or not?

2. The majority rule applicable to non-necessities, under which the minor need only return the article (if able) in order to recover the full purchase price, obviously causes a loss to the competent party in many cases. Such a result is, in fact, one of the basic purposes of the majority rule, since this result tends to make sellers <u>refuse</u> <u>to</u> <u>deal</u> <u>with</u> <u>minors</u> <u>at</u> <u>all</u> (unless, of course, their parent or guardian consents). By thus making it somewhat more difficult for minors to find persons who will enter contracts with them, the law to this extent "protects the minors from their follies" --- i.e., the fewer contracts made by minors, the fewer foolish or one-sided contracts will result.

CASE BRIEFS:

<u>Hogue et. al. v. Wilkinson</u>

<u>Facts</u>: Wilkinson, a minor, brought this action to recover the full purchase price of a number of chinchillas he had purchased from defendants Hogue and

McCoy. Defendants contended that plaintiff was not entitled to the full price because some of the chinchillas had died as a result of plaintiff's negligence. The trial court rejected this contention and permitted plaintiff to recover the full price. Defendants appealed.

Holding: Judgment affirmed. Under the majority (and Texas) rule, a minor who has purchased a non-necessity need only return that portion of the consideration that he is <u>able to return</u> in order to recover his full payment. The fact that his inability to return the full consideration was the result of negligence on his part is immaterial.

Gastonia Personnel Corporation v. Rogers

Facts: Rogers, a minor, contracted to pay Gastonia Personnel Corporation (GPC) a fee of $295 if it found him a suitable job. After it did so, he disaffirmed the contract. GPC then sued to recover its fee, contending that its services constituted a "necessity" for which he was liable. The trial court ruled as a matter of law that the services were not a necessity, and GPC appealed.

Holding: Judgment reversed, and case remanded. The facts were that Rogers was a high school graduate, married, and a college student before having to drop out of school because his wife was expecting a child. Under those circumstances, it was error for the trial court to rule as a matter of law that Rogers could not obligate himself to pay for services rendered him in obtaining a job suitable to provide the necessities of life for himself, his wife, and expected child. The law should not, and does not, deny to "older minors" the opportunities and right to obligate themselves for property or services needed to support their dependents.

Hanks v. McNeill Coal Corporation

Facts: Hanks sold coal lands in Colorado to the defendant corporation in 1937. In 1940, Hanks was adjudicated insane by a court, and his son brought this action to set aside the 1937 sale of land on the theory that the senior Hanks was <u>insane in fact</u> in 1937. At the trial, there was evidence tending to prove that Hanks was totally irrational in regard to many matters during 1937, but there was other evidence tending to show that Hanks did understand the nature of this particular contract, and was entirely rational at the time that it was entered into. On this conflicting evidence the trial court found Hanks to be sane at the time of contracting, and dismissed plaintiff's action.

Holding: Judgment affirmed. A person can have insane delusions with regard to some matters, yet be entirely sane in regard to other matters. Here the evidence of business associates clearly indicated that at the time the senior Hanks made the 1937 contract he was fully aware of what he was doing, and hence, from a legal standpoint, he was sane insofar as that contract is concerned. Thus cancellation was not permitted.

ANSWERS TO QUESTIONS AND PROBLEMS:

1. The seller's argument (that McAllister's failure to disaffirm for more than three years after he became an adult constituted a ratification) was rejected by the Supreme Court of Rhode Island. The court followed the rule that "a ratification of an infant's executory contract will not be implied from his mere failure to disaffirm it after he becomes of age, even though the former infant remains silent and inactive in the matter for a long period of time" after reaching the age of majority. (Note: The courts of a number of states have adopted a contrary rule --- i.e., that a minor has a duty to disaffirm the contract within a reasonable time after he attains the age of majority, and that a failure to do so does constitute an implied ratification. Note also that the minor did not retain possession of the car after becoming an adult. If this had been the case, retention for more than a reasonable period of time would constitute an implied ratification in all states.)

2. In Robertson, the court ruled that the evidence sustained the jury finding that the son, after reaching the age of majority, did ratify the agreements to repay his father for the funds expensed for his education. Evidence showed that the son had received and accepted the benefits of his father's loan; that the son orally affirmed the agreement after he reached the age of majority; that the son wrote a letter which affirmed the agreement after he reached the age of majority; and lastly, that there was evidence showing monthly payments over a period of three years, specifically noted as "college payment."

3. Assuming that the TV set is not a necessity (normally a safe assumption), Hughes may recover the full purchase price. The rule of most states is that the minor must only return the consideration if he is able --- regardless of its condition. In other words, Hughes is not charged with the decrease in value that resulted from the damage caused by the fire.

4. The court felt that the trailer home was not a necessary because it was not "actually required" in this particular situation. While it is true that a married couple needs a place to live, the evidence of the defendants showing that they have in fact been living with the husband's parents indicates that the house trailer was not a necessary to them, in these particular circumstances.

5. The Supreme Court of Oklahoma held that the medical expenses and the expenses connected with the automobile accident were necessaries. Therefore, this was a valid agreement releasing all his claims resulting from the accident, and that agreement could not be disaffirmed. The fact that

minor was married, had a child, and was gainfully employed shows that he was emancipated from parental control. The combination of emancipation with necessity often enlarges and extends necessity for the purpose of determining liability of an infant on his contract.

6. Chauncey will be able to disaffirm the contract and recover the car. Because the right to disaffirm is based on minority alone, the fact that Chang did not take advantage of Chauncey in any way (i.e., the fact that Chang honestly believed the car was worth only $500) does _not_ prevent the disaffirmance. In other words, a minor wishing to disaffirm a contract does not have to show that the other party took advantage of him in any way.

7. The Probate Court held that the evidence established that the deceased was incompetent to make a valid contract. The decedent was not capable of carrying on the ordinary business affairs of life. The Court felt that the deceased had changed his accounts to joint and survivorship accounts in order to authorize relatives to withdraw limited funds for his support, and not with the intent to make a gift to the nephew and niece. Therefore, the plaintiffs (other relatives of Moore) were successful in having the joint accounts set aside.

8. St. Pierre's right to recover the snowmobile from the third party, Owens, depends entirely upon whether or not Owens knew that Derek had purchased it from a minor. If Owens had no such knowledge, he is a "good faith purchaser" and thus entitled to retain the vehicle. This result comes from a part of our sales law, Sec. 2-403 of the Uniform Commercial Code, which provides that a person with _voidable_ title (here, Derek) has power to transfer _good_ title to "a good faith purchaser for value."

CHAPTER 7

ILLEGALITY

AUTHORS' SUGGESTIONS:

1. Under the heading of "Licensing Statutes," the text indicates that unlicensed persons generally are not entitled to recover fees for services which they have rendered. It may be noted further that, in "real life" litigation, cases involving unlicensed real estate brokers seem to be one of the most common of those arising in this general area. In that regard, there are two further points. First, many statutes affecting such brokers expressly provide that unlicensed persons may not enforce their brokerage contracts. Secondly, even if a broker is licensed in one state, he is not entitled --- as a general rule --- to recover a commission arising out of the sale of land located in another state unless he is also licensed in that state.

2. As the text indicates, most states have statutes that prohibit the carrying on of certain kinds of business activities on Sundays. Thus there is always the possibility that a business contract entered into on a Sunday may actually be illegal (and thus unenforceable). While this is true, in order to recognize the practicalities of life, the other side of the coin should also probably be cited in class --- that is, that in many jurisdictions there is little attempt by the authorities to enforce the Sunday statutes even where the goods being sold (frequently at retail) rather clearly do violate the statutes.

3. The topic of illegal contracts provides a good lead-in for a discussion of government regulation, since many areas of government regulation place constraints on freedom of contract. Examples include antitrust, labor law, and consumer credit regulation. There are others, of course. This approach works well if the instructor wishes to spend a relatively limited amount of class time on government regulations, and it provides a nice temporary diversion from contracts. However, if the instructor wishes to devote substantial time to government regulation in a separate portion of the course, this approach probably would not be suitable.

CASE BRIEFS:

Bremmeyer v. Peter Kiewit & Sons Co.

Facts: Peter Kiewit had the prime contract for a highway in Washington State, and made a subcontract with Bremmeyer for clearing the right-of-way. Bremmeyer paid Kiewit $35,000 for the right to take timber from right-of-way. The State cancelled Kiewit's contract and Kiewit cancelled Bremmeyer's before the clearing was finished. The State paid Kiewit about $1.75 million for "cancellation costs," but Kiewit offered Bremmeyer only $38. Bremmeyer sued Kiewit for the value of the remaining uncut timber. Kiewit defended on the ground that Bremmeyer was not registered with the state, as required by statute for contractors. The trial court ruled for defendant Kiewit and plaintiff Bremmeyer appealed.

Holding: Reversed, and remanded for trial. The purpose of the registration statute was to protect the _public_ from contractors, not to protect contractors from _each_ _other_.

Gann v. Morris

Facts: The Ganns bought a silk screening business in Tucson from Morris. The contract included a covenant not to compete within 100 miles of Tucson for 10 years. Morris violated the covenant and the Ganns sued. The trial court ruled for the Plaintiff Ganns, and defendant Morris appealed.

Holding: Judgment for plaintiffs affirmed. This ancillary covenant was reasonably restricted as to time and area, and is thus enforceable. Covenants in sales of businesses are not scrutinized as closely as in employment contracts.

Fong et. al. v. Miller

Facts: The Fongs leased a restaurant from Ms. Miller. Under the lease, they were to retain all proceeds from the restaurant, and one-fourth of the profits made from operation of the illegal slot machines, punch boards, and roulette tables. Soon after the Fongs took possession Ms. Miller, without cause, locked them out of the premises. The Fongs then brought this action to recover damages for breach of contract. Defendant Miller contended that the unlawful portions of the contract made the entire contract illegal and unenforceable. The trial court agreed, and dismissed the action.

Holding: Judgment for defendant affirmed. In this case, the lawful part of the lease (the operation of the restaurant) cannot be separated from the illegal part (the operation of the amusement devices) in view of the fact that the consideration being received by the Fongs was not solely the receipt of restaurant profits, but those profits _plus_ a share of the profits of the illegal machines. And, additionally, the _main_ consideration being received by Miller came from the operation of the illegal machines. Thus the entire contract is illegal, and the Fongs cannot get damages resulting from Miller's eviction, even though it was unjustified.

ANSWERS TO QUESTIONS AND PROBLEMS:

1. No. The court held that, although the licensing statute requiring _initial_ registration of architects _was_ designed to protect the public from incompetent practitioners, the provisions requiring annual renewal of registration were merely revenue-raising measures. The renewal procedure involved no reexamination or reinvestigation, but merely payment of the fee.

2. In the cited case, it was held that the licensing statute was applicable to Bonasera.

The Court of Appeals of Arizona, in denying recovery by Bonasera, said: "The purpose underlying the (various) statutes governing those occupied in real estate activities is to protect the public from unscrupulous and unqualified persons. Our Supreme Court has adhered to a strict application (of the licensing statute) to implement the intent expressed in those statutes. Accordingly, the court will not be a party to the collection of fees sought in violation of the law."

"The underlying public purpose is not served in subjecting an unsuspecting public to untested, unregulated practitioners of isolated transactions. We are of the opinion that these statutes are broad enough to include a business negotiation of the type involved here."

3. Yes. Even though the lease was initially valid, the change in the law rendered it void and unenforceable.

4. Resale price maintenance contracts are those in which a seller of goods sells them to a buyer on the condition that the buyer will not resell them below a stated price. For example, the S Company sells 1,000 widgets to the B Company for $1,000, the contract providing that the B Company will not resell the widgets below $1.50 each.

These contracts, when used in interstate commerce, are today illegal because the U.S. Supreme Court has ruled that they unreasonably restrain trade as a matter of law --- that is, no matter how insignificant the volume of goods that is subject to a particular contract --- and that they therefore violate Section 1 of the Sherman Act (which prohibits contracts that unreasonably restrain trade or commerce). (_Note_: Presumably, as a result of this view of the court, the use of resale price maintenance contracts in interstate commerce today occurs very seldom. Until 1975, however, when such contracts were protected by the now-repealed Miller-Tydings Act, they were in common use.)

5. Lally's contention that the restrictive clause was unreasonable, and therefore illegal, was rejected by the court.

In so ruling, the Supreme Court of Errors of Connecticut made these statements: "This is a contract in restraint of trade. The test of its validity is the reasonableness of the restraint it imposes. To meet this test, successfully, the restraint must be limited in its operation with respect to time and place, and afford no more than a fair and just protection to the interests of the party in whose favor it is to operate, without unduly interfering with the public interest." The court then ruled that the trial court's finding (that the plaintiff's business required the protection of these particular restrictions) would not be set aside, saying, "The trial court correctly concluded that the limitations as to area and time were fairly and justly calculated to protect the business sold and that they were not unreasonable."

6. The court held the contract to be a violation of public policy and, therefore, void and unenforceable. A contingent fee arrangement with an expert witness subverts justice because his testimony inevitably is influenced by the contingency.

7. The clause (purporting to free Constantine of all liability in case of damage) was held to be contrary to public policy and thus illegal.

The Supreme Court of Ohio first ruled that a bailor-bailee relationship existed between Mrs. Bova and Constantine, and further noted that under the general law of bailments a negligent bailee is liable for any damage caused to the property of the bailor which results from such negligence.

The court indicated that it would not permit a bailee, by private contract, to escape this liability, saying: "This bailor (Mrs. Bova) was not bound by the conditions (appearing on the back of the parking ticket) for the reason that they are _contrary_ _to_ _law_ _and_ _against_ _public_ _policy_. By that language the bailee attempted to avoid liability for his own negligence as well as that of his agents and servants, and, if the printed conditions are enforceable, the language is broad enough to avoid liability for any wanton or willful misconduct on the part of such bailee, his agents or servants (as well)."

8. In unusual circumstances, the application of the general rule (to the effect that neither party may enforce an illegal contract) brings about manifestly unfair results.

Accordingly, the courts are likely to enforce the following kinds of contracts, among others, although they are tainted with illegality: (1) contracts which are illegal only because they do not conform to statutes which have as their purpose the protection of a certain class of persons, and where the persons seeking to enforce such contracts are within the protected class; (2) contracts in which one party did not know, (and did not have reason to know) of the contract's illegal nature; and (3) contracts in which one portion of the agreement is lawful, which portion can be reasonably separated from that portion of the contract which is illegal.

CHAPTER 8

REALITY OF CONSENT

AUTHORS' SUGGESTIONS:

1. In previous chapters the view has been taken that a contract requires only four elements --- agreement, consideration, capacity, and legality. In this chapter, however, we find that even if all these elements exist a contract may still be set aside (not enforced) if fraud, mistake, duress or undue influence are shown to exist. On this basis, one could say that "reality of consent" is thus a fifth requirement that must be met in order for an agreement to constitute an enforceable contract.

2. When the subject of fraud is discussed, students usually show special interest in instances in which a seller of a used car "rolls back" the odometer so that it appears that the car has been driven fewer miles than is actually the case. In this regard, there are two points.

First, up until a few years ago, a buyer of such a car who wished to set aside the contract could do so, in most states, only on ground that the seller was guilty of fraud. This meant he not only had to convince the jury or court that the seller actually was responsible for the turning back of the odometer (instead of an earlier owner), but, additionally, he had to convince the court that an odometer reading constitutes a "statement of fact," and, further, that he (buyer) "reasonably relied" on the reading even if he did not specifically ask the seller if the reading was correct. In a substantial number of these earlier cases, the buyer's claim of fraud failed because he could not prove who caused the rollback to occur, or because the court rejected his "statement of fact" or "reasonable reliance" arguments.

Secondly, it should be pointed out that today a much different situation exists insofar as the position of the buyer in such a case is concerned. In recent years both federal and state statutes generally afford the buyer relief if he can show that the odometer was, in fact, incorrect; proof of fraud is thus unnecessary. While these statutes vary to some extent, in general they permit the buyer to cancel the contract, or to keep the car and recover damages, and frequently impose criminal penalties on the seller as well, unless the seller, at the time of the contract, gave a signed statement to the buyer indicating that he (seller) did not know whether the odometer reading was correct, and that this statement was in fact true. (I.e., if the jury found that seller either had the odometer turned back or did at least know the reading was incorrect, the buyer's rights are preserved.)

CASE BRIEFS:

Steinberg v. Chicago Medical School

Facts: Steinberg applied for admission to Chicago Medical School, and was rejected. He then learned that, contrary to statements in the school bulletin, "nonacademic criteria" were used in admitting applicants: the ability to make large pledges to the school. Steinberg then sued for fraud, the trial and intermediate appellate courts ruled summarily for defendant school, and plaintiff appealed.

Holding: Reversed and remanded for trial. Plaintiff had stated a cause of action and should have the chance to prove it. The court took notice of the school's modus operandi (from another recent case): a very high percentage of entering students had large pledges of money made in their behalves. Although a misrepresentation of intention or future conduct does not usually amount to fraud, there is an exception where the statements of intention are themselves the scheme employed to accomplish the fraud. Thus Steinberg's allegation that there were misstatements in the school's bulletin concerning how they would evaluate applicants was a sufficient allegation of fraud.

Kallgren v. Steele

Facts: The Kallgrens purchased a property in a national forest from the Steeles, on which there were several small buildings. Later the government told the Kallgrens that it was revoking their use permit for the reason that some of the buildings encroached upon state highway right-of-way, a fact unknown to the Kallgrens. They then brought this action to recover damages, contending that the Steeles' failure to inform them of this encroachment constituted fraud. The trial court agreed with this contention and entered judgment for the Kallgrens.

Holding: Judgment affirmed. While, as a general rule, silence does not constitute fraud, the "concealment" of a fact by one contracting party may constitute fraud where it results in the other party's believing something is true that is not. The court further felt that there was a concealment here, within the meaning of the above rule, where the Steeles --- knowing of the encroachment --- did not call it to the Kallgrens' attention. (Note: The same result could have been reached --- and many courts have done so --- simply by saying that this was a "latent defect" case, in view of the fact that the property had something wrong with it and that the buyers did not, as a practical matter, have any reasonable way of knowing of this at the time of purchase.)

Beachcomber Coins, Inc. v. Boskett

Facts: After a representative of Beachcomber examined a rare coin owned by Boskett, he was convinced it was genuine and bought it for $500. It was later discovered that the "D" on it (which made it valuable) was counterfeit. Beachcomber sued for rescission and a refund. The trial court ruled for defendant Boskett on the ground that the purchaser had assumed the risk that it might be counterfeit, and plaintiff Beachcomber appealed.

Holding: Reversed. This is a classic example of mutual mistake, and the contract should be rescinded. Both parties thought the coin was genuine; they did not consciously contract with reference to a doubtful fact. Also, there was insufficient evidence to establish a custom in the coin business for buyers to assume the risk.

Totem Marine T. & B. v. Alyeska Pipeline

Facts: Totem and Alyeska had a contract under which Totem was to transport materials for Alyeska from Houston to Alaska. Alyeska wrongfully terminated the contract at a time when it owed Totem about $300,000. The two parties settled the claim for $97,000. Totem later sued to rescind the settlement agreement, claiming that Alyseka deliberately withheld payment of an acknowledged debt, knowing that Totem was in financial trouble and about to go bankrupt, and that it had no choice but to accept an immediate but inadequate cash settlement. The trial court ruled summarily for defendant Alyeska on the ground that no cause of action for duress had been stated, and plaintiff Totem appealed.

Holding: Reversed and remanded for trial. Totem had stated a cause of action for economic duress.

ANSWERS TO QUESTIONS AND PROBLEMS:

1. Yes. The court held that the evidence was ample to show misrepresentation, intent to deceive, reliance, and injury. In addition to actual damages, plaintiffs also recovered punitive damages of $100,000.

2. No. Plaintiff was permitted to rescind. The court said, "If the relationship between insurer and insured requires the existence of utmost good faith, how much more demanding must we be of the ultimate integrity of the parties in the relationship between a pastor and his flock, or a minister

and his congregation, or a rabbi and his synagogue?" Thus, this was one of those cases in which there was a "duty to speak up," and nondisclosure amounted to fraud.

3. (a) The court said the evidence did _not_ establish fraud. There was no evidence of any misrepresentation by defendant. Plaintiff simply signed the contract without reading it because she was in a hurry. The evidence indicated that she was an intelligent, capable person. (b) To show fraud, plaintiff would have had to prove that she was induced to sign by a misrepresentation of fact, or that there were special circumstances creating a duty on the part of defendant to call the material terms of the contract to her attention. To show duress, plaintiff would have had to prove a wrongful threat that had impaired her free will.

4. The court did not accept this defense, and held that the seller had committed fraud. Even though value is a matter of opinion, the seller was in a far better position to know the rental value than the buyer, the seller in fact _knew_ that the building had _zero_ rental value, and expressed the opinion with the purpose of having it accepted as a fact and with the intent to deceive.

5. Clifford will be successful, for the reason that his payment of the $200 was clearly made under duress. In this case, the court applied the general rule to the effect that a threat of criminal prosecution constitutes duress.

(_Note_: The fact that Clifford might very well have been convicted of the crime of larceny, had a criminal prosecution actually taken place, does not change matters. While the general rule is especially applicable to cases in which the threatened party is entirely innocent of the alleged crime, it is also held by many courts, as here, to be equally applicable to situations in which the criminal prosecution might, in fact, have been successful.)

6. The buyer, White, may set aside the contract; this an example of a situation in which a classic "mutual mistake of fact" exists. The mistake, of course, went to the _identity of the craftsman_ making the respective violins.

Undoubtedly, as a result of this mistake of fact, the _value_ of the violins was much less than it would otherwise have been. But this was simply a _consequence_ of the mistake, rather than simply being a "mistake of value" alone.

7. The court did not accept this defense. This was a unilateral mistake, but the buyer was not negligent in making the mistake. A South Dakota statutory definition of "mistake of fact" made no distinction between unilateral and mutual mistakes.

8. "Home solicitation sales" statutes were passed in many states primarily because (1) high-pressure sales tactics and resultant "rip-offs" by door-to-door salespeople were rather widespread, and (2) it often was practically impossible to prove fraud, mistake, duress, or undue influence in such cases.

CHAPTER 9

CONTRACTS IN WRITING

AUTHORS' SUGGESTIONS:

1. This chapter is essentially concerned only with examining those types of contracts which are <u>required</u> <u>by</u> <u>law</u> to be in writing. As an introductory observation, however, it should be stressed that virtually all contracts of any real importance ought to be in writing as a practical matter --- first, because this overcomes the difficulty of proving by one person's testimony alone that the contract was actually ever entered into, and, secondly, because it ordinarily eliminates disputes as to what the terms of the agreement really were.

2. It should be made clear throughout that the courts of the various states have engrafted by judicial decision a number of exceptions to the statutory language; that is, have exempted certain contracts from the operation of the statute in various circumstances. Of these, the text cites <u>only</u> <u>two</u> exceptions (contracts calling for the sale of land where the buyer has substantially performed his part of the bargain, and promises to pay debts of another where the promisor is shown to have benefitted by the creditor-promisee's conduct taken as a result of the promise).

3. In regard to those <u>sales</u> <u>contracts</u> that are required to be in writing by the Uniform Commercial Code, the text sets forth the major portion of the basic provision, Section 2-201(1), and certain exceptions contained in 2-201(3). In this regard the students should probably be <u>required</u> <u>to</u> <u>read</u> <u>all</u> of subsection 3 (appearing in the Appendix) in order to get a full understanding of all of the exceptions contained in that subsection, especially the special manufacture exception.

CASE BRIEF :

<u>Harmon v. Tanner Motor Tours of Nevada, Ltd.</u>

Facts: Tanner submitted a written bid to provide limousine service at the
Las Vegas airport, which bid was orally accepted by the Board of Clark
County Commissioners (governing authority of the airport). The Board then
made a written contract with another firm, LTR, giving it the exclusive
limousine rights. Tanner sued Harmon, a representative of the Board, and
LTR, seeking specific performance of his contract with the Board. Defendants claimed that, since Tanner's contract was for a ten-year term and was
not in writing, it was unenforceable. The trial court ruled for plaintiff
Tanner, and defendants appealed.

Holding: Judgment for plaintiff affirmed. An exception to the Statute of
Frauds requirement of a writing existed here because (1) plaintiff had relied
upon the Board's promise that they would put the agreement in writing and
(2) there had been part performance by Tanner (provided service for a time,
bought two new limousines, and paid $3600 as the minimum guarantee for the
ensuing year).

ANSWERS TO QUESTIONS AND PROBLEMS:

1. Yes. The court ruled for plaintiffs and issued a decree of specific
performance. There had been sufficient acts of performance by defendants
to except the agreement from the Statute of Frauds. These acts, the court
said, were clearly referable to the contract and didn't make much sense without reference to the contract.

2. The railroad's contention is not correct, for the reason that it was
possible for the agreement to have been fully performed within one year
after it was made.

   The U.S. Supreme Court, in awarding Warner damages, explained this view
by saying, "The obligation of the railroad company to maintain the switch
was in terms limited or restricted by the qualification 'for the plaintiff's
benefit for shipping purposes as long as he needed it.' If, within a year
after the making of the contract, the plaintiff had died, or had abandoned
his whole business at this place, or for any other reason had ceased to
need the switch for the shipping of lumber, the railroad company would have
been no longer under any obligation to maintain the switch, and the contract
would have been brought to an end by having been fully performed. The
complete performance of the contract depending upon a contingency which might
happen within the year, the contract is not within the statute of frauds."

3. Harris is not liable on his oral promise. This is a typical example of
a promise falling within the "debt of another" section of the Statute of
Frauds, since the original debt was clearly that of another, Daisy Martin.

   It may be noted in passing that if Harris had made his promise on condition that Griffin release Daisy from liability, and such a release was

given, then her debt is extinguished and Harris' oral promise would be enforceable.

The Supreme Court of Mississippi, in this regard, said "the test whether a promise to answer for another's debt must be in writing to be enforceable is whether the party originally liable for the debt <u>continues liable</u>. (Emphasis added.) In the instant case, Daisy Martin *** is still subject to suit (since there was no release). We, therefore, are of the opinion that the oral promise of the defendant to pay the damages to plaintiff's car comes within the statute of frauds (and is not enforceable)."

4. No, Presti's claim is not correct. The court held that the contract was not enforceable. It was for a sale of goods for a price of $500 or more, and was required to be in writing. It takes payment <u>and acceptance of payment</u> (there was no sufficient memorandum no admission in court, and no delivery and acceptance of goods) to create the exception to the Statute of Frauds that Presti is relying on. There was payment, but no acceptance of that payment.

5. No. The contract was not enforceable. These actions by the construction company were <u>not</u> "unequivocally referable to the contract." These actions could reasonably have been taken by a buyer who was merely negotiating for the purchase, but who had not yet obtained a contract.

6. No, this is not a good defense. Under UCC 2-201(3)(a), an exception to the requirement of a writing exists in the case of goods to be specially manufactured for the buyer, if (1) at the time the buyer repudiates, the seller has already made a substantial beginning in the manufacture of the goods (or a commitment for their procurement), and (2) the goods are of a type that the seller will not be able to sell to others in the ordinary course of business. These elements appear to be present in this case.

7. No. A contract for the sale of land must be in writing, and the writing must be signed by the party against whom enforcement is sought. Here, B did not sign anything.

8. The <u>parol evidence rule</u> provides, in essence, that once a written agreement has been made, neither party will be permitted to prove in court that different or additional terms were also agreed upon <u>orally</u>.

Some of the situations in which the rule is held <u>not</u> to be applicable --- quite logically --- are those where the written contract itself is obviously incomplete; where the written contract is ambiguous; or where the oral testimony of one party indicates that the other party was guilty of fraud.

CHAPTER 10

RIGHTS OF THIRD PARTIES

AUTHORS' SUGGESTIONS:

1. Insofar as <u>sales contracts</u> are concerned, Section 2-201 of the Uniform Commercial Code specifies in what situations a party to a sales contract may delegate his <u>duties</u> to a third party. In general, under that section, one party to a sales contract may delegate his duties "unless otherwise agreed" (under the sales contract), or "unless the other (non-delegating) party has a substantial interest in having his original promisor perform or control the acts required by the contract." This latter clause means, for example, that if a seller delegates his obligation to sell and deliver the goods to a third party, and if the buyer objects to this delegation, the delegation will be permitted (and the buyer must accept the delegated performance) unless the buyer can show a bona fide and acceptable reason why he in fact desired the contract to be performed by the original seller, and by no one else. (Section 2-210 contains additional provisions relative to the assignment of <u>rights</u> arising under sales contracts, so it is advisable to read that section in its entirety.)

2. It should perhaps be noted expressly that, as a general rule, claims for money (due or to become due in the future) are assignable by the party originally entitled to receive the money, without the debtor's consent. In that regard, however, it should also be noted that when employees assign a part of their wages (due or to become due), state statutes today often restrict or limit that right to varying extents.

3. A footnote in this chapter refers to the status of a third party who purchases a negotiable instrument (instead of an ordinary, non-negotiable contract) and contrasts that status with the position of a mere assignee of a non-negotiable contract. This superior position occupied by the holder in due course of a negotiable instrument perhaps ought to receive more visibility in the text than it presently enjoys, so this fact probably ought to receive express attention in class. (And, if one is interested further in the precise rights of a holder in due course of negotiable instruments, he should

examine Chapters 20 and 21 in the area of "Commercial Paper".)

CASE BRIEF:

Schupach v. McDonald's System, Inc.

<u>Facts</u>: Copeland received a McDonald's franchise in Omaha, as well as a right of first refusal on other franchises in the area. Copeland exercised this right and opened five additional stores during the next few years. Copeland then sold all his franchises to Schupach with McDonald's consent. McDonald's later granted a franchise in the area to a third party without first offering it to Schupach. Schupach sued McDonald's, claiming that Copeland had assigned the right of first refusal to him. The trial court ruled for plaintiff Schupach, and defendant McDonald's appealed.

<u>Holding</u>: Reversed. The court agreed with the trial court's holding that the right of first refusal was personal and nonassignable, because the skill and personal characteristics of franchisees were an integral part of McDonald's overall policy and planning. However, the court disagreed with the trial court on the issue of consent, and held that the evidence was not sufficient to show that McDonald's had consented to an assignment of this right.

ANSWERS TO QUESTIONS AND PROBLEMS:

1. Yes. The court said that the contract between the State and the union was not intended, even partially or remotely, to benefit resort owners. They were "incidental beneficiaries" and had no right to enforce the contract.

2. Yes. The court ruled that even though the policy provided coverage for medical payments in behalf of injured passengers, Dr. Jones was not an intended beneficiary of the contract and could not sue to enforce it. He was, at best, an incidental beneficiary.

3. While it is literally true that Springer was not a party to the contract between the company and the union, the company's contention (that he could not maintain the action) is not correct. The Supreme Court of Oregon, following what it termed "the great weight of modern authority," expressly held that Springer could enforce the contract on the ground that he was a "third party beneficiary" of the contract.

(The court also observed that the courts of some other states reached the same result --- i.e., enforcement of the contract by the employee --- on the theory that in a collective bargaining agreement the "real contracting parties" are the company <u>and its employees</u>, with the union merely signing the contract as an "agent" for the employees. Under this view, of course, resort to the beneficiary theory is unnecessary in order to permit the employee to maintain the action.)

4. No. The court ruled that they were only incidental beneficiaries.

5. The court ruled that the covenant <u>could</u> be enforced against Abramov by the corporation. There had been nothing more involved than incorporation and a name change, so the corporation could enforce the covenant even without an express assignment. (There was another fact not set forth in the question, which provided an alternate basis for the ruling: Before leaving the partnership, Abramov and his partners had signed an agreement supplementing their original partnership agreement. In it they agreed to incorporate the business and change its name. This, the court said, was a before-the-fact consent to the assignability of the covenant Abramov later made.)

6. No. The court said that Smith, Bell and Hauck could not enforce the covenant. It was a completely separate entity from the company with which Cullins had made the covenant. The covenant, as part of an employment contract, could not be assigned by the former employer to Smith, Bell and Hauck without Cullins' consent. The employment contract, including the covenant, was a personal one.

7. The school district's defense is valid. Because of the type of the work that was called for under this contract, it is quite clear that the board's selection of a driver was based on the <u>personal skills</u> and <u>character traits</u> of the applicants. That being the case, the board had no duty to accept the services of a third party in place of those originally to be rendered by Paul Folquet, Sr.

The Supreme Court of Oregon, in dismissing the son's action, said, "The subject matter of this contract was the conveyance daily of children to and from school over a long period of time. When the safety of these children is taken into consideration, the necessity of the exercise by the district of great care in the election *** of a trustworthy, competent and careful driver *** is obvious."

"The contention that, in entering into a contract of this character where the lives and safety of children are involved, the district was not entitled to choose the person with whom it was willing to contract, or that, in making such selection, the relation of personal trust and confidence was not involved, we think is wholly unsound."

8. (a) Under the majority rule, the insurance company, as the first "in time," would win. (b) Under the "minority" rule, the bank, as the first to give notice, would win. In this case, the Florida Supreme Court adopted the minority (English) rule.

CHAPTER 11

DISCHARGE OF CONTRACTS

AUTHORS' SUGGESTIONS:

1. To keep things in perspective, it perhaps should be noted in class that the overwhelming majority of contracts are, in actuality, fully performed by both parties. And, in regard to the situations where this is not true, many of the resulting disputes are settled without resort to legal action. Therefore, the kinds of problems that are discussed in this chapter --- and especially those presented by the cases --- are exceptional in nature.

2. The text notes the fact that, traditionally, under <u>contract law</u> a contracting party is generally not freed of his obligations unless he can show that a "legal impossibility" occurred, whereas a more liberal view is taken under <u>sales law</u>. (That is, under sales law a seller is freed simply by showing that his performance has been rendered "commercially impracticable" by the occurrence of some event or condition after the contract was made.) In that regard, it can be observed that in recent cases involving the application of <u>contract law</u> there is a discernible tendency among the courts --- in scattered cases --- to recognize the theory of commercial impracticability. To illustrate: X and Y make a contract under the terms of which X is to render certain services for Y. Before the time of performance arrives some event occurs which, though it does not qualify as a legal impossibility, will make X's performance more costly or otherwise burdensome than was anticipated. In such a case X may --- under this trend --- be excused from his obligations if the added cost of performance is shown to be <u>markedly more</u> than it would have been otherwise. (While it is difficult to summarize the cases, the term "markedly more" usually means two or three times more than the original anticipated cost, as distinguished from 20, 30 or 40% more.) Thus it may be, a few years hence, that the doctrine of commercial impracticality will be as fully accepted under ordinary contract law as it is today under sales law.

3. The subjects of "impossibility," "commercial impracticability," and "frustration of purpose" are all somewhat related in that any one of them may --- if accepted by a court --- result in a contracting party being freed

of his obligations. However, there is a basic "structural" difference in one respect. Whenever a party seeks to get out of a contract on the grounds of impossibility or commercial impracticability, he is arguing that some event has occurred making his performance much more difficult than anticipated. On the other hand, when the doctrine of commercial frustration is being argued, the contracting party is contending simply that some event has occurred which now makes the contract of little or no use to him.

CASE BRIEFS:

Butkovich & Sons v. State Bank of St. Charles

Facts: Butkovich contracted to perform construction work for Grane. The bank was a party to the suit because it was Grane's mortgagee. The work involved enlargement of a basement, construction of a room over the basement, and a new garage floor and patio for a total of $19,290. After completion, Grane refused to pay the remaining $9,290 because Butkovich had (a) failed to install water stops (apparently causing water seepage into house), (b) failed to reinforce patio floor with wire, and (c) built the addition nine inches lower than in specifications. Plaintiff Butkovich sued for the balance, and the trial court ruled in his favor. Defendant Grane appealed.

Holding: Reversed. These defects were of sufficient magnitude to require a conclusion that Butkovich had not substantially performed.

Pearce-Young-Angel Co. v. Charles R. Allen, Inc.

Facts: The Allen Company, defendant, did not deliver a quantity of blackeye peas to the Pearce-Young-Angel Company as it had contracted to do. When the Pearce-Young-Angel Company brought this action to recover damages for breach of contract, the Allen Company explained that the pea crop in the area of Texas where it had expected to buy the peas had been ruined by torrential rains. On that basis, the Allen Company contended that a legal impossibility had occurred (destruction of the subject-matter of the contract) and that it was thus freed of its obligations under the contract. The trial court, on the evidence, ruled that the parties did not contemplate that the peas were necessarily to come from the Dilley area of Texas; that the Allen Company could thus have purchased peas elsewhere; and that the ruination of the pea crop in the Dilley area did not create a legal impossibility. The Allen Company appealed.

Holding: Judgment reversed. The higher court agreed with the general proposition that in a case such as this the "destruction of the subject-matter" defense was acceptable only if the contract, or surrounding circumstances, indicated that the peas were to be acquired by the Allen Company only from the Dilley area, and that in fact there was no pea crop in that area. However, the court (disagreeing with the view of the evidence taken by the trial court) ruled that it was reasonably clear that the parties to this contract <u>did</u> expect that the peas were to come from the Dilley area only, and thus it further ruled that the Allen Company's contention that it was excused (by virtue of the destruction of the subject-matter) from its contractual obligations was <u>correct</u>.

La Gasse Pool Const. Co. v. City of Fort Lauderdale

<u>Facts</u>: La Gasse contracted to renovate one of the city's pools. When the job was almost done, vandals damaged the pool so badly that most of the work had to be redone. The city refused to pay more than the contract price, and La Gasse sued for compensation for the additional work. The trial court ruled for defendant city, and plaintiff La Gasse appealed.

<u>Holding</u>: Judgment for defendant affirmed. In the case of a contract to perform work on an existing structure, damage to the structure before completion of the work is the burden of the contractor, unless the structure has been totally destroyed.

Northern Corp. v. Chugach Electric Association

<u>Facts</u>: Northern contracted to put large quantities of rock on the upstream face of a dam owned by Chugach. The rock was to be quarried on the other side of the lake and hauled across on the ice to the dam. The trucks and loaders kept falling through the ice during two successive winters, and Northern ceased its attempts to perform. Northern sued, claiming that performance was impossible and that it should receive damages for its costs in attempting to perform. Chugach counterclaimed for damages for Northern's nonperformance. The trial court ruled that both parties should be discharged because of impossibility, and denied both parties' damage claims. Both appealed.

<u>Holding</u>: Judgment affirmed in part, reversed in part, and remanded. The trial court correctly held that Northern's duty to perform was discharged by impossibility. The contract specifically called for transport across the lake when the ice was sufficiently thick, and it never achieved that thickness. Alternate methods of transport were prohibitively expensive. The court said that another basis for the holding was commercial impracticability (this was not a sales contract, but commercial impracticability is also in Second Restatement). The court ruled, however, that Northern should have received damages for its costs in attempting to perform.

ANSWERS TO QUESTIONS AND PROBLEMS:

1. Yes, these factors led the court to conclude that the parties had not

intended the cattle and machinery deal to be a condition precedent to the ranch sale contract. The court said that a condition precedent will not be implied unless surrounding circumstances very clearly show that a condition precedent was intended by the parties.

2. Yes. The court ruled for the purchasers. The parties had explicitly agreed to a condition precedent, and the condition did not occur.

3. The first contention of Cayias (and the main reason why this case was cited) is correct. The clause in the contract between him and the buyer of his business which provided that the contract was to be void "if the buyer could not thereafter obtain a new lease on the building at $150 per month" was clearly a condition subsequent. That being the case, the buyer of the business was freed if it were true that he attempted to obtain such a lease, and was unable to do so.

In regard to the second contention of Cayias --- that he was thereby freed of his obligation to pay a commission to his broker --- the Supreme Court of Utah ruled that this was also a correct statement of law if he could prove that the buyer was, in fact, unable to obtain the new lease. Because Cayias' evidence on this point was not persuasive, the court said, judgment was entered against him in the amount of the commission.

4. The Court of Appeals of New York ruled that both of the requirements necessary for the application of the doctrine of substantial performance were met in this case. Accordingly, judgment was entered for the plaintiff.

First, the court ruled that if --- as the plaintiff contended --- the Cohoes pipe "was the same in quality, in appearance, in market value, and in cost" as the Reading pipe, then the breach was clearly of a "trivial and insignificant" nature. In other words, if all of the other performance of the plaintiff was in conformity with the terms of the contract, its total performance (even considering the breach) was clearly substanial when measured against the totality of plaintiff's obligations.

Secondly, the court found that the substitution of the Cohoes pipe was not the result of bad faith on plaintiff's part --- i.e., it was "neither fraudulent nor willful." Rather, the court said, the evidence indicated that the substitution was merely "the result of oversight and inattention" (that is, simple negligence) on the part of the contractor.

5. No. The court did not let MTK Potato Co. out of the contract. It stated that the doctrines of impossibility and commercial impracticability did not apply because (1) there was no evidence that performance (payment) was impossible or impracticable as a result of extreme and unreasonable difficulty, expense, injury, or loss; and (2) the co-op's meeting of its payment schedule with MTK was not a basic assumption of the contract between MTK and Tallackson.

6. Yes. The court said that the parties were excused from further performance because of impossibility. There was no governing provision in the contract, and it was not reasonably foreseeable that the league would fold so quickly, according to the court.

7. (a) Because this case was decided in 1924, long before the Uniform Commercial Code was even thought of, the Supreme Court of Minnesota applied <u>general contract law</u> to the dispute. On this basis, the court ruled that the company's claim of "impossibility" was <u>not valid</u>.

In effect, the company was asking the court to rule that, under the circumstances, it was <u>impliedly understood</u> that if a national box car shortage occurred, then the company was to be relieved of its contractual obligations. The court rejected the company's contention, for the reason that the facts of the case did not fall within the established "true impossibility" cases. Therefore, the court said, the only way in which the company could have legally escaped its obligations was by including in the contract an <u>express</u> condition subsequent clause to that effect, which it had not done.

(b) Under present sales law, Article 2 of the Uniform Commercial Code, it appears that the company would be <u>freed of liability</u> in such a fact-pattern. Section 2-615, as the text indicates, provides that delay in delivery is not a breach (by the seller) if performance has been made "impracticable" by the "occurrence of a contingency the non-occurrence of which was a basic assumption on which the contract was made." Under the examples given by the drafters of the Code in a "comment" following Section 2-615, a national box car shortage would presumably be one sort of "contingency" which would fall within that section.

8. Yes, this evidence did cause the court to rule that the frustration of purpose doctrine was not applicable and that lessee was still bound by the contract. What happened was reasonably foreseeable, and lessee could have provided for it in the contract.

PART THREE: COMMERCIAL TRANSACTIONS

CHAPTER 12

SALES: INTRODUCTION TO THE LAW OF SALES

AUTHORS' SUGGESTIONS:

1. It has been found that students frequently have difficulty with the concept of goods. If they have not studied property law at this point (and they probably haven't), the instructor might find it useful to point out that (a) There are two types of property --- real and personal, (b) Real property is comprised basically of land and many of the things attached to it, (c) Personal property is everything else, (d) Personal property may be either tangible or intangible, and (e) Items of tangible personal property are goods.

2. Sometimes students form the misconception that coverage of Article 2 is dependent upon whether the parties are merchants. Emphasis should be placed on the fact that the status of the parties as merchants is important only if the particular UCC provision being applied so states.

3. It was felt that a detailed treatment of documents of title would require far more time of the students than its importance warrants. However, some knowledge of the subject is essential to understand the problems relating to passage of title and risk of loss. Thus, the textual coverage of documents of title was made brief, with only enough detail to accomplish its intended objective. An instructor wishing to further emphasize this area may do so by lecture, using the reading material as a basic framework.

CASE BRIEFS:

De Filippo v. Ford Motor Co.

Facts: De Filippo and Fleishman, plaintiffs, contracted to buy the assets (excluding the real estate, which was to be leased) of an existing new car dealership from Ford. Ford backed out and plaintiffs sued under the antitrust laws and for breach of contract. The federal district court held for plaintiffs on the antitrust claim, but held for Ford on the contract claim.

<u>Holding</u>: Judgment for plaintiffs on antitrust claim reversed. Judgment for Ford on contract claim affirmed. Thus, Ford won. Issue was whether this was a contract for the sale of goods. If so, it was for more than $500 and was required to be written and signed by Ford. Ford hadn't signed. The court of appeals said that it was a contract for the sale of goods because the aggregate value of the assets of the dealership classified as goods was over three times the value of "nongoods" assets (such as receivables).

Bonebrake v. Cox

<u>Facts</u>: Donald and Claude Cox owned a bowling alley which was gutted by fire. They contracted with Simek, who agreed to sell and install equipment necessary for rebuilding. Simek died with the contract only partly performed by both sides. Simek's administratrix, Bonebrake, sued for the unpaid balance of the contract price, and the Coxes counterclaimed for damages. The federal district court held for Bonebrake, the plaintiff, on her claim and on the Coxes counterclaim.

<u>Holding</u>: Judgment for plaintiff reversed and case remanded to trial court. At issue was whether certain provisions of the UCC should apply regarding performance and damages. The lower court had held that Article 2 did not apply. The court of appeals, however, held that it did apply because the primary object of the contract was the sale of equipment, the installation services being only incidental.

Loeb & Company, Inc. v. Schreiner

<u>Facts</u>: Loeb, a cotton dealer, contracted to buy cotton from Schreiner, a farmer. Schreiner later refused to sell when prices jumped. Loeb sued and the trial court held for Schreiner.

<u>Holding</u>: Judgment for defendant affirmed. The contract was required to be in writing, but the only writing in this case was a confirmation signed by Loeb and sent to Schreiner who didn't sign. This would be sufficient to hold Schreiner to the bargain under 2-201(2) only if both parties were merchants. The court held that a farmer is not a merchant and thus there was no writing sufficient to make the contract enforceable.

ANSWERS TO QUESTIONS AND PROBLEMS:

1. The law merchant was the body of unofficial rules established by early merchants for the resolution of mercantile disputes. It was eventually absorbed into the common law and ultimately formed the basis for many of the provisions of the Uniform Sales Act and the Uniform Commercial Code.

2. In a bailment (such as a lease of goods), no title is transferred, but only temporary possession. In a gift, no price is paid.

3. The issue would be whether electricity should be classified as goods. It was held in <u>Helvey v. Wabash County REMC</u>, 278 N.E.2d 608 (Ind. App. 1972), that electricity is a "good" and such a contract is governed by Article 2 of the UCC. Electricity is both tangible and movable.

4. Yes, Article 2 would govern the matters relating to delivery of the airplane. An airplane would be a "good", and the contract involved the passing of title for a price. The price for the airplane was the real estate. There is no requirement that the price be paid in money. Any questions relating to transfer of the title to the real estate would <u>not</u> be governed by the UCC, however.

5. No, because investment securities such as shares of common stock are not goods. They are intangible personal property. In any event, sales of investment securities are specifically governed by another part of the UCC (Article 8).

6. In <u>Playboy Clubs International, Inc. v. Loomskill, Inc.</u>, 13 UCC Rep. Serv. 765 (N.Y. Sup. 1974), the court said "no." It was said at p. 766: "We must find that petitioner was not a 'merchant' in the textile business, but an ultimate consumer. Petitioner is in the service business of purveying lodging, meals and drinks, and entertainment. It purchased fabric which another 'merchant' would manufacture into costumes. A merchant buys for resale, not for use."

While the court's decision was probably correct on its facts, some of the language employed is rather questionable. It seems that a party buying for consumption could in some circumstances fall within the UCC's definition of a merchant.

7. The ultimate objective of a farmer is not to just grow crops but to sell them and make a profit. That is his business. He should be considered no less a professional because he produces what he sells rather than buying and reselling it. Why wouldn't producing and selling come within the phrase "deals in goods of the kind" in UCC 2-104? And the court itself in the <u>Loeb</u> case appears to approve the suggestion in <u>Fear Ranches, Inc. v. Berry</u> that whether or not a farmer is a merchant should turn upon whether or not he has engaged in a particular type of sale in the past. A farmer who sells his crops to a dealer each season would seem to be a merchant under such a test.

8. Yes. Comment 3 to UCC 2-104 states: "The 'or to whom such knowledge or skill may be attributed by his employment of an agent or broker . . .' clause of the definition of merchant means that even persons such as universities, for example, can come within the definition of merchant if they have regular purchasing departments or business personnel who are familiar with business practices and who are equipped to take any action required."

9. It is very common for goods to be shipped to the buyer by way of a carrier, such as a trucking, railway, or air cargo company. It is also quite common for a seller to store goods at a warehouse before selling them, at which time the buyer might pick them up. In either case, whether the goods are shipped by a carrier or stored in a warehouse, the seller is turning over temporary possession of them to a third party. When an owner of goods parts with possession in such a manner, he will be given a receipt for those goods. When the goods are being shipped and the bailee is a carrier, this receipt is called a "bill of lading." When the goods are being stored and the bailee is a warehouseman, it is called a "warehouse receipt." In addition to being a receipt for goods, a bill of lading will contain instructions to the carrier regarding destination and the like, as well as the terms of the shipping agreement. A warehouse receipt will similarly contain the terms of the sotrage agreement. Both bills of lading and warehouse receipts are referred to as "documents of title," because such documents provide evidence of title to goods.

10. A document of title is negotiable if, by its terms, the goods are to be delivered to "bearer" or to the "order" of a named person. Otherwise, it is non-negotiable.

A negotiable document is actually more than a mere receipt for the goods and a contract for their carriage or storage. Rather, the person who is in legal possession of a negotiable document is entitled to the possession of the goods described therein. Legal possession of the document is tantamount to ownership of the goods. Thus, whoever is in legal possession and presents to the bailee a document which states that delivery is to be made to "bearer" is entitled to the goods. If the document had stated that delivery was to be to the "order of Roscoe Sweeney," whoever is in legal possession of the document and presents it to the bailee is entitled to the goods, if Roscoe Sweeney had properly endorsed it.

Legal possession of a non-negotiable document, on the other hand, is not tantamount to ownership of the goods. Regardless of who presents the document to the bailee, that party will be governed by the instructions of the bailor. The bailee is under a duty to ensure that he is delivering the goods to the party who is supposed to receive them under the bailor's instructions.

CHAPTER 13

SALES: FORMATION AND INTERPRETATION OF THE SALES CONTRACTS

AUTHORS' SUGGESTIONS:

1. Students sometimes seem to think that a firm offer under 2-205 remains open for three months, no matter what. A little extra class time might be needed to forestall such a misconception.

2. It might be wise to urge students not to rely upon the UCC's more liberal approach to the requirement of definiteness, but to strive to make all their agreements as definite and certain as circumstances allow.

3. Section 2-207 is probably the most difficult in all of Article 2 for students to grasp. Particular emphasis in class discussion should be placed on the fact that subsections (1) and (2) are completely divorced. In other words, the occurrence of one of the three events in subsection (2) has nothing at all to do with whether a contract was formed under subsection (1).

4. It is suggested that extra time be spent on the written confirmation under 2-201(2). The primary reason, besides its obvious practicality, is that it has found widespread acceptance and very frequent usage in the commercial world.

CASE BRIEFS:

Just Born, Inc. v. Stein, Hall & Co.

Facts: Plaintiff, a candy manufacturer, made several purchases of gelatin from defendant. Plaintiff filed this suit alleging that, according to their agreement, the dispute should be submitted to arbitration.

Holding: This was a trial court decision. The court held that the arbitration clauses which had been contained in defendant's acceptances of plaintiff's orders did not become part of their contract. The reason was that plaintiff hadn't expressly agreed to this provision, and it materially altered the contract so as to be excluded under 2-207(2).

Fortune Furniture Co. v. Mid-South Plastic Co.

Facts: Mid-South sued Fortune for the purchase price of plastic goods sold to Fortune by Mid-South under a requirements contract. Fortune admitted owing the amount sued for, but filed a counterclaim in which it asserted that Mid-South had not supplied Fortune's plastics requirements as agreed. The jury found for Fortune on its counterclaim, but the trial court rendered a judgment n.o.v. for Mid-South, and Fortune appealed.

Holding: Reversed and judgment rendered in favor of Fortune for the amount by which its counterclaim exceeded Mid-South's claim. The issue was whether a letter to Fortune from Mid-South's president was a sufficient written memorandum to satisfy the Statute of Frauds. The court held that it was, since it indicated that a contract of sale had been made and stated a quantity. The quantity term was sufficient even though it was stated in terms of Fortune's requirements.

Brooklyn Union Gas Co. v. Jimeniz

Facts: Jimeniz purchased a gas conversion burner from the gas company for the purpose of heating a tenement which he either owned or managed. The gas company did not negotiate with Jimeniz personally, but induced his tenant's to pressure him into making the purchase. Although Jimeniz had a very limited comprehension of English, the written contract presented to him by the gas company's employee was in English only. When Jimeniz asked for an explanation of the contract, he was just told to "sign it." One month after signing, Jimeniz tried to make a payment at the gas company's office, but was told that he need not pay for another year, as provided in the written contract. After a year he began making payments, but during that second year the unit ceased functioning. Jimeniz complained and one of the gas company's repairmen found that a transformer had burned out. An order was placed for the part, but no further action was taken to supply it because no payments had been made during the first year. The unit was never repaired and Jimeniz stopped making payments. The gas company sued.

Holding: This was a trial court decision. Judgment for defendant Jimeniz. The court held that the contract was unconscionable, and thus unenforceable, under UCC 2-302.

ANSWERS TO QUESTIONS AND PROBLEMS:

1. (a) As a general rule, an offer may be revoked at any time before it is

accepted. R communicated a revocation to B before B accepted, so the offer was <u>not</u> still open unless it was irrevocable for some reason. It was <u>not</u> an <u>option</u>, because B gave <u>no consideration</u> for R's promise to hold the offer open. Even though this is a sale of goods, UCC 2-205 would not make the offer irrevocable because it was <u>not in writing</u>.

(b) At common law, B's note would not be an acceptance because it stated additional terms (relating to credit) that had not been in the offer. But since this is a sale of goods, the UCC will apply. Sec. 2-207 provides that an attempted acceptance is valid even though it states additional terms, so long as the acceptance is not expressly conditional upon the offeror's consent to these additional terms. B's acceptance was not so conditioned, and would be effective. The additional credit terms would not be part of the agreement unless both parties were merchants. R is obviously a merchant, but B quite likely is not. He doesn't "deal" in lumber as a livelihood, nor does he "by his occupation hold himself out as having knowledge or skill peculiar to the goods or practices involved in the transaction." Carpentry is his hobby, not his occupation. Even if both parties were merchants, the terms will not become part of the agreement if they are <u>material</u>. Unless R and B had been dealing on similar credit terms in the past, it seems likely that something as important as credit would be material.

2. Even if the offer had been in writing (which we don't know) as required by 2-205 of the UCC, the offer could be irrevocable under that section for only three months; four months had passed. Roberts gave no consideration for the promise to keep the offer open, but the facts indicate that <u>promissory estoppel</u> could be used as a substitute for consideration. Thus, a common law <u>option</u> would exist.

3. Yes, it is sufficiently definite under UCC 2-305 according to <u>Silver v. The Sloop Silver Cloud</u>, 259 F. Supp. 187 (S.D.N.Y. 1966).

4. This phrase refers to the use by sellers and buyers of printed forms which contain conflicting terms, sometimes resulting in no contract being formed by the exchange of communications even though they probably so intended. The situation led to the drafting of UCC 2-207.

5. The court in <u>Dorton v. Collins & Aikman Corp.</u>, 453 F.2d 1161 (6th Cir. 1972), held that it was an acceptance under UCC 2-207. It was conditional, <u>but</u> it was <u>not expressly conditional upon the offeror's consent to the additional terms</u>.

6. Assuming that both parties are merchants, it would depend on whether the court viewed an arbitration clause as being a material alteration of the agreement, as the court did in <u>Just Born, Inc. v. Stein</u>, presented earlier in this chapter.

7. The pre-existing duty rule as applied to modifications was intended to prevent one party from coercing a modification, such as additional money,

after performance had begun and the other party was in some sort of predicament. Yes, the UCC replaces the protection formerly provided by this rule with a general good faith requirement and with the "unconscionability" provisions of 2-302.

8. Yes, it just needs to indicate that a contract of sale has been made. See Cohn v. Fisher, 287 A.2d 222 (N.J. Super. 1972).

9. No. It does not indicate that a contract of sale has been made. See Arcuri v. Weiss, 184 A.2d 24 (Pa. Super. 1962).

10. The contract was found to be unconscionable in Jones v. Star Credit Corp., 298 N.Y.S.2d 264 (1969).

CHAPTER 14

SALES: TITLE, RISK OF LOSS, AND INSURABLE INTEREST

AUTHORS' SUGGESTIONS:

1. Students will find it necessary to spend a substantial amount of time differentiating between the rules for passage of title and those for risk of loss. The rules for the shifting of risk of loss are by far the most important. Thus, if time is at a premium, the instructor might wish to merely point out when title might still be important, refer to the rules, and not discuss or hold students responsible for the title rules. More time could then be spent on discussing and grasping the rules relating to risk of loss.

2. The instructor might want to take time to point out that acquisition of goods by fraud creates a <u>voidable</u> title, whereas acquisition by outright <u>theft</u> creates no title at all. This distinction is observed by the UCC even though state <u>criminal</u> laws might treat the two identically.

3. Be sure to note the difference between a BFP and a buyer in the ordinary course of business. The latter is essentially a BFP who has bought in the usual way that such items are bought from this seller.

CASE BRIEFS:

Lane v. Honeycutt

<u>Facts</u>: Willis gave a hot check to Lane for a boat, motor, and trailer. Garrett acquired the goods from Willis, then Honeycutt bought them from Garrett. Lane sued Honeycutt to recover the items. Lane claimed to have good title as a good faith purchaser for value under 2-403. The trial court ruled for plaintiff, and defendant appealed.

<u>Holding</u>: Judgment for plaintiff affirmed. Garrett had nothing to indicate he was the owner, and told Honeycutt he was selling for someone else but

didn't identify the owner. On the documents accompanying the sale, Garrett signed someone else's name as seller and signed a name other than Honeycutt's as buyer. Furthermore, the price was about one-third of what the items had been sold for a few months before. Since defendant consciously ignored such suspicious circumstances, he did not act in good faith.

Lumber Sales, Inc. v. Brown

Facts: Brown bought five carloads of lumber from Lumber Sales. Brown admitted receiving four carloads but denied receiving the fifth, for which he refused to pay. The fifth carload was delivered to a railroad siding about one-half mile from defendant's business, as they had agreed. One of defendant's employees was notified of the delivery, but the lumber was not immediately unloaded. The lumber then disappeared. The seller, plaintiff, sued for the price of the fifth carload. The trial court ruled for plaintiff and defendant appealed.

Holding: Judgment for plaintiff affirmed. Risk of loss passed to defendant when delivery was tendered at the destination. Since the loss occurred after that time, defendant must pay for the lumber.

Multiplastics, Inc. v. Arch Industries

Facts: Multiplastics, plaintiff, agreed to manufacture and deliver 40,000 lbs. of plastic pellets to Arch, defendant. Arch was to accept delivery of 1,000 lbs. per day, but later refused to accept deliveries. A month later the pellets were destroyed by a fire, and plaintiff's insurance did not cover the loss. Plaintiff sued to recover the purchase price. The trial court ruled for plaintiff and defendant appealed.

Holding: Judgment for plaintiff affirmed. When defendant breached, risk of loss immediately shifted to him and remained there for a commercially reasonable time. The fire loss shortly over a month later occurred within a reasonable time and defendant must bear the loss.

Bowman v. American Home Assurance Co.

Facts: Bowman, plaintiff, and his partner Moeller owned an airplane which was insured by American, defendant. They contracted to sell the plane to Hemmer, who borrowed it before the transaction was complete. While in Hemmer's possession, the plane was wrecked and Bowman sought to recover from the insurance company. The company claimed plaintiff no longer had an insurable interest. The trial court ruled for plaintiff and defendant appealed.

Holding: Judgment for plaintiff affirmed. The evidence indicated that

(1) physical delivery had not yet been completed because the plane was just on loan to the buyer prior to completing the transaction and (2) the parties had agreed when title was to pass and the agreed steps had not been completed. Thus plaintiff still had title and an insurable interest.

ANSWERS TO QUESTIONS AND PROBLEMS:

1. Prior to the UCC, questions such as risk of loss were resolved on the basis of who had title. Today, the location of risk of loss is determined by a separate set of rules. The rules as to title have limited application.

2. Lieber will prevail. The chauffeur was a thief and could not pass good title to even a BFP. It was no defense that Lieber himself was a thief and that the German government was allegedly the true owner. The dispute was between Lieber and defendant, and as between those two, Lieber had the better claim. (He was a "prior thief.") See Lieber v. Mohawk Arms, Inc., 64 Misc.2d 206 (N.Y. Sup. Ct. 1970).

3. A void title is no title at all; a voidable title is one which is okay until someone with a better claim asserts it. The holder of a void title can convey no title to anyone; the holder of a voidable title can convey good title to a BFP.

4. A will not be successful. C took good title as a buyer in the ordinary course of business from B. The fact that C paid for the goods by paying a debt B owed to X did not prevent C from being a buyer in the ordinary course of business. If C had paid simply by releasing a prior debt owed to him by B, C would not have been a buyer in the ordinary course of business. See First National Bank v. Crone, 301 N.E.2d 378 (Ind. App. 1973).

5. The purpose is to protect a seller's creditors from a sudden, but non-fraudulent, depletion of his assets.

6. Williams would recover the price from Sanders. The boat was in the possession of a bailee and risk of loss passed to Sanders when the bailee acknowledged Sanders' right to possession. See Whately v. Tetrault, 29 Mass. App. 112 (1964).

7. Lair will prevail. In Lair Distrib. Co. v. Crump, 261 So.2d 904 (Ala. App. 1972), the court did not buy such an argument. It held that the buyer had received the antenna in a physical sense, which was all that was required. Risk of loss had passed to the buyer prior to the fire and he was obligated to pay the price.

8. X will not win. X Co. was a merchant, and risk would pass only when Z Co. actually received the goods. In addition, the court in Consolidated Bottling Co. v. Jaco Equipment Corp., 8 UCC Rep. Serv. 966 (2d Cir. 1971),

indicated that risk would not have passed until Z Co. actually took possession even if X Co. had not been a merchant. The reason was that the term "FOB purchaser's truck" showed specific agreement that risk would not pass until the purchaser took possession. A mere tender would not have been enough had X Co. not been a merchant.

9. Graybar will not prevail. The seller breached the contract, so risk of loss did not pass to the buyer as it would have if the proper cable had been delivered. The buyer's only duty was to take reasonable care in the safekeeping of the goods, which he did, according to the court in Graybar Elec. Co. v. Shook, 195 S.E.2d 514 (N.C. 1973).

10. Scarola will prevail. The court in Scarola v. Insurance Co. of North America, 292 N.E.2d 776 (N.Y. 1972), held that a good faith purchaser from a thief does have an insurable interest in the goods even though he has no title. UCC rules on insurable interest were not analyzed.

CHAPTER 15

SALES: WARRANTIES

AUTHORS' SUGGESTIONS:

1. The UCC parol evidence rule was not separately discussed in Chapter 18 on Formation and Interpretation of Sales Contracts because it is not significantly different from the common law rule. However, the parol evidence rule can be so crucial in warranty cases (thus the discussion in this chapter) that the instructor will probably want to take class time discussing its applicability.

2. Regarding the Mohasco Industries case (carpet in Stardust Hotel), students might be asked whether the result would have been different had the Stardust not hired its own decorator but had instead just told Mohasco what its needs were and relied upon Mohasco to fulfill them. In such a case Mohasco might be under a duty to furnish "twist yarn" because of the warranty of fitness for a particular purpose, assuming Stardust's willingness to pay a higher price.

3. The instructor might want to emphasize that, where a consumer has suffered bodily injury because of a defective product, it is not unusual for the UCC warranty rules to be ignored and the rules of strict liability applied.

CASE BRIEFS:

Community Television Services, Inc. v. Dresser Industries, Inc.

Facts: Two TV stations formed a separate corporation, Community, for the purpose of constructing and operating a 2,000 foot broadcasting tower. Community contracted with Dresser, who designed, manufactured, and erected the tower. During a blizzard, the tower collapsed, and Community sued Dresser for breach of an express warranty. The federal district court ruled for Community, the plaintiff, and awarded damages of over $1.25 million. Dresser, the defendant, appealed.

Holding: Judgment for plaintiff affirmed. The tower did conform to the technical specifications contained in the contract (warranty by description). Apparently, ice had formed on the upper members of the tower, increasing the size of flat surfaces and greatly increasing wind resistance. The court ruled that the warranty created by the technical specifications had been expanded by statements in Dresser's advertising literature. Essentially, these statements amounted to promises that Dresser would design a tower that would withstand the weather conditions to which it ordinarily be subjected in the particular locale. The evidence indicated that the storm was not unprecedented. The court also held that, since this advertising had been provided by Community before contracting, for the purpose of inducing Community to deal with Dresser, the statements in the literature were "part of the basis of the bargain."

Burrus v. Itek Corp.

Facts: Burrus, a printer, purchased a printing press from Itek. The press did not feed properly, had paper jam-ups, failed to "register" (superimpose symbols) properly, streaked and smeared the printing surface, was improperly timed, was slow, and produced crooked printing. Itek, the defendant, refused to replace the press, and Burrus, the plaintiff, sued for breach of the implied warranty of merchantability. The trial court held for plaintiff, and defendant appealed.

Holding: Judgment for plaintiff affirmed. It is not necessary to have expert testimony regarding specific defects in an item; the lay testimony of those having personal knowledge of the functioning of the press was sufficient to support the verdict for plaintiff. Also, there was no evidence to support defendant's contention that the press had been improperly maintained; indeed, the fact that the defects were apparent immediately after delivery was strong evidence against such a contention. There also was no evidence of operation by incompetent individuals. The evidence showed that minor modifications made on the press by plaintiff had nothing to do with its problems. Finally, the court said that presses ordinarily don't do the things this press did, and that it was not fit for the ordinary purposes for which such presses are used.

Mohasco Industries, Inc. v. Anderson Halverson Corp.

Facts: Defendant, owner of the Stardust Hotel in Las Vegas, ordered carpet from plaintiff Mohasco for the lobby and showroom of the hotel. The defendant's own decorator specified the particular type of carpet to be supplied. After installation defendant refused to pay, contending that the carpet "shaded" excessively. Plaintiff sued for the purchase price and defendant defended on the basis of breach of the implied warranty of merchantability. The trial court ruled for defendant and plaintiff appealed.

Holding: Judgment for defendant reversed. There was no breach of warranty by plaintiff and defendant must pay for the carpet. Shading was a natural characteristic of the type of carpet ordered. A higher priced carpet would not have shaded, but plaintiff simply supplied what defendant (through its decorator) specified. To hold otherwise would force the plaintiff to breach either an express warranty of description or an implied warranty of merchantability.

Johnson v. Lappo Lumber Co.

Facts: Johnson, plaintiff, raised hogs. He needed ventilating fans for the hog barn. He told the supplier's representative of his needs and was advised to buy certain fans with "open" motors not sealed off from outside air. He bought them but they malfunctioned because of clogging from humidity and feed dust. He sued the supplier and manufacturer, among others, for breach of the implied warranty of fitness for a particular purpose. The trial court ruled for defendants and plaintiff appealed.

Holding: Judgment for defendants affirmed. In response to the queries of the supplier's representative, plaintiff said there were no unusual humidity or dust problems, and this was not true. The supplier acted on the misinformation Johnson gave, and therefore no breach of the fitness warranty occurred.

Hauter v. Zogarts

Facts: The Hauters, plaintiffs, purchased a "Golfing Gizmo" for their son from defendants. The device was designed to provide driving practice for novice golfers. On the package it said, "Completely safe ball will not hit player." But the Hauters son, while using it as directed, was hit in the head by the ball and severely injured. The jury returned a verdict for defendants, but the trial judge rendered a judgment n.o.v. for plaintiffs. Defendants appealed.

Holding: Judgment for plaintiffs affirmed. There was a breach of express warranty and implied warranty of merchantability. A drawing on the package and instructions had depicted a golfer hitting the ball "properly", but the court refused to imply from this a disclaimer limiting the warranty to situations where the ball was hit squarely. The device was made for duffers, who rarely hit the ball right.

ANSWERS TO QUESTIONS AND PROBLEMS:

1. Arthur's contention is not correct. The court in Jones v. Linebaugh,

191 N.W.2d 143 (Mich. App. 1971) was not sufficiently specific to exclude the warranty of title. Precise and unambiguous language must be used.

2. Probably not. This language is too vague and general to be an "affirmation of fact." It would probably not be treated as a "promise," either, but rather as mere "puffing" or "sales talk." See Carpenter v. Alberto Culver Co., 184 N.W.2d 547 (Mich. App. 1970).

3. Yes, the buyer prevailed. An express warranty by description was created even though the seller made the statement in order to comply with state law. Walcott & Steeler Inc. v. Carpenter, 436 S.W.2d 820 (Ark. 1969).

4. No, the buyer was not successful. The gas was sold, not the meter. Thus, only the gas and not the meter carried with it an implied warranty of merchantability. The gas was not defective. The buyer would have to prove that the gas co. was negligent. See Pioneer Hi-Bred Co. of Illinois v. Northern Illinois Gas, 17 UCC Rep. Serv. 61 (Ill. 1975).

5. Courts traditionally have distinguished between "foreign" objects found in food and objects which occurred naturally. The former constituted a breach of the implied warranty of merchantability; the latter did not. Some courts have recently abandoned this distinction and have applied a test based on the "reasonable expectations of the consumer."

6. The seller's contention was not correct, and the buyer would prevail. A product must not only do the job for which it is intended; it must also do it safely. The feed was intended for breeding cattle; it was not merchantable if it caused sterility even if it did the job it was supposed to do. Kassab v. Central Soya, 246 A.2d 848 (Pa. 1968).

7. Yes, the buyer would probably win because the affirmation of fact in the advertisement very likely created an express warranty. Also, there appears to be liability on an implied warranty of fitness for a particular purpose. See Filler v. Rayex Corp., 8 UCC Rep. Serv. 323 (7th Cir. 1970).

8. The question is whether the disclaimer was conspicuous. Was it written so that a reasonable person against whom it operates ought to have noticed it? The court in Restigiacomo v. Crane & Clark Lumber Corp., 9 UCC Rep. Serv. 1367 (N.Y. Sup. Ct. 1971), said that the disclaimer was not conspicuous.

9. In addition to not having to prove a specific instance of negligence occurred or that a warranty was made and relied upon, a plaintiff suing under the strict liability theory is not subject to most of the defenses which can be asserted against claims of negligence or breach of warranty. But in some states strict liability has not been recognized or has been given only limited recognition. Also, a statute of limitations may sometimes prevent suit on one theory but not another.

10. The Act applies only to express written warranties given in consumer

transactions. It does not require such a warranty, but if one is given on a product costing ten dollars or more, it must be designated as "full" or "limited". The warranty must conform to certain minimum standards to be designated "full". A seller is allowed to provide in the contract for informal settlement procedures, and if these procedures meet FTC regulations, the buyer must resort to them before going to court.

CHAPTER 16

SALES: PERFORMANCE AND REMEDIES

AUTHORS' SUGGESTIONS:

1. Be sure that students understand that acceptance of goods is an entirely different concept than acceptance of an offer.

2. During the times of economic instability and sometimes dramatic inflation which our country has been experiencing, the doctrine of commercial impracticability takes on added significance. It is worthy of substantial class time. Students should also be made aware of the importance of using contractual force majeure clauses.

3. Some instructors might want to expand upon the text discussion of "reasonable basis for insecurity" and "adequate assurance." The comments to the Code section, 2-609, are a good source for additional material.

CASE BRIEFS:

Eastern Airlines, Inc. v. Gulf Oil Co.

Facts: Gulf had been a major supplier of jet fuel to Eastern for a number of years. Their most recent requirements contract, made in 1972, contained an "escalator" clause. This clause permitted Gulf to raise the price on future deliveries in accordance with increases in the government-regulated price of domestically produced crude oil. Several things subsequently happened: (1) The government removed the price ceiling on a portion ("new" oil) of domestically produced crude, letting it rise to market levels, (2) OPEC raised the price of imported oil by 400 percent, and (3) more and more oil began to be imported. Thus, Gulf's costs of producing jet fuel rose much more than it was able to pass along under the escalator clause. Gulf refused to honor its contract, claiming "commercial impracticability," and Eastern sued. The decision is that of the federal district court.

Holding: Judgment for plaintiff Eastern; decree of specific performance issued. Gulf had not proved sufficient hardship to show commercial impracticability. It produced no meaningful data on its costs; all of its cost data included intracompany profits on transfers between its overseas and domestic production departments and its refining department. Also, the company as a whole was earning record profits. On the issue of foreseeability, the court said: (1) Deregulation of the price of a part of domestic crude production should have been no surprise to Gulf; they had been lobbying for deregulation for years and had been in constant contact with federal officials; and (2) The action by OPEC also was foreseeable, because oil had been used as a political weapon with increasing success over the years, and the volatility of the Mideast was well known.

Oloffson v. Coomer

Facts: Oloffson, plaintiff, was a grain dealer; Coomer, defendant, a farmer. They contracted in April for the sale of 40,000 bushels of corn to be grown by Coomer and delivered in October and December. On June 3, Coomer informed Oloffson that the corn would not be planted because of too much rain, and that Oloffson should obtain the corn elsewhere to fulfill obligations Oloffson had to third parties. Oloffson did not do so but waited for Coomer to perform. Oloffson covered only after the contractual delivery dates had passed. He then sued Coomer for damages. The trial court ruled for Oloffson but awarded him damages based on the June 3 market price rather than the actual cover price. Oloffson disputed this method of computation (the actual cover price paid later on was higher than the market price on June 3) and appealed.

Holding: Judgment affirmed. Oloffson's choices upon Coomer's anticipatory repudiation were to immediately pursue his remedies or to await performance for a reasonable time. The court said that since the repudiation was so definite and the market price was rising, it was unreasonable to wait any time at all for performance. Thus, Oloffson should have stirred himself immediately on June 3, and his damages should be computed based on the market price on that date.

Baden v. Curtiss Breeding Service

Facts: Baden, plaintiff, was a rancher who purchased bull semen from Curtiss, defendant, for purposes of artificial insemination. The semen proved defective and no calves were born in 1972. Plaintiff sued for breach of warranty, claiming damages not only for the loss of this calf crop but also for loss of the 1974 calf crop which would have been expected from the calves born in 1972. This was a trial court decision.

Holding: Judgement for plaintiff for damages caused by loss of 1972 calf crop only. Loss of 1974 calf crop was not a reasonably foreseeable result of the breach of warranty.

Conte v. Dwan Lincoln-Mercury, Inc.

Facts: Conte bought a new 1970 Continental from Dwan, a dealer. It was a lemon: oil leaks, windshield wipers and cigarette lighter wouldn't work, electric windows malfunctioned, paint blistered, fan belt broke more than once, alternator failed. Over a 14 month period, the car was taken back to the dealer eight times; five of those times it had to be towed. The last time, Conte refused to pick up the car and sued Dwan, seeking to revoke acceptance and get his money back. The trial court held in favor of Conte, the plaintiff, and Dwan, the defendant, appealed.

Holding: Jugment for plaintiff affirmed. The defects did substantially impair the value of the car and were not reasonably discoverable at the time of acceptance. Revocation of acceptance was made within a reasonable time, because Conte was in continual contact with Dwan during the 14 months and Dwan continually assured Conte that the car would be fixed satisfactorily. Finally, the "repair or replace within 12 months" provision in the sales contract was a limitation of remedies that had "failed of its essential purpose" because the car had not been put in proper working order within a reasonable time after sale.

ANSWERS TO QUESTIONS AND PROBLEMS:

1. If the place designated after the FOB term is the place of shipment, it is a shipment contract; if the place is the destination, it is a destination contract.

2. The dealer will not prevail. If Smith had not yet accepted, he could reject. Even if he had accepted, he could revoke his acceptance because a defective transmission "substanially impairs the value" of the car, and the other requirements for revocation of acceptance seem to be present. Smith was not obligated to accept the dealer's offer to cure; the dealer had no right to cure under 2-508(1) or 2-508(2). Zabriskie Chevrolet, Inc. v. Smith, 240 A.2d 195 (N.J. Sup. 1968).

3. The buyer is not correct. Such a transaction was held to be an installment contract in Gulf Chemical & Metallurgical Corp. v. Sylvan Chemical Corp., 12 UCC Rep. Serv. 117 (N.J. Super. 1973). Buyer could reject the third delivery only if the defect substantially impaired the value of that installment. The defect would be a breach of the whole contract only if it substantially impaired the value of the whole contract. Installment contracts are an exception to the perfect tender rule.

4. If a particular occurrence is felt by the court to have been fore-

seeable at the time of contracting, but the parties did not make provision for it in the contract, the promisor usually will be treated as having assumed the risk of such an occurrence. If it does happen, he is not excused under the doctrine of commerical impracticability even if performance actually is rendered impracticable.

5. In Maple Farms, Inc. v. City School Dist. of the City of Elmira, 352 N.Y.S.2d 784 (N.Y. Sup. 1974), the court denied the requested relief, stating that the seller was familiar, or should have been familiar, with recent substantial price increases. Thus the increase in question was foreseeable and the seller assumed the risk that it might occur. Furthermore, the court indicated that, even if unforeseeable, increased costs of this magnitude by themselves would not constitute impracticability.

6. Zippy's manager is correct. According to the court in Bowen v. Young, 14 UCC Rep. Serv. 403 (Tex. Civ. App. 1974), such conduct by a buyer is inconsistent with the seller's ownership. The buyer accepted the mobile home when he moved in and repaired the leak. Of course, the buyer can still recover damages resulting from the defect. (And it does not appear that the circumstances would allow a revocation of acceptance.)

7. A commercial unit is a unit of goods which is recognized in commercial practice as being a "single whole" for purposes of sale, and division of which materially impairs its value. If part of a delivery is conforming and part is not, the buyer may if he chooses make a partial acceptance. But he may not accept less than a commercial unit.

8. The seller is not correct. The court in Puget Sound Marina, Inc. v. Jorgensen, 475 P.2d 919 (Wash. App. 1970) said that a seller's claim for additional money amounted to an anticipatory repudiation. Buyer does not have to await the agreed date for delivery but may go ahead and cancel and sue for damages.

9. The seller's contention is not correct. Although the goods are not really unique, the UCC says that specific performance may be granted where the goods are unique or in "other proper circumstances". The court in La Clede Gas Co. v. Amoco Oil Co., 17 UCC Rep. Serv. 447 (8th Cir. 1975), said that under circumstances like this, specific performance was an appropriate remedy.

10. Buyer is correct. A seller has a duty to notify the buyer prior to a private resale. The seller's failure to give such notice is an affirmative defense which a buyer may assert against seller's suit for the deficiency. See Alco Standard Corp. v. F&B Mfg. Co., 265 N.E.2d 507 (Ill. App. 1970).

CHAPTER 17

COMMERCIAL PAPER: TYPES, PARTIES, AND BASIC CONCEPTS

AUTHORS' SUGGESTIONS:

1. Until the topic of defenses is reached, the subject of commercial paper must be essentially "compartmentalized" --- that is, the initial topics (such as requirements of negotiability, and requirements of a holder in due course) are best discussed separately, without too much emphasis on how they fit together. However, a minor exception to this concept is made in this chapter --- particularly in regard to the status of a holder in due course as contrasted with that of a mere assignee of a simple contract right --- so that students will have at the outset at least some idea as to how the succeeding topics are related, and thus possess practical significance.

2. Insofar as types of commercial paper are concerned, the authors have found that notes are easy for students to understand, but that drafts are not. This is particularly true when the status of the maker of a note is contrasted with that of the drawer of a draft. So that students will not be "gunshy" insofar as drafts are concerned, it is very helpful during the introductory hour to make clear the drawee-drawer relationship, and especially the fact that while a maker of a note is making a promise to pay the instrument, the drawer of a draft is ordering a third party (drawee) to pay the instrument. Among other things, this distinction makes it easier for students to understand later why a maker is a "primary" party and a drawer is a "secondary" party.

CASE BRIEFS:

(no cases)

ANSWERS TO QUESTIONS AND PROBLEMS:

1. If the note is non-negotiable, Y is not liable to the bank. In such a

case, Y may successfully assert the defense of "breach of contract" (i.e., the breach of contract on X's part) against the bank. In other words, the bank's ability to collect on the note is no better than X's would have been if he (X) had retained the note himself.

2. At a very early time, merchants carried quantities of gold and silver with them in order to pay for the goods that they purchased. Later, in order to eliminate this difficulty and attendant risks, they deposited their gold and sliver with bankers located in safe areas. The traders were then able to pay for goods by drawing "orders" on the bankers, and giving these orders to the sellers in exchange for the goods. The traders would then obtain payment by presenting the orders to the bankers upon whom they were drawn.

3. When a holder of a time note discounts it he receives payment (cash) immediately, instead of having to wait until the due date arrives. The bank benefits from the transaction, too, because the amount of cash that it pays to the holder is somewhat less than the face amount of the note.

4. This is a draft, because it contains an _order_ to pay instead of a _promise_ to pay (i.e., Tom has ordered Dick to make a payment of money to Harry).

5. The drawer of the trade acceptance would be the Gray Company (the seller of the snowmobiles); the drawee would be the Scarlet Company (the buyer/debtor); and the Scarlet Company would also be the acceptor after its name was signed to the draft by an authorized official.

6. Y's defense is not good. If a note is non-negotiable, this merely permits the maker of the note (Y) to assert a defense against the holder of the note _if_ the maker has a defense. In this case Y has no assertable defense because there was no breach of contract on X's part.

7. The statement is false. All negotiable instruments are governed by Article 3 of the UCC, regardless of whether they are payable to bearer or payable to the order of a specified payee. (It is only non-negotiable instruments that are governed by contract law.)

8. If B had issued the note to C in payment for services which C was obligated to perform at a later time, and if C never did perform such services, D can enforce the note against B if he (D) is a holder in due course. On the other hand, if D were only an ordinary holder, he would recover nothing from B.

CHAPTER 18

COMMERCIAL PAPER: NEGOTIABILITY

AUTHORS' SUGGESTIONS:

1. In this chapter, where the first of the basic portions of commercial law is encountered, two general observations about the format of Article 3 of the Uniform Commercial Code are useful. First, each of the major topics of commercial paper (e.g., requirements of negotiability, requirements of the holder in due course, etc.), is primarily governed by one basic section of the code. This basic section is then immediately followed by several clarifying sections. For example, the primary section setting forth the general requirements is Sec. 3-104. The following sections, through 3-114, then define in detail the basic requirements found in 3-104. Sec. 3-105, for example, indicates what kinds of clauses meet (or do not meet) the requirement that the promise or order be "unconditional" in nature.

Secondly, the clarifying or explanatory sections are often very long and detailed. For this reason the authors, in the text material, have made references only to those subsections of the clarifying sections which in their opinion are felt to be significant. (Even with this approach some instructors may find that, within the class time allotted to the subject, occasional subsections that _are_ covered in the text are too time-consuming, and thus will wish to make specific deletions in their reading assignments.)

2. It cannot be stressed too forcefully that the negotiability of an instrument depends entirely upon its _form_; that is, the written terms of the instrument either do or do not conform to the requirements of negotiability found in Sec. 3-104. Thus the fact that the parties to the instrument may have _intended_ that the instrument be negotiable, or non-negotiable, is entirely irrelevant.

3. Because continuous references to Article 3 of the Code will be made in successive chapters, students should be made aware that the provisions of Article 3 apply _only_ to negotiable instruments. Thus, for example, if a section provides that the "holder of an instrument" has certain rights that

are then set forth, the section means "the holder of a negotiable instrument." Thus the holder of an instrument which is ruled to be non-negotiable would not acquire rights under that particular section, or any other section of Article 3.

CASE BRIEFS:

Walls v. Morris Chevrolet, Inc.

Facts: This is an action by Walls against the defendant company, brought by Walls under an Oklahoma statute which provided that if a seller of goods took a negotiable instrument in conjunction with a consumer credit sale, the buyer (as a penalty) could recover three times the amount of the credit charges from the seller. The defendant company contended that the instrument it received from Walls was non-negotiable (for reasons appearing below). The trial court agreed with this contention and entered judgment for the defendant.

Holding: Judgment affirmed. The provisions of the note itself did not meet the tests of negotiability, because they indicated that a finance charge was to be paid but did not specify what that charge would be. Thus the note did not meet the "sum certain" requirement. The fact that a "security agreement" appeared on the same sheet of paper on which the note was written, and the fact that this agreement did indicate the amount of the finance charge, does not supply the missing element of negotiability. A non-negotiable instrument cannot be made negotiable where it is necessary to refer to some separate writing or agreement in order to find additional terms that might (if incorporated into the instrument) cause it to be negotiable.

Ferri v. Sylvia

Facts: The Sylvias, defendants, signed a promissory note which was payable "within 10 years after date" (i.e., date of issue). Ferri demanded payment before the ten years were up, and the defendants contended that the instrument was not due until the ten years had elapsed. The trial court ruled that the due date of the instrument was ambiguous, and allowed oral testimony as to what the parties' intentions were as to the due date. On the basis of this testimony the court concluded that the plaintiff had the right to demand payment at any time after the instrument was issued, and entered judgment for plaintiff.

Holding: Judgment reversed; the instrument is not due and payable until the 10 years have elapsed. The court first observed that Sec. 3-109 of the UCC provides that an instrument is payable at a definite time (rather than being payable on demand) "if by its terms it is payable on or before a stated date." The court further observed that under case law it has been established that "on or before" instruments give the <u>maker</u> the right to pay the instrument before the stated due date if he wishes, rather than giving the <u>holder</u> the right to demand payment before that time. The court then concluded that the "within 10 years after date" language of the instant note was, legally speaking, the same as "on or before" language, and thus the holder had no right to payment until the 10 years had elapsed.

United States v. The First National Bank of Boston

<u>Facts</u>: 63 false U.S. postal money orders were fraudulently prepared by one MacDonald, who cashed them at the defendant bank. That bank then received payment for them from the federal government. The government, after learning that the orders were bogus, brought this action to recover back the amount of the money orders from the bank. One issue in the case affecting the government's ability to recover payment was whether the orders qualified as negotiable instruments.

<u>Holding</u>: (of the trial court) The court did not expressly rule that the money orders failed to meet the requirements of negotiability contained in Sec. 3-104. It did, however, say that the provision to the effect that "more than one indorsement is prohibited by law" was in direct conflict with Sec. 3-301 of the UCC, which provides that the holder (of any negotiable instrument) "may transfer and negotiate it." For this reason the court ruled that, essentially, postal money orders were <u>different from</u> negotiable instruments. (<u>Note</u>: Despite this ruling, which rejected the bank's contention, the court nevertheless freed the bank of liability on grounds of "public policy.")

ANSWERS TO QUESTIONS AND PROBLEMS:

1. The inscription does not destroy negotiability. First, the court quoted Sec. 3-10f(1)(c) of the UCC, which provides that an unconditional promise to pay "is not made conditional by the fact that the instrument refers to or states that it arises out of a separate agreement." It then held that the inscription in question was clearly a <u>mere reference</u> to the contract that existed between the maker and the payee (as distinguished from a "subject to" inscription). Therefore, the inscription <u>did not condition</u> the maker's promise to pay in any way, and the note thus met all requirements for negotiability.

2. The note is probably negotiable. While it is payable out of a fund (monies received from special assessments), the note is issued by a <u>government</u> and thus falls under Sec. 3-105(1)(g), which provides that instruments payable out of particular funds do not lose negotiability "if the instrument is issued by a government or governmental agency or unit."

3. The Georgia court held that the promise was not a negotiable instrument, because it was merely payable "to your firm," rather than payable "to the order of your firm." (I.e., the writing did not contain words of negotiability.) Therefore, the writing did not meet the requirement of Sec. 3-104 (1)(d) that a nego-instrument must "be payable to order or to bearer."

4. (a) The instrument is a bearer instrument. Sec. 3-110(3) provides that an instrument made out in this way is an order instrument "unless the bearer words are handwritten or typewritten" --- (i.e., not part of a printed form). In this case, since the words "or bearer" were handwritten, the instrument is payable to bearer.

(b) The acceleration clause does not destroy negotiability. Any instrument that is not payable on demand must be payable at a "definite time." This instrument meets the definite time requirement because Sec. 3-109(c) provides that all instruments with acceleration clauses meet that requirement. In other words, the drafters of the UCC have taken the position that if an instrument contains a fixed deadline (in this instance, January 2, 1983), it is payable at a definite time even if it contains a clause under which the time of payment might be moved up (accelerated).

5. The Florida appellate court held that the writing destroyed the negotiability of the note. Because the terms of the mortgage were expressly incorporated into the note, this means that the promise contained in the note was, in effect, subject to all the terms of that extrinsic document (the mortgage), whatever those terms might be. Therefore, the promise (under Sec. 3-105(2)(a)) of the UCC is clearly a conditional promise that causes the instrument to be non-negotiable. (In reaching its decision, the court made the traditional observation that an incorporation clause is much different than a clause that merely "refers to the existence" of some extrinsic document. The latter type of clause, of course, has no effect upon the negotiability of the instrument in which it appears.)

6. In the Walls case, the court rejected the argument that the "sum certain" requirement was met (in view of the fact that the attached security agreement did specify the amount of the finance charge) for two reasons. First, the court said that while there was case law supporting the proposition that an instrument otherwise negotiable could be rendered non-negotiable because of a reference to a separate agreement, it could find no cases supporting the view that a non-negotiable instrument could be rendered negotiable because of a reference to a separate agreement. (The court also noted that Sec. 3-119(2) of the UCC provides that "A separate agreement does not affect the negotiability of an instrument," and that, by inference, this means the separate agreement cannot supply negotiability.) Secondly, the court said that if it ruled the note in question to be negotiable, it was distinctly possible that such notes in future cases could become detached from the security agreements that originally appeared on the same piece of paper, with the result that in such cases it would have to rule the notes non-negotiable (thus introducing an undesirable uncertainty to the law).

7. (a) The clause cited here permits the maker of the note to pay the instrument before June 1, 1983 if he wishes; it does not give the holder the right to demand payment before June 1, 1983. Authority for this answer is found in the Ferri case in this chapter.

(b) The clause does not destroy negotiability of the note. Because of the reasoning expressed in "a" above, the instrument meets the "definite time" requirement.

8. The quoted clause does not destroy negotiability. A clause in a note giving the maker the right to extend the time of payment does not violate the "definite time" requirement if --- as here --- the extension is limited "to a further definite time." (Sec. 3-109(1)(d)). Under the clause quoted, the note will come due in any event no later than November 1, 1984 --- that is, six months after the original due date.

CHAPTER 19

COMMERCIAL PAPER: TRANSFER AND NEGOTIATION

AUTHORS' SUGGESTIONS:

1. As a practical matter, most transfers of negotiable instruments probably do qualify as "negotiations." Nonetheless, the negotiation requirements are of considerable importance in specific situations for the reason that if a particular transfer does not qualify as a negotiation, then the transferee --- for most purposes --- is no better off than if the instrument were non-negotiable.

2. Restrictive indorsements are inherently more complicated in nature than are the other kinds of indorsements, and it is impossible because of time limitations in an introductory course to analyze the legal effect of each type of restrictive indorsement in all situations. Thus if class time requires an even more abbreviated discussion of these kinds of indorsements than the text presents, the basic ideas that should be stressed are probably these: (a) Restrictive indorsements are essentially different from blank and special indorsements in that they usually give the indorser certain rights against the indorsee if he fails to abide by the terms of the indorsement which other indorsers do not have. (b) Except for the "pay any bank or banker" indorsements used by banks in the collection process, the "for deposit only" indorsements are the most common of restrictive indorsements and should thus be given some class time in any event. And (c) it should be observed that intermediary banks in the bank collection process which routinely receive instruments from other banks that are indorsed restrictively generally do not have the special liability that other restrictive indorsees normally possess.

CASE BRIEFS:

Westerly Hospital v. Higgins

Facts: Higgins was maker of a promissory note which he issued to the hospital, the payee. An authorized agent of the hospital indorsed the note in blank and negotiated it to a bank. When Higgins defaulted on his payment the note was redelivered by the bank to the hospital. The hospital then brought this action to recover the balance due against Higgins. In the trial court Higgins contended that redelivery of the note from the bank to the hospital was not a negotiation (and that the hospital was thus not a "holder") for the reason that the agent of the bank who indorsed the instrument as part of the redelivery did not have authority from the bank to do so. The trial court, for reasons appearing below, rejected this contention and entered judgment for the plaintiff hospital.

Holding: Judgment affirmed. When the agent of the hospital indorsed the note to the bank, an indorsement in blank was utilized. This converted the note into a bearer instrument, with the result that the indorsee, the bank, could thereafter negotiate the note further without any indorsement at all. That being true, the delivery of the note by the bank back to the hospital constituted a negotiation of the instrument even if the purported indorsement of the bank was entirely unauthorized. Thus the trial court was correct in concluding that the plaintiff hospital was a holder of the instrument, and entitled to judgment.

In Re Quantum Development Corporation

Facts: As part of a bankruptcy proceeding, the American Fidelity Fire Insurance Company, plaintiff, issued a certified check for $84,858 payable to the order of "Charles R. Joy, Receiver." Joy indorsed the check restrictively, "For deposit in Quantum Acct. Quantum Bankruptcy," and negotiated it to Bank of Nova Scotia, which in return issued certificates of deposit to Joy that were payable to Joy personally. Joy later cashed the certificates, absconded with the money, and American Fidelity then brought this action to recover the amount of the check from the BNS. American Fidelity's major contention was that defendant bank's actions were inconsistent with the terms of the restrictive endorsement.

Holding: (of trial court) Judgment for plaintiff. The Bank of Nova Scotia was legally put on notice, by virtue of the restrictive indorsement, that Joy had received the check only in his capacity as receiver for the bankrupt Quantum firm and not for his personal use. Therefore, when BNS received the check its use of the proceeds was restricted --- that is, it had the duty to see that the proceeds went only into the Quantum account, and nowhere else. By giving Joy certificates of deposit payable to him personally the bank violated this duty and thus must be responsible for the subsequent loss of the funds occasioned by Joy's absconding with the money. (Note: Ordinarily it is only the restrictive indorser who can recover from the restrictive indorsee when the latter does not obey the terms of the indorsement. In this case, however, it was the drawer of the check who was permitted to recover, apparently for two reasons. First, the check was not payable to Joy personally, and thus when he indorsed restrictively it was only in a representative capacity --- i.e., Joy was never the owner of the check personally, as the usual indorser is. And, secondly, it is only fair for American Fidelity to recover in this action since it appears it may still be liable as surety to Quantum's creditors.)

Cole v. First National Bank of Gillette

Facts: The Coles (through a company owned by them) drew a check payable to the order of Wyoming Homes and issued the check to Wyoming Homes in partial payment for a home purchase. The Wyoming Homes salesman, without indorsing the check, deposited it in Wyoming Homes' account in the Gillette Bank, which credited the account. The Gillette Bank put the check into channels of collection and it was duly charged to the Coles' account in the drawee bank, First National Bank of Buffalo.

The Coles then discovered that Wyoming Homes was guilty of fraud, and it brought this action against the Gillette bank (where the check was originally deposited by Wyoming Homes) on the theory that the bank was merely a transferee of the check --- rather than a holder --- since Wyoming Homes did not indorse the check to the bank. If that theory is correct, then the bank took the check subject to all defenses existing in favor of the Coles, and is liable in this action. The trial court (for reasons appearing below) rejected the Coles' contention and gave judgment for the bank.

Holding: Judgment affirmed. Normally, a transferee of unindorsed order paper does not qualify as a holder of the instrument, and thus certainly is not a holder in due course. However, Sec. 4-205 expressly permits a bank which has taken a check for collection to indicate on the back of the check by stamp (as the Gillette Bank did) that the item was deposited by that bank in the customer's account. When that is done, such a notation constitutes an indorsement of the customer from a legal standpoint. Thus the Gillette Bank was a holder, and, the check having been honored by the drawee bank, it has no liability to the Coles.

ANSWERS TO QUESTIONS AND PROBLEMS:

1. The X Corporation's contention is not correct. When the payee, Gladys Nall, indorsed the check in blank it thereby became a bearer instrument. Because such an instrument may be negotiated by "delivery only" --- i.e., without additional indorsements --- it is immaterial that the Y Company did not indorse its name to the check. H thus became a holder of the bearer instrument the moment that it was delivered to him.

2. (a) P's indorsement is a qualified indorsement; A's indorsement is a restrictive one; and B's indorsement is a special one. (b) No. An indorsement "Pay to A" has the same legal effect as one that reads "Pay to the order

of A." Thus A's transfer of the instrument to B _is_ a negotiation. (c) All of the transferees (A, B and C) qualify as holders of the instrument.

3. The bank would not be a holder. The first indorsement, "Pay to the order of Gulf Oil, (signed) P Company," was a special indorsement. As a result, the check could not thereafter be negotiated until Gulf Oil indorsed it. Because the purported indorsement of Gulf Oil proved to be a _forgery_, the ownership of the check remained in Gulf, and thus the bank that subsequently took the check does _not_ qualify as a holder. And this is true even if the bank had no reason to suspect that the indorsement of Gulf was forged.

4. The difficulty in this case is the fact that when an instrument is payable to two persons jointly, both payees have to indorse it in order for it to be negotiated further. Here, the ABC Auto Repair Company will probably refuse to indorse the check.

5. As the text indicates, a blank indorsement converts an order instrument into a bearer instrument. This means that if you (indorser) thereafter lose it, it can be negotiated further without indorsement and any subsequent good faith purchaser would become the owner of it.

6. A bearer instrument may be converted into an order instrument by the holder simply indorsing it specially. Thus if B is holder of an instrument payable to bearer, all he need do is indorse it, for example, "Pay to X, (signed) B."

7. No; Y is a holder of the instrument. A minor does not have the right to disaffirm his indorsement of an instrument after the instrument has been negotiated to an innocent third party (in this case, Y).

8. The new trustee can hold the Baltimore bank liable for the amount of the instrument, but can not hold the Chicago bank. (The Baltimore bank is liable because it disobeyed the restrictive indorsement when it gave cash to Chandler, personally. The Chicago bank, however, has no liability because it is merely an intermediary bank in this situation.)

CHAPTER 20

COMMERCIAL PAPER: HOLDERS IN DUE COURSE

AUTHORS' SUGGESTIONS:

1. As was indicated in the suggestions in this manual relative to Chapter 23, we again have a situation where the basic section, Sec. 3-302, is followed by two explanatory sections. While that section should obviously receive primary attention insofar as class discussion is concerned, Sec. 3-304 --- especially in subsections (1), (3), and (4) --- should receive almost "equal billing" because of the many situations which are expressly clarified by that section.

2. While this chapter is shorter than its original version in the first edition (at the suggestion of a number of users) some instructors may still feel it is somewhat more detailed than necessary. Such persons should find it easy to omit, in class assignments, a number of paragraphs on narrow points. An alternative, of course, is to make no assigned omissions but to indicate to the class (in advance) those points that are felt not to justify class discussion time. The question as to the circumstances in which a bank may qualify as a holder in due course (with the applicable first-in, first-out rule), might be an example of one narrow topic that could be deleted.

3. Since most holders of commercial paper fall into one of two classes (i.e., they are holders in due course, or they are not), students are somewhat surprised when a third category of holder is reached, the "holder through a holder in due course." However, once the basic idea is explained students usually have no difficulty with this category.

CASE BRIEFS:

Norman v. World Wide Distributors et al.

Facts: The Normans signed a promissory note as purchase price of a piece

of furniture (breakfront) which they bought from State Wide/World Wide
Distributors. World Wide negotiated the note to defendant Peoples National
Fund, which obtained a judgment against the Normans at maturity date. The
Normans then brought this action to have the judgment set aside, alleging
(a) that World Wide was guilty of fraud in acquiring the note from them, and
(b) that defendant Peoples Fund --- which obtained the judgment --- was not
a holder in due course, and thus stood in no better position than World
Wide. The trial court set the judgment aside, and Peoples Fund appealed.

Holding: Judgment affirmed. Peoples Fund did <u>not</u> take the note in good
faith, in view of the fact that it knew of the general nature of the referral
racket carried on by World Wide; that it was so suspicious of the legality
of the referral plan that an officer called the Normans to say that Peoples
had no connection with the plan; and that Peoples knew that State Wide and
World Wide operators had changed the company name three times in one year.

Salter v. Vanotti

Facts: The Vanottis purchased a lot in a subdivision from Cochise College
Park, and gave their promissory note to Cochise in payment for it. After
the Vanottis made several monthly payments, Cochise negotiated the note to
Salter, plaintiff. The Vanottis later refused to pay the balance due, contending that they had several defenses against Cochise, and further contending that Salter was not a holder in due course.

Holding: The trial court was correct in ruling that Salter was <u>not</u> a holder
in due course, because he had knowledge (at the time that he acquired the
note) that the purchase contract which the Vanottis had with Cochise gave
them the right to rescind the contract within six months from the time of
their purchase. Salter also knew that the Vanottis were entitled to a deed
to the property after three payments were made, and that a deed had not
been given them. Thus, Salter took the instrument with knowledge of a claim
or defense against the instrument, which disqualified him from HDC status.

ANSWERS TO QUESTIONS AND PROBLEMS:

1. The Supreme Court of Minnesota held that Merrill Lynch (ML) <u>was</u> a
holder in due course of the check. Therefore, ML had the legal right to
give value for the check to Drexler, as it did.

The issue was whether ML took the check "with notice" of a possible
claim to the instrument on the part of Eldon's, the drawer, or "with notice"
of a possible dispute of some sort between Eldon's and Drexler, from whom ML
received the check. The starting point is this: if the check had been
payable to Drexler, and if Drexler had indorsed it to ML, ML would clearly
have taken the instrument without notice of a claim, and would clearly have

qualified as a holder in due course. The only issue, therefore, is whether the fact that the instrument was payable to ML rather than to Drexler (with ML being a company that had had no earlier dealings with Eldon's) should by itself have put ML on notice of a claim or defense in favor of Eldon's. The court held that this fact alone did not put ML on notice, saying, "Merrill Lynch was entitled to conclude that Drexler, known (by Merrill Lynch) to be an attorney (for Eldon's), had lawfully obtained and was delivering the instrument to discharge the debt incurred by his own stock purchase." On the contrary, the court said, ML was justified in assuming that the check was in payment for legal services rendered by Drexler to Eldon's, and that Drexler had simply asked Eldon's to make the check out directly to ML in payment of the debt Drexler owed to ML.

2. The Supreme Court of Wyoming held that Wood (third party/purchaser) was a holder in due course only to the extent of the amount of the loan. Thus, where Wood brought this action against Willman (maker) and Willman had a personal defense against the payee, Wood was entitled to recover the amount of the loan, because he had given value for the instrument to that extent. But he was not permitted to recover the full amount of the note. (For example, if the amount of the note were $1,000 and the amount of the debt owed by the payee to Wood were $400, Wood will recover $400. As to the balance of $600 Willman may successfully assert his defense.)

3. (a) H qualifies as a holder in due course. He took the instrument for value, in good faith, before it was overdue, and with no notice of any defense against it. (b) Under Sec. 3-303, a holder has given value "to the extent that the agreed consideration has been performed" --- i.e., performed before the holder learns of a defense. Thus H has given value to the extent of $600, but not as to the $400 balance. Thus if H were to sue M on the note, he is entitled only to $600. (I.e., as to the balance of $400, M's defense may be asserted.)

4. In the preceding case, if H had purchased the note on October 20, he would not qualify as a holder in due course. The reason is that the note, being payable 90 days after July 1, would have been overdue as of September 29.

5. The bank may charge P's account with the amount of the check (assuming, of course, that it then returns the check to him). The reason is that the typical bank/depositor contract provides that the crediting of an account on any check deposited by the bank's customers is conditional upon the check being honored by the drawee bank when the check reaches that bank.

6. S is not correct. Once it is established that S knew (or, under the circumstances, should have known) of the dishonor before he acquired the note on June 20, he does not qualify as a holder in due course even though he acquired it within a reasonable time after issue. Sec. 3-302(1)(c) provides that a person is disqualified if he takes an overdue instrument knowing it is overdue, or if he has notice that it has been dishonored.

Notice of _either_ fact disqualifies the taker as a holder in due course.

7. (a) D is not a holder in due course since she did not give value for the note. (b) While D is not a holder in due course, the prior holder (H) did qualify as a holder in due course. Thus D is a _holder_ _through_ _a_ _holder_ _in_ _due_ _course_ and is entitled to judgment against M on that basis.

8. (a) The Griffey Corporation was not a holder in due course when it received the instrument because at that time it had not given value (i.e., its consideration had not yet been performed). (b) In this case the Griffey Corporation does _not_ have all the rights of a holder in due course even though it acquired the note the second time from Concepcion, who did qualify as a holder in due course. The "reacquirer rule" provides that when a holder of an instrument acquires an instrument that he had owned earlier, his status is determined as of the first time he acquired the instrument. Sec. 3-201(1) provides that the reacquirer "cannot improve his position" by repurchasing the instrument.

CHAPTER 21

COMMERCIAL PAPER: DEFENSES

AUTHORS' SUGGESTIONS:

1. The study of the subject of defenses permits students, for the first time, to see precisely the several kinds of situations in which holders in due course are entitled to payment, whereas ordinary holders are not. Thus this chapter pulls together the various topics (requirements of negotiability, and requirements of the HDC) that have previously been studied somewhat in isolation.

2. When the time for distinguishing between personal and real defenses is reached in class, it is well at the outset to make it clear that three general kinds of defenses may be either personal or real, depending upon their degree of surrounding circumstances. These are the defenses of fraud, illegality, and incapacity. (The text mentions these as they are discussed individually, but it avoids confusion to remind the class of this apparent overlapping at the very beginning.)

3. In regard to the discussion of the "FTC Rule," a minor conceptual problem may exist. While it is clear that the rule prevents the acquirer of a consumer credit contract (which contains the required notice) from enforcing the instrument against the purchaser of the consumer goods if such purchaser has a defense against the seller, the FTC Rule does not speak in terms of holder in due course. In other words, it does not say the acquirer of such a contract is clearly not a holder in due course; it simply says that the acquirer cannot enforce the instrument if a defense exists. (Presumably we should not call the acquirer an HDC, because an HDC knows he takes the instrument free of personal defenses, while the acquirer of a consumer credit contract under FTC rule knows that he takes it subject to such defenses.)

CASE BRIEFS:

Commercial Bank & Trust Co. v. Middle Georgia Livestock Sales

Facts: Middle Georgia Livestock Sales (MGLS) drew a check and issued it to a seller of cattle. Thereafter MGLS learned the cattle it had purchased were stolen, so it issued a stop payment order to the drawee bank. MGLS (drawer) is now sued on the check by Commercial Bank and Trust Company, a holder in due course. The trial court ruled in favor of Commercial Bank.

Holding: Judgment reversed. Under Sec. 3-305(2), a holder in due course does not take the instrument from the defense of illegality if the illegality is such as to render the transaction (in payment for which the instrument was issued) "a nullity." Here the sale of the cattle was a totally illegal act insofar as the seller was concerned, and hence the innocent drawer of the check (MGLS) may assert the defense of illegality successfully.

ANSWERS TO QUESTIONS AND PROBLEMS:

1. The New York appellate court held that Rochman _could_ assert his defense against the bank. Thus the bank recovered nothing. When Rochman indorsed the instrument and delivered it to the bank with the understanding that he would not be liable until D'Onofrio also indorsed it, Rochman's delivery of the instrument to the bank was a _conditional delivery_. This being the case, when the condition (indorsement by D'Onofrio) never occurred, Rochman could assert the defense of "conditional delivery" against the bank (which was obviously not an HDC since it was fully aware of the agreement when it took the instrument).

2. The evidence that was introduced by the trust company as to the Hutchinsons' intelligence caused the Pennsylvania Common Pleas Court to rule that the Hutchinsons' defense of "misrepresentation" was invalid. The Hutchinsons contended that they did not know, and had no reason to know, that they were signing a promissory note, in view of the fact that the salesman told them that they were merely signing a proof-of-demonstration document. However, the court noted, the evidence indicated (a) that Hutchinson was a high school graduate and employed as a clerk in a responsible job; (b) that his wife had three years of high school; and (c) that the depositions which they prepared indicated a high degree of intelligence. In view of this evidence, the court said, the Hutchinsons clearly _could_ have determined that they were signing a note if they had exercised reasonable care. Since they did not exercise such care, their claim of misrepresentation was rejected.

3. H is entitled to the $1,000. The defense which D has against P, the payee, is "failure of consideration" --- i.e., essentially breach of contract, resulting from P's failure to install the fence in a workmanlike and acceptable manner. This is only a personal defense, and cannot be asserted against a holder in due course.

4. (a) The name of D's defense is "unauthorized completion."

   (b) If H did not qualify as an HDC, he will recover nothing from D. Under Sec. 3-407(2)(b) an ordinary holder recovers nothing if the wrongful completion (as here) is both "fraudulent and material."

5. The defense of illegality is a personal defense unless --- under Sec. 3-305(2) --- the illegality of the transaction between the payee and drawer was so illegal as to render the obligation of the drawer a *nullity*. Thus, unless the transaction is entirely illegal under local law --- that is, null and void --- the defense of illegality is only personal.

6. Even if the P Company qualifies as an HDC, it ordinarily is not entitled to judgment against D. The defense of "minority" is a real defense in most jurisdictions.

7. Assuming no negligence on M's part, H is entitled to recover $500 --- the original amount of the note, only --- from M. Sec. 3-407(3) provides that where there has been a material alteration, an HDC "may in all cases enforce the instrument according to its original tenor."

8. (a) The FTC rule is designed to eliminate situations in which a buyer purchases a consumer product, signs a credit instrument in payment, and later has to pay the instrument in full to an HDC even if the product which he received from the seller turns out to be defective, or is not delivered at all.

   (b) The FTC rule is applicable to consumer credit obligations where (a) the buyer of the goods gives a note or other credit instrument directly to the seller, and (b) where the buyer takes the proceeds of a "purchase money loan" and gives such proceeds to the seller in payment of his purchase.

CHAPTER 22

COMMERCIAL PAPER: LIABILITY OF THE PARTIES

AUTHORS' SUGGESTIONS:

1. The subject of "liability of the parties" is generally felt to be the most difficult part of commercial paper law, and thus adequate class time should be allocated to it. Three class periods are probably desirable; one period would ordinarily not be.

2. As is true of other areas of commercial paper, certain topics in this chapter must also be kept separate from others. For example, the liability of primary parties must at least initially be discussed apart from that of secondary parties (though a later comparison is certainly helpful). Similarly, when discussing the liability of secondary parties, care must be taken to distinguish warranty liability from secondary or conditional liability.

3. The fact that there are only two kinds of primary parties should be emphasized at the outset: makers of notes and acceptors of drafts. In this regard, it is sometimes initially difficult for students to accept the idea that drawers of checks (and other drafts) are secondary parties. This difficulty can be allayed by noting two facts: (a) what the conditions are that must be met in order to hold the drawer of a check on his or her conditional liability, and (b) the fact that drawers of checks --- despite their "secondary" label --- are not discharged of conditional liability as a result of late presentment except in the limited circumstances set forth in Sec. 3-502(1)(b). Since these limited circumstances do not usually exist, the drawer's conditional liability in ordinary cases is thus closer to that of a primary party than to that of the usual secondary party (such as an indorser).

4. The various rules in the UCC as to when presentment of different kinds of instruments is required, the times at which such presentments must be made, and the times within which notice of dishonor must be given are un-questionably complicated. Certainly no one can or should memorize all of Sections 3-501, 503, and 508. Rather, it is hoped that only the most

important provisions of these sections --- which the text highlights --- can be concentrated on, and thus substantially understood.

CASE BRIEFS:

Pollin v. Cindy Mfg. Co. and Apfelbaum

Facts: Pollin, a holder of 36 payroll checks of the Cindy Manufacturing Company, brought this action against the company and its president, Apfelbaum, after the checks were not honored by the drawee bank. Pollin contended that Apfelbaum was personally liable on the checks since he simply signed his name, as drawer, without words indicating that he was signing only as a representative of the company. The trial court agreed, and entered judgment for Pollin.

Holding: Judgment reversed. The court said that Apfelbaum would be personally liable if his signature alone were considered. However, the court ruled that, under Sec. 3-402 of the UCC, a person who claims to have signed in a representative capacity (but where the signature does not indicate this) is personally liable only where the instrument _in its entirety_ fails to show that such person signed in a representative capacity. In this case, the instrument did indicate Apfelbaum was only a representative, since the Cindy Manufacturing Company name was printed on the checks in two places, and since the checks were also labelled "payroll checks." Hence Apfelbaum has no personal liability on the checks.

Hane v. Exten

Facts: The Extens indorsed an installment note containing a provision that if any payment were missed, the entire instrument became due. A payment was missed by the maker (apparently in November of 1965) but the holder, Hane, did not present the instrument for payment to the maker until April of 1967. Payment was refused, and Hane got a judgment (by virtue of the confession of judgment clause in the note) against the Extens, indorsers. They now bring this action against Hane to have the judgment set aside. The trial court did so.

Holding: Judgment affirmed. Where an instrument is accelerated, presentment for payment is due within a reasonable time after the acceleration. Here the presentment was not made until almost 18 months after the acceleration, which was clearly not reasonable. Thus the Extens are freed of liability.

Fair Finance Co. v. Fourco, Inc.

Facts: Fourco, defendant, took a promissory note in payment for goods which it sold. It then indorsed the note "without recourse" and negotiated it to Fair Finance. Fair Finance was not able to recover the full amount of the note from the maker because Fourco, in filling out the note, had computed the interest at a rate higher than that allowed by Ohio law. Fair Finance then brought this action to recover the balance from Fourco, the indorser. Fourco defended on the ground that a qualified indorser, rather than guaranteeing there are no defenses, merely guarantees he has no knowledge of defenses. The trial court found that Fourco had no knowledge of the excess interest and entered judgment for it.

Holding: Judgment reversed. Where Fourco itself prepared the note, including computation of the interest, it cannot contend that it has "no knowledge" of the wrongful computation. In the eyes of the law it possessed knowledge of the illegal computation, even though it did not intentionally charge more than the law allowed. Thus Fourco is liable on its warranty that it has no knowledge of a defense (Sec. 3-417(C)).

ANSWERS TO QUESTIONS AND PROBLEMS:

1. The Georgia Appeals Court held that the trial court was correct in admitting Johnson's evidence. The court observed, first, that if the plaintiff in this suit had been a third party (i.e., a purchaser of the instrument), Johnson would have been absolutely liable on the instrument personally, and his evidence would thus not be allowed. However, where the plaintiff is the payee in a case such as this, as was true here, the defendant/maker is permitted to introduce evidence that would show that the plaintiff/payee did know that the maker (here, Johnson) was simply signing in a representative capacity. This result is brought about by Sec. 3-403 of the UCC, which provides, in effect, that evidence indicating that the maker signed in a representative capacity is not allowed "except as otherwise established between the immediate parties."

2. This evidence should not be admitted. As indicated in the answer to Question 1 above, where the plaintiff is a third party/purchaser of the instrument (here, the Last National Bank), the maker (Vance) is not allowed to introduce evidence indicating that the payee knew that he (the maker) was signing merely in a representative capacity. Thus Vance is personally liable to the bank. (Thus, as the text indicates, Sec. 3-403(2)(b) applies to the situation presented by Question 1 --- where the defendant's signature includes words of representation but the principal's name does not appear --- and also to the situation presented by Question 2 --- where the principal's name appears, but the defendant's signature does not include words of representation.)

3. The Supreme Court of Nebraska held that the telephone inquiry was not a valid presentment. Thus the reply by the bank employee (to the effect that

there were insufficient funds to cover the check) did not constitute a dishonor of the instrument. The court said that, under Sec. 3-504 of the UCC, "It seems obvious that payment of a personal check or refusal of payment and dishonor by the drawee bank necessitate exhibition or delivery of the instrument, under current banking practices."

4. The Nebraska Supreme Court agreed with Mrs. Fisher's contention. The court first observed that one of the "preconditions" to an indorser's liability is "timely notice of dishonor." In this case, the court conceded, the last bank to receive notice of dishonor (Nevada State Bank) did act promptly by giving Mrs. Fisher notice of dishonor the day following its receipt of notice of dishonor. However, the court continued, the fact that this notice did not occur until 90 days after the date of Mrs. Fisher's indorsement made it obvious that one of the banks involved in the bank collection process (i.e., some bank other than Nevada State Bank) "violated its midnight deadline" obligation. In other words, that other bank held the dishonored check for a long period of time before giving notice of the dishonor to Nevada State Bank, rather than giving notice by midnight of the day following the dishonor. In these circumstances, the court held, Mrs. Fisher is no longer liable as an indorser, saying "prompt action by all parties to the transaction is contemplated before an indorser may be held liable. The Nevada State Bank (therefore) may look only to the violator bank for its recovery," rather than to Mrs. Fisher.

5. M is not correct. The rule that he is relying on is applicable only where two conditions exist: (a) the holder presents the note late, and (b) the bank failed after the due date but before the late presentment occurred. In the instant case neither of these conditions exists. (I.e., the holder presented the note at the proper time, and the bank had failed before that time.) Thus the maker, M, is fully liable on the note.

6. Y's defense is not good. First, it should be noted that although Y indorsed the note "without recourse," such an indorsement does carry with it the warranty of good title (the same as any other type of indorsement). Second, and more importantly, the warranty of title is a guarantee that the indorser's title is absolutely good, rather than a warranty to the effect that the indorser believes his title is good. Thus, in this case, Y is liable to Z (who did not receive title because of the forged indorsement of X) even though Y --- at the time of his indorsement --- was not aware of the forgery.

7. X is not liable to H. A person who negotiates an instrument without indorsing it has no conditional (promissory) liability. In other words, a person who negotiates a check in this manner does not promise to pay the instrument in case the drawer has insufficient funds in the drawee bank when the check is presented for payment.

8. The maker has continuing liability to the current holder (Bravo), and also to the first indorser (Alpha) if Alhpa discharges his liability to

Bravo by taking up the instrument from him (Bravo). Insofar as Alpha is concerned, he remains liable to Bravo if Bravo never receives payment from the maker. (I.e., as indicated above, Bravo has the right to demand that Alpha take up the instrument if he (Bravo) never receives payment from the maker. Charlie, the third indorser, is freed of liability completely.)

CHAPTER 23

COMMERCIAL PAPER: CHECKS AND THE BANK-DEPOSITOR RELATIONSHIP

AUTHORS' SUGGESTIONS:

1. The subject of checks has several characteristics that makes it easier to teach than those aspects of commercial paper covered in prior chapters. First, students are much more familiar with checks than other kinds of instruments, so the special check rules have an obvious real-life usefulness. Secondly, checks present fewer "mechanical" problems than do other drafts, since there is no acceptor and, generally, they are outstanding for shorter periods of time. Thirdly, unlike some of the rules encountered earlier, we here come across a number of rules applicable to checks alone.

2. In order to answer selected problems presented in this chapter, certain references to sections in Article 4 of the UCC (Bank Deposits and Collections) have been made. However, it should be clear to the instructor that no attempt has been made to cover that Article comprehensively.

3. Most of the problems arising out of the bank-depositor relationship are today resolved by specific sections of Articles 3 and 4 of the UCC. But despite this relative certainty, cases often arise which either require judicial interpretation of particular sections of the UCC, or which require courts to harmonize two or more sections of the UCC insofar as possible (as in the Granite Equipment case).

CASE BRIEFS:

Phillips Home Furnishings, Inc. v. Continental Bank

Facts: Schectman, plaintiff, put $5,669 in his regular deposit bag and placed it in defendant bank's night depository safe after regular banking hours. The bag was not in the safe when opened the next day. Schectman brought this action to recover damages when the bank refused to credit his account. The bank defended on the ground that a provision in its night depository agreement, signed by Schectman, absolved it of liability. The trial court ruled that the defense was good, and entered judgment for the bank.

Holding: Judgment reversed. (1) While there is a split of authority, Pennsylvania has adopted the view that a bailee (here, the bank) cannot by contract legally relieve itself of liability for its own negligence. (2) Leaving aside bailment law, in view of the great public necessity for banking services, and in view of the fact that depositors have no bargaining power when it comes to preparation of bank-customer contracts, exculpatory clauses utilized by banks in agreements such as this one are contrary to public policy. (The court then returned the case to the trial court for the purpose of having it determine whether the bank was or was not negligent.)

Granite Equipment Leasing Corp. v. Hempstead Bank

Facts: Plaintiff (Granite) stopped payment on a check it drew on defendant bank. The stop payment order was not renewed, and a year later the check was presented to defendant bank through the bank collection process. The bank honored it and charged plaintiff's account. Plaintiff then brought this action to recover the amount of the check, claiming wrongful payment by the bank.

Holding: (of the trial court) Judgment for the bank. (1) A written stop payment order is good only six months, unless renewed. (Sec. 4-403). Once the order expired, it had no further effect. Therefore, the most plaintiff can argue is that the check was stale. (2) However, a bank may honor a stale check without liability to the drawer if its payment is made in good faith. (Sec. 4-404) Here there was no evidence of lack of good faith.

ANSWERS TO QUESTIONS AND PROBLEMS:

1. If the bank became insolvent between August 1 and August 10, D may discharge his liability to P by giving him a written assignment of his rights to his funds in the bank, to the extent of the checks. (Under the 30-day rule, P had the duty to present the check no later than July 31. Because he did not, the risk that the bank might fail thereafter is thus shifted from the drawer to the holder.)

2. With rare exception, certification of a check makes the bank absolutely liable on the instrument, and certification (at the request of a holder) discharges the drawer and indorsers. Additionally, certification extinguishes the drawer's right to stop payment.

3. Since the check is stale, the bank has no duty to honor it. Despite this fact, however, the bank may honor the check if it wishes to do so. (Sec. 4-404)

4. The bank may not charge D's account. An oral stop payment order is good for 14 days. (Sec. 4-403) Therefore, the bank had the duty to honor the oral order through June 24, even if no written stop payment order had been issued by D at all.

5. The bank may be able to show that D suffered no loss in at least two general situations. The first would be where the bank can prove that D had no legally adequate reason for stopping payment (i.e., D had no defense at all against the instrument). The second would be where D had a personal defense only, and where the person it paid qualified as a holder in due course. In both of these cases the holder would have had a legal right to recover the amount of the check from D even if the bank had obeyed the order.

6. H's defense is not valid. A person who surrenders a check to a payor bank thereby warrants that he has a good title to the instrument. (Sec. 4-207(1)(a)). In this case, H did not have good title because of the forged indorsement. The fact that he had no reason to suspect the indorsement is thus immaterial.

7. H's defense is not good. Under Sec. 4-207(1)(c) of the UCC, a person who obtains payment of a check from a drawee bank warrants to that bank (subject to limited exceptions) that the instrument "has not been materially altered." Therefore, where the instrument was altered from $100 to $700, H is usually liable to the bank for the $600 despite the fact that he was not aware of the alteration.

8. As the text indicates under the heading "Exception to the Rule; Negligent Drawer," a drawer may be guilty of negligence if he fails to use reasonable care in preventing unauthorized persons from having access to a check writing machine. Additionally, he may be guilty of negligence if he does not examine his cancelled checks within 14 days of receiving them, if one of such checks was a forgery and if, after the 14 days had elapsed, the bank in good faith honored a second check forged by the same wrongdoer. (Sec. 4-406(2)(b))

CHAPTER 24

SECURED TRANSACTIONS

AUTHORS' SUGGESTIONS:

1. The status of the secured party upon a debtor's default, as compared to the unsecured party, should be stressed. This will give the instructor the opportunity to review or introduce areas such as bankruptcy and exemption laws.

2. The instructor should clearly distinguish between the <u>creation</u> of a security interest and the <u>perfection</u> of the security interest. The former establishes rights and duties between the debtor and the secured party, the latter any priority the secured party may have as against other parties with an interest in the same collateral.

3. The floating lien concept is perpetuated by the Code. It is important to note that once a security interest is properly perfected, this one perfection may give the secured party priority even though the collateral is moved to another jurisdiction. Also this one perfection can cover after-acquired collateral, future advances made on the same collateral, proceeds from the sale of the collateral, and continue to exist where the collateral has been commingled with other goods. This concept can become a problem for <u>subsequent</u> secured parties who have security interests in the same collateral.

4. Perfection does not assure the secured party that his rights in the collateral will prevail over <u>all third persons</u> who may have an interest in the same collateral. Three classes of third persons deserve special attention: the buyer in the ordinary course of business, the buyer not in the ordinary course of business, and a subsequent perfected secured party with a purchase money security interest. (§9-307 and §9-312)

5. Rights of the secured party upon a debtor's default are important. The "self-help" repossession problem needs a thorough discussion, as well as the situation where a secured party may keep the collateral in satisfaction of the debt as opposed to exercising his right to sell the collateral.

CASE BRIEFS:

M. Rutkin Electric Supply Co., Inc. v. Burdette Electric Inc.

Facts: Burdette allegedly assigned an account receivable to one Rabin. Burdette is adjudicated insolvent and the appointed receiver wants to set aside this assignment. Rabin claims he has an enforceable security interest in the account receivable and introduced into evidence a financing statement signed by both parties. At the trial, the receiver demanded Rabin produce a security agreement, which Rabin failed to do. The trial court concluded there was none and held for the receiver.

Holding: Judgment for receiver affirmed. To have a security interest, the secured party must show the collateral to be in the possession of the secured party or a security agreement describing the collateral signed by the debtor. An account receivable cannot be possessed, thus a security agreement must be proved and such must be in writing. The financing statement is not a substitute for a security agreement. Since Rabin could not produce a written security agreement, Rabin did not have a security interest in the account receivable and the collateral is vested in the receiver.

Kimbrell's Furniture Co., Inc. v. Friedman

Facts: Plaintiff Kimbrell sold a new television set and tape player by a conditional sale contract designated as a purchase money security agreement. The purchasers, O'Neal and his wife, took the purchased goods to defendant pawnbroker Friedman as security for a loan. Kimbrell did not file a financing statement. Upon the default of the O'Neals, Kimbrell wanted the collateral to satisfy the balance owed on the conditional sale contracts. Friedman contended his possessory lien had priority over the unrecorded purchase money security interest of Kimbrell. The lower court held for Friedman

Holding: Judgment for Friedman reversed. The court held first that Kimbrell had a purchase money security interest in consumer goods and had a perfected security interest without a filing. This perfection became effective upon the execution of the security agreement and possession of the collateral by the O'Neals (§9-312(4) and §9-312(5)(b)). Second, the court held Friedman could not be a buyer in the ordinary course of business (as he had alleged) who would take free of a perfected security in the collateral. For Friedman to be a buyer in the ordinary course of business, the O'Neals would have to be persons in the business of selling goods of that kind, and they obviously were not.

Hunt v. Marine Midland Bank-Central

Facts: The plaintiff purchased a car from co-defendant Heritage car dealership and financed it through co-defendant Bank on a retail installment contract. The plaintiff was in default when the Bank learned that a mechanic's lien was held by co-defendant car dealership for repairs. The Bank paid for the repairs, took possession and sold the car despite a loan payment made by plaintiff. Apparently proceeds from the sale were insufficient to cover all costs and the balance of the loan. The Bank requested that plaintiff pay the deficiency. Plaintiff not only refused but filed suit claiming Bank and Heritage committed a tort of conversion and/or in the manner of repossession violated her constitutional rights of due process. Defendants filed motions (primarily) for summary judgment dismissing plaintiff's complaint.

<u>Holding</u>: Summary judgment dismissing plaintiff's complaint was granted. The court held that the security interest created by the installment sales contract gave both parties interests in the collateral. To determine the constitutional issue, the court stated it was not only prepared to protect the buyer's possessory interest to use and enjoy, but at the same time the seller's right to be paid in full. Thus, the court held that when the contract agreed to by the debtor provided for repossession ("self-help") of the collateral upon default in accordance with the Code, such agreement is constitutional. Even though the Bank accepted a late payment, plaintiff was in default and subject to repossession of the collateral. The tort of coversion claim was disallowed as Heritage has a lien as provided by statute and upon payment by Bank (who had right to possession) had no choice but to transfer the collateral to the bank.

<u>ANSWERS TO QUESTIONS AND PROBLEMS</u>:

1. (a) To create a security interest, unless the possession of the collateral is with the secured party, a written security agreement signed by the debtor and describing the collateral is required. The secured party must also give value and the debtor must have rights in the collateral.

   (b) The classification of collateral between A-W is <u>inventory</u>, and perfection would be by a central filing. The classification of the collateral between A-B will depend on B's use. If the use is for the home, it will be classified as a <u>consumer good</u>. If B was a doctor and purchased it for his office, the sofa would be classified as <u>equipment</u>. If a consumer good, A could perfect by attachment (automatic upon signing of security agreement without a filing, since it is a purchase money security interest) <u>or</u> A could perfect by filing locally. If the collateral is equipment, A would file centrally.

   (c) W has no rights in the sofa purchased by B, because B is a bona fide purchaser in the ordinary course of business and takes free of W's perfected security interest.

   (d) Upon B's default, A can pursue any judicial remedy available, as well as his rights under the Code. He can repossess the sofa by judicial or peaceful nonjudicial process. Once the sofa is repossessed, A must sell it (he cannot keep it in satisfaction of the debt) <u>if it is a consumer good</u>, since B has paid 60% or more of the purchase price. A's sale must be in a commercially reasonable manner. Proceeds from the sale would go first to repossession and sale costs, second to the balance of the debt owed A, third to junior security interests who have made written demand, and the balance, if any, to the debtor. If the proceeds do not cover the costs and A's debt, A is entitled to a deficiency judgment. If the sofa is equipment, A does not have to resell it, but may keep it in full satisfaction of the debt if he gives notice to W and any other secured party who has filed a written notice of claim, and no objection is received within 21 days after notice is sent.

The debtor has a right to redeem the collateral at anytime prior to A's disposal of it unless the debtor has waived this right in writing <u>after default</u>. To exercise his right of redemption, B must tender payment of all obligations as well as all reasonable costs incurred by A.

2. Unless the collateral is consumer goods and 60% or more has been paid, the secured party may keep it in full satisfaction of the debt, providing the secured party gives the debtor and (except for consumer goods) other secured parties, who have given the secured party written notice of their claim, notice of his intent. If no objection is received within <u>twenty-one days</u> after this notice is <u>sent</u>, the secured party may keep the collateral subject to debtor's right of redemption. If objection is received, the secured party must sell the collateral.

3. (a) A secured party in possession of the collateral must use reasonable care in the custody and preservation of it. Failure to exercise reasonable care subjects the secured party to liability. In this case, P must milk the cows to preserve their value, as failure could cause sickness and/or death of the cows. P is under an obligation to milk the cows even in absence of permission by D. The secured party is entitled (unless he waives the right) to any increase in the value of the collateral in his possession as additional security, except if the increase is money. Money must be used to reduce the debt or turned over to the debtor. Although the milk is an increase in value for security purposes, it must be sold to preserve its value (it will spoil). Thus the cash from the sale of the milk would have to be turned over to D or be used to reduce D's debt.

(b) In absence of agreement the secured party is entitled to keep any increase in value of the collateral in his possession as additional security. P could keep the calf as additional security.

4. (a) The secured party must keep the collateral (except fungible goods) identifiable and cannot commingle debtor's goods with others. If a secured party wrongfully commingles the collateral, he is liable for any loss suffered by the debtor. The question here is whether milk cows are fungible goods. In most states they are not.

(b) Unless the security agreement provides to the contrary, the debtor is responsible for all reasonable charges incurred in the custody and preservation of the collateral in the secured party's possession.

5. If the debtor were in default, the secured party could employ any judicial remedy available, or repossess under the Code. However, if the secured party really feels that all the debtor needs is a little more time to pay, the secured party should file a continuation statement to retain his priority. A properly filed perfected security interest is effective for five years from date of filing. To continue this perfected interest (priority), the secured party should file a continuation statement within six months prior to the expiration date. This will continue his perfection for another five years.

6. (a) Collateral would be classified as <u>inventory</u>. Since the retailer would obviously have possession, the wholesaler would perfect by filing <u>centrally</u>.

   (b) Collateral would be classified as <u>consumer goods</u>. Perfection would be by <u>attachment</u>, as this is a purchase money security interest in consumer goods, or by filing <u>locally</u>.

   (c) Collateral would be classified as <u>farm equipment</u>. Since the use of the collateral deals with the business of a farmer, perfection would be by filing <u>locally</u>.

7. You, as the debtor, should send the secured party a signed statement indicating what you believe to be the amount of the unpaid indebtedness owed and a list of collateral covered by the security agreement, requesting that the secured party approve or correct the statement and list. The secured party must comply with your request within two weeks of receipt (unless delay is excused) or he is liable for any loss suffered by you. You are entitled to such a request every six months without charge.

8. (a) Under the 1972 amendments to Article 9, for <u>consumer goods</u> the secured party must file a termination statement within <u>one month</u> after a debtor's final payment or within <u>ten days</u> after a written demand is made by the debtor, whichever is earlier. Failure to do so will result in the secured party being liable for any loss caused to the debtor <u>plus</u> $100.

   (b) If the collateral is <u>equipment</u>, a termination does not have to be filed until the debtor makes a written demand. Upon receipt of the written demand, the secured party must file a termination statement within 10 days or be liable as in (a) above.

CHAPTER 25

BANKRUPTCY

AUTHORS' SUGGESTIONS:

1. The instructor may want to point out that the Bankruptcy Reform Act of 1978 is generally viewed as much more debtor-oriented than the previous bankruptcy statute. This view seems to be supported by the great increase in bankruptcy petitions almost immediately after the new law took effect on October 1, 1979, and by the increased scrutiny many firms have given their credit policies.

2. It will be worthwhile to distribute and discuss with your students the exemption laws of your particular state. Dictate to them a list of property you own, and then have them pretend that each has a $100,000 judgment against you. Using your state's exemption laws, have them determine how much, if any, of the judgment they can collect. Then declare bankruptcy and have them determine whether you, the debtor, should use the state or federal exemptions.

3. Although no space has been given in this chapter to the United States Trustee pilot program which is under way in several parts of the country, the instructor may wish to make students aware of the program and point out that official U.S. Trustees may take the place of court-appointed trustees in future years.

CASE BRIEFS:

Mickelson v. Detlefsen

Facts: Detlefsen became subject to bankruptcy proceedings about six weeks before his mother's death. After her death, he filed in an Illinois court a disclaimer of his inheritance. Under Illinois law, this disclaimer was effective, and would make Detlefsen's children entitled to the inheritance. Mickelson, the trustee in Detlefsen's bankruptcy case, sued both Detlefsen and the securities dealer who had custody of the cash and securities comprising the inheritance. The Bankruptcy Court ruled for the plaintiff trustee, holding that the disclaimer was invalid and the inherited property was part of Detlefsen's estate subject to the bankruptcy proceeding. Defendant Detlefsen appealed.

Holding: Judgment for plaintiff affirmed. The state law permitting such a disclaimer of inheritance must give way, under the Supremacy Clause of the Constitution, to the federal bankruptcy law. The state law in this situation would clearly conflict with the intent of Congress in enacting the bankruptcy law.

Feinblatt v. Block

Facts: Block, who agreed to buy real estate from Kline for $100,000, put that amount in an escrow account at City Title & Escrow Co. The money was to be released to Kline only after Block's attorney approved certain documents relating to the sale. Under a shady arrangement with City Title's president, Kline obtained the money from the escrow account before the documents were approved. Block discovered what had happened, demanded his money, and City Title refused. Block sued City Title and Kline. Kline sold other property and used the proceeds to pay Block the $100,000. Block dropped the suit. One month later, Kline was forced into bankruptcy. Feinblatt, the trustee in bankruptcy, sued Block to recover the $100,000. This is the trial court's decision.

Holding: Judgment for plaintiff Feinblatt. When Kline misappropriated Block's money, he became Block's debtor. The payment was made within the period for a voidable preference, and Block received more of his claim than he would have received in the bankruptcy proceeding. Thus, this was a voidable preference and Block must return the money to the debtor's estate.

Wood v. Sears, Roebuck, & Co.

Facts: Danny Wood and his wife used their charge account to buy $700 worth of merchandise from Sears. A little more than a month later, Wood filed for bankruptcy and obtained a discharge. Sears then sued Wood, claiming that the debt was not discharged because it had been obtained by fraud. Both the Bankruptcy Court and the U.S. District Court ruled for defendant Wood, and plaintiff Sears appealed.

Holding: Judgment for defendant affirmed. There was no evidence that Wood did not intend to pay when he bought the merchandise or that he concealed his financial condition. Nothing was ever said about his ability to pay.

ANSWERS TO QUESTIONS AND PROBLEMS:

1. Almost certainly yes. Three creditors have joined in the petition, which is a sufficient number regardless of the total number of creditors. The claims of these three ($6200) total over the required $5,000 and are unsecured, so this requirement is met so long as these claims are noncontingent. (They probably are noncontingent.) If Monroe contests the petition, the creditors will prevail by showing that he has not been paying his debts as they fell due, even though his assets exceed liabilities.

2. Yes, Slonim's contention was correct. The court dismissed Moore's suit because Moore's trustee had exclusive authority to file the suit.

3. The court held that Gay must turn over the records to the trustee. The trustee had a statutory duty to investigate the debtor's financial affairs, and the records in question were necessary for a complete investigation. The court did, however, issue an order preserving the priority of the attorney's retaining lien.

4. Yes, Suval was required to act for the debtor in the proceedings. Even though he had no formal employment relationship with La Staiti, he was a "person in control," which is what the bankruptcy law requires.

5. (d) This probably would be his homestead, and would be at least partially exempt under state or federal exemption laws. (f) Since he became entitled to receive it within 180 days of the petition filing, it would be part of the estate, but if he uses the federal exemptions, he can claim a $500 exemption for the ring if it is primarily for personal, family, or household uses. (g) Earnings from labor or personal service after the filing date are not included in the debtor's estate. (h) The pension would be exempt under the federal law, if this is used.

6. Yes, it was exempt. The court said the word "value" in the statute referred to the value of the debtor's interest. Thus, Levin can keep the car. If her interest in the car had been valued at more than $700, the car would have been turned over to the trustee and sold, but Levin would have received $700 from the proceeds to buy another car.

7. The court ruled that the termination of the lease and retaking of the premises by Atkinson was a transfer of a property interest from Ferris to Atkinson. The transfer was not for a fair consideration and Ferris was insolvent at the time. Therefore, it was a fraudulent transfer and was voidable by the trustee. The court invalidated the lease termination, and the premises (for the term of the lease) was part of the debtor's estate.

8. No, the trustee was not successful. The Scanlons were creditors of the subsidiary, not of the bankrupt parent.

9. The Bankruptcy Court's ruling was reversed. On appeal, the court held that the law penalized inadequate record keeping only in the absence of justification and only where the inadequacy interfered with the administra-

tion of the case. The Bankruptcy Court was ordered to permit Martin to introduce evidence that the stubs were sent but lost in transit, and also to permit him to produce other records to prove the transactions in question.

10. (a) Fraudulent transfers by the debtor can be set aside by the trustee; (b) Voidable preferences by the debtor, which can be set aside by the trustee, frequently involve less than completely pure motives; (c) Claims resulting from the debtor's dishonest (fraudulent) conduct are not dischargeable; (d) Dishonesty by the debtor during the bankruptcy proceeding will offer result in a denial of his discharge.

PART FOUR: AGENCY

CHAPTER 26

AGENCY: NATURE, CREATION, DUTIES, AND TERMINATION

AUTHORS' SUGGESTIONS:

1. Perhaps in no other area of law has the legal profession been so unable to agree on what to call the various parties as it has been in the law of agency. The instructor should, at the outset, set forth whatever ground-rules he wishes to use regarding terminology, and then be careful to follow them.

2. It is crucial for students to obtain a thorough grasp of the agent's fiduciary duties, because the fiduciary concept arises throughout the law and will be confronted by students on other occasions.

3. Students sometimes have difficulty with the idea that an ordinary agency relationship can be terminated by one party without the consent of the other, regardless of the existence of an enforceable contract. Although not used in the text, an instructor might wish to employ the power vs. right dichotomy in explaining the concept.

CASE BRIEFS:

Bloom v. Weiser

Facts: Joseph Weinberg bought a condominium and had the title placed in his name and that of his fiance, Rachela Weiser, as "joint tenants with rights of survivorship." About a month later, Weinberg gave a general power of attorney to his son, Arthur Winters. Winters then executed and delivered a deed transferring Weinberg's one-half interest in the condo to Miriam Bloom, Weinberg's daughter. Weinberg died shortly thereafter. Bloom then filed suit against Weiser, claiming (1) the deed creating a joint tenancy between Weiser and Weinberg had been obtained by undue influence and was void and, alternatively, (2) Bloom had a one-half interest in the condo by her deed from Winters, which terminated Weiser's right of survivorship. The trial court ruled for defendant Weiser on both claims and plaintiff Bloom appealed.

Holding: Judgment for defendant affirmed. (1) There was no evidence of undue influence. (2) It takes very specific language in a power of attorney to give an agent the authority to sell real estate. There was no such language in the power of attorney given Winters by Weinberg, so Winters had no authority to execute the deed to Bloom. The deed to Bloom was void; Weiser owns the whole thing.

Thompson v. Hoagland

Facts: Thompson, plaintiff, was a real estate broker who entered into an "exclusive right-to-sell" agreement with the Hoaglands, defendants, covering a 76-acre tract of land for $65,000. Thompson obtained a buyer willing to pay the price, which ordinarily would have entitled him to his commission. The Hoaglands refused to sell (they now wanted more for the land) and refused to pay Thompson his commission. Thompson sued for the commission (10%). The trial court dismissed the suit and Thompson appealed.

Holding: Judgment reversed and remanded for a new trial. Thompson was required to disclose to the Hoaglands beforehand that in the past he had engaged in several partnership arrangements with the prospective purchaser. The mere possibility of an adverse interest must be disclosed. However, the trial court should not have dismissed the suit; a trial must be conducted to determine if the disclosure was or was not made.

ANSWERS TO QUESTIONS AND PROBLEMS:

1. "Attorney-in-fact" is simply an agent; the term is often used when the agent has been given a formal power of attorney. An "attorney-at-law" is a lawyer.

2. Except for a very few agency relationships which must be created by a written authorization (and even more rarely, accompanied by a seal), no formalities are required. There must merely be evidence that the principal and agent consented, by words and/or conduct, to a relationship in which the agent is authorized to represent the principal.

3. Todd is not correct. The agent's capacity has nothing to do with it --- only the principal's capacity is important in determining whether his contract with a third party is binding.

4. Anderson is required to refund the price and take back the stock. Even though he sold at the current market price, he violated his fiduciary duty to Pointer by failing to disclose his personal (and adverse) interest in the

transaction.

5. Carter was entitled to refuse to pay Hines a commission. Again, Hines violated his fiduciary duty by failing to disclose his "double dealing." One cannot serve two masters. The existence or possibility of an adverse interest must be disclosed by the agent and the principal's consent obtained, before representing him.

6. Thompson is probably liable for violating his duty of due care. Unless specifically authorized, very speculative investments (such as mining stock, ordinarily) would be negligent on the part of an agent given general investment authority.

7. Yes, the principal was justified in claiming the additional $90. The agent was authorized to get the best price he could (but at least $700) and to get 10% of the actual selling price. He was entitled to a commission of $80 (10% of $800); thus the principal should have received $720.

8. Harkins was probably entitled to his commission. In most cases, a salesman of goods is only authorized to take orders. And not only is that usually the extent of his authority, but the extent of his duty as well. Thus, in the ordinary situation, the service performed by Harkins was a full performance of his obligation and he would be entitled to the commission. Of course, principal and agent can agree otherwise in a given case.

9. Ordinarily a principal may revoke the agent's authority without the latter's consent, even if the termination constitutes a breach of contract. However, if the agent has an "interest in the subject matter" of the agency (such as a lien), the principal may not unilaterally terminate the agent's authority during the agreed duration.

10. An agent's bankruptcy automatically terminates his authority if it impairs his ability to act for the principal --- in other words, in a situation where the agent ought to realize that the principal probably would not want the agent to continue representing him if the principal knew the facts.

CHAPTER 27

AGENCY: LIABILITY OF THE PARTIES

AUTHORS' SUGGESTIONS:

1. In class discussion, the instructor may wish to actually subdivide implied authority into "customary" and "incidental" authority. We have found it to work fairly well, but not making a distinct subdivision has worked at least as well.

2. Regarding the method of notifying third parties of a terminated agency relationship, the instructor might point out to students that although a newspaper notice is sufficient to protect the principal against all third parties who haven't actually dealt with the agent in the past, it is really only important with respect to those who had known of the existence of the relationship. There is no duty of notification whatever to one who did not even have any prior knowledge of the agency relationship.

3. In both the Bruton and Wing cases, the courts indicated that the quasi contract theory could not be used because of an absence of pleading and/or proof. If time permits, the instructor might give students a good refresher by discussing whether plaintiff could have prevailed on such an alternate theory if proper procedures had been followed.

CASE BRIEFS:

Industrial Molded Plastic Products v. J. Gross & Son, Inc.

Facts: Industrial, a plastics manufacturer, was contacted by Stanley Waxman, president of Gross, a wholesaler to the retail clothing industry. Waxman and his son Peter spoke with Industrial's president, Ulansey, about obtaining plastic clothing clips for resale to retail clothiers. Nothing was said about Peter's authority. After the meeting with Industrial's president, Waxman authorized his son to buy a "trial" amount from Industrial. Peter, misrepresenting himself to be Gross's vice president, contacted Ulansey and signed a contract for five million clips. Before signing the agreement, Ulansey called Waxman, who said that Peter could act for Gross, but he said nothing about specific terms of purchase or any limitation on Peter's authority. Peter picked up the first 772,000 clips and Waxman paid the invoice for them, thinking this was the "trial" amount. Industrial produced the remainder of the clips and billed Gross for them. Peter refused to take delivery and Industrial sued. Waxman then learned that his son had ordered five million clips. The trial court ruled for plaintiff, Industrial, but awarded damages of only $2400. The court did not reveal how this amount was computed. Defendant Gross appealed, and plaintiff also appealed, seeking the entire unpaid contract price of over $31,000.

Holding: Judgment for plaintiff for total contract price. Because of Waxman's actions, Industrial was misled into thinking Peter had authority to do what he did. Thus Gross was bound under the doctrine of apparent authority.

Wing v. Lederer

Facts: Mrs. Lederer asked her yardman whether a certain tree on the Lederer property needed care. He said that it did and that he would send a tree surgeon to see her. Instead, the yardman purported to hire the tree surgeon, plaintiff Wing, to do this and other work. After doing the work, Wing sent a bill for $500 to the Lederers, who tried unsuccessfully to discuss it with him. The bill was not paid, and Wing sued the Lederers and their yardman. The trial court held that Lederer, but not the yardman, was liable. Lederer appealed.

Holding: Judgment for plaintiff reversed. The yardman had no authority to enter such a transaction, there was no apparent authority, and no ratification.

Singleton v. International Dairy Queen, Inc.

Facts: Singleton, nine years old, was leaving the local Dairy Queen. When she pushed on the door, it shattered, she fell through it, and was injured. In her behalf, her father sued the owner of the local franchise plus International Dairy Queen, the franchisor, claiming there was a master-servant relationship between franchisor and franchisee. The franchisor filed a motion for a summary judgment, claiming there was not even a fact issue as to a master-servant relationship, and that it should be dismissed from the case because the franchisee was an independent contractor. This is the trial court's ruling on the motion.

Holding: Motion denied; the case against both franchisor and franchisee should go to trial. Because of the great control actually exercised by franchisor over minute details of franchisee's business, a fact issue existed as to whether there was a master-servant or employer-independent contractor relationship, despite a disclaimer of control over business operations in the contract. Also, there was a fact issue as to whether the franchisee was an "apparent servant." Note: These were the crucial questions, because the question of liability for failing to maintain a safe premises was rather clearcut.

Bridger v. International Business Machines Corp.

Facts: Teasely worked for IBM as a route serviceman. He only worked during normal hours, but was on call seven days a week, twenty-four hours a day. He had not actually received an emergency call for at least two years, and it was unclear how well IBM could even reach him in the field. On the way home from work he was involved in an auto accident which injured Bridger, plaintiff, and killed his wife. Bridger sued IBM. The trial court granted summary judgment for IBM, and Bridger appealed.

Holding: Judgment for defendant reversed and case remanded for new trial. Although an employee driving to and from work is ordinarily not in the scope of his employment, when the employee uses a car in his work and is on call, an exception exists. A trial is necessary to determine whether Teasely could actually be reached in the field, so as to truly be on call. If so, IBM would be liable.

Rappaport v. International Playtex Corp.

Facts: Davis was a salaried traveling salesman for Playtex. He had no set hours and worked when necessary, including evenings and weekends. On a Sunday he was planning to go to his girlfriend's house to have dinner and do some paperwork. (He apparently took work with him wherever he went.) On the way, he was involved in an auto accident with Barnum. Barnum died, and Rappaport, his executor, brought suit against Playtex. The trial court denied defendant's motion to dismiss, and defendant appealed that action.

Holding: Judgment reversed and case dismissed. When an employee has a dual purpose, both personal and work-oriented, for making a trip, he is in the scope of employment while making the trip only if it would have been made anyway had there been no personal motive. This obviously was not the case here, and defendant's motion to dismiss should have been granted.

ANSWERS TO QUESTIONS AND PROBLEMS:

1. Yes, the principal's contention is correct. Unless the principal and agent expressly agree otherwise, the word "sell" in the context of an authorization concerning real property includes only the procurement of a

willing and able buyer and the making of a contract with that buyer. It does not include the authority to actually transfer title. The word "convey" in the authorization would, however, extend authority to transfer title. Seavey, Handbook of the Law of Agency §28B (West Pub. Co. 1964).

2. Yes, the wife will prevail. The marital relationship does not automatically create an agency relationship, except for a wife's purchase of necessaries. Here, the wife had not given her husband authority to cash the check and there was no basis for finding apparent authority or ratification. The bank is liable for its negligence and will have to pursue the husband to recoup its loss.

3. The wife would probably lose in such a case. Her action would quite likely confer implied authority upon the husband. Or, if not, it would create a reasonable appearance of authority and clothe the husband with apparent authority.

4. The court held that the NFL was not bound by the agreement. Bell's statement during negotiations made it clear to everyone that he had no authority to bind the NFL. Also, the players' representatives who negotiated with Bell had themselves been NFL players for several years prior to 1959 and understood the structure of the NFL and the authority of the commissioner. They were not misled by NFL owners into thinking that Bell had authority to make the agreement.

5. The customer must comply with the demand. There obviously was no express authority to sell the tray, nor does there appear to be any basis for finding implied authority. A reasonable person in the janitor's position would not believe he had authority to sell something below the marked price (or to even sell it at all). He was just asked to "watch the store." There also does not seem to be any basis for finding apparent authority, since a reasonable customer would certainly not think that someone dressed like Jones would have such authority.

6. The only possible difference would relate to the question of apparent authority. It is much more likely that the bookkeeper would be dressed in a manner similar to a salesclerk. Thus, there is a greater possibility that a reasonable customer might be misled into thinking the bookkeeper had authority to sell. However, if the customer was a regular one and knew the store's employees, he probably would know that the person watching the store was not a salesclerk, and there would be no apparent authority.

7. The court ruled for Amy, on the ground that Rodriguez had acted with apparent authority, stating on page 733: "By virtue of this staffing arrangement, defendant placed Rodriguez in a position where it could be logically inferred by a job seeker of ordinary prudence, reasonably conversant with business custom, that he was in a position to hire sales personnel for the store. And, it would follow that he had concomitant authority to state the terms of employment, absent any reasonable and

timely contrary notice to an individual employed by him."

8. The court ruled for Bruton, holding that there had been neither apparent authority nor ratification. Bruton had not said or done anything to lead AWS to believe that Eckvall had authority to have such major repairs done. Merely giving Eckvall possession of the Cat did not create an appearance of such authority. Bruton's words and actions at the AWS shop could not create apparent authority because it was after the fact. There was no ratification because Eckvall had not given any indication to AWS that he was acting in behalf of Bruton. Also, when Bruton saw his Cat in the shop and talked to the mechanic, he did not ratify by failing to object, because it was reasonable for him to believe that Eckvall was having the repairs done at Eckvall's own expense.

9. The appellate court reversed the trial court's dismissal and remanded for a trial. The evidence showed that Barrickman had known in the past when Estell and other passengers had ridden with employees, and he had never objected. The court said that there was a fact issue as to whether Chipman had authority to take Estell as a passenger. Although this result seems correct, the court should have spoken of "foreseeability" and "scope of employment" rather than "authority."

10. According to the court in Son v. Hartford Ice Cream Co., 129 Atl. 778 (Conn. 1925), Hartford is liable for the driver's actions. The court said that the driver was directed by Hartford to collect payment for deliveries, and the driver's attempt to do so resulted in a series of acts constituting one continuous transaction. The beating occurred in the course of the driver's attempts to perform Hartford's business.

PART FIVE: BUSINESS ORGANIZATIONS

CHAPTER 28

FORMS OF BUSINESS ORGANIZATIONS

AUTHORS' SUGGESTIONS:

1. Students should be made aware of the fact that the limited liability enjoyed by limited partners and by shareholders in a corporation is a statutorily created exception to the general rule of owners' liability. Limited liability simply does not exist unless created by statute. It is for this reason that fairly strict adherence to the requirements of the particular statute is necessary for the enjoyment of limited liability.

2. One point cannot be overemphasized --- even if a party is granted limited liability by the law, he may have to bargain it away before a creditor will extend credit to the business.

3. Although business taxation is beyond the scope of this text, an instructor who is well-versed in the subject may use this chapter as a starting point and expand the coverage by lecture.

CASE BRIEFS:

(no cases)

ANSWERS TO QUESTIONS AND PROBLEMS:

1. No. Many provisions of the UPA are merely gap fillers and may be altered by the partners' agreement. But those provisions aimed at protecting the rights of third parties, such as partnership creditors, cannot be changed by the partners' agreement.

2. The question is whether E took part in the management of the business. Performing bookkeeping services would not constitute control, regardless of

whether compensation was received. Therefore, E would not be personally liable.

3. If E had performed consulting services relating to management of the business, a closer question would be presented as to whether he had exercised any control. It would appear more likely that E would be deemed to have participated in management, and thus would incur personal liability, if he performed the consulting services without compensation. The receipt of compensation would make E more of an independent contractor than a general partner. But the question would still be close.

4. Yes. These similarities would include centralization of management, limited liability of limited partners and shareholders, and transferability of the interests of limited partners and shareholders.

5. The answer is found in Sec. 11 of the ULPA: "A person who has contributed to the capital of a business conducted by a person or partnership erroneously believing that he has become a limited partner in a limited partnership, is not, by reason of his exercise of the rights of a limited partner, a general partner with the person or in the partnership carrying on the business, or bound by the obligations of such person or partnership; provided that on ascertaining the mistake he promptly renounces his interest in the profits of the business, or other compensation by way of income."

6. A joint stock company in some ways resembles a corporation, but for most purposes is treated like a partnership. Management is usually centralized, and ownership is evidenced by shares of transferable stock. This organizational form may exist without an authorizing statute. Each shareholder is personally liable as is true of a partner, but shareholders are generally not treated as agents of one another the way partners are.

7. No, because the word "syndicate" has no particular legal meaning. The precise nature of the organization will depend on the parties' agreement and how the enterprise is actually operated.

8. As an example, a shareholder in a corporation having inadequate business assets may be required by a prospective corporate creditor to assume personal liability as a precondition to the receipt of credit by the corporation.

9. Essentially, the inclusion of more investors, whether partners, limited partners, or shareholders, not only brings more capital directly into the business but also may increase the borrowing power of the company.

10. Under existing law, a corporation's income is taxed by the federal government. Upon distribution of these profits as dividends to shareholders, the same money is taxed again as personal income to those receiving it.

CHAPTER 29

PARTNERSHIPS: NATURE, FORMATION, AND PROPERTY

AUTHORS' SUGGESTIONS:

1. If students learn nothing else about **partnerships**, they should learn that <u>agreement</u> is the key to creation of this organizational form. The agreement should be carefully drafted and reduced to writing, but it may be oral or even implied from the actions of the parties.

2. A "buy-sell" provision in a partnership agreement is a practical must. Such a provision entitles surviving partners to buy out the interest of a deceased or retiring partner. A method for computing the value of this interest should also be included.

3. Regarding the question of whether an item of property belongs to the partnership or to one or more individual partners, classroom emphasis should be given to the practical point that a clear statement on the matter in the partnership agreement will forestall almost all such problems.

CASE BRIEFS:

Gelder Medical Group v. Webber

<u>Facts</u>: Dr. Webber was admitted to a pre-existing medical partnership in a small town in New York. One provision of the partnership agreement provided for involuntary withdrawal of a partner by majority vote of the others. Another provision contained a covenant not to compete within 30 miles of the town for five years after termination. Dr. Webber couldn't get along with anybody, was voted out, and paid his interest after an accounting. He then violated the covenant, and the partnership sued for an injunction. Dr. Webber also sued for damages resulting from his expulsion. The two suits were consolidated; both the trial court and the intermediate appellate court ruled for the partnership on all issues, and Dr. Webber appealed.

Holding: Judgment for the partnership affirmed. The termination of Dr. Webber was entirely proper because of the provision in the partnership agreement. The covenant was reasonable, and an injunction was issued to enforce it.

Grissum v. Reesman

Facts: Nora Grissum, plaintiff, had worked with her brother Elwood Grissum in a farming operation for many years. No formal partnership agreement was ever executed. Elwood died and Nora was the sole beneficiary under his will. As a result of the large amount of property she would receive, state inheritance and federal estate taxes in substantial sums would be due. She filed suit against Reesman, Elwood's administrator, asking the court to hold that she and her brother had been partners. A ruling in her favor would mean that she already owned a proportionate interest in the business, rather than receiving everything through her brother's will. The result would be a tax savings of about $57,000. The trial court ruled in plaintiff's favor. The state of Missouri (also a defendant because of the taxes) appealed.

Holding: Judgment for plaintiff affirmed. The conduct and words of Nora and Elwood over a period of forty years clearly showed their intent to engage in business as partners.

Shawn v. England

Facts: England was the weatherman for a TV station in Oklahoma City. Shawn, a stock broker, was a stock market reporter for the station. England had for sometime referred on his program to a mythical "thunder lizard." Shawn came up with the idea of a thunder lizard doll. Shawn liked it, and they brought in May, an artist, to assist the project. The three agreed to be partners. They held weekly meetings, had a drawing contest, and the doll idea gradually evolved into a weather coloring book and then into a regular weather booklet about Oklahoma weather. All three helped produce the booklet, and as it was nearing completion, with very good prospects for profitability, England and May kicked Shawn out of the group. Shawn sued, claiming that they still had a partnership, and asking for one-third of the profits. Jury verdict was for plaintiff Shawn, but the trial judge granted defendants' motion for judgment n.o.v., and plaintiff appealed.

Holding: Judgment for defendant reversed, and jury verdict for plaintiff reinstated. The early oral partnership agreement continued in existence with the evolution of the project, and plaintiff is entitled to one-third of the profits.

Kay v. Gitomer

Facts: Kay and Eckles engaged in the plumbing business as partners. They purchased real estate, consisting of "lot 5" and a portion of "lots 1 to 4". Title to the property was held in the names of Kay and Eckles, individually, as co-owners, and not in the partnership name. They conducted their business from a building on lots 1 to 4, but rented out lot 5 as a parking lot. In need of cash, they decided to sell lot 5. Kay by himself signed a contract to sell lot 5 to Gitomer. Kay and Eckles later refused to sell, and Gitomer, plaintiff, sued for specific performance. The trial court held for plaintiff, and defendants appealed.

Holding: Judgment for plaintiff affirmed. All the evidence considered together indicates that they intended lot 5 to be partnership property, rather than individually co-owned property. The most important factor was the treatment in the partnership books of rental income from, depreciation on, and taxes on lot 5 as partnership income and expenses. The court held that the contract signed by Kay did bind the partnership in this case, and that Gitomer was entitled to specific performance.

ANSWERS TO QUESTIONS AND PROBLEMS:

1. The UPA does not expressly adopt either theory. The definition of a partnership as an "association of persons * * *" seems to point to the aggregate theory. But the UPA treats the partnership as a legal entity for some purposes, such as the ownership of property.

2. They probably are not partners. A partnership exists only if a _business_ is being carried on for profit. The UPA defines "business" as "every trade, occupation, or profession." It is quite possible that a court would find the activities of Johnson and Watkins not to be a business.

3. There is no partnership. Nelson took no part in managing the business. Everything points to the fact that he was an employee, not a co-owner. His share of the profits was received merely as _wages_. UPA Sec. 7.

4. X's widow is not a partner. Her share of the profits was received only as a settlement for her deceased husband's interest. Such a sharing of profits creates no presumption of partnership under Sec. 7 of the UPA. And the other evidence, such as that of an absence of management power, does not indicate a partnership.

5. No, this agreement by itself did not make Winn a partner. Again under Sec. 7 of the UPA, profits received as rent create no presumption of partnership.

6. A partnership did exist. It appears that they created an "association to carry on as co-owners a business for profit." Neither a written nor an express oral agreement to become partners is essential.

7. No, her claim will not be upheld. Property purchased with partnership funds is partnership property, even though held in the name of one or more individual partners. Neither a partner nor his heirs have any right or interest in a specific item of partnership property. What is owned by a partner and passes to his heirs is an "interest in the partnership". Partnership property belongs to the partnership as an entity.

8. This is a statute found in most states which requires the owners of any unincorporated business, including a partnership, operating under an assumed name to register with a designated state official. The true names and addresses of the owners are included in the registration, thus enabling business creditors to ascertain who is personally liable.

9. An attorney will have experience with the type of problems which may be encountered and will be able to assist the parties in planning for them. Legal advice on the potential tax problems of a partnership may be crucial. A well-drafted partnership agreement can, among other advantages, prevent possible future misunderstandings about the various rights and obligations of the parties, provide for continuity of the business in case of death or withdrawal, and force the parties beforehand to think about and plan for contingencies they might not otherwise contemplate.

10. (a) Matters of taxation; (b) Distribution of assets upon dissolution; and (c) Rights of individual partners to use the property. Another factor would be the varying rights of partnership and personal creditors.

CHAPTER 30

PARTNERSHIPS: OPERATING THE BUSINESS

AUTHORS' SUGGESTIONS:

1. Students often seem to have difficulty with the concept of partners' rights in specific partnership property. Their difficulty is lessened if they clearly understand that a partnership, for the purpose of property ownership, is treated as a <u>legal entity</u> --- a "person". The <u>partnership</u> owns partnership property, not individual partners. All that an individual partner has is the equal <u>right</u> with other partners to use partnership property for partnership purposes.

2. The instructor might want to specially emphasize that a partner's payment of money into the partnership is <u>very strongly</u> presumed to be a contribution to capital, not a loan.

3. The trading-nontrading distinction is on its way out, a fact generally not recognized by business law texts. But the terminology continues to appear, and probably will do so for many more years, despite its decreasing importance as a determinative rule. The instructor is urged to convey this to students.

CASE BRIEFS:

Madison National Bank v. Newrath

Facts: Haft, Weiss, and Wine engaged in the business of operating a shopping center as partners. One of the assets of the partnership was a long-term leasehold on the land on which the shopping center was located. Weiss was also involved in other business enterprises. He borrowed money for use in connection with these other enterprises. To secure one such loan, he gave the lender (Fidelity) a mortgage by way of deed of trust on the partnership leasehold. When Weiss defaulted on this loan, Fidelity, acting through its agent Newrath, sought to foreclose the mortgage. Another of

Weiss' creditors, Madison, which held a lien on Weiss' interest in the partnership, sued Fidelity (Newrath was the named defendant) to prevent the foreclosure. The trial court ruled for Fidelity, and Madison appealed.

Holding: Judgment for defendant reversed. The leasehold was partnership property and Weiss could not mortgage it to secure a nonpartnership debt. Thus, the mortgage given to Fidelity was void and could not be enforced by foreclosure. (Of course, Madison's stake in all this was that Fidelity's foreclosure would deplete partnership assets and indirectly reduce the value of Weiss' interest in the partnership, on which Madison held a lien.)

Burns v. Gonzalez

Facts: Bosquez and Gonzalez were partners in an advertising agency. The sole business of the partnership was the sale of broadcast time on XERF, a radio station owned by a Mexican corporation which was also owned by Bosquez and Gonzalez. Burns purchased broadcast time, but labor difficulties shut the station down and the broadcast time, with some exceptions, was not available. Later the station was placed in receivership and it was unlikely that broadcast time would be available for at least two years. Bosquez, acting individually and supposedly in behalf of the partnership as well, executed a promissory note to Burns for $40,000 in settlement of Burns' claim for the unavailable broadcast time. The note was not paid when due, and Burns sued the partnership and Bosquez and Gonzalez as individuals. The trial court rendered judgment for plaintiff Burns against Bosquez, but it held that neither the partnership nor Gonzalez was liable. Bosquez did not appeal the judgment against him, but Burns appealed the court's denial of recovery from the partnership and Gonzalez.

Holding: Judgment affirmed. Bosquez had no authority to bind the partnership by executing a note like this. (Apparently the two partners had earlier agreed that Bosquez could not take such action alone.) Therefore, the partnership will be liable only if the act of Bosquez was "for apparently carrying on in the usual way the business of the partnership." The act of Bosquez was not of this nature and did not bind the partnership or Gonzalez.

Oswald v. Leckey

Facts: Oswald and Leckey, CPA's, formed a partnership. Each continued to bill the clients he personally served. They couldn't get along, and dissolved the partnership. Oswald filed suit for an accounting and claimed that Leckey had improperly "written down" (accepted less than the amount billed) several accounts before dissolution. The trial court agreed with plaintiff Oswald, and held that defendant Leckey was responsible to the partnership for the amounts written down. Defendant appealed.

Holding: Judgment for plaintiff affirmed. Settling a claim in behalf of the partnership *is* within the implied authority of a partner. However, in this case Leckey's motive --- to make several clients happy so that they would follow him after dissolution --- was improper. He violated the fiduciary duty of good faith.

ANSWERS TO QUESTIONS AND PROBLEMS:

1. X is not correct. An individual partner does not *own* any part of the partnership property. He has only the equal right with other partners to use partnership property for partnership purposes.

2. In the absence of a specific agreement on the sharing of profits, each partner receives an equal share regardless of the amounts of their capital contributions. Therefore, each partner would receive $1,500.

3. Unless agreed otherwise, losses are to be shared in the same proportions as profits. Thus, each partner would bear an equal part of the loss --- $1,000.

4. Although a majority vote usually governs the management of a partnership, this action constitutes a modification of the partnership agreement and would require *unanimous* consent.

5. Wilkes and Watkins could take this action over Weston's objection. It would not constitute a change in their partnership agreement, but rather would be an ordinary management decision and would be governed by the wishes of the majority.

6. A trading partnership is one which engages in the business of buying and selling goods. A nontrading partnership is one engaged in any other type of business. Under the traditional approach, a partner in a trading partnership had implied authority to borrow money and issue negotiable instruments while a partner in a nontrading partnership did not have such authority unless expressly granted. This distinction is on the wane, however, and is becoming less important in court decisions.

7. The partnership would nevertheless be bound by the warranty if D had implied authority. Was D's act for the purpose of carrying on the partnership business in the *usual* way? In other words, was it customary for used car dealers in that locale to give warranties of this type? If so, the partnership would be liable.

8. Here there could be no implied authority because D knew that he was not authorized to make warranties. But if the transaction was *apparently* for carrying on the partnership business in the usual way (that is, if it was customary), and if Johnson had no knowledge of the restriction in the part-

nership agreement, the partnership would be bound by the warranty under the theory of apparent authority.

9. The partnership would be liable because Jurgenson obviously committed the tort while acting in the ordinary course of partnership business.

10. Driver could hold Jurgenson and Taylor personally responsible after exhausting partnership assets. Individual partners do not enjoy limited liability as do limited partners in a limited partnership or shareholders in a corporation. If Leonard had been admitted <u>after</u> Jurgenson's negligence, his liability would extend only to his investment in the partnership --- if partnership assets were exhausted he would not be personally liable. But if he had been admitted <u>prior to</u> Jurgenson's negligence, he would be personally liable as would any other partner.

CHAPTER 31

PARTNERSHIPS: TERMINATION

AUTHORS' SUGGESTIONS:

1. Some care must be taken in the use of descriptive terminology in this area. "Dissolution" does not mean "termination." Dissolution plus "winding up" does mean termination. On the other hand, termination does not necessarily mean "liquidation." The termination might pertain only to the organization, and not to the business itself. If the business itself is terminated, then the word termination does include liquidation.

2. Different texts make conflicting statements about whether the partnership agreement may effectively provide that death or withdrawal of a partner will not cause dissolution. The prevailing view is that which is expressed in this chapter. As a technical matter, the partnership agreement may not prevent dissolution from occurring in such a case. But this agreement can provide for a smooth changeover to a new organization and continuation of the old business.

3. It has been found that students rarely gain a complete understanding of the mechanics of asset distribution after dissolution without substantial exposure to problem solving exercises. They probably should be led through at least one such problem in class.

CASE BRIEFS:

Smith v. Kennebeck

Facts: Thomas Smith and his brother Charles formed a partnership in 1963. The next year they dissolved the partnership and formed another one with Kennebeck as an additional partner. Several months later, Thomas and Kennebeck notified Charles that they were dissolving this partnership and would form a corporation to operate the business. Charles refused to consent to this change. Thomas and Kennebeck offered to buy Charles' interest in the partnership, but Charles rejected the offer. He filed suit asking the court to formally dissolve the partnership and compute the value of Charles' interest. The trial court ruled that there had been a dissolution and valid winding up, and that Charles was entitled only to the offered amount. Charles, plaintiff, appealed.

<u>Holding</u>: Judgment reversed and case remanded for new trial. The amount of the offer, which the trial court viewed as correctly representing the value of Charles' interest, had not been correctly computed. In valuing partnership assets, work in process should have been included, but was not. Also, the evidence showed that the inventory had missed other items as well.

Cauble v. Handler

<u>Facts</u>: Tom Handler and Thomas Cauble were equal partners in the furniture and appliance business. Cauble died and Anice Cauble, his administratrix, brought this suit as plaintiff against Handler for an accounting of partnership assets. The trial court based its valuation of partnership assets on their <u>book value</u>. In addition, it allowed plaintiff <u>interest</u> since dissolution on the value of Cauble's share, refusing her claim to a share of the profits earned since dissolution. Plaintiff appealed.

<u>Holding</u>: Judgment reversed and case remanded for a new trial. The trial court should have used <u>market value</u>, not book value for valuing partnership assets. Furthermore, since Handler had continued the business, plaintiff had a choice of receiving either interest on the value of Cauble's **share** or a proportionate part of the profits earned since dissolution. Plaintiff was entitled to share in those profits and could not be compelled to take interest instead.

<u>ANSWERS TO QUESTIONS AND PROBLEMS:</u>

1. <u>Dissolution</u> marks that point in time when the object of the partnership changes from continuation in its present form to termination. <u>Winding up</u> refers to the actual process of bringing the organization to an end, whether this process be only paperwork where the business itself is to be continued or actual liquidation where the business is not to be continued.

2. Alden's death causes dissolution of the partnership. However, the partnership is not terminated but continues until completion of the winding up process.

3. Henderson has the right to wind up partnership affairs. He may complete transactions which were unfinished at the time of Alden's death. Henderson is also entitled to be compensated for the reasonable value of his services in winding up.

4. Alden's widow does not have any interest in specific partnership property (the theaters). Ownership of partnership property remains with the surviving partner, Henderson. Mrs. Alden has a right to receive the value of her husband's interest <u>in the partnership</u>. She has a right to insist that the partnership be wound up, but she has no right to take part in either managing the business or winding it up. To insure that she receives the value of her husband's interest, she is entitled to an <u>accounting</u> from Henderson.

5. After dissolution a partner's authority is limited to acts which are necessary to complete unfinished transactions or which are otherwise appropriate for winding up partnership affairs. Examples would include making arrangements to ship goods which the partnership had already contracted to sell, making new contracts to sell existing inventory, and hiring an accountant to take inventory and perform an audit.

6. No. The business may be continued as a new partnership or other form of organization, the winding up process in such case merely consisting of bookkeeping entries and settling with those former partners or their estates who will not be participating any longer.

7. The loss position of the partnership would be $285,000 (liabilities and partners equity of $685,000 minus assets of $400,000). Liabilities to outside partnership creditors ($500,000) exceeded partnership assets ($400,000) by $100,000. Thus, the individual assets of Parsons and Raymond would be used to pay this amount. However, Parsons had already borne $135,000 of the total partnership loss (unpaid loan of $60,000 and unreturned capital contribution of $75,000), while Raymond had already borne only $50,000 of this loss (unreturned capital contribution). Therefore, to make their shares of the total $285,000 loss equal, Parsons should be required to use only $7,500 of his personal assets ($285,000 divided by 2 = $142,500 minus $135,000 = $7,500). The remaining $92,500 owed to partnership creditors should be taken from Raymond's personal assets ($142,000 minus $50,000 = $92,500).

8. In that case, Raymond's net personal assets would be only $50,000 and thus insufficient to pay his part of the amount owing to partnership creditors. (Remember that his personal creditors have priority on his personal assets.) Thus, Parsons would have to use $50,000 of his personal assets to pay partnership creditors (instead of $7,500), Raymond would pay $50,000, and Parsons would have a claim remaining against Raymond for $42,500.

9. Although the partnership had suffered an overall loss of $15,000 (liabilities and partners' equity of $95,000 minus assets of $80,000), partnership assets ($80,000) would be sufficient to pay outside partnership creditors ($55,000). After paying partnership creditors, remaining partnership assets would amount to $25,000. Of this amount, $10,000 would be used for the next item of priority, repayment of the loan Atkins had made to the partnership. Partnership assets of $15,000 are then remaining, which is insufficient to cover the next distribution priority --- return of partners' capital contributions. This deficiency of $15,000 ($30,000 of capital con-

tributions minus $15,000 of available assets), of course, represents the partnership's overall $15,000 loss. This loss must be shared equally ($5,000 each) by the partners, since profits were agreed to be shared equally and there was no agreement regarding sharing of losses. Therefore, Atkins should receive a net of $15,000 (capital contribution of $20,000 minus his $5,000 share of the loss); Benson should receive a net of $5,000 (capital contribution of $10,000 minus his $5,000 share of the loss); and Collier, assuming his personal assets are sufficient, must contribute $5,000 (his share of the loss, since he made no loans or capital contributions). The $5,000 paid by Collier plus the remaining partnership assets of $15,000 will equal the amount to be received by Atkins and Benson.

10. Since book value is an arbitrary figure and may or may not be accurately reflective of true value, market value should be used for valuation of partnership assets, as held in Cauble v. Handler.

CHAPTER 32

CORPORATIONS: NATURE AND FORMATION

AUTHORS' SUGGESTIONS:

1. Students are usually fascinated by the law's treatment of a corporation as a person. Thus, if time permits, this is a concept which the instructor might want to expand upon by assigning supplemental readings.

2. The instructor may want to discuss current proposals for eliminating the tax on corporate income, thus eliminating the double taxation phenomenon. Those who propose such a measure cite encouragement of capital formation as their reason.

3. The concept of the de jure and de facto corporation had to be included, it was felt, for the coverage to be complete. But their importance as issues in modern times is rather minute. As a result, the instructor may wish to skip this material.

4. The SEC Rule (146) on private offerings was not mentioned because it would require an inordinate investment of time on the part of students and instructor alike, especially in light of the fact that the SEC was considering its repeal at the time of this writing. Compliance with the rule apparently has been about as burdensome as filing a registration statement.

CASE BRIEFS:

First National Bank of Boston v. Bellotti

Facts: There had been public debate for sometime concerning a voter referendum on a Massachusetts constitutional amendment to permit a state income tax. Although the tax would be on the income of individuals, not corporations, the First National Bank of Boston and several other corporations wanted to publicly express their opposition to it. However, the Massachusetts legislature passed a statute which, in effect, prohibited corporations from expending corporate funds to publicly express their opinions on the issue. The Bank and several other corporations filed suit against Bellotti, the Massachusetts Attorney General, claiming that the statute was unconstitutional. The Massachusetts courts ruled for defendant Bellotti, and plaintiffs appealed to the U.S. Supreme Court.

Holding: Judgment for defendant reversed. The statute infringed the corporations' First Amendment right of free speech. Corporate speech is protected by the First Amendment to the U.S. Constitution, and this was an arbitrary, unjustifiable suppression of that right.

Tigrett v. Pointer

Facts: Tigrett was hurt on the job while working for Heritage Building Company. She received a judgment against the company for approximately $20,000 in workmen's compensation benefits. At the time of her injury, the company's liabilities exceeded its assets. About a month after her injury, before she received the judgment, Pointer (the company's president and sole stockholder) transferred most of the company's assets to himself. Consideration for the transfer was a reduction of the company's indebtedness to him. He then transferred the assets to another one of "his" corporations, Heritage Corporation. Tigrett sued Pointer and Heritage Corporation for the $20,000. The trial court ruled for defendants Pointer and Heritage Corporation, and plaintiff Tigrett appealed.

Holding: Judgment for defendants reversed. Plaintiff should be allowed to recover the money from Pointer and Heritage Corporation. Tigrett's employer, Heritage Building Company, was grossly undercapitalized from the beginning, using loans from Pointer for most of its working capital. Thus, Pointer had abused the separateness of the corporate entity and the "corporate veil" should be "pierced." An alternate basis for holding Pointer liable is his violation of the fiduciary duty owed by a dominant stockholder to an insolvent corporation. The transferee corporation, Heritage Corporation, was also held liable because it was completely controlled by Pointer and was part of the overall "device."

Krause v. Mason

Facts: The Masons and the Krauses formed a corporation (Golden Age Distributors) for the sale of carpets. After its formation but before it began doing business, the Krauses gave Mr. Mason $7,900 with which to purchase carpets. He did so, but used the funds to buy carpets not only for Golden Age but also for another carpet business he owned. The carpets bought for his own business were resold at a profit. Later on, he gave equivalent carpets to Golden Age as replacements. After Mason refused the Krauses demand for an accounting, the Krauses filed suit claiming misappropriation of corporate assets. The trial court ruled for the Masons, and plaintiffs appealed.

Holding: Judgment for defendants reversed, and case remanded for a new trial. The Masons breached their fiduciary duty to the Krauses. Even though they replaced the misappropriated carpets, they are liable for any profit made on the misappropriation.

Henderson v. Joplin

Facts: Joplin operated a retail liquor business as sole proprietor. She induced Henderson to join the business. They agreed that a corporation would be formed, with Henderson buying 25% of the stock and Joplin receiving 75% in return for the assets she would contribute. It was further agreed that Joplin would be President and Treasurer, while Henderson would be Vice President, Secretary, and General Manager. Each was to receive a salary of $700 per month. After three years Henderson became disillusioned and proposed that he buy out Joplin, that she buy him out, or that they sell the business to a third party. She refused and fired him. Henderson sued for breach of contract. The trial court ruled for plaintiff Henderson and defendant Joplin appealed.

Holding: Judgment for plaintiff affirmed. This was a valid contract. Before formation of a corporation, its promoters may make an enforceable contract providing for the structure and division of capital stock, the election of themselves as officers, and their salaried employment.

SEC v. Ralston Purina Co.

Facts: Ralston Purina offered shares of treasury stock to "key employees." As the phrase key employee was defined by Ralston, it included just about any employee who inquired about owning stock in the company. The SEC filed suit against Ralston, seeking an injunction to prevent the unregistered offerings. The district court held that no public offering was involved and thus no registration statement was required. The court of appeals affirmed and the SEC appealed to the U.S. Supreme Court.

Holding: Judgment for Defendant reversed. The employees here were not shown to have access to the kind of information which registration would disclose. The obvious opportunities for pressure and imposition make it advisable that they be entitled to Ralston's compliance with registration requirements.

ANSWERS TO QUESTIONS AND PROBLEMS:

1. The FTC should prevail, according to the court in Progress Tailoring Co.

v. FTC, 153 F.2d 103 (7th Cir. 1946). The advertising is deceptive because Progress and its subsidiary are separate entities.

2. Yes, there was a violation. The separateness of the corporate entity will be disregarded where its purpose is to evade a statute. See United States v. Milwaukee Refrigerator Transit Co., 142 F. 247 (E.D. Wisc. 1905).

3. As a corporation, such an organization will be able to own property, make contracts, and transact other business as an entity. Otherwise, such things would have to be done in the names of individual members, who will be personally liable.

4. Yes, they will recover from Boss. In Stanley J. How & Associates v. Boss, 222 F. Supp. 936 (S.D. Iowa 1963), the court said that since 3/4 of the contract price was to have been paid by the time the drawings were completed, "it clearly tends to show that the parties intended that there be a present obligor * * *. The words 'who will be the obligor' are not enough to offset the rule that the person signing for the nonexistent corporation is normally to be personally liable."

5. No, the creditor will not prevail against the corporation. Caparella did not even purport to act in behalf of the corporation. He bought the equipment in his own behalf and the corporation assumed no liability by accepting it. Caparella is the responsible party. And knowledge acquired by corporate officers while acting for themselves cannot be imputed to the corporation. See C&H Contractors, Inc. v. McKee, 177 So.2d 851 (Fla. D.Ct. App. 1965).

6. It might be a useful maneuver where there is an insufficient number of interested parties or for convenience and speed where some or all of the interested parties are unavailable.

7. No, the shareholders will not prevail. After 1941, Baum was a de facto corporation, the existence of which could be challenged only by the state. See Baum v. Baum Holding Co., 62 N.W.2d 864 (Neb. 1954).

8. Yes, the plaintiff should recover. There was not substantial compliance with statutory requirements and, therefore, no de facto corporation. See Beck v. Stimmel, 177 N.E. 920 (Ohio App. 1931).

9. Many state securities agencies actually pass judgment on the merits of securities issues, and can forbid them. But the SEC has no such power. It merely requires full and fair disclosure of facts relevant to the issue. It can prevent an issue only where the disclosure is inadequate.

10. An offering to all of Ralston's employees would be public because it would in no way be limited to those having access to the kind of information which a registration statement would disclose and who would be sophisticated enough to fend for themselves.

CHAPTER 33

CORPORATIONS: CORPORATE POWERS AND MANAGEMENT

AUTHORS' SUGGESTIONS:

1. Ultra vires is another dying concept, but was included for completeness. An instructor wishing to save time could skip it and do very little violence to students' practical education.

2. The instructor might point out that directors of some corporations frequently engage in long distance "conference calls" over the telephone. These are only for discussion, however, and do not substitute for directors' meetings.

3. It might be emphasized in class that cumulative voting does not automatically mean that every minority shareholder or group will be able to elect a director. But it does at least make minority representation on the board a possibility in many situations.

4. Not all courts hold as the court did in Campbell v. Loew's, Inc., that shareholders may remove a director for cause even if he was elected by cumulative voting. A few courts hold otherwise when the director was elected by cumulative voting.

CASE BRIEFS:

Campbell v. Loew's, Inc.

Facts: Fighting for control of Loew's were two factions, one headed by Tomlinson and the other by the president of Loew's, Vogel. Vogel called a shareholders meeting for several purposes, including the removal of Tomlinson and another party from the board of directors. A shareholder, Campbell, filed this suit as plaintiff asking the court to prevent the holding of the meeting or to prevent the meeting from considering the removal of the named directors. This was a trial decision.

Holding: Judgment for defendant. The meeting had been validly called and the shareholders could vote on the removal of Tomlinson and the other director from the board. Shareholders have the power to remove directors for cause even if those directors were elected by cumulative voting.

In Re William Faehndrich, Inc.

Facts: Rudolf owned 161 shares and his father William 157 shares in the corporation. After a protracted dispute, Rudolf as president called a special shareholders meeting. He sent a notice beforehand to his father, but the latter did not attend. At the meeting Rudolf voted his shares for himself and his wife as directors. After their election they held a directors meeting and elected themselves officers. The father's employment and position as an officer were terminated. The father filed suit asking the court to declare that the election was illegal and that it be voided. The trial court ruled for the plaintiff, father, and the son appealed. The intermediate-level court affirmed and the son appealed to the state's highest court.

Holding: Judgment for plaintiff reversed and case dismissed. The father was given a sufficient prior notice of the shareholders meeting. Since the son held over a majority of the shares, a quorum of shares was present at the meeting. (The bylaws required two-thirds of the shares for a quorum at a special meeting, but this was held invalid because a state statute provided that a quorum could not exceed a majority of the shares.) Therefore, the action taken at the meeting in electing directors was valid, as were the actions of the newly elected directors.

Stone v. American Lacquer Solvents Co.

Facts: Harold Stone was chairman of the board of American Lacquer Solvents. Part of his compensation was a pension to be paid to his wife by American after his death. Stone and his wife later had marital difficulties, and he told American's president that he wanted the pension cancelled. The president called a board meeting to consider the matter, but Stone was not notified of and did not attend the meeting. At the meeting 5 of the 7 board members were present and, after seeing a letter from Stone indicating his wishes, they voted unanimously to rescind the pension. Several months later Stone died and his widow sued American when the corporation refused to pay the pension. The trial court ruled for the defendant corporation and plaintiff appealed.

Holding: Judgment for defendant reversed, and case remanded for a new trial. The action of the board in cancelling the pension was void because: (1) Stone was not notified of the meeting, (2) his letter to the board could not serve as a written consent because such a consent is a legal method for board action only if signed by all directors, and (3) Stone's later silence and failure to object was not a ratification of the board's action because there was no evidence that he was ever made aware that the meeting had taken place or that the pension had been cancelled.

Hallahan v. Haltom Corp.

Facts: Two brothers, Paul and Peter Hallahan, joined with Charles and Errol Thompson, also brothers, to open a drinking and eating place. A cousin of the Thompsons assisted by performing carpentry work. They then decided to incorporate as Haltom Corp., it being understood that power was to be equally divided among the Thompson brothers and the Hallahan brothers. Haltom Corp. issued 100 shares of stock, 23-3/4 to each of the four, and 5 shares to the cousin as compensation for his carpentry work. Shortly thereafter, one of the Thompson brothers obtained a proxy from the cousin for his 5 shares. Relations deteriorated, and the Thompsons called a shareholders' meeting without notice of the business to be transacted. Saying there had been complaints about the Hallahans' bartending (there hadn't), the Thompsons used their superior voting strength (with the cousin's 5 shares) to fire the Hallahans as employees of the corporation. The Hallahans, plaintiffs, sued the three Thompsons and the corporation, defendants. The trial court ruled for plaintiffs and ordered the cousin to return the 5 shares to the corporation in exchange for the repurchase price set forth in the articles of incorporation. Defendants appealed.

Holding: Judgment for plaintiffs affirmed. In a closely held corporation, compensation as an employee is often the primary benefit received by a stockholder. By "freezing out" the plaintiffs from this benefit, without justification, defendants violated their duty of good faith.

ANSWERS TO QUESTIONS AND PROBLEMS:

1. The traditional common law rule was that a corporation could not be a partner, because the other partners would exercise control that only the corporation's elected board should exercise. Strangely, the courts normally did permit corporate membership in a joint venture. Today, however, a majority of states, by statute, permit corporations to join partnerships.

2. The Model Act and the statutes of many states have abolished ultra vires as a contractual defense, although other legal consequences may still result. Also, many states now allow extremely broad statements of corporate purpose in the articles of incorporation.

3. The board acted properly in ignoring the committee because the vote appointing the committee was void under the quoted statute. See Charlestown Boot and Shoe Co. v. Dunsmore, 60 N.H. 85 (1880).

4. According to the court in Berger v. Amana Society, 111 N.W.2d 753 (Iowa 1962), the amendment was invalid because once the notice undertook to describe the proposed amendment, it had to describe it fully.

5. The shareholder may or may not be correct, because the court decisions interpreting such an ambiguous bylaw provision are in conflict. Cirrincione v. Polizzi, 220 N.Y.S.2d 741 (1961), held that a bylaw provision using this language required a majority of the whole number for a quorum. A contrary result was reached in Gearing v. Kelly, 222 N.Y.S.2d 474 (1961), affirmed on other grounds at 182 N.E.2d 391 (N.Y. 1962).

6. Girard would not have this authority unless expressly granted, according to Kagan v. Levenson, 134 N.E.2d 415 (Mass. 1956).

7. No, the corporation was not correct. Under these particular facts the president had authority to act as he did, according to the court in Hessler, Inc. v. Farrell, 226 A.2d 708 (Del. 1967).

8. Yes, the contract was valid. See Storer v. Florida Sportservice, Inc., 125 So.2d 906 (Fla. Dist. Ct. App. 1961).

9. No, the agreement is not valid. The court in Marvin v. Solventol Chemical Products, 298 N.W. 782 (Mich. 1941), held such an agreement to be void as an abdication of the directors' duty to manage.

10. Many of the older cases held that such contracts could not be made because a board of directors, in selecting the management personnel of the corporation, should not be allowed to hamstring future boards in the overall supervision of the enterprise and the implementation of changing corporate policy. See 2 Fletcher, Corporations §514. The trend of modern decisions, however, is to allow such long term contracts. It is often reasoned that a later board can always fire the employee if it chooses, even if the action subjects the corporation to a breach of contract suit.

CHAPTER 34

CORPORATIONS: RIGHTS AND LIABILITIES OF SHAREHOLDERS AND MANAGERS

AUTHORS' SUGGESTIONS:

1. The instructor may want to point out to students that a shareholder attempting to exercise a legitimate right to inspect corporate records will frequently encounter varying degrees of hostility from management. Such hostility is almost inevitable because an inspection demand often portends a challenge to existing management.

2. In connection with the Pillsbury case, a lively class discussion might be generated by posing the question whether Pillsbury was "too honest for his own good." This, of course, would raise moral as well as legal issues.

3. Potential problems concerning watered stock today are usually caught in their incipiency by state or federal regulatory agencies. It is thus an infrequently litigated issue in modern times, but students do at least need to be aware of its existence.

CASE BRIEFS:

Pillsbury v. Honeywell, Inc.

Facts: Pillsbury, an opponent of American involvement in the Vietnam war, bought a few shares of Honeywell stock, admittedly for the sole purpose of challenging Honeywell's production of munitions used in that war. He demanded the right to inspect the corporation's records for the purposes of determining the extent of Honeywell's munitions production and obtaining the names and addresses of other shareholders so that he could attempt to persuade them to join his effort. Honeywell refused and Pillsbury sued. The trial court ruled for defendant Honeywell and plaintiff Pillsbury appealed.

Holding: Judgment for defendant affirmed. A shareholder's demand for inspection of corporate records must have some type of economic motivation.

Shlensky v. Wrigley

Facts: Plaintiff Shlensky was a minority shareholder in the corporation which owned the Chicago Cubs baseball team. He filed a derivative suit against Wrigley and the other directors of the corporation, claiming that the corporation had been damaged by the directors' negligence in failing to install lights in Wrigley Field, the Cubs' home park. The trial court held that plaintiff had not asserted a legally recognizable claim and dismissed the suit. Plaintiff appealed.

Holding: Judgment for defendants affirmed. The motive of the directors (preserving the neighborhood surrounding the field) was not improper but was arguably in the long-term interests of the corporation. Furthermore, the failure to follow the example of other major league clubs in scheduling night games did not constitute negligence.

Francis v. United Jersey Bank

Facts: Pritchard and Baird Intermediaries Corporation was a reinsurance broker. The founder, Charles Pritchard, Sr., was a lousy bookkeeper, but was honest and there were no real problems. As he became older, his two sons Charles, Jr. and William played an increasingly dominant role. After the father's death in 1973, they took complete control. They also were lousy bookkeepers, but were not honest. The sons looted the firm of millions of dollars (much of it was clients' money) and plunged it into bankruptcy by 1975. During all of this time Lillian Pritchard, the elder Pritchard's wife and the mother of the two scoundrels, was a director of the firm. The firm's trustee in bankruptcy, Francis, sued the father's estate (United Jersey Bank was administrator) and Lillian Pritchard's estate (she died after the bankruptcy proceedings began). Apparently because of the size of her personal estate, the primary question was whether Lillian Pritchard, as a director, had been negligent in not discovering and stopping the illegal activity. This is the trial court decision.

Holding: Judgment for plaintiff Francis against Lillian Pritchard's estate for $10.3 million. Although the court felt that Lillian had no knowledge of the looting, even a casual glance at the firm's annual financial statements would have informed her that something was terribly wrong. She completely neglected her duties as a director, and was liable for that neglect.

Morad v. Coupounas

Facts: Bio-Lab, Inc. was formed in 1972 by Morad, Thompson, Coupounas, and Shaw for the purpose of establishing a plasmapheresis (separating red blood cells from plasma) business in Birmingham, Alabama. By mid-1973, dissension arose over Morad's compensation. In 1974, Morad and Thompson incorporated another plasmapheresis business (Med-Lab, Inc.) in Tuscaloosa, Alabama. Morad served as president of both corporations. Both firms were profitable. Coupounas, in his own behalf and in behalf of Bio-Lab, sued Morad, Thompson, and Med-Lab, alleging a breach of the fiduciary duty owed to Bio-Lab. The trial court held for plaintiff Coupounas, and ordered defendants to offer him 30% of the stock of Med-Lab (this was the percentage of interest he held in Bio-Lab). Defendants appealed.

Holding: Judgment for plaintiff affirmed. Since one of the original purposes of Bio-Lab was to expand into specific new areas, including Tuscaloosa, the formation of Med-Lab was a violation of the "corporate opportunity" doctrine. The court said, however, that Coupounas shouldn't have to buy into Med-Lab to obtain what is due him. Instead, a constructive trust should be imposed on the profits of Med-Lab for the benefit of Bio-Lab.

ANSWERS TO QUESTIONS AND PROBLEMS:

1. Hanrahan will win; his demand for inspection had a proper purpose. See Hanrahan v. Puget Sound Power & Light Co., 126 N.E.2d 499 (Mass. 1955).

2. No. At this point, the corporation cannot cancel the issue. Barsan v. Pioneer Savings & Loan Co., 121 N.E.2d 76 (Ohio App. 1954).

3. Pre-emptive rights are extremely important in a closely held corporation because each shareholder usually possesses a very substantial interest in the business and often takes an active role in managment. In a publicly held corporation, however, the number of shareholders frequently is quite large, with each shareholder usually owning a relatively small portion of the total shares and having no significant role in running the enterprise. Thus, pre-emptive rights generally are not of the same importance in publicly held corporations.

4. In Arizona Western Ins. Co. v. L. L. Constantin & Co., 247 F.2d 388 (3rd Cir. 1957), the federal court ruled in favor of the shareholder. The directors had no discretion as to dividends when profits were sufficient because, unlike most situations, the articles had made dividends mandatory. However, Constantin & Co. later filed suit in a New Jersey state court seeking a declaratory judgment as to the meaning of the quoted provision. The New Jersey court held that the federal court decision was only binding with respect to the particular shareholder who had sued. The court then held that the mandatory dividend provision was contrary to a state statute which vested discretion in the directors as to dividend declarations. Therefore, declaration of dividends was a decision for the board despite the mandatory provision in the articles. L. L. Constantin & Co. v. R. P. Holding Corp., 153 A.2d 378 (N.J. Super. 1959).

5. The preferred shareholders are not correct. The court in State ex rel.

Cullitan v. Campbell, 20 N.E.2d 366 (Ohio 1939), held that in the absence of very explicit language to the contrary, the normal rule that each share, preferred or common, is entitled to one vote would remain in effect.

6.   The bank directors were held to have been guilty of negligence in Ford v. Taylor, 4 S.W.2d 938 (Ark. 1928). It should be mentioned that courts tend to place a higher standard of care on bank directors than on other directors.

7.   Reese would be liable. In such a case it is the director's duty to resign because of age or ill health, or else suffer the consequences of continuing to owe a duty to participate in the company's affairs. See Gamble v. Brown, 29 F.2d 366 (4th Cir. 1929).

8.   Wembley does not have a valid excuse and would be liable. See, for example, Bowerman v. Hamner, 250 U.S. 504 (1919).

9.   The basic rationale behind the corporate opportunity rule is that since a director or other manager occupies a fiduciary position, he must subordinate personal interests to the interests of the corporation.

10. The shareholder instituting the suit would lose --- there was nothing wrong with the transaction. A non-controlling shareholder owes no fiduciary duty to the corporation.

CHAPTER 35

CORPORATIONS: MERGER, CONSOLIDATION, AND TERMINATION

AUTHORS' SUGGESTIONS:

1. Students' interest in mergers can usually be stimulated by showing them several articles from the Wall St. Journal. Reports of merger activity may be found in almost every issue.

2. The instructor may want to mention that since 1968, the Securities Exchange Act of 1934 has specifically regulated tender offers. If the intent behind the tender offer is to give the offeror more than 5% of the target company's shares, the offeror must fully disclose to the SEC and to the offerees all relevant material information needed by those offerees to make an informed decision.

3. Despite the fact that a state has the power to dissolve corporations in a number of situations, this is a power which is very rarely exercised. The instructor may wish to impart this information to students.

CASE BRIEFS:

Ray v. Alad Corp.

Facts: In 1968 Alad Corp. ("Alad I"), which made ladders, sold all assets, including trade name and goodwill, to Lighting Maintenance Corp. Alad I was dissolved, and Lighting Maintenance created a new corporation, also named Alad Corp. ("Alad II"). Alad II used the acquired assets and the same factory workers (but with new management) to continue the business with only a week's interruption. Alad II used the same salesmen and manufacturers' representatives and solicited the same customer list as Alad I. In 1969, Ray was injured in a fall from one of the ladders made by Alad I. Claiming that the ladder was defective, he sued Alad II. The trial court granted summary judgment for defendant Alad II, and plaintiff Ray appealed.

Holding: Reversed. Although this situation does not come within one of the four recognized exceptions to the general rule that a purchaser of assets isn't subject to the seller's obligations, the court held that a separate exception should be created for this set of circumstances. This exception makes the asset purchaser liable for the defective products of the seller, where (1) the plaintiff has no practical remedies against the original manufacturer, (2) the asset purchaser has the ability to estimate and plan for this type liability, and (3) the asset purchaser continues to use and benefit from the original manufacturer's goodwill.

Crane Co. v. Westinghouse Air Brake Co.

Facts: Crane made a tender offer to Air Brake's shareholders at $50 per share, to expire on April 19. American Standard owned just under 10% in Air Brake and also wanted to accomplish a merger with Air Brake. American Standard knew that most of Air Brake's shareholders would put off a decision on the Crane tender offer until April 19. On that date American Standard bought a large volume of Air Brake shares in a series of transactions on the open market. It then made a secret resale of most of these shares on the same day. The public purchases created the impression of a great deal of activity in Air Brake shares and caused the market value of those shares to rise above $50. When this happened, few Air Brake shareholders accepted the Crane tender offer and it was defeated. Later, American Standard sought to consummate a merger with Air Brake, and Crane sued to prevent it. The trial court ruled for defendants, and Crane appealed.

Holding: Judgment for defendants reversed. In attempting to defeat Crane's tender offer, American Standard violated Sec. 9(a)(2) of the Securities Exchange Act of 1934, which prohibits market manipulation. For this reason, its merger with Air Brake should be prohibited.

Lynch v. Vickers Energy Corp.

Facts: Vickers offered to buy all outstanding common stock of Trans Ocean Oil, Inc. at $12 per share. Vickers already owned 53.5% of these shares. As a result of the offer, Vickers increased its interest to 87%. Lynch responded to the offer by selling her 100 shares. Later, she filed suit against Vickers and its directors, claiming that Vickers had not made a full and frank disclosure of the value of Trans Ocean's assets. The trial court granted summary judgment for defendants and plaintiff Lynch appealed.

Holding: Reversed. Vickers, as controlling shareholder in Trans Ocean, violated its fiduciary duty to the minority shareholders by failing to disclose (1) that a "highly qualified" petroleum engineer, who was a member of Trans Ocean's management, had calculated the net asset value to be significantly higher than the "minimum" amount disclosed in the tender offer; and (2) that Vicker's management had authorized open market purchases of Trans

Ocean's stock at up to $15 per share during the period immediately preceding the $12 tender offer.

Gruenberg v. Goldmine Plantation, Inc.

Facts: Goldmine's principal asset was a 900-acre tract of land which it used solely for growing sugar cane. Returns from the sugar cane operation were dismal, but the land had appreciated greatly because of tremendous industrial potential. The board, however, would not sell the land. Ten shareholders, collectively owning 40% of the firm's stock, sued to obtain court-ordered dissolution on the grounds of mismanagement. Their goal was to have the land sold and get their money out of the unprofitable operation. The trial court dismissed the suit, and plaintiffs appealed.

Holding: Judgment affirmed. The corporation was not being so grossly mismanaged as to require dissolution. Even though the operation was not profitable, the land was increasing in value and probably would continue to do so. The plaintiff's investment was not in danger; they just weren't getting any present return. The court sympathized with minority shareholders trapped in a close corporation, but said that the law provided no relief.

ANSWERS TO QUESTIONS AND PROBLEMS:

1. The board should consider, among others, the following factors: (a) Is the athletic shoe business one with high entry barriers (such as firmly entrenched consumer preferences for certain name brands), so that independent entry would be difficult? (b) Does the manufacture of athletic shoes require expertise and facilities X Co. doesn't have? (c) How difficult would it be to develop distribution channels for a new brand of athletic shoes? (d) Does an attractive takeover target exist in the athletic shoe business, perhaps with shares currently undervalued on the open market? (e) Would there be possible antitrust implications of an acquisition in such a closely related industry?

2. The appraisal right exists to prevent a shareholder from being forced into a situation where he finds himself to be an unwilling investor in a business which is quite different from the one he originally invested in.

3. No. The surviving corporation is responsible for all unpaid debts of the acquired company, regardless of whether the debt was expressly assumed.

4. Alad II's use of these intangible assets showed that it was obtaining the benefits of Alad I's reputation as a going concern, and the court felt that Alad II should also shoulder some of the responsibilities derived from Alad I's prior operations.

5. Their suit will not be successful. Under identical facts the court in

<u>Skelly v. Dockweiler</u>, 75 F.Supp. 11 (S.D. Calif. 1947), denied the minority shareholders' request for an injunction. According to the court, it was not demonstrated that the proposed merger was unfair and the minority still had their appraisal rights.

6. The creditor is not correct. Tandem did not acquire Kilmer's liabilities when it acquired its assets. The creditor will have to collect from Kilmer, which does still exist, and Kilmer received cash for its assets, so it should be able to pay the debt.

7. In a majority of states, their challenge will be successful. They are correct in claiming that the situation is "different." Under Sections 60 and 73 of the Model Business Corporation Act, nonvoting shares may vote as a class on matters which will result in fundamental changes in their rights and privileges.

8. The tender offer can be used to deal directly with shareholders of the target company if that company's management would oppose a formal merger. A tender offer, since it is addressed to <u>all</u> shareholders, avoids any possible claims that the acquiring company dealt selectively with only controlling shareholders. And a tender offer, in and of itself, will not affect the market value of the shares as individual negotiations with shareholders might.

9. Most susceptible to a deadlock is a closely held corporation with an even number of directors and an even number of equally divided shares.

10. There is no preference as to the distribution of assets unless it is expressly provided for in the articles of incorporation. Therefore, the two classes of stock will be treated equally, each shareholder receiving $20 per share.

PART SIX: PROPERTY AND BAILMENTS

CHAPTER 36

REAL PROPERTY

AUTHORS' SUGGESTIONS:

1. It might be well to advise students that even though fixtures are considered to be real property, security interests in such items are governed by Article 9 of the Code rather than real property mortgage law.

2. It probably should be pointed out to students that the word "tenant" is used in various ways. It doesn't just mean a lessee.

3. In those areas where reference to the government survey is used to describe land in a deed, the instructor may want to give an example of this descriptive method. An excellent source is R. Kratovil, Real Estate Law (6th ed. 1974) §49.

4. Also, in those few areas such as New York City which employ the Torrens system of title registration, the instructor will probably want to explain its operation. Again, the 6th ed. of Kratovil, §273, is a good source.

CASE BRIEFS:

Cook v. Beerman

Facts: Cook purchased 62 acres from Beerman. While inspecting the premises prior to buying it, Cook saw an irrigation well complete with pump and motor. The pump was in the well and the motor was bolted to a concrete foundation next to the well and was connected to a natural gas line. The irrigation pipe and sprinkler system were unassembled and stacked behind the house, 1500 feet from the well. Cook told the agent he would have no use for the pipe or sprinkler system. The sale contract they subsequently executed included a typewritten provision that had been added to the printed form, which stated, "The irrigation equipment is not included in this sale." Before Cook took possession, Beerman gave notice that the pump and motor didn't go with the land. Cook disputed this, but Beerman sold these items to a third party. Cook sued Beerman for the value of the pump and motor. The trial court ruled for plaintiff Cook and awarded damages of $1750. Both sides appealed, Cook asserting that the damage award was inadequate.

Holding: Judgment for plaintiff Cook affirmed, but damages should be $3500, which the evidence showed the items' value to be. The pump and motor clearly were fixtures, and the quoted provision was inserted to formalize Cook's statement that he didn't need the irrigation pipe and sprinkler system. Since the contract language was ambiguous, oral testimony was admissible, and the testimony of Cook, the Real Estate agent, and Beerman's attorney indicated that the provision was not intended to exclude the pump and motor from the sale.

Baker v. Zingelman

Facts: Margaret DeBow (later Zingelman) owned property which was mostly farmland, but on which there also were a house, several sheds and garages, and a barn containing an antique shop. Margaret asked her sister and the sister's husband (the Bakers) to move from Ohio to Pennsylvania, live in the farmhouse, and operate the shop. The Bakers agreed, and Margaret prepared a deed supposedly conveying that part of the land on which all the buildings were located. The description of the land to be conveyed was derived from Margaret's measurement, accomplished by "walking off." Later, there was a falling out between Margaret and the Bakers. It was discovered that the deed description was inaccurate, and that the boundary it established went through the middle of the barn, garage, and some sheds. Margaret told them that the buildings encroaching on her property would be forcibly removed, unless they paid her $10,000 for the strip of land that would clear up the location problem of the buildings. The Bakers, plaintiffs, sued Margaret, defendant, asking the court to enjoin Margaret from using or removing the disputed portion of the buildings. The trial court ruled for plaintiffs, and defendant appealed.

Holding: Judgment for plaintiffs affirmed. An injunction should be issued prohibiting Margaret from trespassing on the disputed property. It was clearly the parties' original intention to include sufficient land in the deed to encompass all the buildings. Allowing the deed to stand as written would sanction the absurd; Margaret must convey the disputed portion to the Bakers.

Kline v. Kramer

Facts: The Klines and the Kramers were adjoining landowners who both claimed ownership of a strip of land one to four feet wide and 309 feet long. The Klines based their claim on the description in their deed, which included the strip. The Kramers based their claim on title by adverse possession established by the previous owners of the Kramer property, the Britts. The Kramers, plaintiffs, sued the Klines, defendants, seeking to establish ownership. The trial court granted plaintiff's motion for summary judgment, and defendants appealed.

Holding: Judgment for plaintiffs affirmed. The Britts had fenced, and used as their own, the disputed strip for longer than the required ten-year period. Thus they owned the strip by adverse possession, and the Kramers became owners when they bought from the Britts.

ANSWERS TO QUESTIONS AND PROBLEMS:

1. Warren will not prevail, so long as Talley uses proper methods of drilling and extraction. Talley has a right to draw oil from the common reservoir, subject to the doctrine of "correlative rights", which was established in Ohio Oil Co. v. Indiana, 177 U.S. 190 (1900), and is now generally followed. Under this rule, Talley will be liable to Warren if he uses improper methods in an attempt to produce too much oil too quickly and thereby reduces the ultimate recoverable capacity.

2. Warren will win in this case, period. Talley has committed a subsurface trespass and will be liable to Warren for the value of the oil he takes. This is true both in those states following the "ownership in place" rule and in those that don't. A good example of a slant well case is Alphonzo E. Bell Corp. v. Bell View Oil Syndicate, 76 P.2d 167 (Cal. App. 1938).

3. The issue is whether the hutches were fixtures. If so, ownership of them passed to Watkins along with the rest of the real property since they were not expressly excluded from the sale. It would be a fairly close question, but under the standards applied by the courts, as discussed in this chapter, it seems most likely they would not be fixtures.

4. Wall-to-wall carpet is installed in various ways. It may be glued or just tacked, but even if merely tacked to the floor, the carpet has been cut to fit a particular room and might not fit perfectly in any other. Another factor in determining if there was an intent that the carpet be a permanent addition is whether it is on top of a finished floor or not. The courts are divided on the question, although it seems more logical to treat it as a fixture in most cases.

5. The most obvious reason is the fact that an owner should logically be expected to say so if he does not intend to convey his entire interest.

6. Kempin will be allowed to cut timber for firewood but not for sale. He will not be allowed to extract the lignite at all unless a mine existed when he acquired his life estate.

7. An easement is the right to <u>do something</u> on someone else's premises; a profit is the right to <u>take something</u> from someone else's premises; and a license is an <u>unenforceable permission</u> to <u>go upon</u> someone else's premises.

8. An open listing entitles the broker to his commission only if <u>he</u> procures a willing and able buyer. An exclusive agency entitles the broker to his commission if he procures a willing and able buyer <u>or</u> if the land is actually sold <u>by anyone other than the owner</u> (such as another broker). An exclusive right to sell entitles the broker to his commission if he procures a willing and able buyer <u>or</u> if the land is actually sold by <u>anyone</u>, including the owner.

9. In most states an unrecorded deed, although valid between grantor and grantee, is void as against a subsequent good faith purchaser for value. Under these facts, Rosser would have title. In most states the same would be true regardless of whether Rosser recorded <u>his</u> deed. If Samuelson was already in possession when Rosser purchased, this possession would serve as constructive notice to Rosser (that is, whether he actually knew of the possession or not) of Samuelson's interest. In such a case Rosser would not be deemed to have acted in good faith, and Samuelson would have title.

10. Ross would still own the cave beneath his land. Arnold did not acquire title to the cave by adverse possession because his possession had not been <u>open</u> and <u>notorious</u> --- it had been concealed. <u>Marengo Cave Co. v. Ross</u>, 10 N.E.2d 917 (Ind. 1937).

CHAPTER 37

PERSONAL PROPERTY

AUTHORS' SUGGESTIONS:

1. The subject of gifts causa mortis is a good take-off point for a short lecture on wills if the instructor wishes to do so.

2. A lively class discussion can sometimes be generated by querying whether the rationale for the different treatment of lost and mislaid property is necessarily valid. It is arguable, in fact.

3. An interesting discussion might also ensue from asking students whether they can see, in Humble v. West, any underlying public policy considerations in the court's decision that Humble's injection did not divest it of title to the natural gas.

CASE BRIEFS:

Gordon v. Bialystoker Center & Bikur Cholim, Inc.

Facts: Ida Gorodetsky, 85, suffered a stroke and was partially paralyzed, confused, and sometimes semicomatose. At the suggestion of an acquaintance, the Bialystoker nursing home sent a social worker to visit her in the hospital. After learning she had money, the home sent another worker who obtained Ida's signature on a withdrawal slip for $15,000. Using the slip, the home obtained a check payable to the home for Ida's benefit. She was then moved to the home and was immediately visited by the home's executive director, its fund raiser, one of its social workers, and a notary. Her mark was obtained on several documents, including another withdrawal slip for over $12,000. She died a month later and Gordon, her brother and administrator of her estate, sued the home to recover these funds, less Ida's actual expenses. The trial court ruled for the defendant home, the intermediate level appellate court reversed, and the home appealed.

Holding: Judgment of the intermediate level appellate court for plaintiff Gordon is affirmed. The home must return all the money less Ida's actual, provable expenses. Although a gift was made, the home had the status of a fiduciary because of its control over Ida. Thus, the gift is presumed void, and the home has the burden of proving the absence of undue influence, fraud, or mistake. It has not met this burden.

Paset v. Old Orchard Bank & Trust Co.

Facts: Paset, a safety deposit box holder at the bank, found $6,325 on the seat of a chair in a booth in the vault. She turned the money over to officers of the bank. The bank contacted everyone who had been in the vault area on the day of, or on the day before, the discovery. No one came forth and the money remained unclaimed for over a year. Under the Illinois "estray" statute, the finder becomes owner after a year if notice has been advertised. The bank refused to turn over the money, claiming that it was "mislaid," not lost, and that the bank should continue to hold the money for the true owner. Paset filed suit and the trial court ruled for defendant bank.

Holding: Reversed. Paset, the finder, is now owner of the money. To effectuate purposes of the estray statute --- finding true owner by advertising notice, and rewarding honest finder --- the statute should be applied unless evidence very clearly shows that property was not lost (i.e., a presumption that property was lost). Here, it wasn't clear, so court ruled that property was lost, not mislaid, and estray statute applied.

Humble Oil & Refining Co. v. West

Facts: The Wests in 1938 conveyed to Humble a tract of land in a natural gas field. The Wests reserved, however, a one-sixth royalty interest which entitled them to one-sixth of the value of all natural gas produced from the land. In 1969 Humble began injecting gas back into the natural underground reservoir for the purpose of storage and to prevent the seepage of salt water from destroying the reservoir's capacity. In 1970 the Wests sued Humble, asking for an injunction prohibiting Humble from continuing its injection activities. Alternatively, they asked the court to declare them to be entitled to a one-sixth royalty on *all* gas subsequently taken from the reservoir, both native and "extraneous" (injected). The trial court refused to grant the injunction but granted the alternative request. The Court of Civil appeals reversed, holding that an injunction should have been granted. Humble appealed.

Holding: Judgment reversed, and case remanded for a new trial. The Wests were not entitled to an injunction because the result would be destruction of natural gas storage capacity vital to the Southeast Texas area. Also, Humble became the owner of the gas when it was extracted, and Humble did not lose title by injecting it back into the ground. However, by doing so, it commingled its gas (on which royalties had already been paid) with native gas in which the Wests had a royalty interest. Since Humble had caused the confusion, it has the burden of proving which part of the gas later taken out is native and which is extraneous. If it cannot prove this on retrial, Humble must pay royalties on <u>all</u> gas subsequently extracted.

ANSWERS TO QUESTIONS AND PROBLEMS:

1. A lease of personal property merely creates a bailment and does not give the lessee an ownership interest in the property. A lessee of real property, on the other hand, acquires a legal interest in the property.

2. The court in <u>Liebe v. Battman</u>, 54 Pac. 179 (Ore. 1898), held that Schutz was not the owner of the note and that Liebe, the administrator, should prevail. There had not been a valid gift <u>causa mortis</u> because there had been no delivery of possession to Schutz before Closter's death.

3. The ring does not belong to the sister. Walters' recovery automatically terminated the gift <u>causa mortis</u>, even though he ultimately died from the same condition. An example of this rule is found in <u>Weston v. Hight</u>, 17 Me. 287 (1840), where there was a recovery from consumption and then death only eight months later. The court there held that the donor's recovery revoked the gift.

In the hypothetical case, if Walters had not asked for the return of the ring, but had just allowed her to keep it for such a long period, a court might be justified in holding that he intended to make a gift <u>inter vivos after</u> his recovery. And, of course, the sister already had the ring and a new delivery would not be necessary.

4. If there is no delivery, all that exists is a promise to make a gift in the future. Such a promise obviously is not supported by consideration and is not enforceable as a contract.

5. According to the court in <u>Hillebrant v. Brewer</u>, 6 Tex. 45 (1851), the branding conferred sufficient control so as to constitute constructive delivery. Thus, a valid gift was made.

6. A gift was not made. Although such an account creates a presumption of an intent to make a gift, the evidence here clearly overcomes this presumption. Since the sole purpose for opening the joint account was to allow Kuntz to assist Harkness, and since the funds were never used for any other purpose, there was no intent to make a gift to Kuntz.

7. Property is classified as lost if it is discovered in a place where the true owner had not intentionally left it. Property is mislaid if it is discovered in a place where it had been intentionally put by the true owner,

but then forgotten. Property is abandoned if it is discovered in a place where the prior owner had left it with no intention to reclaim it. The rationale behind favoring the owner of the premises where the item is discovered, in the case of mislaid property, is that the true owner is more likely to remember where he left it and return for it than in the case of lost property. The finder is favored in the case of lost property because it was his effort that brought about the discovery, and because it is felt to be much less likely that the true owner will return to the place. The first party to take possession of abandoned (unowned) property becomes the owner because of a policy in favor of putting property to use rather than letting it be in a state of disuse.

8.   In Keron v. Cashman, 33 Atl. 1055 (N.J. Ch. 1896), all the boys were treated as joint finders, each entitled to an equal share. Even though Crawford first picked up the sock, he was unaware of the presence of the money. One cannot "find" or "possess" something without knowing of its existence.

9.   If the mixing was by consent, X and Y would be tenants in common of the total mass, each owning a proportionate undivided interest. The same result would obtain if a third party such as Z caused the confusion by accident. Where X has brought about the confusion willfully, knowing he had no right to do so, the parties nevertheless will be tenants in common if the goods of X and Y are identical as is probably true here. If not, X will lose title to his goods unless he can prove the specific identity of his goods, which will be very difficult.

10. Courts tend to require a greater change before holding that title has passed to a bad faith improver than they do in the case of a good faith improver. Also, if an improver does acquire title, he has to compensate the original owner only for the value of the property in its unimproved condition if he acted in good faith. But a bad faith improver who acquires title must compensate the original owner for the value of the property in its improved state.

CHAPTER 38

WILLS, TRUSTS, AND ESTATES

AUTHORS' SUGGESTIONS:

1. Reference to Picasso's intestacy is of course to a factual event. The instructor, and students, may have other examples of the problems created by the failure to provide for the orderly disposition of one's property at death. While not emphasized in the chapter, it may be worth mentioning that considerable family dissension occurs when a member dies intestate and the squabble immediately begins over what property goes to which survivor.

2. Most states' laws are reasonably clear in their will requirements but careful compliance should be stressed. Terms may give the students some trouble so it may be helpful to devise a drill or exercise in which the students are required to define and apply the more common terms and expressions. The Holladay case is somewhat of a classic as regards contest of wills for lack of testamentary capacity while the Thompson case illustrates the necessity for strict compliance with state law in revoking a will.

3. The point is made in the section on intestacy that one who fails to make a valid will, or otherwise provide for the distribution of his estate, is leaving the selection of his heirs to the state. It should, of course, be pointed out that the state doesn't benefit or become an heir. Nevertheless, the decedent has failed to take advantage of his right to leave his property to whomever he wishes.

4. The discussion of trusts intentionally omits any reference to the Rule Against Perpetuities. It is a complex theory, difficult to explain, and even more difficult to understand. The instructor might want to mention it in passing as a limitation on the duration of trusts. With regard to the "spendthrift trust," it should be pointed out that it is not a trust but is merely a provision in a private express trust.

5. The authors have tried to emphasize that estate planning is a complex procedure calling for the advice of experts. It should not be left to amateurs. Quite simply, the larger the estate the greater the need for competent advice

and counsel.

CASE BRIEFS:

Holladay v. Holladay

Facts: Testator, Lewis Holladay, died leaving a will in which his brother was named as the sole beneficiary. The testator's three sisters contested the will claiming that the testator lacked the mental or testamentary capacity to execute a will. The sisters produced testimony to the effect that the testator was emotionally upset by his mother's death; that he shot his pet dog for no apparent reason; that he sat under trees during electrical storms; that he roamed his farm at night and often stood "like a statue" in the middle of the road; and that he frequently bathed at night in a pond that was "little more than a hog wallow." Opposed to this testimony were twenty-six of Holladay's neighbors, associates and business acquaintances who testified that he was sane, normal, a good farmer and successful businessman.

Holding: The Court of Appeals of Kentucky affirmed the trial court's verdict (jury trial) that Lewis Holladay did possess the mental capacity to make a will despite some otherwise strange behavior.

Thompson v. Royall

Facts: Testatrix, a Mrs. Kroll, executed a will of five typewritten pages, signed by her and three witnesses as required by statute. Two weeks later she informed her attorney that she would like to destroy the will. He suggested that she retain it as a memorandum in case she later decided to make a new will. She agreed, so to cancel the will, the attorney wrote in longhand, on the cover page of the will: "This will null and void and to be only held by H. P. Brittain instead of being destroyed as a memorandum for another will if I desire to make same. This 19 Sept. 1932." Mrs. Kroll signed her name below this writing in her attorney's presence. She died the following month, leaving an estate of $200,000, and having made no new will. When the will was offered for probate it was contested by Mrs. Kroll's heirs who had not been named as beneficiaries. The trial jury found that the attempted revocation did not comply with Virginia law and that the will was therefore valid. The heirs appealed.

Holding: Since Virginia law requires the same formalities for revoking as for executing a will, the writing by the attorney, though signed by Mrs. Kroll, fell short of meeting the requirements for revocation. Neither was it a canceling of the will since it was not words, marks or lines written across the provisions of the will itself; nor was it a physical defacement or mutilation.

Comford v. Cantrell

Facts: Testator, James Cantrell, devised certain real estate to his wife "to be her absolute state forever." He further provided, in the next paragraph: "It is my request that upon her death my said wife, Clara Augusta Cantrell, shall give, devise and bequeath my interest (in the specified real estate), to each of my brothers, Harvey W. Cantrell, Lee Cantrell, and Julian W. Cantrell, or their heirs." Mrs. Cantrell's will, she having survived her husband, devised the real estate in question to her nephew and his wife. At her death the nephew contended that she received a fee simple interest in the property under her husband's will. The brothers claim that she took the property subject to a trust in their favor. The brothers appealed a trial court ruling in favor of the nephew.

Holding: Judgment affirmed. The language used by the testator, a devise to his wife's "absolute estate forever," clearly indicates a fee simple estate. On the other hand, the language of the following paragraph of the will amounted merely to a request and was simply precatory in nature. No trust was created.

ANSWERS TO QUESTIONS AND PROBLEMS:

1. No. Holographic wills must be entirely in the handwriting of the testatrix and must be signed. The decedent in this case had not signed the will; her name in the opening paragraph and on the envelope did not constitute a "signature."

2. A purchase money resulting trust is created since it was the father's intention that the stock purchases benefit the children and due to the fact that the childrens' money was used to make the purchase. The mother, therefore, holds the stock in trust for the benefit of the children.

3. No. It did not comply with the state's requirement that the testatrix and witnesses sign at the "end of the will." This case points out the dangers in using a do-it-yourself, fill-in-the-blanks type form.

4. Yes. The surviving spouse will take the estate under the terms of the will. The revocation requested by the testator was ineffective and the will was admitted to probate. However, due to the wife's fraudulent conduct, she will take the estate subject to a constructive trust for the benefit of the children who would have taken had the will been revoked.

5. A per stirpes distribution will be made. The three children will each take one-fourth of the estate with the two grandchildren of decedent sharing the remaining one-fourth, their parent's share.

6. A trust creates a fiduciary relationship between the trustee and the

beneficiaries. The conduct of the trustee in using trust property for his own gain is a breach of his fiduciary duty. He can of course be liable for this breach and the sale can be set aside or the profit recovered for the trust.

7. No. The wording by testatrix did not convey an intent to benefit the public or some particular class of persons, indefinite in number. The dominant thought was that the interest from a certain fund be used to help educate some (one) individual to be selected, on a one-time basis by Paul Gill.

8. The fifth page is of no effect. The law of wills requires that codicils be executed with the same formalities as are wills. Here the writing was not attested by two or more competent witnesses.

9. Since the language used by the testator is largely precatory it is doubtful that a trust was intended. John took a fee simple estate in the real estate and the $5,000 was an outright gift. Language creating a trust must be directive in nature, expressing something more than a mere request, hope or desire.

10. The 1,000 acre farm and the auto owned solely by the decedent will be subject to administration. The property owned jointly will pass to the surviving joint tenant and not to the estate. The life insurance proceeds would be paid to the named beneficiary. However, even though jointly owned property may bypass the estate it may nevertheless be subjected to estate or inheritance taxes.

CHAPTER 39

BAILMENTS

AUTHORS' SUGGESTIONS:

1. Bailments is yet another subject that students find particularly interesting, as it involves transactions that they encounter in everyday life. Since one of the authors (at least) has found this subject to be a useful introduction to sales law, instructors may want to assign this chapter just before Chapters 17-21.

2. Because there are many kinds of bailments, the rights and duties of the bailor and bailee vary widely. For that reason, when fielding particular questions in class in this area, the instructor has to make sure (and make known to other students) what particular type of bailment the student who is asking the question has in mind.

3. Students often have the preconceived idea that commercial bailees are liable for any loss or damage to the property while in their hands, even when they are not at fault. This is generally not true, and (hopefully) the text makes this perfectly clear.

CASE BRIEFS:

The Broadview Apartments Co. v. Baughman

Facts: Baughman, plaintiff, was a tenant of Broadview Apartments, and he parked his car in Broadview's garage for $15 a month. When his car was stolen he sued Broadview for damages, alleging that a bailment existed and that his proof of loss of the car made out a prima facie case of negligence on the part of defendant Broadview. The trial court agreed and entered judgment for Baughman.

Holding: Reversed. Where Baughman merely rented space in the garage, parked his own car, and kept the keys when he left the car overnight, no bailment existed. In such a case, Broadview did not have sufficient control over the car for it to be a bailee.

Lissie v. Southern New England Telephone Co.

Facts: The plaintiffs, employees of the telephone company, brought this action against the company when their coats were stolen while they were at work. They contended that the company was a bailee of the coats (for reasons appearing below), and thus liable for the loss unless the company could prove it was not negligent. The trial court agreed and entered judgment for plaintiffs.

Holding: Judgment affirmed. The court first observed that whether or not a transaction creates a bailment is determined by the degree of custody or control given the one having possession. Here, where the company required the coats to be kept in a particular room (and on a floor different from that where plaintiffs' offices were located), the company implicitly assumed sufficient control over the coats to constitute it a bailee. Therefore, since the presumption of negligence rule applies and the company did not rebut the presumption, it is liable for the loss.

Buchanan v. Byrd

Facts: The defendants, Byrd and Barksdale, kept and fed Buchanan's horse on their small acreage for $40 a month. One night the horse got out and was killed when struck by a train. Buchanan brought his action, contending that the defendant-bailees were negligent in letting the horse escape. Defendants claimed that they had explained and rebutted the presumption of negligence. The trial court entered judgment for plaintiff, Buchanan, but an appellate court reversed the judgment. Buchanan then appealed to the Supreme Court of Texas.

Holding: Judgment of the appeals court reversed, and judgment of trial court in favor of Buchanan reinstated. The evidence of defendants is inadequate to rebut the presumption that they were negligent. The fact that the fences were in good repair; that a caretaker lived on the premises; and that plaintiff had never complained about the care of the horse does not legally explain why the gate was open, or why the horses were left to run loose at night on the acreage, especially in light of the fact that the caretaker was away til midnight and there was no evidence that he had checked the gate upon his return.

Cintrone v. Hertz Truck Leasing and Rental Service, Inc.

Facts: Hertz, defendant, leased trucks to Contract Packers on a long-term basis. Cintrone, plaintiff, was an employee of Contract Packers who was injured when the brakes of the truck in which he was riding failed. He sued Hertz on two theories: negligence and breach of implied warranty. The trial court ruled that Hertz made no implied warranties and dismissed plaintiff's claim based on that theory, and the jury found no negligence on Hertz's part. Judgment was thus for defendant Hertz.

<u>Holding</u>: Judgment reversed, and case remanded for new trial. The trial court was wrong in dismissing plaintiff's warranty claim. Where Hertz was a commercial bailor, there arose an "implied continuing promissory warranty" that the truck was fit for the purposes for which Contract Packers rented it --- i.e., operation and transportation of goods on public highways. The court said if Hertz had <u>sold</u> the truck to Contract Packers an implied warranty of fitness for operation would have come into existence, and that there was no logical reason for not extending such a warranty to <u>bailments</u> of this type.

ANSWERS TO QUESTIONS AND PROBLEMS:

1. Hanson's contention is not correct. A pledge --- i.e., a transfer of possession of personal property from a debtor to a creditor as security for the debt --- is considered to be a bailment even though the creditor has no duty to return the property to the bailor/debtor if he fails to pay the debt when it comes due. We thus have another exception (in addition to the two mentioned in this chapter) to the general rule that a bailment contract <u>always</u> requires a return of the identical goods by the bailee.

2. (a) A bailor-bailee relationship would almost certainly be <u>ruled out</u> in this instance. One of the requirements of a bailment is that the purported bailee knows (or should know) of the transfer of possession.

(b) This change in facts moves us much closer to a bailment relationship. A court might easily say that though there was no physical handing of the bag to the receptionist, a constructive bailment existed. On the other hand, a court might say <u>no bailment</u> on the ground that Miss X was able (physically and legally) to retake possession of the bag with no notice to the receptionist, and that the receptionist therefore did not have exclusive control. (<u>Note</u>: Even if a court were to rule no bailment, the receptionist still has a duty to use reasonable care to prevent loss of the bag.)

3. (a) No bailment. As long as Gray has the right to return a different car than the one he got from Scarlet, a necessary element of a bailment is lacking.

(b) This would be a bailment with the option to purchase. Where the one taking possession merely has the option of returning the property <u>or</u> of paying the money instead, this is an exception to the general rule that the specific property must <u>always</u> be returned.

4. The company was receiving a benefit because it was to the company's

advantage to have the coats in an area where they would not interfere with the employees' work, and where the employees would normally not have to worry about the safety of their coats. (Additionally, it is possible that the company might even have had a legal obligation to furnish reasonable space for this purpose.)

5. A bailee does not have the right to use the property if the contract expressly so provides. Also, in a storage contract the bailee by implication has no right to use the property.

6. If the relationship is that of lessee and lessor, with X being the lessee, X must ordinarily prove a specific act of negligence on the Y Company's part in order to recover a judgment. On the other hand, if the relationship is bailor-bailee, the Y Company is liable for the loss unless it can clearly prove that it was not negligent.

7. Byrd's evidence --- the fact that the fences were in good repair before the incident; the fact that there was no evidence that the fences gave way; and the fact plaintiff had made no complaint about the care of the horse --- does not explain two possibilities of negligence: (1) that one of the defendants negligently left the gate open, or (2) that the caretaker negligently failed to see if the gate was closed when he arrived back late at night.

8. The carrier's argument was rejected. The New York Court applied the usual rule to the effect that "the phrase 'public enemy' connotes the existence of an actual state of war, and refers to the government of a foreign nation at war with" the United States. Thus, thieves, rioteers, robbers (and hijackers), "although at war with the social order, are not to be classed as 'public enemies' in the legal sense. Result: the carrier was liable to David Crystal, Inc.

TEST BANK

Chapter 1

The American Legal System

True-False

1. In general, our law has been little influenced by community mores, thoughts and conduct.

2. There is no single definition of "law" that is universally accepted or universally approved by legal authorities.

3. Our federal law is entirely statutory (there is no general, federal "common law" today).

4. Today, the great bulk of law in the U.S. is federal (rather than state) law.

5. The subjects of corporation law, sales law, and taxation law are governed by statutes.

6. The process of interpreting statutes after they are passed is generally in the hands of the legislative bodies.

7. The subjects of criminal law and constitutional law fall within the "public law" category.

8. The issuance of a summons is procedural and is not considered a part of the pleadings of a case.

9. If a case that presents a federal question is initiated by the plaintiff in a state court, the defendant ordinarily has a right to ask that the case be removed to a federal court.

10. As a general rule, there is no jury in a civil action unless plaintiff and defendant both request a jury.

11. One of the differences between state and federal court systems is that the federal system has no courts of "limited jurisdiction."

12. Courts of equity evolved in England primarily because the courts of law were too busy to hear all the cases coming before them.

13. Motions to dismiss are always sustained because they would not be filed unless they did not state a cause of action.

14. The term "process of adjudication" refers to the action or conduct engaged in only by appellate courts.

15. When an appellate court reverses the judgment of the trial court, this means -- in most cases -- that the loser in the trial court has "won" and the case will not be sent back to the trial court for further proceedings.

Chapter 1

Multiple Choice

1. The basic difference between the traditional and environmental approaches to the subject of Business Law lies in the fact that the traditional approach:

    a) emphasizes the older rules of law, while the environmental approach emphasizes modern rules of law.
    b) places much more emphasis upon the content of the existing rule of law that comprise the various legal subjects than does the environmental approach.
    c) is essentially concerned with the traditional processes by which the rules of law are made, and is little concerned with the content of the rules themselves.
    d) none of the above.

2. Which of the following bodies of law are essentially "statutory" in nature?

    a) torts
    b) agency
    c) contracts
    d) none of the above
    e) b and c only

3. The term "common law" has several different meanings. As used in this course, it refers to:

    a) only those rules of law in effect today in the U.S. which were earlier formulated by the English courts.
    b) only those rules of law that have resulted from cases in which state or federal statutes had to be interpreted by the courts.
    c) only those rules or principles of law that have been made up and applied by the courts over the years in those areas of law where the legislatures and Congress have not enacted statutes.
    d) none of the above.

4. In regard to "actions in equity," which of the following is (are) true today?

    a) there is no jury.
    b) such actions may ordinarily be brought only in the federal courts.
    c) the proceedings are less formal and technical than those governing actions at law.
    d) all of the above.
    e) a and c.

5. Which of the following is (are) not equitable remedies?

    a) decree of specific performance
    b) injunction
    c) mortgage foreclosures
    d) damages (recovery of money)
    e) c and d

Chapter 1

6. In a civil action in which the plaintiff is asking for a money judgment (or remedy at law), questions of fact are resolved by:

   a) the jury.
   b) the court (judge), the jury deciding the questions of law.
   c) the jury and the judge who instructs the jury as to the facts.
   d) the judge who gives the jury written instruction dealing with the law.

7. Peremptory challenges to prospective jurors are those which:

   a) require the challenging attorney to show some reason why the prospective juror is not capable of rendering an impartial verdict, or is otherwise unfit to serve.
   b) only the trial judge can make.
   c) permit the attorney to have a juror removed arbitrarily without assigning a reason for doing so.
   d) none of the above.

8. The work of higher courts in ruling on appeals differs from the trial courts in that:

   a) appellate courts are concerned only with questions of law.
   b) appellate courts are comprised of three or more judges.
   c) there is no reintroduction of the evidence.
   d) all of the above.

Short Essay

1. a) Give the major reasons why equity courts were created.

   b) Briefly describe the two primary remedies that courts of equity may provide.

2. X, a Pennsylvania manufacturer, is owed a debt of $8,000 by Y, an Indiana retailer. Y owns a farm in Pennsylvania, but that property has no relation to the debt. If you are an attorney for X, who now wants to collect the debt by court action, would you file this suit in a state court in Pennsylvania where the land is located, in the federal court in Indiana having jurisdiction of Y's residence, in a state court in Indiana within whose jurisdiction Y's residence is located, or in some other court? Explain your answer, indicating, among other things, which of the courts suggested could not hear the case.

Chapter 2

Major Bodies of Law

True-False

1. Most branches of our law today are statutory (rather than common-law) in nature.

2. The subjects of contracts, torts, and agency are our three major areas of law that are still essentially governed by common-law principles.

3. In actual practice courts almost never overrule a precedent even when they realize it has no logical basis.

4. A state statute defines a motor vehicle as "an automobile, an automobile truck, a motorcycle, or any other self-propelled vehicle not designed for running on rails." If this statute were interpreted literally, airplanes would fall within its scope and be "motor vehicles."

5. If a court, when interpreting a statute, finds that the statute's "circumstantial context" leads to one interpretation and its "textual context" to another, the court is required to apply the textual context interpretation.

6. The Uniform Commercial Code (UCC) governs, among other things, the subject of "corporation law."

7. Because the First Amendment simply provides that "Congress shall make no law respecting the establishment of a religion, . . ." there is no legal rule or principle today that prohibits a state from making such a law.

8. If a case is appealed to the U.S. Supreme Court and it refuses to hear the appeal, the judgment being appealed from is, in effect, upheld by the Supreme Court.

9. Today, under Supreme Court decisions, the "freedom of speech" clause is given such sweeping protection by that court that state statutes forbidding obscenity are held to be illegal under the free speech clause even if such statutes define obscenity in terms which the Supreme Court concedes to be legally correct.

10. Because of the "separation of powers" concept of the federal constitution, very few federal agencies possess investigative, rule-making, and adjudicative powers.

11. One of the factors explaining the emergence of the modern administrative agency is the fact that many complex problems exist today which require for their solution technical expertise which the courts and legislatures usually do not possess.

Chapter 2

12. Because the courts are increasingly hostile to the dual role of "prosecutor and judge" played by agencies in earlier years, most state and federal agencies today are rarely given adjudicatory powers.

13. It is possible for a single wrongful act to constitute a tort and a crime.

14. One of the requirements for the bringing of a successful _slander_ action is proof that the false statement was "communicated" to a _third_ party.

15. One essential element of all torts is the _intent_ to injure another or his property.

16. The principles of negligence law are designed to protect persons from unintentional harm resulting from the careless conduct of others.

17. A majority of states today, by statute or judicial decision, have adopted some form of comparative negligence rule.

Multiple Choice

1. Which of the following bodies of law are essentially made up of common-law rules?

    a) contracts
    b) agency law
    c) corporation law
    d) b and c
    e) a and b

2. Prior to the _Flagiello v. Pennsylvania Hospital_ case, the common-law rule in Pennsylvania was that charitable institutions were not liable for the torts of their employees. The Supreme Court of Pennsylvania, in _Flagiello_, overruled the early view because it felt that:

    a) the entire _stare decisis_ doctrine had outlived its usefulness.
    b) the hospital did not qualify as a charitable institution.
    c) the plaintiff did not prove her claim of negligence.
    d) none of the above.

3. In the case of _Holy Trinity Church v. U.S._, the U.S. Supreme Court examined several factors in an effort to interpret a federal statute. Which of the following factors was _not_ examined?

    a) the title of the statute.
    b) the extent to which churches have historically been exempt from state and federal statutes in this country, expressly or impliedly.
    c) the legislative history of the statute.
    d) the "evil" which the statute was presumably designed to eliminate.
    e) none of the above. (I.e., the court examined all of the above factors.)

Chapter 2

4. The phrase "the constitution is not self-executing" means that:

   a) generally, governmental actions that may be unconstitutional will not be prohibited or set aside unless their legality is challenged in court.
   b) it is the Supreme Court that executes (carries into action) the constitutional guarantees.
   c) it is the federal courts that execute the constitutional guarantees.
   d) none of the above.

5. In regard to the subject of <u>administrative agencies</u>, which of the following observations is/are correct?

   a) A primary reason for the growth of administrative agencies in the last 40 years is political in nature -- i.e., the desire of elected officials to have a large source of jobs for political supporters.
   b) The courts have been increasingly hostile to agencies' rulings and actions.
   c) Agencies' rulings that are strictly discretionary in nature may not be set aside by the courts even if they are found to be totally without reason.
   d) b and c.
   e) none of the above.

6. Sometimes an agency's ruling is challenged in court on the ground that the statute creating the agency is an "unconstitutional delegation of legislative power." A party making such a challenge is contending that:

   a) the statute lacks reasonable standards by which the agency is to be guided and limited in performing its duties.
   b) the legislative body that passed the statute did not itself possess the particular power which it was attempting to delegate to the agency.
   c) the statute was in clear conflict with a state or federal constitutional provision.
   d) none of the above.

7. On the subject of <u>comparative negligence</u> statutes, which of the following observations is/are correct?

   a) Because of various problems that such statutes have produced in actual practice, the number of states having such statutes has declined in the last few years.
   b) In states having them, such statutes are applicable not only to negligence actions, but to several other types of tort actions as well.
   c) The basic reason for the enactment of such statutes has been legislative dissatisfaction with the common-law rules of negligence.
   d) a and b.
   e) a and c.

8. Which of the following is <u>not</u> a tort?

   a) breach of contract.
   b) a crime that produces no injury (e.g., running a traffic light).
   c) a breach of a duty owed by one person to another which produces an

168

Chapter 2

        injury, if the latter (the actor) did not actually know of the duty.
- d) all of the above are true. (I.e., none of the actions above constitutes a tort.)
- e) a and b.

9. Proximate cause problems arise:

   a) more often in negligence cases than in other tort cases.
   b) about as often in breach of contract cases as in tort cases.
   c) often in criminal actions, but seldom in tort cases.
   d) none of the above.

10. The most common defense to assault and battery is:

    a) consent and privilege.
    b) self-defense.
    c) trespass on the land.
    d) a and b.
    e) b and c.

Short Essay

1. In the school segregation case of Brown v. Board of Education, the U.S. Supreme Court held that state segregation of students on the basis of the color of their skin violated the equal protection clause of the federal constitution. In that case, did the court overrule the earlier "separate but equal" doctrine, or did it simply say that the doctrine was not applicable to this case? Explain.

2. Do administrative agencies really "make law?" If so, how? If not, why not?

3. Explain, as specifically as possible, how wrongs known as "torts" differ from a) crimes and b) breaches of contract.

Chapter 3

Nature and Classification of Contracts

True-False

1. A contract is an agreement that the law will enforce in case of a breach.

2. A bilateral contract is a promise for a promise.

3. A unilateral contract is an act for a promise.

4. A promise for an act is considered to be an inverted unilateral contract.

5. An express contract states fully and explicitly, orally or in writing, the entire agreement between the parties.

6. The conduct of the parties is never a basis for a contract.

7. Quasi-contracts are based on a genuine valid agreement between parties.

8. A void contract allows one of the parties, at his option, to withdraw from the contract without liability.

9. A contract may be rendered unenforceable by a special rule of law.

10. A formal contract is any agreement that is set in writing.

11. An executed contract is a contract that has been signed by all parties.

12. Specific performance is a remedy issued by a court of law.

13. The terms "unenforceable contract" and "void contract" both refer to agreements that, in the eyes of the law, never possessed a legal existence.

14. "Speculative damages" refers to losses which actually flow from one person's wrongful act (such as breach of a contract), but are of such a nature that the wrongdoer did not know, and had no reason to know under the circumstances, that they would result from his breach.

15. B buys S's hardware store in a small town, and the contract contains a promise by S that he will not engage in the hardware business in that town for the next six months. If S breaks this promise, B would be entitled to damages but would not be entitled to an injunction. (I.e., this is not a situation in which injunctions can be issued.)

Chapter 3

16. On Monday O hands a written proposal to P, offering to pay him $50 if he (P) performs a specified act no later than the following Friday noon. P, unbeknownst to O, performs the requested act the following Saturday morning. In such a case, most courts will probably refuse to rule that a unilateral contract was formed on Saturday morning, even if P can give a good reason why he was unable to perform the act earlier.

17. In the case of Judd Realty, Inc., v. Tedesco, Judd Realty had an exclusive right to sell the property. A buyer was found and Tedesco refused to sell. In this case the Supreme Court of Rhode Island determined that the contract was unilateral in nature.

18. In the case of Deskovick v. Porzio, two Deskovick brothers sought to recover from their father's estate the amount of hospital bills which they had paid on behalf of their father out of their own funds. In that case the higher court ruled (a) that they could not recover on the implied contract ground since their father did not know they were making the payments, and (b) that they could recover on the quasi-contract theory, however, because otherwise the father's estate would be unjustly enriched.

Multiple Choice

1. Professor H, soon after posting the results of a test, is stabbed by an unhappy student. While H is hospitalized, his brother (B) pays all of his hospital expenses under the honest impression that H is financially unable to do so. Later B learns that H is in fact quite wealthy, and he brings suit against H to recover the money he has spent.

    a) If B bases his action on the implied contract theory, he will have to show (among other things) that H knew he was paying the bills, and that H in some manner indicated that he would pay B back.
    b) If B bases his action on the quasi-contract theory, he will not have to prove either of the facts referred to in choice "a" above.
    c) neither of the above is correct.
    d) a and b are both correct.

2. The primary difference between a unilateral contract and a bilateral contract is the fact that:

    a) in a bilateral contract the apparent intentions of the two parties are not important in determining whether such a contract has or has not been formed.
    b) the formation of a unilateral contract necessarily involves the performance of an act by the offeree, while this is not necessary in the formation of a bilateral contract.
    c) neither of the above.

Chapter 3

3. For introductory purposes, a contract can be defined as:

   a) any agreement that a court will enforce.
   b) any written agreement that shows that the contracting parties have intended to make a binding contract, even if the elements of "consideration" and "capacity" are not present.
   c) any relationship existing between two (or more) adults, as a result of which the law recognizes that certain duties are owed by each party to the other.
   d) none of the above.

4. The offer made by a homeowner to a real estate agent that results from the signing of a "listing contract" by the homeowner:

   a) may, as a general rule, be legally revoked by the homeowner by giving notice of revocation to the agent at any time before he has produced a buyer for the property.
   b) is normally considered to be a unilateral offer.
   c) usually contains a stated future expiration date.
   d) all of the above are correct.
   e) b and c only.

5. An <u>implied contract</u> can best be defined as one:

   a) which lacks one or more elements of a true contract, but which may nevertheless be enforced by the courts if they feel it is in the best interests of the parties to do so.
   b) which is formed entirely without the use of words, either written or oral.
   c) in which the intentions of the contracting parties must be inferred by the courts in large part from their conduct and the circumstances surrounding their conduct.
   d) which exists in the eyes of the law, even though the parties have not in any way manifested an intent to contract.
   e) none of the above is an acceptable definition.

6. X asks Y to do a particular job for him, and Y does it. Later Y seeks to recover the reasonable value of the work. In such a case X is obligated to pay because of the formation of a:

   a) bilateral contract.
   b) unilateral contract.
   c) contract implied in law.
   d) contract implied in fact.

7. A contract that is <u>totally illegal</u> is properly called:

   a) void.
   b) void, unless the exception in "d" below is applicable.
   c) voidable; i.e., either party may ask to have it set aside.
   d) valid, <u>if</u> a court is convinced that the performance of the contract would not appreciably harm either party or society in general.

Chapter 3

8. <u>Nominal damages</u> are those which:

   a) are "named" in the contract--i.e., a specific sum of money that one party agrees to pay to the other in the event that he breaches the contract.
   b) are "in name only"--i.e., a small sum awarded to a plaintiff whose rights have been infringed upon as a result of the defendants breach of contract or other misconduct, but who has suffered no real or actual loss as a result of the defendant's wrong.
   c) are awarded by a court where a "liquidated damages" clause in a contract is felt by the court to be excessive; that is, nominal damages are those that are given in lieu of liquidated damages.
   d) none of the above.

9. A contract can be defined as:

   a) an agreement to do or not to do a certain thing.
   b) a promise or set of promises for the breach of which the law gives a remedy or the performance of which the law in some way recognizes as a duty.
   c) a legal relationship created when 2 or more parties agree to perform or refrain from performing a legal act.
   d) all of the above.

10. A bilateral contract comes into existence upon the exchange of:

    a) performance for a forbearance.
    b) a promise for an act.
    c) a promised forbearance for a promised act.
    d) an act for a promise.

11. A unilateral contract is formed by:

    a) an act for a promise.
    b) mutual promises to act.
    c) a promise to act upon the performing of an act.
    d) three or more parties.

12. An implied contract can best be defined as:

    a) one which will not be recognized as enforceable by the courts.
    b) a true form of a formal contract.
    c) one in which the intentions of the parties are inferred from their conduct by the court as well as the circumstances of the contract.
    d) one which exists in the eyes of the law, even though the parties have not in any way intended to form the contract.

Chapter 3

Short Essay

1. Accurately describe the characteristics that distinguish express, implied, and quasi-contracts.

2. X lived in a state which by law obligated school districts to furnish free transportation to children within a district who lived more than two miles from their school. X's children, who lived more than two miles from school, were wrongfully refused transportation by their district. Thereafter X drove the children to and from school for an entire year, at the end of which time he asked the district to reimburse him for his expenses, $175. The district refused to pay X, and he brought suit to recover the $175.

   In the suit of X vs. the school district, do you think that X has any contractual grounds for recovering his expenses? (I.e., do you think any kind of contract, from a legal standpoint, might exist between X and the district?) Explain your answer.

Chapter 4

The Agreement

True-False

1. In determining whether an intent to contract exists in a particular situation, the general rule is that it is the apparent intentions of the parties that are controlling (as opposed to their actual or subjective intentions.)

2. X receives an unordered article (car wax) in the U.S. mail from the Y Co., together with a bill for $3.95. Today, because of a federal statute, X may use the wax without incurring liability to the Y Co. even if it can prove that X clearly knew that the wax was not meant to be a gift.

3. Inquiries generally do not constitute offers, even when they contain a specific price. (E.g., "Would you sell your car for $900?")

4. The historical distinction between "preliminary negotiations" and "offers" has been essentially abandoned by the courts in recent years.

5. A common form of rejection is a counter-offer.

6. A counter-offer is a proposal made by the offeree to the offeror that differs in any material terms from the original offer.

7. On June 1 a retailer offers (by telephone) to sell certain pieces of office furniture to a prospective buyer for $1,400, and the retailer further promises that he will hold the offer open until June 15. Under present sales law (Article 2 of the UCC), the retailer is bound by this promise since he is a merchant (even though the promise was only made orally).

8. Placing an order with a mail-order catalogue is the acceptance of an offer rather than an offer to purchase.

9. An advertisement quoting a special price for a specific item is generally considered by the court to be an offer.

10. Despite the well-established rule that a contract must be "reasonably definite," the courts as a general rule try to avoid setting contracts aside on the ground of indefiniteness if they can reasonably do so.

11. In the case of Rivers v. Beadle, the appellate court ruled that the term "speculative home" in the contract was too indefinite a term to enforce in view of the fact that nowhere in the written contract were there additional terms indicating what the parties meant by this term.

Chapter 4

12. The rule that an offer must be "communicated" to the offeree before it can be accepted does not necessarily require proof--in the case of a written offer--that the offeree <u>actually read</u> the offer.

13. Offers can be terminated in only three ways--by revocation, rejection, and lapse of time.

14. The mailing of a revocation of an offer takes effect the moment it is placed in the mail if the offer itself was made by mail.

15. The mailing of a rejection does not take effect the moment it is placed in the mail even if the offer was made by mail.

16. It is a general rule that a party contracting by mail, when no time limit is made for acceptance of the contract, must act with due diligence and within a reasonable time or the offer will lapse.

17. If an offer is made and the offeror dies soon thereafter, most courts today rule that the offer remains open until the offeree receives notice of the death.

18. Under the UCC, an "acceptance" of an offer to buy or sell goods usually constitutes a legal acceptance even if it contains a term additional to or different from the terms expressly contained in the offer.

19. The general rule that "silence is not an acceptance" is not applicable to the situation where the offeree replies that the offeror may conclude a contract has been formed if he (the offeror) does not hear from him (the offeree) within a stated time.

20. Under contract law an "acceptance" which contains a material term or condition that does not expressly appear in the offer itself may constitute a legal acceptance in some circumstances.

Multiple Choice

1. S makes an offer to G by mail, the offer saying nothing as to what means G should use in replying. Which of the following answers best illustrates the modern rule of acceptance.

    a) If G promptly mails a letter of acceptance, there is a contract formed the moment the acceptance is placed in the mail if--and only if--the acceptance reaches S within a reasonable time of being mailed.
    b) If G telephones S soon after receiving the offer and says "I accept," a contract has been formed since G did use a medium of communication reasonable under the circumstances.
    c) Both of the above.
    d) None of the above.

Chapter 4

2. As a general rule, the acceptance of a unilateral offer legally occurs:

   a) when the requested act is fully performed, even if notification of this fact is not given to the offeror until a later time.
   b) when the offeree gives the offeror his unconditional promise that he will perform the act at a time agreeable to the offeror.
   c) only after the act is fully performed and the offeror is given notice of its completion.
   d) none of the above.

3. X makes an offer to Y by mail, requiring Y's acceptance to be made by telegram. In such a case:

   a) an acceptance by mail would take effect the moment that it was placed in the mail, despite X's condition that the acceptance be made by telegram.
   b) an acceptance by telegram would take effect the moment it was placed in the hands of the telegraph company, even if that company thereafter never delivered it to X.
   c) both of the above.
   d) none of the above.

4. In the case of Green's Executors v. Smith Garage, Smith (plaintiff) was contending that he and Mrs. Green had entered into a new contract arising from a "note" which he had delivered to her. In that case, the precise legal issue in the higher court was whether or not:

   a) Mrs. Green had actually read the note.
   b) the note (offer) had been legally communicated to Mrs. Green.
   c) Mr. Smith reasonably believed that Mrs. Green, by continuing to have her car garaged in his facilities, thereby accepted his offer.
   d) none of the above.

5. Silence on the part of the offeree:

   a) constitutes an acceptance if the offer clearly states that it will be considered to be such by the offeror.
   b) does not constitute an acceptance under any circumstances.
   c) constitutes an acceptance in those exceptional circumstances where the courts feel that the offeror is justified in treating it as such and where the offeree might reasonably expect him to do so.
   d) constitutes an acceptance only when the offeror and offeree are in an industry or association where such view is well established.
   e) a and c.

6. A contract of adhesion is one:

   a) which is so inherently one-sided that courts will ordinarily refuse to enforce it.
   b) which "adheres to" both parties; that is, legally binds both parties.
   c) which is usually recognized only under sales law.
   d) the terms of which are prepared by one party, usually in a standardized form, and which are presented to the other prospective contracting party on a "take it or leave it" basis.

177

Chapter 4

7. As a general rule, the law requires acceptances to be in writing:

   a) if the offer is in writing.
   b) if the proposed contract is a sales contract.
   c) if the offer contains new terms that might possibly be construed by the offeror to be a counter-offer.
   d) a and b.
   e) none of the above.

8. Which of the following events do not terminate an offer "by operation of law"?

   a) revocation by the offeror.
   b) subsequent (or intervening) illegality.
   c) adjudication of insanity of the offeror.
   d) adjudication of insanity of the offeree.

9. In determining what is a reasonable time for an offer to remain open, which of the following factors are significant?

   a) the language of the offer, if relevant.
   b) past dealings of the parties, if any.
   c) means by which the offer was communicated.
   d) all of the above.

10. When goods are placed on sale at an ordinary auction, a contract is formed at the moment that:

    a) the highest (last) bid is made.
    b) the auctioneer "knocks down the goods"--that is, accepts a particular bid.
    c) the bidder whose bid has been accepted pays for (or makes suitable arrangements to pay for) the purchased item.
    d) none of the above.

Short Essay

1. The drafters of the UCC, in Sec. 2-207, have provided that, in certain circumstances, a "definite expression of acceptance" on the part of the offeree (in response to an offer contemplating the sale of goods) operates as an acceptance even though it contains additional terms.

   Describe the situation existing prior to the drafting of the UCC which Sec. 2-207 was designed to remedy.

Chapter 4

2. Professor X, in response to an advertisement placed by his university, submitted a bid to the Board of Trustees of the university on August 10, offering to perform janitorial services in Brown Hall for the next school year "at a salary of $175 per week." On August 13 the Board passed this resolution: "Voted to award Brown janitorial contract to Prof. X for sum of $35 per day." On August 15 Prof. X received in the mail a copy of the resolution.

   a) In the above case, does a contract exist? Why or why not?
   b) Suppose, in the above case, that the resolution passed by the board read "at a salary of $175 per week." At that point, that is, the moment that the resolution was formally passed, would a contract exist between Professor X and the Board? Why or why not?

Chapter 5

Consideration

True-False

1. Today, most courts will enforce written contracts even though consideration is totally lacking.

2. The doctrine of promissory estoppel is limited in application and is only a limited means of enforcing promises that fail to pass the test of consideration.

3. Under sales law, modification contracts need no consideration in order to be binding.

4. The terms "promissory estoppel" and "detrimental reliance" are essentially synonymous.

5. An existing contract that is modified is enforceable only if additional consideration is given.

6. When a creditor cashes a check marked "paid in full," the general rule today is that this bars any further recovery by him, regardless of whether or not the original debt was a "liquidated" one.

7. The general rule today is that if an existing debt is a liquidated debt, a settlement agreement under which the debtor pays a lesser sum than admittedly owed is not binding even if the debtor pays the lesser sum a few days early (e.g., $1,000 due July 15, and settlement agreement of $900 is made July 5).

8. Under the Federal Bankruptcy Reform Act of 1978, a particular promise to repay a discharged debt is not binding unless supported by consideration.

9. People incur legal detriments when they do something they are not otherwise legally obligated to do.

10. In order for a promisee's act to constitute legal consideration, it must be the one asked for by the promisor.

11. In order for a contract to be enforceable, there must be mutuality of obligation.

12. Creditors' composition agreements are usually upheld by the courts--that is, are binding on the creditors--only when the debts owed to the participating creditors were unliquidated debts.

13. Requirement contracts generally have terms such as, "wish," "may want," or "desire" included in them.

Chapter 5

14. Today, in most states, a sealed contract is unenforceable unless consideration is present.

15. The "detriment test" and the "benefit-detriment test" for determining whether consideration is present bring about substantially different results.

16. The performance of a preexisting legal duty does not constitute consideration.

17. If a person (in response to an offer) refrains from a specified activity, this constitutes the giving of consideration even if it was an activity which he ordinarily would never have engaged in anyway (i.e., in the absence of the offer).

18. The performance of a preexisting obligation does not constitute consideration if the obligation is one required by statute, but it does constitute consideration if the preexisting obligation was merely required by a prior contract.

19. If the parties to a contract clearly cancel it and then make a new agreement (regarding the same subject-matter), the new agreement is supported by consideration even though some of its provisions are the same as those contained in the earlier contract.

20. Application of the unforeseen difficulties rule, where properly applied, results in the promisor being held liable on his promise even though true consideration is lacking on the part of the promisee.

Multiple Choice

1. If a "contract" lacks consideration, it is:

    a) unenforceable.
    b) illegal.
    c) contrary to public policy.
    d) enforceable if both parties clearly intended it to be binding at the time that they entered into it.

2. A promise is supported by consideration if:

    a) the promisor has received a benefit.
    b) the promisor has incurred a detriment.
    c) the promisee has incurred a detriment.
    d) both a and c.
    e) none of the above.

3. A promise which is unsupported by consideration is nonetheless enforceable if:

Chapter 5

   a) the promisor clearly intended to be bound by it when he made it.
   b) the doctrine of promissory estoppel is applicable to it.
   c) the promise is in writing.
   d) the promisee received a benefit.
   e) none of the above.

4. Homer agrees to pay Jethro $900 for blacktopping his driveway, and Jethro promises to do the job ("Contract #1"). Before the work is finished, Homer agrees to pay an extra $200 for completion of the work. Jethro finishes the job and Homer refuses to pay the additional sum ("Contract #2"). In such a case:

   a) as a general rule--that is, in most circumstances--the completion of the work by Jethro is considered to <u>constitute consideration</u> regardless of whether or not the first contract was cancelled (and Jethro is thus entitled to the extra $200).
   b) in some situations presented by the basic fact-pattern (that is, Contract #1 followed by Contract #2), the courts will rule that the "unforeseen difficulties rule" is applicable. In such situations, Jethro is definitely entitled to the extra $200. (Assume here--and also in choice "a"--that Contract #2 is <u>not</u> prompted by any threat on Jethro's part to quit unless he gets more money.)
   c) both of the above.
   d) none of the above.

5. The unforeseen difficulties rule is:

   a) rarely applied by the courts.
   b) usually applied only in a situation where the doctrine of promissory estoppel is also applicable.
   c) applied only in construction cases.
   d) a creature of statute (i.e., courts in a state connot apply it unless a state statute so permits).
   e) c and d.

6. Consideration can consist of:

   a) a promise.
   b) performance of an act.
   c) nonperformance of a act (i.e., abstaining from performance of an act).
   d) all of the above.
   e) a and b.

7. An <u>illusory</u> contract is one in which:

   a) consideration appears to exist, but upon closer examination is found to be absent.
   b) the consideration of one party is so inadequate in value as to suggest fraud is present.
   c) consideration appears <u>not</u> to exist, but upon closer examination is found to be present.
   d) a and c.
   e) none of the above.

Chapter 5

8. The "requirement of mutuality of obligation" means, in general, that:

   a) an agreement is enforceable even though consideration is lacking if the contract expressly so provides (i.e., the parties have mutually agreed when making the agreement that it shall be binding).
   b) there must be an offer and an acceptance in order to have a contract.
   c) if one party to a "contract" is not bound (because consideration does not exist, then the other party is not bound either.
   d) none of the above.

9. If a court finds, in a particular situation, that a valid <u>requirements contract</u> exists, the result is that:

   a) consideration (of some kind) exists and both parties are usually bound by the contract.
   b) the seller is bound by the contract but the buyer is not (in view of the fact that his exact requirements are not known when the contract is made).
   c) the buyer is bound by the contract (since the term "requirements" refers to his requirements) but the seller is not bound by it.
   d) no consideration is present, but the court will nevertheless enforce the contract because of public policy considerations.
   e) none of the above.

10. When a creditor accepts a payment of money from a debtor, with the creditor promising at the same time that he thereby releases the debtor of any further liability, the creditor (as a general rule) is legally bound by his promise to release:

    a) if the debtor can clearly prove that the promise was made (regardless of other circumstances).
    b) only if the original debt was a liquidated debt.
    c) only if the original debt was an unliquidated debt.
    d) just as long as the statute of limitations had not run before the payment was made (regardless of other circumstances).
    e) none of the above.

Short Essay

1. Briefly explain the doctrine of promissory estoppel, and explain the reason for its existence. (That is, what sort of injustice was the doctrine meant to eliminate?)

2. In 1975 the Seller Co. agreed to sell, and the Buyer Co. agreed to buy, "all the automatic chicken pluckers that the Buyer Co. will need in the operation of its business during 1976, at a price of $150 each." In March of 1976 Buyer Co. ordered five pluckers, but the Seller Co. refused to deliver them, claiming that it (Seller Co.) was under no legal obligation to do so.

Chapter 5

More specifically, the Seller Co. contends that, under the contract, there was no consideration on the Buyer Co.'s part in view of the fact that (at that time) it was possible that Buyer Co. would not need any chicken pluckers.

Is Seller Co. correct in its contention? Explain precisely why or why not.

Chapter 6

Contractual Capacity

True-False

1. In order for a minor to disaffirm a contract, the courts <u>do</u> <u>not</u> <u>require</u> the minor to show that the contract was unfair to him in any way.

2. A minor may disaffirm most contracts, and the courts also allow minors to disaffirm tort liability.

3. Some states have adopted the rule, by statute, that minors who have misrepresented their age are bound by such contracts to the same extent as adults (that is, the right to disaffirm on the grounds of <u>minority</u> is totally lost).

4. It is not possible for a minor to legally ratify a contract before he reaches adulthood.

5. Most courts feel that the importance of protecting minors, by permitting disaffirmance in most cases, outweighs the occasional hardship that such protection causes other parties.

6. If a person is <u>formally declared</u> to be insane by a court after holding the prescribed <u>hearings</u> and examinations, and if the person later makes a "contract" with some third party, the "contract" is <u>void</u> (rather than voidable).

7. The early English view (i.e., minors may disaffirm their contracts only when they are shown to be "harmful" to them) is, today, still the basic rule followed by the courts in this country.

8. If a minor wishes to disaffirm a contract, he must always do so before reaching the age of majority.

9. As a result of a federal statute, the age of majority has been reduced in all states to 18.

10. In general, minors' liability under "ordinary" contracts is the same as under contracts calling for the purchase of "necessities."

11. A minor may disaffirm an executory contract without liability.

12. A minor may disaffirm an executed contract without liability.

13. Some executed contracts--such as those made with common carriers--can <u>not</u> be disaffirmed on the grounds of minority.

Chapter 6

14. As a general rule, minors' "ordinary" contracts can be disaffirmed only if the other party to the contract knew that he was dealing with a minor when making the contract.

15. If a plaintiff seeks to hold a minor liable on the theory that the goods purchased by the minor constituted necessities of life (e.g., clothes), he will not recover on this theory if the minor can prove he had a parent willing and able to supply him with all the clothes he needed.

16. Most states today take the view that a minor who has misrepresented his age will not be allowed to disaffirm a contract, even if the disaffirmance will not cause a loss to the other party.

17. Under statutes of most states, minors cannot disaffirm contracts made with banks and insurance companies.

18. A contract entered into by a person who is at a later date adjudicated insane may, at the option of the insane party's guardian, be disaffirmed up to one year after the date of adjudication.

19. A convict, while incarcerated, is legally dead and does not have the capacity to contract.

20. As a general rule, once a person has been found to be so intoxicated at the time of making a contract that he did not understand the nature of the agreement, disaffirmance is allowed even if he is unable to return any of the consideration which he received.

Multiple Choice

1. Which of the following best describes minors' contracts?

    a) invalid
    b) void
    c) voidable
    d) unenforceable
    e) conditional

2. If a person is adjudicated insane and subsequently makes a "contract," the contract is:

    a) void.
    b) illegal.
    c) voidable.
    d) a and b.
    e) none of the above.

3. In order for a minor to disaffirm a contract, he must usually show--in addition to his minority--that:

Chapter 6

    a) the contract was unfair to him.
    b) the other party had had more business experience than he.
    c) the contract was an oral one, and that there was at least some disagreement as to its terms.
    d) a specific state statute permits him to disaffirm.
    e) none of the above.

4. In order for a person to disaffirm a contract based on insanity, he must show:

    a) the eccentric acts the person committed.
    b) the court hearing and adjudication of insanity.
    c) the party was "insane in fact" and was incapable of understanding the nature and consequences of the agreement.
    d) a and c.
    e) b and/or c.

5. "Fang" Ellis, while intoxicated, signs a contract to support "Ravishing Ruby" for a period of 18 months. In order to disaffirm the contract "Fang" must prove:

    a) that it is against public policy.
    b) the agreement is immoral, therefore illegal.
    c) he was so intoxicated that he did not understand the nature of the purported agreement.
    d) he is married, and the contract is not in accord with a preexisting legal obligation under the marriage contract.

6. Ratification of a contract is a statement or other conduct on the part of a minor:

    a) before he reaches the age of majority, indicating that he is reserving his right to disaffirm the contract at a later time if he wishes.
    b) after reaching the age of majority, indicating he will be bound by the contract.
    c) either before or very shortly after reaching the age of majority (i.e., within a reasonable time), indicating he will be bound by the contract.
    d) none of the above.

7. Indicate which of the following types of contracts usually can not be disaffirmed on the ground of minority:

    a) purchases of consumer goods made under installment contracts.
    b) contracts with common carriers.
    c) purchases of goods at retail, where the purchaser-minor makes full payment of the purchase price when the contract is made.
    d) a and b.
    e) b and c.

Chapter 6

8. Civil liability arising out of torts committed by minors:

   a) may be disaffirmed much like contractual liability, under many modern state statutes.
   b) may be disaffirmed under common-law principles, but only if the injured party was also a minor.
   c) may be disaffirmed under common-law principles, but only if the wrongful act--the tort--was not a crime.
   d) may not, as a general rule, be disaffirmed at all.
   e) none of the above.

9. A contract entered into by an adult with a minor may be disaffirmed by:

   a) either party.
   b) the minor only.
   c) the minor's parent.
   d) the adult at his option.

10. Criminal liability as well as contractual liability may be disaffirmed by a minor:

    a) of "tender years," so young they cannot formulate the intent to commit a crime.
    b) so intoxicated he did not understand the nature and consequence of the act.
    c) when charged with a crime involving moral terpitude.
    d) a and b.

Short Essay

1. Jennifer Lea Dingbatski, a 17-year-old minor, purchased a Quadrophonic Sound System for her apartment from "Fang" Ellis, a feared and crusty old professor at the university she attended. Jennifer made payments for 13 months then ceased paying. "Fang" pointed out her legal responsibilities, and she made paymants for an additional 5 months and then stopped paying again. "Fang" promptly filed suit and Jennifer disaffirms the contract and pleads minority as a defense. What results?

2. Ravishing Ruby, a convicted felon, jumped the fence at Juliet, the ladies' state prison, and made good her escape in a pickup truck stolen from the train station. Ruby married a minister and changed her ways and became a "good" woman. Ruby entered into a series of contracts for purchase of mineral interests near Gotebo, Oklahoma and became wealthy overnight when a huge natural gas field was discovered. Her new-found wealth and ensuing publicity bring about her capture and return to prison. The parties that sold her the mineral interests bring suit to set aside the contracts. What results?

Chapter 7

Illegality

True-False

1. Contracts are often held by the courts to be illegal even though they are neither contrary to statute nor contrary to public policy.

2. If a statute prohibits the making of a particular kind of a contract, the contract is illegal even if the statute does not impose criminal liability (fines or imprisonment) upon violators.

3. It is possible for a contract--or a portion of a contract--to be illegal yet still be enforceable by one of the parties against the other.

4. While state statutes used to vary a great deal as to which kinds of Sunday contracts were legal and which were not, practically all of this uncertainty has been eliminated today as a result of the widespread adoption of uniform legislation on this subject.

5. A resale price maintenance contract that involves the sale of goods in interstate commerce are clearly illegal.

6. Exculpatory clauses provide that one party agrees to free the other of all liability and are against the public policy.

7. "Friendly bets" are often lawful under modern statutes.

8. In general, risk-shifting and risk-creating contracts are both illegal.

9. The main reason why insurance contracts today are _not_ wagers is because most states have statutes that expressly so provide.

10. An insurance contract is a wager if the insured does not possess an _insurable_ _interest_ in the property or life that is being insured.

11. Unlicensed workers are generally permitted to recover the value of their services if the statute or ordinance requiring them to have a license is _money-raising_ in nature.

12. If the object of a statute is to protect the public from unauthorized practices of a profession or trade, it is usually considered regulatory in nature.

13. Whether a particular contract that is entered into on a Sunday is legal or illegal depends primarily upon the statutes of the state in which it was entered into.

Chapter 7

14. A contract calling for a borrower of money to pay interest in excess of the maximum permitted by state law is illegal <u>even if</u> the borrower knows of, and readily agrees to pay, the higher interest.

15. Many state usury statutes do <u>not</u> apply to loans made by national and state banks.

16. "Small loan laws" expressly permit small loan companies to charge rates of interest that are higher than general interest statutes.

17. Contracts not to compete are often held to be lawful if they are "ancillary" to a valid contract.

18. Exculpatory clauses are usually made illegal <u>by statute</u>, regardless of whether or not they substantially affect the <u>public</u> interest.

19. In those contracts where exculpatory clauses are held to be illegal, it is usually because they are held to be contrary to public policy (as distinguished from being contrary to statute).

20. As a general rule, bailees are legally liable for any damage done to the bailed property while it is in their possession even if they were not at fault in any way.

21. Resale price maintenance contracts in interstate commerce today are illegal for the reason that they are contrary to modern common-law rules.

Multiple Choice

1. Snippy sells his barber business to Flattop for $9,000. The contract provides that "Snippy promises not to engage in the barbering business for a period of one year within a one mile radius of the shop being sold." In regard to this situation:

   a) the clause quoted above is "in restraint of trade," but it is not necessarily illegal.
   b) the clause, since it is "ancillary to" a valid contract of sale, would--under general common-law principles--be <u>lawful</u> if the courts concluded that its terms were "reasonable under the circumstances."
   c) both of the above.
   d) none of the above.

2. If the parties to an illegal contract are equally at fault, this means (among other things) that:

   a) it can be said that the parties are <u>in pari delicto</u>.
   b) it can be said that the parties are <u>not in pari delicto</u>.

190

Chapter 7

   c) neither party can enforce it against the other.
   d) each party can enforce it against the other, despite the contract's illegality.
   e) a and c.

3. In which of the following cases might one party to an illegal contract be able to enforce it (or a part of it) against the other party?

   a) Where the contract is "severable" in nature.
   b) Where the parties are "at equal fault."
   c) Where the contract is a fire insurance contract, and where the insured does not have an insurable interest in the insured property.
   d) none of the above.

4. An insurance company issues a fire insurance policy to X, whose insured property is in a state where the company is not licensed to do business. When the property is destroyed by fire, the insurance company refuses to pay X, claiming the defense of illegality. In such a case:

   a) the defense is probably good (company freed of liability).
   b) the defense is probably good if the officers of the company can clearly establish good faith (i.e., if they can prove they did not know of the licensing requirement).
   c) the defense is probably bad (i.e., despite the technical illegality the company is liable to X).
   d) none of the above.

5. When a lobbyist seeks a fee he claims is due him under a contingent fee contract:

   a) many courts refuse recovery of the fee under any circumstances on the grounds that the tendency of such contract is to induce improper activities.
   b) some courts permit recovery of the fee if the lobbyist can prove that, in fact, his actual conduct is proven to be entirely proper.
   c) most courts today allow the lobbyist to recover his fee regardless of whether his actual conduct was proper, on the theory that contingent fee contracts of this type are not illegal at all.
   d) all of the above.
   e) a and b.

6. X goes to work for the Y Company under a contract providing that he cannot go to work for a competing company (upon leaving employment with the Y Company) for a specified time in a specified area. Which of the following considerations is usually not relevant to a determination of the contract's legality?

   a) whether the contract affords more protection to the Y Company than is necessary or reasonable.
   b) whether the contract is injurious to the public.
   c) whether the contract is unreasonably oppressive to X.
   d) whether the contract is unreasonably oppressive to the Y Company.
   e) none of the above (i.e., all of the above factors are relevant).

Chapter 7

7. Resale price maintenance contracts in interstate commerce are today illegal because:

   a) they violate the Sherman Act.
   b) they violate the Miller-Tydings Act.
   c) they violate the Sherman Act (<u>unless</u> the buyer's state has a fair trade law).
   d) none of the above.

8. Exculpatory clauses in bailees' contracts are usually held to be:

   a) illegal, if the court feels that they were not properly communicated to the bailor.
   b) illegal--even if they are properly communicated to the bailor--if their terms purport to free the bailee from liability arising out of the bailee's negligence.
   c) legal, if properly communicated to the bailor (even if they purport to free the bailee from liability arising out of the bailee's negligence).
   d) a and c.

9. A contract under which the seller contracts to sell at a specified price a quantity of goods that he does not presently own, with delivery to be made in the future is:

   a) illegal, because it is a gambling contract.
   b) a risk shifting contract.
   c) a lottery.
   d) a futures contract.

10. The Hardly Able Co., Inc. an Oklahoma corporation, is duly licensed in the State of Kansas. The company opens an office in Ness, Kansas but fails to purchase a city business license. It will be:

    a) unable to enforce its contracts.
    b) permitted to enforce its contracts because city licensing ordinances are revenue raising.
    c) unable to enforce its contracts because corporations are charged with greater degrees of care.
    d) none of the above.

Short Essay

1. Wiley Fouler, a senior law student, established a business selling "divorce kits," "bankruptcy kits," and other handy legal forms. For an additional $50.00, Wiley would tell the customer how to use the kit and how to fill in the blanks. Debra Deevorsay bought a "divorce kit" and the advice, and entered into a written contract. Debra failed to pay and Wiley sued Debra in small claims court. What results?

Chapter 8

Reality of Consent

True-False

1. A fraud is the intentional misrepresentation of a material fact with the intent to deceive, and there was reliance on the misrepresentation and there was injury.

2. X, a retailer, tells a prospective buyer, "This masonry paint will keep moisture out of your basement for four years after its application, if applied according to the instructions." Under sales law this statement is a warranty, as opposed to dealer's puffing.

3. The statement that the income from a certain business wil be $15,000 in the coming year is a statement of fact.

4. If the declarant of a statement is considered an "expert," his opinion is likely to be viewed as a statement of fact and thus fraudulent if false.

5. The statement of a homeowner that his home is worth $81,763.00 is a statement of fact and is basis for a fraud action.

6. Today, most courts will set aside a contract if it was entered into under a "mutual mistake of law" (i.e., mutual mistakes as to law are treated like mutual mistakes of fact).

7. The intentional misrepresentation of law by a bank cashier about a banking transaction is not considered fraudulent because it referred to the law.

8. Vermin fills out an application for a policy of life insurance and knowingly fails to mention a material fact regarding his physical condition (e.g., that he has had stomach surgery in the past year). Because of the general rule that silence is not fraudulent, the insurance company may not later cancel its policy on the ground of fraud.

9. S sells a painting to B for $200, S having no idea who the artist is. Later S learns that it was a work of Wyeth, that its value was thus at least $4,000, and that B knew it was a Wyeth when he bought it. If S can prove all of these facts, plus the fact that B knew that S was ignorant as to the identity of the artist, most courts will permit S to rescind the contract on the ground of fraud. (Assume that neither S nor B was an art expert.)

10. In the case Beachcomber Coins, Inc. v. Boskett, a coin was sold to the plaintiff that was later discovered to be counterfeit. This is a unilateral mistake of fact and cannot be rescinded.

Chapter 8

11. Where only one party to a contract is mistaken about a material fact, rescission is ordinarily not allowed.

12. A mutual mistake as to value is generally considered a mistake of opinion rather than fact, and rescission is not permitted.

13. Generally, a statement as to a building's rental value is held to be a statement of opinion rather than one of fact.

14. Since fraud must involve a "misrepresentation," or "misstatement" of fact, a mere withholding of information very rarely could constitute fraud.

15. If a person sells a car possessing a hidden defect, under the "latent defect" rule he may be guilty of fraud (in not pointing out the defect) even if he (the seller) did not actually know of the defect.

16. In a fraud action, if the plaintiff can prove that the defendant's statement was absolutely known by him (defendant) to be false when he made it, then the plaintiff is entitled to damages even if the plaintiff knew the statement was false at the time that it was made.

17. If a plaintiff seeks to disaffirm a contract on the ground of mutual mistake of fact, he generally has to prove the same elements in this action as if he were relying on the unilateral mistake theory. (That is, in a mutual mistake action, the things which the plaintiff must prove in order to win are substantially the same things he must prove in a unilateral mistake action.)

18. X buys a violin from Y, thinking it to be made by a respected local woodworker. In fact, X is wrong. X in this case can not have the contract set aside on the basis of mistake unless he can prove that Y knew (or should have known) of his mistake when the contract was made.

19. In some cases courts allow rescission on the basis of mistake of fact with little or no consideration being given to the factors of mutual mistake and unilateral mistake.

20. In some states, by statute, a contract may be rescinded on the basis of unilateral mistake even if the other party to the contract can clearly prove that he was not aware of the mistake when the contract was made (and had no way of knowing of the mistake at that time).

Multiple Choice

1. The first element of a fraud has been established if the innocent party can prove:

    a) the other party lied.
    b) the other party lied about an existing fact.
    c) the other party gave an erroneous opinion.
    d) none of the above.

Chapter 8

2. Innocent misrepresentation is the same as fraud, insofar as the required elements are concerned, except that in innocent misrepresentation:

   a) the person making the misstatement of fact honestly thought his statement was true.
   b) the person making the misstatement of fact may have known that it was not material to the other party (i.e., did not induce the innocent party to enter into the contract).
   c) the innocent party need not prove that he relied on the misstatement in any way in order to have the contract rescinded.
   d) none of the above.

3. X sells land to Y, both of them believing that a particular event is very likely to take place in the future that will substantially affect the property's value (e.g., they believe an interstate highway is soon to be built in the area). If it turns out that the anticipated event never occurs:

   a) either party may rescind the contract on the ground of mutual mistake of fact.
   b) the buyer is usually permitted to rescind if he wishes, but not the seller.
   c) neither party may rescind.
   d) none of the above.

4. A mutual mistake is <u>not</u> grounds for rescinding a contract if the mistake merely involves:

   a) the existence of the subject-matter.
   b) the identity of the subject-matter.
   c) reasonableness of the contract price.
   d) the character of the subject-matter.
   e) none of the above (i.e., a mutual mistake as to any of the above is grounds for rescission).

5. If a person can prove that he was honestly mistaken as to the <u>terms</u> of a contract that he has made, even though it was not apparent to the other party, as a general rule he:

   a) can rescind the contract.
   b) can not rescind the contract.
   c) can rescind the contract <u>if</u> he can show that the mistake was not the result of negligence on <u>his</u> part.
   d) none of the above.

6. Which of the following best describes <u>duress</u>?

   a) <u>any intentional wrongdoing</u> that causes another to make a contract he otherwise would not have made.
   b) <u>application of physical force</u> that causes another to make a contract he otherwise would not have made.

Chapter 8

    c) the inducing of fear in one person by another, through the latter's use of force or threat to use force, inducing the former to make a contract he otherwise would not have made.
    d) a threat to break an existing contract that causes the other party to take an action he otherwise might not have taken.

7. The essence of undue influence is the obtaining of control over one person's will by another (the dominant party):

    a) usually as a result of the former's increasing reliance on the latter person's (dominant party's) judgment and apparent trustworthiness over a period of time.
    b) usually as a result of fear on the former's part, which results from their prior dealings over a period of time.
    c) usually as a result of the existence of what the courts call constructive fraud, which is brought about by the dominant party's misconduct.
    d) usually as a result of the dominant party's proven ability over a period of time to make money for the former (the dominated) party.
    e) none of the above.

8. Under the typical "home solicitation" statute, the buyer of goods may rescind his contract within a specified time only if he can show:

    a) fraud or duress, or high-pressure salesmanship, on the part of the seller.
    b) that the value of the goods was actually much less than the selling price.
    c) that the goods were in some way defective, no matter how slight the defect.
    d) none of the above.

9. In Totem Marine T. & B. v. Alyeska Pipeline the Supreme Court of Alaska stated that economic duress exists where:

    a) one party involuntarily accepted the terms of another.
    b) circumstances permitted no other alternative.
    c) such circumstances were the result of coercive acts of the other party.
    d) a and c.
    e) all of the above.

10. Undue influence is generally considered to be:

    a) where one party nags the other party into entering a contract.
    b) where one party dominates the other and the latter's volition actually is destroyed.
    c) where one party threatens to bring shame on the latter party.
    d) none of the above.

Chapter 8

Short Essay

1. A person can escape liability under a contract if he can show that there was, in fact, no real or genuine consent on his part when he made the contract. In other words, he wants to prove that his apparent consent was _not_ genuine. Briefly describe the four major types of misconduct (or conditions surrounding the making of a contract) that are responsible for such a result--that is, where "reality of consent" is lacking.

2. B buys the Eastward Ho Motel from S for $250,000, after being shown, among other things, income tax returns by S which show that S made a net profit of $31,000 on the operation of the motel in the last calendar year. B later learns that the tax returns contained several erroneous entries, and that S's true net profit was about $10,000. B now brings an action to recover damage from S, claiming S was guilty of fraud. On the basis of these facts, and others appearing below, answer the following:

   a) Suppose, at the trial of B vs. S, one of S's contentions is that the statement in regard to the net profits was dealer's puffing rather than a statement of fact; that is, "everyone knows that a seller overstates his profits." Comment on the validity of this contention.

   b) Suppose, at the trial, that one of S's contentions is that even if the statement as to profits was one of fact, still he is not guilty of fraud because he gave all of his income and expense statements to his accountant, that the accountant came up with the $31,000 figure, and that he (S) honestly and reasonably thought that figure was entirely correct. If the jury finds that S honestly thought the statement was true, is he guilty of fraud? If yes, explain how this could be; if no, explain why not.

Chapter 9

Contracts in Writing

True-False

1. While <u>leases</u> of real estate are, strictly speaking, "sales of interests in land," many states have statutes which provide that oral leases of a year or less are lawful and binding.

2. In view of the widespread adoption of the Statute of Frauds among the states of this country, it is probably correct to say that, today, most types of contracts are required by law to be in writing.

3. The "parol evidence rule" applies only to those written contracts which fall within the Statute of Frauds (that is, it would <u>not</u> be applicable to a written contract that clearly did not have to be in writing in the first place).

4. Under the UCC, an oral sales contract (calling for the sale of goods having a value of $500 or more) is valid--despite the fact it is not in writing--if, after the contract is made, the seller delivers the goods and the buyer accepts them.

5. In May of 1978 H and J enter into an oral contract of employment, under the terms of which J is to perform certain tasks during the months of July and August of <u>1979</u>. Because J's actual performance is only going to take two months, this contract does not have to be in writing.

6. S orally agrees to sell his farm to B for $100,000, and B orally agrees to pay that price. If, thereafter, the contract is completely performed by both parties--that is, S gives B a deed and possession, and B pays the full price--neither party may thereafter have the agreement rescinded or cancelled simply for the reason that the agreement was in writing.

7. While <u>easements</u> are technically "interests in land," the general rule is that contracts that create or convey easements do <u>not</u> have to be in writing.

8. In <u>most</u> situations, the fact that one of the parties to an oral contract (falling within the Statute of Frauds) has partially performed his part of the contract does <u>not</u>, in itself, cause the contract to be enforceable.

9. It is correct to say that, <u>in general</u>, contracts need not be in writing (assuming that their terms can be proven in court if a dispute arises).

10. Most of the Statute of Frauds provisions that we find in state statutes today <u>vary widely</u> from those of the original English statute.

Chapter 9

11. The courts of this country have, by judicial decision, engrafted a number of exceptions to the basic Statute of Frauds provisions.

12. If a contract is required by the Statute of Frauds to be in writing, as a general rule it is <u>valid and enforceable</u> (when in writing) even if it possesses a defect (such as lack of consideration or reality of consent) that would <u>otherwise</u> cause it to be invalid.

13. An oral contract calling for the sale of land is valid, as a result of judicial decisions in most states, if it is clearly established that both parties, at the time of contracting, expressly agreed that it need not be in writing.

14. If the buyer under a contract calling for the sale of land brings suit asking for specific performance of the contract, the buyer's action will be an action in equity if the contract is an oral one, and an action at law if the contract is in writing.

15. X orally agrees to work for Y "as long as I shall live" for a specified monthly salary. Two years later X quits his job without legal excuse, and Y seeks damages for breach of contract. If X's defense is "the Statute of Frauds," the defense is <u>not good</u> for the reason that X could have died within a year after making the contract (i.e., X is liable to Y).

16. X tells Y, "If you will sell your car to Z, I will pay you $1,000." This promise is outside the Statute of Frauds (i.e., this is <u>not</u> a promise to pay the debt of another, and thus X is liable on his <u>oral</u> promise).

17. If some of the terms of a contract (that falls within the Statute of Frauds) are in writing, but other terms are not in writing, as a general rule the written part of the agreement will be enforced even if it is clear to the court that the writing was not complete, and even if the parties are in complete disagreement as to what the oral terms of the contract were.

18. The parol evidence rule does <u>not</u> apply to written employment contracts.

19. The parol evidence rule does <u>not</u> apply to oral contracts.

20. If a contract has actually been formed, but the writing that evidences the contract is only signed by one of the parties, as a <u>general rule</u> neither party can enforce it against the other.

Multiple Choice

1. Which of the following kinds of promises or contracts are <u>not</u> required by the Statute of Frauds to be in writing?

Chapter 9

a) promises made in consideration of marriage.
b) promises made by executors of estates to personally pay estate debts.
c) contracts calling for the sale of land.
d) contracts that have actually taken more than a year to perform, even though it was possible for full performance to have taken place within a year.
e) none of the above (i.e., all of the above kinds of contracts are required to be in writing).

2. As a general rule, an oral contract that is required by the Statute of Frauds to be in writing is:

a) illegal.
b) unenforceable.
c) contrary to public policy.
d) voidable.
e) void.

3. While the general rule is that contracts calling for the sale of land must be in writing, most courts will nevertheless permit a buyer of land under an oral contract to enforce that contract against the seller if:

a) he (buyer) has taken possession of the land with the seller's permission.
b) he (buyer) has taken possession of the land with the seller's permission and can clearly prove in court what the terms of the oral contract were.
c) he (buyer) has paid part of the purchase price, has taken possession with seller's permission, and has substantially improved the land.
d) both parties admit in court making the contract in question.
e) none of the above.

4. In most situations, the fact that one of the parties to an oral contract (falling within the Statute of Frauds) has partially performed his part of the contract:

a) causes the contract to be enforceable against the other party.
b) causes the contract to be enforceable against the other party (except for contracts which cannot possibly be performed within one year).
c) does not, of and by itself, cause the contract to be enforceable.
d) causes the contract to be enforceable against the other party if the partial performance was clearly above and beyond what was required of him (the performing party) by the contract.
e) none of the above.

5. Under common exceptions to the parol evidence rule, in which of the following situations (among others) may oral testimony be allowed?

a) if the testimony shows fraud.
b) if the contract is incomplete (as to very minor matters only).
c) if the oral testimony offered by one party clearly is in conflict with

Chapter 9

a material provision of the written contract.
d) all of the above.
e) b and c.

6. A question arises as to whether a particular oral contract falls within that provision of the Statute of Frauds requiring contracts to be in writing that "are not to be performed within one year from the making thereof." In such a case the usual test applied by the courts is:

   a) under the terms of the contract, was it possible, under any circumstances, for the contract to have been fully performed within one year?
   b) did the parties, at the time of making the contract, apparently and reasonably intend that full performance would have occurred within the year?
   c) under the terms of the contract, was it possible, under any circumstances, that performance might have become illegal within a year?
   d) was performance of the contract actually carried on for more than a year after the contract was made?
   e) none of the above.

7. Under sales law (the UCC), contracts calling for the sale of goods must, as a general rule, be in writing:

   a) in all cases if interstate commerce is involved.
   b) if at the time that the contract is made the buyer does not take possession of the goods.
   c) if the market value of the goods at the time of the sale is $500 or more (regardless of amount of the stated purchase price).
   d) if the purchase price of the goods is $500 or more and if the goods are "commercial (non consumer) goods."
   e) none of the above.

8. X and Y make an oral contract calling for the sale of goods which, under the UCC, was required to be in writing. Which (if any) of the following events will cause the contract to become valid and enforceable?

   a) delivery of the goods by the seller and acceptance of them by the buyer.
   b) delivery of the goods by the seller to the buyer's warehouse (the delivery being unknown to the buyer).
   c) mere sending of a check by the buyer to the seller in payment for the goods. ("Mere sending" means regardless of whether or not seller cashes the check.)
   d) all of the above.
   e) a and c.

9. Jim Dandy was injured while helping Wiley Fowler remove a small fish from Wiley's hook. Wiley rushed Jim Dandy to the doctor and told the doctor, "If Dandy does not pay, I will." The statement:

Chapter 9

    a) is not enforceable because it falls within the Statute of Frauds.
    b) is enforceable because it is a moral obligation.
    c) is not enforceable because it is the "extravagant exclamation of an excited man."
    d) is enforceable because it was a primary promise.

10. A prenuptial agreement that expressly states the interests in each parties property is invalid:

    a) because it is contrary to the intent of the marriage vow and against public policy.
    b) if oral.
    c) if prepared in one state and taken to a neighboring state for application.
    d) all of the above.

Short Essay

1. The courts, by judicial decision, have engrafted a number of exceptions to the Statute of Frauds provisions. Simply list three of these exceptions. (That is, simply list three situations in which oral contracts—that normally fall within the Statute of Frauds—will probably be enforced by the courts.)

2. X is a Cheyenne, Wyoming, contractor, and Y owns a service station next door. The two make an oral contract, under the terms of which X was to blacktop the parking lot at Y's station, with Y agreeing in return to let X park his trucks on the lot at any time of day or night, free of charge, "as long as you (X) operate your business in the city of Cheyenne." X blacktopped the area, but three years later Y reneged on his promise and refused to let X park his trucks there any more.

    X now sues Y to recover damages for breach of contract. Y defends on the ground that the contract was one "not to be performed within one year," and thus had to be in writing under the Statute of Frauds. Is Y's defense good? Why or why not?

Chapter 10

Rights of Third Parties

True-False

1. As a general rule, all types of beneficiaries (creditor, donee, and incidental) are entitled to enforce contracts made by others.

2. As a general rule, an assignee of a contractual right can not enforce the contract if he did not give consideration to the assignor in exchange for the assignment.

3. As a general rule, assignments must be evidenced by a writing in order to be enforceable.

4. Whenever an assignment takes place, the assignee acquires no greater rights than those possessed by the assignor.

5. Assignees and third-party beneficiaries are similar in this respect: they are both third parties for whose benefit the contract was originally made.

6. Life insurance policies comprise a common type of contract that may be enforced by donee beneficiaries.

7. Incidental beneficiaries usually are not permitted to enforce contracts.

8. In general, the assignment of one's rights under a contract--without the consent of the other party--is more likely to be permitted by the law than is the delegation of one's duties.

9. A contract which a party promises to render a certain performance not to a promisee but to a third person is a third party beneficiary contract.

10. The only two situations in which the assignment of contractual rights can not occur without the consent of the other contracting party are these: 1) when the contract so provides, and 2) when a statute so provides.

11. The assignment of contracts falling within the Statute of Frauds must, as a general rule, be in writing.

12. When an assignment is made for which the assignee gives no consideration, the assignor can rescind the assignment at any time before the obligor performs his duties under the contract.

13. Tom owes Dick $100. Dick assigns his right to collect the money to a third party, Harry. In such a case, if Tom has no notice of the assignment and pays the $100 to Dick when the debt comes due, he still is legally liable to Harry for the $100.

Chapter 10

14. The delegation of one's duties under a contract can be made only if the other contracting party gives his consent to the delegation.

15. Duties as well as rights are assignable.

16. Duties and rights for personal services may never be assigned.

17. If an assignment materially alters the duties of the obligor, the obligor still must complete the contract.

18. An assignee is entitled to enforce the contract against the obligor even if the assignee did not give consideration for the assignment to the assignor.

19. A valid assignment takes effect the moment it is made, regardless of whether the obligor is aware that the assignment has occurred.

20. The delegation of duties is allowed without consent of the promisee if the duties are essentially "routine".

Multiple Choice

1. Indicate which of the following third parties usually can not enforce contracts.

    a) incidental beneficiaries.
    b) donee beneficiaries (with the exception of insurance contracts)
    c) creditor beneficiaries.
    d) assignees, if assignment is not in writing.
    e) a and b.

2. A owns a home, which is mortgaged to B Bank. A sells the home to C, with C agreeing (by his contract with A) to pay off the mortgage. In this situation:

    a) C is a creditor beneficiary of the original contract between A and B Bank.
    b) A is creditor beneficiary of the contract between him (A) and C, since C is promising to pay off his mortgage.
    c) B Bank is a donee beneficiary of the contract between A and C.
    d) B Bank is a creditor beneficiary of the contract between A and C.
    e) none of the above.

3. Going back to the fact-pattern of the previous question, if C fails to pay off the mortgage held by B Bank,

    a) the B Bank can still hold the original debtor, A, liable for the debt, even if it (the Bank) had released A from liability at the time of sale of the home to C. (I.e., the release can be set aside in these circumstances.)

Chapter 10

   b) the B Bank can still hold the original debtor, A, liable only if it did not release him when he sold the home to C.
   c) the B Bank can not hold C liable for the indebtedness, since he did not contract directly with the B Bank.
   d) a and c.
   e) none of the above.

4. A makes a contract with B and then assigns his (A's) rights to a third party, C. In such a case, as a general rule, C:

   a) takes the rights subject to any defenses that B might have against A.
   b) stands in the same position as that of the assignor, A.
   c) is liable to B (on the theory of implied delegation) in case the performance that A rendered to B under the contract is defective, or is never rendered by A at all.
   d) all of the above.
   e) a and b only.

5. Indicate in which of the following cases contractual rights can not be assigned by one party without the consent of the other:

   a) where the rights involve a substantial personal relationship between the contracting parties.
   b) where the assignment would materially alter the duties of the assignor.
   c) where the assignment would materially alter the duties of the obligor (i.e., party to the original contract who is not a party to the assignment).
   d) a and c.
   e) a, b, and c.

6. R owes a debt to S. On January 2, S assigns the claim to T, and on January 10 S assigns the same claim to U. On January 15 U gives R notice of the assignment, and on January 20 T gives R notice of the assignment to him. In such a case:

   a) the courts of some states rule that both assignments are invalid, and neither T nor U recovers from R.
   b) the courts of some states rule that the first assignee to give notice (U) recovers from R, and the other assignee does not.
   c) the courts of some states rule that both T and U can recover from R (in which case R can recover the amount of one payment from S).
   d) all of the above.
   e) a and b.

7. Whenever an assignment takes place, the assignee acquires:

   a) greater rights than those possessed by the assignor.
   b) no greater rights than those possessed by the assignor.
   c) the same rights as those possessed by the assignor except the right to further assignment.
   d) none of the above.

Chapter 10

8. The law recognizes three kinds of beneficiaries:

   a) creditor, donee, and accidental.
   b) creditor, debtor, and incidental.
   c) creditor, donee, and incidental.
   d) creditor, donee, and voluntary.

9. When an assignment is made as a gift, the third party is called:

   a) creditor beneficiary.
   b) donee beneficiary.
   c) incidental beneficiary.
   d) lucky.

10. The assignment of a contract for sale of real property must:

    a) contain implied warranties.
    b) be made in writing.
    c) be considered a subassignment.
    d) be considered a partial assignment.

Short Essay

1. Frank "Cutie" Stein sells has automobile to his next door neighbor Johnny Crashem and includes his liability insurance in the sale. The insurance is paid up for six months, and "Cutie" is retiring to a monastery for a year to recover from a term of summer school and won't need a car or insurance. Johnny pays cash for the car and the insurance and shortly thereafter crashes the car. The insurance company refuses to pay stating they are not required to honor the assignment. What results?

2. F. Elliss took out a $10,000 life insurance policy on his own life with XYZ Insurance, Inc. and named Jim Dazzler as the beneficiary. Elliss paid all the premiums until his death, at the hands of a disgruntled student. The insurance company is refusing to pay Dazzler and Dazzler files suit. The company defends on the grounds of no privity. What results?

Chapter 11

Discharge of Contracts

True-False

1. When a contract is said to be discharged, it means that the duties of the contracting parties have been discharged.

2. X and Y make a contract. Later Y refuses to perform his part of the agreement. In such a case, while Y's breach of contract makes him liable in damages, it does not free X from his obligations under the contract.

3. Conditions precedent may be either express or implied, but conditions subsequent are implied only.

4. All contracts are subject to certain implied conditions.

5. B agrees to buy S's property upon certain terms, "provided that the city council votes within the next 30 days to build a new city hall on Fox Lane." Because the vote of the city council will necessarily come after the making of the contract (if at all), the decision of the city council would be a condition subsequent in this case.

6. If a contract contains an express condition precedent, and if the condition or event never occurs, as a general rule both parties are freed of their obligations under the contract.

7. Satisfaction guaranteed contracts are usually held that such satisfaction is a condition precedent that must be met in order for the promissor to recover under the contract.

8. Tailor agrees to make a custom suit for Chairman for $300, the contract guaranteeing that Chairman would be "totally satisfied" with the job. When the suit is done, Chairman does not like it; Tailor then sues Chairman for the $300. Judge instructs jury: "If you find that a reasonable man would be satisfied with the suit, then Chairman is liable even if he genuinely dislikes it." Under the circumstances, this instruction is probably correct.

9. When a contract contains a completion date, the general rule is that such a provision does not create a condition precedent.

10. Implied conditions subsequent are generally disfavored by the law (i.e., there are relatively few types of situations in which such conditions are recognized by the courts).

Chapter 11

11. The occurrence of a condition precedent <u>imposes</u> upon the parties to a contract a duty of immediate performance, while the occurrence of a condition subsequent <u>removes</u> such a duty.

12. As a general rule, a breach of a condition by one party frees the other party of his contractual obligations, even if the breach is a slight one.

13. Under recent decisions, the courts are likely to rule that a person has substantially performed his contract even if his performance has fallen far short of what the contract originally required of him.

14. In the case of <u>Butkovitch and Sons v. State Bank of St. Charles</u>, the court determined that the ordinary rule applied in cases involving building contracts is that a builder is not required to perform perfectly but rather is held only to a duty of substantial performance in a workmanlike manner.

15. X and Y make a contract, and X, after just beginning his performance, is forced to quit the job because of illness. In such a case, the doctrine of substantial performance is <u>not</u> applicable (though X <u>will</u> probably be allowed to recover the reasonable value of the benefit which Y received as a result of the partial performance).

16. In December of 1977 S leased a gasoline station to Hy Test for a 5-year period beginning January 1, 1978. On January 1, 1979, Congress--because of the imminent possibility of World War III--passed emergency legislation which immediately reduced by 85% the amount of gasoline available to civilian motorists. In such a situation, the enactment of this legislation probably constitutes a commercial impracticability and Hy Test is thus freed of his remaining obligations under the lease.

17. Promisor sues promisee to recover for work done under a contract. Promisee defends on the ground that performance by promisor was not complete. If the rule of substantial performance is applicable, Promisor is entitled to recover "the reasonable value of the work" (as distinguished from "the contract price minus damages").

18. L and V make a contract; later, they and a third party, (X), agree that X will perform V's obligations, with L expressly releasing V from the original contract. In such a case it may be said that V's obligations are discharged by "<u>accord and satisfaction</u>" (as distinguished from "novation").

19. The only clear situation in which the courts will free a promisor of his contractual obligations on the theory of "legal impossibility" is the situation where a personal services contract is entered into, and thereafter the promisor dies or becomes too ill to do the job.

20. When a party to a contract seeks to escape its obligations on the theory of "frustration of purpose," he is not necessarily arguing that some event has caused his performance to be much more difficult or expensive than originally anticipated, but, rather, that some event or condition has caused the contract to be of little use or benefit to him.

Chapter 11

21. The "frustration of purpose" argument is rarely accepted by the courts. (i.e., contracting parties are not often freed of their contractual obligations on this ground).

22. The doctrine of "commercial impracticability" is more widely recognized under sales law than under contract law.

23. X, a manufacturer, contracts to sell 1,000 widgets to Y for $2,000. Before the time of delivery arrives, X's material costs increase 20%. He therefore refuses to perform, and Y sues him for damages for breach of contract. If the doctrine of commercial impracticability were applied to this case, the result is that X would clearly be freed of liability to Y (i.e., X's nonperformance would be excused).

24. Today courts are not likely to free contracting parties because of the doctrine of commercial impracticability.

Multiple Choice

1. If a contract is drawn up that indicates that the promises made by the parties are not to be performed until a <u>specified event</u> takes place, that event is called:

   a) a condition subsequent.
   b) an express qualification.
   c) a condition precedent.
   d) none of the above.

2. If a contract contains either an express or implied <u>condition subsequent</u>, and if the specified condition thereafter does occur, this means that:

   a) both parties must now go ahead and perform their obligations.
   b) both parties are now freed of their obligations under the contract.
   c) both parties are now freed of their obligations if--and only if-- they mutually agree to cancel the contract.

3. Sometimes a person will try to escape contractual liability under the "doctrine of commercial impracticability." In regard to that doctrine, which of the following is/are correct?

   a) the doctrine is more often recognized under sales law than it is under contract law.
   b) cost does excuse performance if "the rise is due to some unforeseen contingency which alters the essential nature of the performance."
   c) a severe shortage of raw materials or of supplies due to a contingency such as war, unforeseen shutdown of major sources of supply which cause a marked increase in cost causes performance.
   d) a and b above.
   e) all of the above.

Chapter 11

4. Sometimes a person will try to escape contractual liability under the "doctrine of frustration of purpose." In regard to that doctrine, which of the following is/are true?

   a) a person who is trying to escape liability on this ground is essentially contending that the happening of some certain event caused the contract to be worthless to him.
   b) the courts, while giving the doctrine due consideration in their decision, actually find it to be inapplicable in the great majority of cases.
   c) both of the above.
   d) none of the above.

5. If the rule of substantial performance is applicable to a particular case, the promisor/plaintiff is entitled to:

   a) recover the contract price.
   b) the contract price plus the damages.
   c) the contract minus the damages.
   d) the contract plus compensatory damages.

6. In order for a person to recover money under the doctrine of <u>substantial performance</u>, he must show:

   a) that the performance was substantial, that it varied only slightly from the terms of the contract.
   b) the variations that do exist were not occasioned by bad faith from the part of the promisor.
   c) that his actual performance was very close to 100% of the obligations of the contract and that the deviations that did exist were not due to bad faith on his part.
   d) a and c.
   e) all of the above.

7. In regard to the subject of "legal impossibility," which of the following statements is/are true?

   a) a true legal impossibility exists only where a court finds that a contract was subject to an <u>implied</u> condition subsequent. (That is, an implied condition subsequent which has been recognized under case law.)
   b) the defense of "legal impossibility" is accepted by the courts in only a very few kinds of situations.
   c) the term "physical impossibility" is not synonymous with "legal impossibility" (i.e., physical impossibilities do <u>not always</u> constitute legal impossibilities).
   d) all of the above.
   e) a and b.

8. X, an interior designer, agrees to decorate Y's living room for a specified price, with the contract providing that X guarantees Y's "total satisfaction" with the job. When the work is done, Y claims he is not satisfied. In such a case:

Chapter 11

    a) if the court feels the contract was one essentially involving <u>subjective matters</u>, such as Y's personal color likes and dislikes, and if Y's dissatisfaction is genuine, Y may escape liability to X.
    b) if the court feels that a reasonable man would have been satisfied with X's performance, even though it essentially involved <u>subjective matters</u> as in (a) above, Y will probably be held liable to X.
    c) if the court feels the contract was one essentially involving matters of <u>utility</u> or <u>mere mechanical fitness</u> (rather than subjective matters), Y will probably be held liable even if he is personally dissatisfied and even if a reasonable man would be dissatisfied with X's work.
    d) b and c.
    e) a and b.

9. A stated time for performance in a contract may constitute a <u>condition precedent</u>:

    a) only if the contract expressly so provides.
    b) only if from the subject-matter of the contract such an intent on the part of the contracting parties can be inferred.
    c) only if the contract is a sales contract.
    d) none of the above.

10. X contracts to deliver 500 pumpkins to Y during the month of October. X is unable to do so because the pumpkin crop in his part of the state failed due to a drouth. This crop failure would furnish X with the defense of "legal impossibility" (destruction of the subject matter):

    a) if the contract provided that X was to get the pumpkins from that part of the state that was affected by the drouth.
    b) if from the circumstances surrounding the making of the contract it was reasonably clear that both parties knew that X meant to get the pumpkins from that one area of the state, even if the contract itself said nothing in that respect.
    c) if X can clearly prove that he <u>actually intended</u> to get the pumpkins from that one area of the state, even if Y did not know this and even if the contract said nothing about it.
    d) a and b.

11. After a contract has been formed, the parties may agree that one of them will accept and the other will render a performance different from what was originally called for. This type of agreement is known as:

    a) the rescission.
    b) a novation.
    c) accord.
    d) accord and satisfaction.

12. One type of discharge by operation of law is a bankruptcy proceeding. After a person receives a discharge in bankruptcy from a bankruptcy court, the discharge will:

Chapter 11

   a) extinguish the debt.
   b) discharge the debt in full.
   c) prohibit creditors from thereafter bringing court action against the debtor to recover any unpaid debt.
   d) all of the above.

Short Essay

1. Joe Roller contracted with Frank Skilled to build and install in his restaurant a 150 gallon wine cask from which Roller would be able to draw wine for his customers. Roller and Skilled signed the contract on May 8, and on June 1 the city council passed a city ordinance making the sale of wine illegal. Skilled had commenced construction and installation of the cask prior to June 1. On June 3, Roller told Skilled to cease work immediately. Skilled sued Roller for breach of contract. What results?

Chapter 12

Introduction to the Law of Sales

True-False

1. Article 2 of the UCC generally applies to both sales and leases of goods.

2. Contracts for the sale of land are governed by Article 2 of the UCC, because land is tangible.

3. A contract for the sale of growing crops is a contract for the sale of goods, regardless of whether they are to be harvested by seller or buyer.

4. Despite the fact that service is an important part of the total product of a restaurant, food sold by such an establishment is treated as a sale of goods.

5. A blood transfusion is treated as a sale of goods in some states, but not in others.

6. The sale of a radio station, including FCC license and various physical assets, was held by a court to be a sale of goods.

7. As was seen in DeFilippo v. Ford Motor Co., the total transaction may be viewed as a sale of goods even though some nongoods items were included.

8. If a transaction is a sale of goods, it is governed by most provisions of Article 2 regardless of whether either the seller or the buyer is a merchant.

9. A party who does not personally meet the definition of a merchant cannot be considered as one in a particular transaction just because he hires a merchant to act in his behalf.

10. The courts have unanimously agreed that a farmer is not a merchant.

11. A party can be considered a merchant only if he regularly "deals" in goods of the kind involved in a particular transaction.

12. A bill of lading and a warehouse receipt are documents of title, although an airbill is not.

13. Both bills of lading and warehouse receipts may be either negotiable or nonnegotiable.

14. A bill of lading which states that the goods are to be "delivered to bearer" is a negotiable document of title.

Chapter 12

15. A warehouse receipt which states that the goods are to be "delivered to Joe Jones" is a nonnegotiable document of title.

16. A warehouse receipt which states that the goods are to be "delivered to the order of Joe Jones" is a nonnegotiable document of title.

17. Whether negotiable or nonnegotiable, a document of title is nothing more than a mere receipt for goods.

Multiple Choice

1. Our law relating to sales of goods

    a) traces its origins back to the rules established by merchants themselves in the "fair courts."
    b) has been contained in the UCC since 1906.
    c) was not put into statutory form until enactment of the UCC.
    d) all of the above.

2. A sale

    a) is the same thing as a bailment under the UCC.
    b) is not the same thing as a gift, because no title passes in the case of a gift.
    c) is the passing of title from the seller to the buyer for a price.
    d) both a and b.
    e) both b and c.

3. A contract for the sale of coal

    a) is a contract for the sale of goods if the coal has already been taken from the ground before the contract is made.
    b) is a contract for the sale of goods if the coal is still in the ground and the contract calls for its removal by the seller.
    c) is a contract for the sale of real estate if the coal is still in the ground and the contract calls for its removal by the buyer.
    d) both b and c.
    e) all of the above.

4. A contract which involves both a sale of goods and the rendition of services

    a) may or may not be governed by the UCC, depending on whether the sale of goods or the rendition of services is the predominant factor in the transaction.
    b) is always governed by the UCC, because goods are involved.
    c) is not governed by the UCC in any situation, because services are involved.
    d) none of the above.

Chapter 12

5. A party's status as a merchant or nonmerchant

    a) is irrelevant.
    b) determines whether his contracts are governed by the UCC rules or common-law rules.
    c) is determined solely by whether he regularly deals in the particular kind of goods involved.
    d) both b and c.
    e) none of the above.

6. Legal possession of a negotiable document of title

    a) entitles the possessor to receive the goods only if he is named in the document.
    b) is tantamount to ownership of the goods.
    c) confers no greater rights than legal possession of a nonnegotiable document.
    d) none of the above.

7. In order for a farmer to be included within the definition of "merchant" he must do one of the following:

    a) deal in goods of the kind.
    b) by his occupation hold himself out as having knowledge or skill peculiar to the practices or goods involved in the transaction.
    c) employ an agent or broker or other intermediary who by his occupation holds himself out as having such knowledge or skill.
    d) all of the above.

8. Documents of title are two basic types:

    a) negotiable and nonnegotiable.
    b) creditor debtor.
    c) possessory or nonpossessory.
    d) all of the above.

9. A negotiable document is more than a mere receipt for the goods and a contract for their carriage or storage. A person who is in legal possession of a negotiable document is:

    a) entitled to the goods described therein.
    b) will be governed by the instructions of the bailor.
    c) is under a duty to insure the goods.
    d) is under a duty to care for the goods.

10. A contract for the sale of anything attached to real estate is a sale of goods:

    a) if it can be severed without material harm to the real estate.
    b) if it is a mineral.
    c) if it is the right to hunt or fish on the property.
    d) if it is attached by growing roots.

Chapter 12

Short Essay

1. Explain the test which is employed in determining whether a "mixed" sale of goods and a service contract is within the coverage of UCC Article 2.

2. George had been an automobile mechanic for many years, but he had never bought and sold cars except for his own personal use. On one occasion, however, George bought a used car because of its very low price. He did not intend to use it, but to sell it at a profit. Shortly thereafter, he contracted to sell the car to William. A dispute arose over the contract, which would be resolved by the UCC in different ways depending on whether George was considered a merchant. Is George a merchant? Discuss.

Chapter 13

Sales/Formation and Interpretation of the Sales Contract

True-False

1. Under the UCC a firm offer is irrevocable for a maximum of 3 months.

2. A written and signed offer to buy or sell goods, made by a merchant, is automatically irrevocable for three months if it gives assurance that it will be held open.

3. The UCC has generally relaxed the common law rules relating to the definiteness of a contract for the sale of goods.

4. If the parties actually intended to be legally bound by a contract for the sale of goods, but left the price for later agreement and then failed to agree, a court will determine a reasonable price at the time for delivery and will enforce the contract.

5. The absence of a delivery date in a contract for the sale of goods renders it null and void.

6. In a contract for the sale of goods where the parties have not agreed otherwise, the buyer has the right to select the assortment.

7. Under the UCC, an offer to make a contract is construed as inviting acceptance in any manner and by any medium reasonable in the circumstances, assuming that the offer is silent on the matter.

8. An offer to buy goods which states "for prompt shipment" is construed an inviting acceptance either by prompt shipment or by a prompt promise to ship.

9. When a buyer offers to buy goods and both parties intend the act of shipment to be the acceptance of that offer, the seller does not have to notify the buyer of the shipment for it to be an acceptance.

10. A shipment of nonconforming goods can be an acceptance of the buyer's offer to buy.

11. As contrasted with common-law rules, the UCC broadens the scope within which an acceptance can deviate from the terms of the offer and yet still be an acceptance.

12. Under the UCC, an attempted acceptance is not really an acceptance if it contains a term not found in the offer and if that term is material.

13. The preexisting duty rule applies to modifications of sale of goods contracts in the same way it applies to modifications of other contracts.

Chapter 13

14. Between merchants, a written confirmation of an oral contract for the sale of goods at a price of $500 or more is sufficient to satisfy the Statute of Frauds, thus making the contract enforceable against the recipient of the confirmation even though he did not sign it, if the sender had signed it, and if the recipient had reason to know of its contents but had not objected to it in writing within ten days after receiving it.

15. Although a contract for the sale of goods at a price of $500 or more generally has to be evidenced by a writing signed by the party against whom enforcement is sought, the UCC provides that in some circumstances a writing is sufficient even though signed only by the party seeking to enforce the contract.

16. Under the UCC, a written document is sufficient to satisfy the Statute of Frauds if it merely indicates that a contract of sale has been made between the parties, and it does not have to contain any of the actual terms of that agreement.

17. The quantity term, which is required to satisfy the Statute of Frauds in a written contract for the sale of goods, can be expressed in terms to the buyer's requirements.

18. Contracts for specially manufactured goods are exempt from the UCC Statute of Frauds requirement for a writing because they involve a transaction in which service is an important factor.

19. "Course of performance" and "course of dealing" both relate to the conduct of the particular seller and buyer involved.

20. From the cases thus far decided on the question of unconscionability, it appears that merchants are the chief beneficiaries of the UCC provision empowering courts to invalidate unconscionable sales contracts.

Multiple Choice

1. Under the UCC, an offer to buy or sell goods is irrevocable

    a) if the offeror promises to hold the offer open and the offeree gives consideration for that promise, regardless of whether either party is a merchant.
    b) The offer clearly states the price and delivery date.
    c) if it expressly states that it is irrevocable.
    d) if made by a merchant, but only for three months.

2. Under the UCC, a sales contract is enforceable even if one or more terms are left open

    a) so long as the court feels that the parties intended to make a binding contract, and there is reasonably certain basis for granting an appropriate remedy.

Chapter 13

    b) if the court has a reasonably certain basis for granting an appropriate remedy, regardless of how the court views the parties' intent.
    c) so long as the terms that actually were agreed upon were put in writing.
    d) none of the above.

3. Suppose that S and B made a sale of goods contract that they intended to be binding but which contained no price term.

    a) The contract is not enforceable.
    b) If the parties had expressly left the price for later agreement and then failed to agree, the contract is enforceable and the price set by the court will be a reasonable price at the time for delivery.
    c) If the agreement had said nothing at all about price, and the price was never settled on due to the fault of one of the parties, the party not at fault can either cancel the contract or set a reasonable price.
    d) both b and c.
    e) none of the above.

4. Where the parties have made a sale of goods contract that they intend to be binding, but which does not state a time and place for delivery,

    a) the contract is not valid.
    b) the delivery must be made at the buyer's place of business within a reasonable time.
    c) the delivery must be made at the seller's place of business within ten days.
    d) the delivery must be made within a reasonable time and, depending on the circumstances, must be made at the seller's place of business, at the seller's residence, or at some other place where the goods are located.
    e) none of the above.

5. Regarding details of delivery omitted by the contracting parties, the UCC provides that

    a) the seller has the right to specify shipping arrangements where the contract contemplates shipment but does not mention arrangements.
    b) the seller has the right to decide whether delivery is to be made in a single lot or in several lots.
    c) both parties must agree on the assortment to be delivered.
    d) both a and c.
    e) none of the above.

6. Regarding a seller's acceptance of a buyer's offer to buy goods,

    a) the UCC provides that the buyer may no longer limit the seller to acceptance by actual shipment rather than by a communicated promise to ship.

Chapter 13

  b) the seller may ship nonconforming goods without thereby accepting the buyer's offer if the seller indicates that the shipment is only an attempt to accommodate the buyer.
  c) where actual shipment constitutes the seller's acceptance the seller has to notify the buyer of the shipment only if the buyer is not likely to learn of the acceptance otherwise.
  d) both b and c.
  e) none of the above.

7. With respect to a contract for the sale of goods, a definite and reasonable expression of acceptance sent within a reasonable time is effective as an acceptance even though it states additional terms not contained in the offer, except in which one of the following situations?

  a) Neither party is a merchant.
  b) The additional terms materially alter the contract.
  c) Acceptance is expressly conditional on the offeror's consent to the additional terms.
  d) The offer expressly limited acceptance to the terms of the offer.
  e) None of the above.

8. Under the UCC an agreement modifying a contract for the sale of goods needs no consideration to be binding. However, such a modification without consideration must be in writing:

  a) unless the parties had expressly agreed that their contract could be modified orally.
  b) if the original agreement had provided that it could be modified only by a writing.
  c) only if the original contract, before the modification, was required to be in writing under the Statute of Frauds.
  d) none of the above.

9. In which of the following situations may a contract for the sale of goods be enforceable despite the absence of any written evidence of it?

  a) where the contract price is less than $500.
  b) where the goods have been delivered and accepted.
  c) where payment in full has been made and accepted.
  d) all of the above.
  e) none of the above.

10. A court can declare a sale of goods contract unconscionable

  a) only in cases involving economically disadvantaged consumers.
  b) whenever it finds an abuse of bargaining power, but can actually refuse to enforce the contract only if fraud or duress was practiced.
  c) in circumstances where the contract is so unfair and oppressively one-sided as to shock the conscience of the court.
  d) both a and c.
  e) none of the above.

Chapter 13

Short Essay

1. What is meant by "course of performance," "course of dealing," and "usage of trade." What part do these concepts play in the law of sales?

2. Havlicek's Athletic Supply Store ordered 200 pairs of basketball shoes at $10 per pair from Chamberlain Shoe Co. Upon receiving Havlicek's written order, Chamberlain replied as follows: "Accept your order. This acceptance subject to the following terms and conditions. (1) These goods are sold without any warranties, express or implied; (2) Any dispute arising from this transaction shall be submitted to binding arbitration."

   a) Assuming that Havlicek made an offer, did Chamberlain accept it? Explain.

   b) Regardless of what you just answered, assume that an acceptance was made. Did the exclusion of warranties and the arbitration clause become part of the agreement? Explain.

Chapter 14

Sales/Title, Risk of Loss, and Insurable Interest

True-False

1. Title to goods is unimportant in resolving most legal issues arising under the UCC.

2. Goods must be both existing and identified before title to them can pass to a buyer.

3. Future goods, such as crops to be grown, cannot be the subject of a sale contract because they are not yet existing goods.

4. A basic difference between a shipment contract and a destination contract is in the extent of the seller's delivery obligation.

5. One who acquires goods through fraud has the same type of title as one who physically steals them.

6. If S purchases goods from a minor, S acquires a voidable title and can thus transfer only a voidable title to another purchaser.

7. A buyer cannot ignore highly suspicious circumstances and then, because he didn't have actual knowledge of the facts causing the seller's title to be voidable, claim to be a BFP.

8. A seller who retains possession of goods for any length of time after they are sold is guilty of fraud against any of his creditors who rely upon his possession in granting credit to him.

9. Even if a bulk transfer is ineffective because proper notice has not been given to the seller's creditors, the buyer can transfer good title to a BFP.

10. A sale made for less than a "fair consideration" is a fraud on the seller's creditors if the seller is insolvent at the time of the sale, but not if he is made insolvent for the first time by the sale itself.

11. The question of whether the seller or the buyer bears the risk of loss is important only if the goods are not insured.

12. Seller and buyer can agree however they wish on the matter of title and risk of loss to existing, identified goods.

13. Where seller and buyer have not agreed as to the placement of risk of loss, the question basically turns on how the goods are to be delivered.

14. According to UCC rules, the passage of both title and risk of loss can sometimes depend on whether a document of title is used.

Chapter 14

15. According to UCC rules, the passage of both title and risk of loss can sometimes depend on whether a document of title is negotiable or non-negotiable.

16. When the buyer is to pick up the goods at a seller's premises, that is not a merchant, risk of loss passes to the buyer when the seller "tenders" delivery.

17. For the purpose of determining who bears the risk of loss on goods that are held by a bailee and are to be picked up there by the buyer, a writing given to the buyer by the seller which directs the bailee to deliver the goods to the buyer is treated the same as a nonnegotiable document of title.

18. The extent to which the risk of loss shifts to a buyer is determined by the extent that the seller's insurance coverage is deficient, regardless of whether there has been a breach of contract by the buyer.

19. A seller retains an insurable interest in goods so long as he still has either title to or a security interest in the goods.

20. A seller and buyer can both have an insurable interest in the same goods at the same time.

Multiple Choice

1. Passage of title from a seller of goods to the buyer

    a) is totally irrelevant.
    b) can be important in determining questions such as tax liability and insurable interest.
    c) is determined by the UCC rules regardless of the agreement of the parties.
    d) both b and c.
    e) none of the above.

2. A buyer has voidable title and can transfer goods title to a BFP

    a) if the buyer fraudulently acquired the goods.
    b) if the buyer bought the goods from a minor.
    c) if the buyer bought the goods in a cash on delivery transaction and paid with a bad check.
    d) all of the above.
    e) none of the above.

3. If goods are taken for repairs to someone who is not only a repairman but also a merchant who deals in goods of that kind,

    a) the merchant can transfer goods title to anyone who is a BFP.
    b) the merchant can transfer goods title to a buyer in the ordinary course of business.

223

Chapter 14

    c) the merchant has voidable title.
    d) both a and c.
    e) none of the above.

4. S is a merchant whose principal business is the sale of major home appliances from inventory. He contracts to sell approximately 60 percent of his inventory at a particular time to B.

    a) Before the actual sale takes place, S must furnish a list of his creditors to B.
    b) S and B must prepare a list of the property to be sold and B must notify the seller's creditors of the sale at least ten days before taking possession of or paying for the goods (whichever occurs first).
    c) Since this is classified as a bulk sale, S's creditors automatically have the right to seize the goods after B takes possession of them.
    d) both a and b.
    e) both a and c.

5. If seller and buyer have made a sale contract in which they have agreed that the goods are to be shipped by carrier and seller's delivery obligation is to be fulfilled upon shipment of the goods;

    a) this is a destination contract and risk of loss passes to buyer when seller duly delivers the goods to a carrier.
    b) this is a shipment contract and risk of loss passes to buyer only when the goods are tendered at the destination.
    c) title and risk of loss probably will shift to the buyer at the same time.
    d) both b and c.
    e) none of the above.

6. Seller S and Buyer B make a sale contract for goods stored with a warehouseman. S and B agree that B will pick up the goods at the warehouse.

    a) Passage of risk of loss to B hinges upon whether a warehouse receipt had been issued by the warehouseman and if so, what type of document it is.
    b) If a negotiable warehouse receipt has been issued for the goods, risk of loss passes to B when S gives him that document.
    c) If no warehouse receipt was issued by the warehouseman, risk of loss passes to B as soon as S obtains from the warehouseman an acknowledgment of B's right to the goods.
    d) all of the above.
    e) both a and b, but not c.

7. M, a manufacturer, and R, a retailer, agreed upon the sale of items from M to R. The contract gave R the privilege of returning the goods.

    a) If the items consist of supplies to be used in R's business office at his store, title to the goods passes to R as soon as the goods are tendered at the destination, unless the parties have agreed otherwise.

Chapter 14

    b) If the items consist of supplies to be used in R's business office at his store, risk of loss immediately passes to R when he receives the goods, but passes back to M if R returns the goods, unless the parties have agreed otherwise.
    c) If the items consist of merchandise to be sold by R to his customers, and R decides to return them to M, the return is at the buyer's risk and expense, unless the parties have agreed otherwise.
    d) If the items consist of merchandise to be sold by R to his customers, the arrangement between M and R is a "sale on approval," unless the parties have agreed otherwise.

8. Seller and buyer made a contract for the sale of goods which were to be shipped to the buyer. The contract of sale stated that delivery was to be "F.O.B. seller's factory." In this situation, unless the parties expressly agree otherwise,

    a) this is a "shipment contract," and title passes to buyer when he receives a negotiable bill of lading.
    b) this is a "shipment contract," and title passes to buyer upon shipment, that is, when the goods are turned over to the carrier.
    c) this is a "shipment contract," and even though title passes to the buyer when the goods are shipped, risk of loss does not pass until the goods are tendered at the destination.
    d) this is a "shipment contract," and the moment at which title and risk of loss pass to the buyer depends upon whether a document of title is used, but not upon the type of document of title.

9. Suppose that the facts are the same as in No. 8, except that the buyer breaches by repudiating the contract before the goods are shipped. The goods conformed to contract requirements and were identified at the time of the buyer's repudiation. In this situation,

    a) the risk of loss immediately shifts to the buyer and remains with him indefinitely, but only to the extent that the seller's insurance coverage is deficient.
    b) the risk of loss immediately passes to the buyer to the extent that the seller's insurance coverage is deficient, but this risk then remains with the buyer only for a commercially reasonable time.
    c) the risk of loss immediately passes to the buyer to the full extent of any loss incurred, but this risk then remains with the buyer only for a commercially reasonable time.
    d) title immediately passes to the buyer.

10. Seller and Buyer contract for the sale of 200 dozen pairs of men's slacks. Each is interested in having the goods insured against loss by fire or theft during the time before actual delivery.

    a) Seller can obtain insurance on the goods only if he still has title.
    b) Buyer can obtain insurance on the goods as soon as a specific 200 dozen pairs have been identified as the subject of the sale contract.
    c) Since it is possible for both Seller and Buyer to obtain insurance on the same goods at the same time, it is possible for both of them to recover the full value of the goods from the insurance company in case of a fire loss.

Chapter 14

   d) both a and c, but not b.
   e) none of the above.

Short Essay

1. Owner O entrusts possession of his TV set for repairs to M, who is a merchant dealing in TV sets. Explain why the UCC allows M to transfer goods title to O's TV set to a buyer in the ordinary course of business.

2. X was in dire financial straits, his liabilities greatly exceeding his assets. Knowing that his creditors were breathing down his neck, he wanted to keep as much of his inventory from them as possible. To do this, he sold a portion of his inventory to his brother. X then squandered the proceeds. What do X's creditors have to prove in order to be able to seize the goods from X's brother?

Chapter 16

Sales/Warranties

True-False

1. To make an express warranty, the seller does not have to use the words "warranty" or "guarantee" or even have the intention to create a warranty.

2. Even without an express exclusion of the warranty, there is no warranty of title on goods seized and sold by a sheriff at a public sale.

3. A statement of opinion or commendation does not create an express warranty on goods, but a statement relating to the value of the goods does create such a warranty.

4. A descriptive word or phrase used in the sale of goods may create an express warranty.

5. Although the UCC makes no distinction between a sample and a model, a sample is more likely to create an express warranty than a model.

6. A sample or model does not always create an express warranty, but only when the parties intend it to establish a standard of quality for the sale.

7. The implied warranty of merchantability requires that goods be fit for the ordinary purposes for which such goods are used and be merely of average or medium grade.

8. Most courts today, in applying the implied warranty of merchantability to food containing an injurious object, base their decision on whether a consumer would reasonably expect such an object to be in the food.

9. In the case of Mohasco Industries, Inc. v. Anderson Halverson Corp. the appellate court followed the general rule that the implied warranty of merchantability is limited by an express warranty of conformity to a precise description supplied by the buyer.

10. An implied warranty of merchantability will exist only if the seller is a merchant dealing in goods of the kind involved, but this is not a requirement for creation of the implied warranty of fitness.

11. The implied warranty of fitness for a particular purpose is created only if the seller actually knows of the particular purpose for which the goods are needed by the buyer.

12. The failure of a buyer to fully inform the seller of all facts relevant to a purchase has no effect on the existence of an implied warranty of fitness, because the rule of caveat emptor is no longer applicable.

Chapter 15

13. It is possible for both types of implied warranties to exist in a single sales transaction.

14. It is not possible for an express warranty and either type of implied warranty to exist in the same sales transaction.

15. A disclaimer of the implied warranty of merchantability must be in writing and must be conspicuous.

16. A disclaimer of the implied warranty of fitness must be in writing and must be conspicuous, although the language used does not have to be as specific as the language used to disclaim the warranty of merchantability.

17. The protection provided by a warranty may extend to others besides the actual purchaser.

18. Privity of contract is not a requirement for a buyer of defective goods to recover under either the strict liability or negligence theories.

19. Contributory negligence on the part of the buyer cannot be used as a defense by the seller if the buyer's claim is based on breach of warranty or strict liability.

20. Under the Magnuson-Moss Warranty Act, a seller is required to give a warranty that is either full or limited, and, if it is full, he must repair or replace any malfunctioning product within a reasonable time and without charge.

Multiple Choice

1. Unless there is an exclusion of such a warranty by specific language, the UCC imposes a warranty in most sales to the effect that

   a) the title conveyed shall be good and its transfer rightful.
   b) the goods shall be delivered free from any security interest or other lien or encumbrance of which the buyer at the time of contracting has no knowledge.
   c) the goods sold do not infringe upon the patent, copyright, or trademark of a third party, but this warranty applies only if the seller is a merchant in the type of goods involved.
   d) all of the above.
   e) both a and b, but not c.

2. The UCC provides that express warranties by a seller of goods are created in which of the following circumstances?

   a) Any affirmation of fact or affirmation of value or promise made by the seller to the buyer which relates to the goods and becomes part of the basis of the bargain creates an express warranty that the

Chapter 15

        goods shall conform to the affirmation or promise.
- b) Any description of the goods which is made part of the basis of the bargain creates an express warranty that the goods shall conform to the description.
- c) both a and b.
- d) none of the above.

3. In a sale of goods under the UCC, the implied warranty of merchantability

- a) exists if the seller is a merchant with respect to goods of that kind, unless the warranty is excluded or modified.
- b) requires that the goods have no defects of any kind.
- c) requires, in the case of fungible goods, that the goods be of high or premium quality.
- d) may not be disclaimed by the seller by general language such as "with all faults" or "as is."

4. An express warranty

- a) cannot be disclaimed.
- b) is the same thing as fraud, if the warranty is actually breached.
- c) is difficult to disclaim.
- d) all of the above.
- e) both b and c, but not a.

5. An express warranty

- a) is created by an affirmation of fact which becomes "part of the basis of the bargain," this quoted phrase being explicitly defined in the UCC.
- b) that the goods conform to the sample is created anytime a sample is used, but this is not necessarily true of a model.
- c) can be created by a description of the goods, but not by a trade name.
- d) all of the above.
- e) none of the above.

6. The implied warranty of merchantability

- a) does not exist unless the seller is a merchant in the type of goods being sold.
- b) is essentially equivalent to "wholesomeness" in the case of food, but does not apply to food sold by a service establishment such as a restaurant.
- c) takes precedence over an inconsistent express warranty.
- d) all of the above.
- e) none of the above.

7. Which of the following is required by the merchantability warranty?

- a) The goods must be fit for any purpose for which the goods might be used.

Chapter 15

- b) The goods must be adequately packaged and labeled.
- c) The goods must be accident-proof.
- d) The goods must be of the highest quality available.
- e) None of the above.

8. Which of the following is <u>not</u> required for the creation of an implied warranty of fitness for a particular purpose?

   a) The seller must have had reason to know of the particular purpose for which the goods are needed by the seller.
   b) The seller must have had reason to know that the buyer was relying on the seller's skill or judgment to select or furnish suitable goods.
   c) The seller must be a merchant.
   d) The facts leading the court to conclude that the seller had reason to know of the buyer's particular purpose and reliance must have existed at the time of contracting.

9. Which of the following statements is applicable to warranty disclaimers?

   a) The parol evidence rule is irrelevant.
   b) Warranty liability, like strict liability and liability based on negligence, can be disclaimed only if the disclaimer is conspicuous.
   c) Where the seller demands that the buyer inspect goods, the buyer's refusal to inspect may exclude warranties on easily observable defects, even though the seller has not made an express disclaimer.
   d) All of the above.
   e) None of the above.

10. The Magnuson-Moss Warranty Act

    a) requires sellers to give written warranties on all goods costing ten dollars or more.
    b) requires sellers to give written warranties on consumer goods costing ten dollars or more.
    c) regulates the safety and quality of consumer goods.
    d) applies only if a seller voluntarily chooses to give a written warranty on consumer goods.

Short Essay

1. Explain why it is rather difficult to completely avoid liability on any type of express warranty.

2. Thompson, a tobacco wholesaler, was about to complete a sale of 500 boxes of cigars to a retailer. Knowing that because of bad weather the tobacco crop from which these cigars had been produced was possibly not of the same quality as in normal years, Thompson wanted to avoid any liability on the implied warranty of merchantability. What should he do and how should he do it?

Chapter 16

Sales/Performance and Remedies

True-False

1. A seller performs his delivery obligation by "tendering" delivery, which means that he must actually put the goods into the buyer's possession.

2. Unless the parties have agreed otherwise, the seller's delivery must be at a reasonable hour.

3. Where, under the sale contract, delivery is to be accomplished by the buyer picking up the goods from a third party warehouseman, the seller can perform his obligation merely by providing the buyer with a negotiable document of title for the goods.

4. Where, under the sale contract, delivery is to be accomplished by the buyer picking up the goods from a third party warehouseman, the seller can perform his obligation by providing the buyer with a nonnegotiable document of title if the buyer does not object.

5. In a shipment contract, the seller performs his delivery obligation by tendering delivery at the point of shipment, which includes (unless the parties have agreed otherwise) the requirement that the seller promptly notify the buyer of the shipment.

6. The phrase FOB New York is indicative of the parties' agreement on shipping terms only if the phrase appears separately in the contract, and not merely in connection with the price.

7. The letters CIF, when used in a sale contract, stand for "cost, interest, and freight."

8. The perfect tender rule applies under the UCC exactly as it did at common law.

9. The principle of "cure" applies only when the agreed time for performance has not yet expired.

10. Under the UCC, an installment contract is defined as one requiring or authorizing the delivery of goods in separate lots to be separately accepted.

11. The seller's failure to make proper shipping arrangements for goods under a shipment contract entitles the buyer to reject the goods only if material loss or delay results.

12. Where an unforeseen occurrence destroys a source of supply that had been

Chapter 16

contemplated by both seller and buyer, the seller is not excused from delivering to the buyer if the seller did not take all reasonable steps to assure himself that the source would not fail.

13. In the case of <u>Eastern Airlines, Inc. v. Gulf Oil Co.</u>, the court felt that Gulf would have prevailed if the energy crisis was foreseeable, because if a contingency is foreseeable, it and its consequences are directly in the scope of UCC 2-615.

14. Unless otherwise agreed, the buyer must furnish facilities that are reasonably suited for receipt of the goods.

15. If the parties have not limited inspection by their agreement, the buyer has a right to inspect the goods, at any reasonable place and time and in any reasonable manner, before accepting or paying for them.

16. Sometimes the parties' agreement obligates the buyer to make payment before inspecting the goods, as when the contract calls for "COD."

17. A mere failure to respond to a request from the other party for an assurance of performance cannot constitute an anticipatory repudiation.

18. The word "cover" refers to the right a buyer has in some circumstances to buy goods elsewhere in a commercially reasonable manner when the seller has breached the contract.

19. If the buyer rightfully rejects goods because they are nonconforming, but the seller does not pick them up or give reasonable instructions as to their handling, the buyer may resell them but he is never required to.

20. If the buyer breaches the contract after the seller has shipped the goods but before they arrive at their destination, the seller cannot stop delivery if he has already sent a negotiable bill of lading to the buyer.

Multiple Choice

1. To perform his part of the contract, the seller must

   a) tender delivery at a reasonable hour.
   b) put and hold conforming goods at the buyers disposition and give the buyer any notification reasonably necessary to enable him to take delivery.
   c) tender delivery at the point of shipment, in the case of a shipment contract.
   d) all of the above.
   e) a and b, but not c.

Chapter 16

2. Which of the following terms indicate that a shipment contract has been made?

   a) ex-ship.
   b) FOB buyer's warehouse.
   c) FAS vessel, New York.
   d) payment against documents.

3. Which of the following do not relate to an exception to the perfect tender rule?

   a) installment contract.
   b) revocation of acceptance.
   c) improper shipping arrangements.
   d) substitute means of delivery.

4. When the available quantity of goods is diminished because of commercial impracticability, the seller must allocate deliveries among

   a) all customers then under contract and, if he chooses, regular customers not currently under contract.
   b) all customers then under contract and, if those customers so choose, regular customers not currently under contract.
   c) all customers, both regular and occasional, on a first-come first-served basis.
   d) none of the above.

5. In which of the following situations is there not an acceptance of goods?

   a) After having had a reasonable opportunity to inspect, the buyer signifies to the seller that the goods are conforming.
   b) After having had a reasonable opportunity to inspect, the buyer fails to reject the goods within a reasonable period of time.
   c) The buyer receives the goods and then resells them to a third party.
   d) The buyer receives the goods and uses a small portion of them for the sole purpose of testing.

6. If a seller delivers goods which do not conform to the contract of sale,

   a) the buyer may reject all of the goods, but the seller will always have a right to "cure" (correct the problem).
   b) the buyer may accept all of the goods, but this prevents him from recovering damages from the seller.
   c) once the buyer accepts the goods he may not under any circumstances revoke his acceptance.
   d) the buyer may accept any commercial unit or units, and reject the rest and recover damages.

7. In order for an occurrence to constitute a commercial impracticability,

   a) it must have been unforeseen.
   b) the party seeking to be excused from performance must promptly notify the other party.

233

Chapter 16

    c) it must be something other than just a change in the market price.
    d) all of the above.
    e) none of the above.

8. X communicates an anticipatory repudiation of their contract to Y. Which of the following actions is Y not entitled to take?

    a) suspend his own performance.
    b) treat the contract as having been breach-d, and immediately pursue the appropriate remedies.
    c) wait for performance until the time for performance that was agreed upon in the contract,

9. When the seller delivers nonconforming goods, the buyer can

    a) cancel the contract.
    b) accept the goods and sue for damages.
    c) accept the goods and later revoke that acceptance under certain circumstances.
    d) all of the above.
    e) a and b, but not c.
    f) a and c, but not b.

10. If the seller has delivered nonconforming goods and the buyer has rejected them, but the seller has not yet taken the goods back,

    a) the buyer does not have to return the goods even if the seller demands it.
    b) the buyer does not have to follow any instructions from the seller for handling the goods, but can just resell or store the goods or reship them to the seller.
    c) the buyer must follow all reasonable instructions of the seller.
    d) a and b, but not c.
    e) none of the above.

11. In the case of Conte v. Dwan Lincoln-Mercury, Inc. the legal issue involved was:

    a) After accepting delivery, can a buyer revoke acceptence?
    b) Does the nonconformity substantially impair the value?
    c) Revocation must occur within a reasonable time after buyer discovers the basis.
    d) a and b.
    e) b and c.

12. If a clause in a contract limiting remedies "fails of its essential purposes," it will:

    a) be ignored by the court.
    b) allow remedies normally available under the UCC to apply.
    c) apply to consumer goods only.
    d) a and b.
    e) b and c.

Chapter 16

Short Essay

1. Explain the circumstances in which a buyer may revoke his acceptance of goods.

2. Bailey, a grower of citrus fruit, shipped 10,000 cases of Florida oranges to Winston, a fruit wholesaler. However, their contract had called for grapefruit. Winston had no need for oranges at that time. He had not yet paid Bailey for them, and Bailey had no agent or office in the area that Winston could contact, so he simply let the oranges sit on the loading dock at his warehouse. They spoiled after a few days and Winston discarded them. Did Winston act within his rights? Explain.

Chapter 17

Commercial Paper/Types, Parties, and Basic Concepts

True-False

1. The adoption of Article 3 of the UCC ("Commercial Paper") in the 1960s brought about <u>sweeping changes</u> in that area of the law.

2. Insofar as their basic elements are concerned, drafts and notes are essentially <u>different kinds</u> of instruments.

3. Drafts necessarily have three parties (drawer, drawee, and payee), while promissory notes have only two parties (maker and payee).

4. A trade acceptance is one kind of check.

5. When a trade acceptance is used in connection with a sale of goods, the seller is the <u>drawer</u> of the instrument and the buyer is the <u>drawee</u>.

6. A <u>bank</u> draft is a draft drawn by a bank on itself.

7. Insofar as their basic elements are concerned, certificates of deposit are more closely related to <u>checks</u> than they are to <u>promissory notes</u>.

8. Certificates of deposit may be either negotiable or nonnegotiable in form.

9. Most certificates of deposit are time instruments (as distinguished from demand instruments).

10. A draft that is drawn on a bank may properly be called a <u>check</u>, regardless of whether it is payable at a fixed future date or payable on demand.

11. In general, the obligations of makers, drawers, and indorsers of negotiable instruments are governed by the same rules of law as are makers, drawers and indorsers of nonnegotiable instruments.

12. It is not possible for a person to qualify as a holder in due course (HDC) of a nonnegotiable instrument.

13. M (maker) signs a promissory note and issues it to the payee, P. P indorses the note to H. Later, P fails to perform his contract with M, in payment for which the note was originally issued by M. In such a case, if H qualifies as an HDC, he is entitled to <u>full payment</u> from M when the note comes due.

14. A person who qualifies as an HDC of an instrument takes the instrument free of all defenses to such instrument.

Chapter 17

15. A person who acquires an instrument from the payee can always be sure that he qualifies as an HDC just as long as the instrument is negotiable.

16. An HDC of an instrument takes the instrument free of "personal" defenses, but subject to "real defenses."

17. If a draft is "accepted" by the drawee, his liability is very similar to that of the maker of a note.

18. A check is payable "to the order of P." P indorses the instrument simply by signing his name on the back of it. The check is now a bearer instrument.

19. A check goes from D (drawer) to P (payee) to X, and X thereafter negotiates it to H. In such a case, if X qualified as an HDC, H would have the same rights as X possessed (i.e., the rights of an HDC) even if he (H) failed to qualify as an HDC.

20. The liability of accommodation parties (e.g., accommodation makers and indorsers) is significantly less than that of ordinary makers and indorsers.

21. The term "commercial paper" refers to written promises or obligations to pay sums of money that arise from the use of such instruments as drafts, credit cards, checks and trade acceptances.

22. Commercial paper came into use primarily after passage of the UCC in the 1960s.

23. The early English courts refused to recognize commercial paper.

24. In 1896 the American Bar Association drafted the UCC, and, by 1920, it was adopted by all the states for application to commercial paper.

25. During the 18th and 19th centuries the principals of commercial paper came to be substantially recognized by English and American courts and thus became a part of the common law of both countries.

Multiple Choice

1. When a trade acceptance is utilized in connection with a sale of goods, the seller of the goods is:

    a) the drawer of the instrument.
    b) the acceptor of the instrument.
    c) often both the drawer and the acceptor of the instrument.
    d) the drawee of the instrument.
    e) a and c.

Chapter 17

2. In order for an instrument to be a <u>check</u>, it must

   a) contain an order to pay money.
   b) be payable on demand.
   c) be drawn on a bank.
   d) all of the above.
   e) a and c.

3. The chief advantage of being a holder in due course (HDC) of a negotiable instrument is the fact that such a holder

   a) can be sure that he will be paid by the primary party when the instrument matures.
   b) takes the instrument free of both universal (real) and limited (personal) defenses.
   c) takes the instrument free of limited (personal) defenses--such as fraud and breach of contract.
   d) a and b.
   e) none of the above.

4. The <u>acceptor</u> of an instrument is a person who

   a) "accepts it"--i.e., purchases it--from the payee or from some subsequent holder of the instrument.
   b) indorses an instrument prior to negotiating it to a third party.
   c) is in physical possession of a bearer instrument. (Assume here that the possession is lawful.)
   d) none of the above.

5. An <u>ordinary holder</u> of a negotiable instrument

   a) stands in about the same legal position as that of an <u>assignee</u> of a <u>nonnegotiable</u> instrument (insofar as his ability to enforce payment of the instrument at maturity is concerned).
   b) can enforce the instrument against the primary party (such as the maker of a note) at maturity <u>if</u> such party has no defense of any kind.
   c) is, by definition, a holder who fails to qualify as an HDC.
   d) b and c.
   e) a, b and c.

6. X is the payee of a check drawn on the Y Bank, and he wishes to cash it at the Z Bank, where he is unknown. At the Z Bank's suggestion, a depositor of the Z Bank, D, (who is also a friend of X's) indorses the check and the bank then cashes it for X. In this case:

   a) D is an accommodation maker.
   b) the Z Bank is the accommodated party.
   c) D is an accommodation indorser.
   d) a and b.
   e) b and d.

238

Chapter 17

7. Commercial paper can be considered as:

   a) substitute for money.
   b) credit devices.
   c) a chose in action.
   d) all of the above.

8. In order for a draft to work:

   a) the drawee must owe the drawer a debt.
   b) some kind of relationship or agreement must exist between the parties under which the drawee has consented to the drawing of the draft upon him.
   c) a and b.
   d) either a or b.

9. A note differs from a draft in which of the following aspects.

   a) contains promises to pay rather than order.
   b) has two parities, maker and payee, rather then three.
   c) always provides for attorney fees for breach.
   d) a and b.
   e) all of the above.

10. The Rules of Article 3 of the UCC apply (with rare exception) to:

    a) negotiable instruments.
    b) nonnegotiable instruments.
    c) sales contracts.
    d) a and b.
    e) a and c.

Short Essay

1. a) Checks, drafts, and trade acceptances all share one common element, or characteristic. What is that element?
   b) In what respects do the instruments in (a) above <u>differ from</u> one another?

2. X, Y, and Z were partners in a car racing enterprise and had all of their assets tied up in that operation. They hoped to run one of their cars in the Indianapolis 500 strictly as a money-making venture. Their best car had a track record that indicated a good possibility of finishing "in the money," but they needed $20,000 for a driver's guarantee and miscellaneous other expenses.

   In order to facilitate the raising of $20,000 through a loan from his bank, X went to one of his creditors, C, and talked C into signing a promissory note for $10,000 so that he, X, could list the note as an account receivable on his personal balance sheet which he would show to the bank. C reluctantly signed the note as maker, believing--probably correctly--that his only hope of having his debt paid by X was for X to win big at Indianapolis.

239

Chapter 17

Soon thereafter X died, and later X's estate sued C on the note. C, after proving all of the facts above, contended that he was an <u>accommodation maker</u> of the note, and in that capacity was not liable to X's estate since X was the <u>accommodated party</u>.

The estate claimed that C did <u>not</u> qualify as an accommodation party in view of the fact that C's signing was not "gratuitous"--that is, was not gratuitous since C stood a much better chance of recovering the original debt which X owed him if the X, Y, and Z organization did in fact win at Indianapolis.

Basing your answer on the <u>Darden</u> case in this chapter, do you agree with the estate's claim that C was <u>not</u> an accommodation party? Why or why not?

Chapter 18

Commercial Paper/Negotiability

True-False

1. An instrument must meet all the requirements of negotiability in order for any holder of it to qualify as a holder in due course (HDC).

2. The negotiability or nonnegotiability of an instrument is entirely dependent upon its form and content.

3. The provisions of Article 3 of the UCC apply only to <u>negotiable</u> instruments.

4. The "signing" of one's name through the use of a rubber stamp does <u>not</u> meet the UCC requirement that an instrument be "signed by the maker or drawer."

5. A note, executed in June, provides that it is payable "on the last day of the next World Series." In July, litigation is commenced between the maker and the holder of the note, and one question is whether or not the instrument--as of July--is a negotiable one. Today, in such a case, most courts will probably rule this instrument to be <u>negotiable</u>, since it is very likely that the World Series will, in fact, be played as scheduled in October.

6. In the above case, if the World Series were played in October and the question as to the note's negotiability did not arise until the following November, a court--in November--would almost certainly rule that the note was negotiable in form as of that time.

7. It is possible for an instrument to be payable out of a designated fund and still be a negotiable instrument.

8. If a note or draft expressly provides that it is "subject to" some other (separate) agreement, the instrument is <u>nonnegotiable</u> even if the language of that other agreement in fact does <u>not in any way</u> condition the promise or order of the instrument.

9. X gives Y an instrument that is clearly nonnegotiable on its face because it lacks one of the elements of negotiability (for example, the amount is not certain). The instrument does, however, contain a provision that it is "subject to" some other (separate) agreement, and the terms of that other agreement do, in fact, contain the missing element. In such a case the courts will probably rule that the instrument is a <u>negotiable</u> one.

10. Bonds issued by State X provide that they are "payable only out of the

241

Chapter 18

turnpike revenues of State X." Under the UCC, this clause does not destroy the bonds' negotiability.

11. On February 1 M gives P a $1,000 note that is due in one year, the note further provides that the interest rate is "6% until maturity date, and if unpaid at that time, 8% thereafter." Under the UCC this note is negotiable (i.e., the quoted clause satisfies the "sum certain" requirement).

12. M gives P a note for $1,000. The note contains a provision permitting M, at maturity, to pay the holder $1000 in U.S. money or its equivalent in gold, at M's option. This instrument is nonnegotiable since it does not satisfy the "sum certain in money" requirement.

13. Acceleration clauses in time instruments do not destroy the negotiability of such instruments, even though it is not known at the time of issue whether the event upon which acceleration is based will ever occur.

14. An instrument payable "on or before" a stated date is nonnegotiable for the reason that it is not known, at the time the instrument is issued, just when payment will actually be made.

15. Clauses in time instruments that permit the maker or drawer to extend the time of payment destroy the negotiability of such instruments unless the extension clause contains a "further definite time" of maturity.

16. Clauses in time instruments that permit the holder to extend the time of payment do not destroy the negotiability of such instruments even if they do not contain a new fixed maturity date.

17. A note "payable to X" fails to qualify as a negotiable instrument because it is neither a bearer instrument nor an order instrument.

18. A check is "payable to the order of Alexis Jones or bearer." (The underlined words of the quoted clause appear in the printed check form, while the words "Alexis Jones or bearer" are written in longhand.) In such a case the instrument is a bearer instrument (as distinguished from an order instrument).

19. A note is "payable to the order of X," but it contains a clause prohibiting more than two transfers of the instrument. This note is nonnegotiable.

20. An instrument obligating the maker or drawer "to deliver additional collateral to the holder (of the instrument) if, prior to maturity, the market value of the original collateral suffers any decline in value" is not negotiable.

21. If an instrument is negotiable, when legal problems arise as to enforceability the rights and obligations of the parties are resolved under ordinary contract law.

Chapter 18

22. If an instrument is nonnegotiable, when legal problems arise as to enforceability the rights and obligations of the parties are resolved under Article 3 of the UCC.

23. Commercial paper cannot serve its "substitute for money" and "extension of credit" roles unless it is freely transferable.

24. The negotiability or nonnegotiability of an instrument is entirely dependent upon its form and content.

25. Negotiability of an instrument has no apparent relationship to a HDC.

Multiple Choice

1. Which of the following choices correctly complete(s) this sentence? "In some situations it is necessary for a court to determine whether an instrument is negotiable or nonnegotiable because:

   a) a holder of an instrument who claims to be a holder in due course (HDC) can acquire this status only if the instrument is negotiable."
   b) nonnegotiable instruments are governed by contract law, while negotiable instruments are governed by Article 3 of the UCC."
   c) nonnegotiable instruments (unlike negotiable instruments) cannot be sold, assigned or otherwise transferred."
   d) all of the above choices correctly complete the sentence.
   e) a and b correctly complete the sentence.

2. In order for an instrument to be negotiable, it must:

   a) contain an unconditional promise to pay a sum certain in money, signed by the maker or drawer.
   b) contain no other promise, order, obligation, or power given by the maker or drawer except as authorized by the Article.
   c) be payable on demand or at a definite time and be payable to order or to bearer.
   d) a and c.
   e) all of the above.

3. A clause in a draft that expressly provides that the order is to take effect only upon the happening of a specified event (e.g., "payable upon the retirement of my father"):

   a) destroys the negotiability of the instrument, regardless of other factors.
   b) does not destroy the negotiability of the instrument if all the other elements of negotiability are present.
   c) destroys the negotiability of the instrument unless a court feels, from the other language of the instrument, that the original parties to it clearly intended for it to be negotiable.
   d) none of the above.

Chapter 18

4. A note that is payable out of a specified fund is

   a) nonnegotiable, unless the note is one issued by a government or governmental unit or agency (i.e., is payable out of a governmental fund).
   b) nonnegotiable if it turns out that the designated fund, at maturity, is not sufficiently large to permit payment in full; otherwise, negotiable.
   c) nonnegotiable, regardless of other factors.
   d) none of the above.

5. Which of the following clauses destroy(s) the negotiability of an instrument?

   a) A provision calling for interest to be paid at maturity "at current rates."
   b) A provision in a foreign note (e.g., the amount is 500 francs) payable in this country, providing that the instrument is payable "with exchange."
   c) A provision in a note providing that the holder, at maturity, is entitled to the face amount of the interest "plus costs of collection, if any."
   d) None of the above destroys negotiability.
   e) b and c both destroy negotiability.

6. On June 1 M signs this note: "June 1, 1980. I promise to pay to the order of P $500. (Signed), M." Because this note contains no express due date, the note is, under the UCC:

   a) payable "a reasonable time" after it is issued to the payee.
   b) payable on demand.
   c) payable entirely at the option of M; that is, the note is payable only when and if M wishes to pay it.
   d) none of the above.

7. A note that is payable "on or before" a stated date in the future is held (by most courts) to be:

   a) a demand instrument, and thus negotiable.
   b) indefinite as to time of payment, and thus nonnegotiable.
   c) payable at the stated date, or earlier at the option of the maker, and thus negotiable. (I.e., the "on or before" clause is simply treated as giving the maker the right to pay early if he wishes.)
   d) none of the above.

8. A note is payable at a fixed future date, but contains a clause permitting the maker to extend the time of payment if he wishes. Such a clause:

   a) destroys negotiability, unless the extension clause contains a new, stated maturity date.
   b) does not destroy negotiability, because in such a case the UCC provides that the time of extension shall be "a reasonable time."

Chapter 18

    c) destroys negotiability of the note.
    d) does not destroy negotiability, because such a clause is treated by the courts in the same manner as is an acceleration clause.
    e) none of the above.

9. Under the terms of the UCC a negotiable instrument is "signed":

    a) by affixing the signature in longhand.
    b) by a rubber stamp.
    c) by affixing one's initials.
    d) a and b.
    e) all of the above.

10. The amount to be paid in a negotiable instrument may be:

    a) a sum certain.
    b) a sum certain in goods.
    c) a sum certain in money.
    d) a sum certain in money and/or goods.

Short Essay

1. Under what circumstances, if any, can an instrument be "subject to" another agreement and still be negotiable? Explain.

2. M gives this note to P: "December 1, 1980. I owe P $500 and I hereby promise that my estate will pay that amount to him, no later than 60 days after my death, out of the proceeds of my estate. (Signed) M."

List three reasons why this note is nonnegotiable.

Chapter 19

Commercial Paper/Transfer and Negotiation

True-False

1. Any transfer of a negotiable instrument that fails to qualify as a "negotiation" means that the status of the transferee (the purchaser of the instrument) is merely that of an <u>assignee.</u>

2. If an instrument is clearly a <u>bearer instrument</u> at the time that it is transferred, it may be negotiated by delivery only (i.e., no indorsement whatever is necessary).

3. While it is legally possible for a <u>finder</u> of a bearer instrument to transfer title to a third party, it <u>is</u> not possible for a <u>thief</u> to do so.

4. A note is "payable to the order of P." A thief (T) steals the note, signs P's name on the back of it, and sells it to H. In such a case, if H knew nothing of the forgery and had no reason to be suspicious of T's possession, he (H) qualifies as a <u>holder</u> of the instrument.

5. A note is "payable to the order of P." If P never indorses this note, and never authorizes any person to sign his name to it, no subsequent person would ever qualify as a holder of the instrument.

6. The payee of a check indorses it in blank--that is, he merely signs his name on the back of it--and negotiates it to H. Thereafter, H writes the following above the blank indorsement: "Pay to the order of H." In this situation, under the UCC, the check <u>remains a bearer instrument</u> (i.e., the additional words have no legal effect).

7. An indorsement "Pay to X, (s) P" has the same legal effect as if it read "Pay to the order of X, (s) P."

8. If an instrument is "payable to bearer" on its face, it remains a bearer instrument for the rest of its life, no matter how it might be indorsed.

9. A primary distinction between a qualified (without recourse) indorsement and a blank indorsement is the fact that a qualified indorser has no conditional liability (i.e., he does <u>not</u> promise to pay the instrument himself in case the primary party fails to pay at maturity).

10. While a qualified indorsement <u>transfers</u> title to the instrument to the indorsee, it does <u>not</u> <u>extend</u> <u>any</u> <u>warranties</u> to the indorsee.

11. While a restrictive indorsement does not prohibit further physical <u>transfers</u> of the instrument, such transfers can not qualify as <u>negotiations</u>.

Chapter 19

12. A conditional indorsement is one type of restrictive indorsement.

13. P indorses a note to H "Pay to H when he delivers to me his stock in the XYZ Corporation, (s) P." If M (maker) pays H not noticing the condition in the indorsement, and if the stock is never delivered to P, P probably is entitled to recover the amount of the note from either H or M.

14. When a check bearing a restrictive indorsement is put into the channels of collection, as a general rule intermediary banks are not put on notice or affected by the indorsement. (I.e., such banks are not liable to the restrictive indorser in case the depositary bank acts inconsistently with the indorsement, which causes the indorser a loss.)

15. Under the UCC, an instrument indorsed "pay to X only" can not be further negotiated by X.

16. P indorses a note "to A for the purpose of collection." Since the indorsement is for a special purpose, it is a "special" indorsement.

17. P, payee of a check, transfers it to H but forgets to indorse it. As a general rule, H is permitted by the UCC to sign P's name on the back of the check, and thereafter is permitted to negotiate the check further.

18. P, payee of a check drawn on the X Bank, deposits it in his own bank (Y Bank) but forgets to indorse it. The Y Bank, without P's knowledge, supplies the missing indorsement by writing his name on the back of the instrument. In such a case, since the "indorsement" was not made with P's consent, the Y Bank does not qualify as a "holder" of the instrument.

19. If a minor indorses a check and negotiates it to a third party, he may rescind the indorsement and recover the instrument from the transferee and any subsequent holder who is not an HDC.

20. O, an officer of the X Co. who has the authority to draw checks in the corporate name, draws a check payable to the order of P, a person to whom the X Co. owes no money. O then "indorses" the check by writing P's name on the back of it and cashes it at the drawee bank. In such a case, if the X Co. now sues the bank to recover the amount of the instrument on the theory that O's signing was not an effective indorsement, the X Co. will probably lose because the "fictitious payee" rule is clearly applicable to this situation.

21. The transfer of a nonnegotiable instrument always constitutes an assignment no matter how the transfer is effected.

22. The issuance of an instrument to the payee technically constitutes negotiation, however, in actual practice negotiation refers only to transfers that occur after an instrument has been issued.

23. The following are the four kinds of indorsements: blank, special, personal and unrestricted.

Chapter 19

24. If an order instrument is transferred without the indorsement of the payee, the transferee is a holder of the instrument and therefore can negotiate it.

25. If a payee or other holder of an instrument transfers it to a third party in such a manner that the transfer qualifies as a negotiation, the transferee is a holder of the instrument.

Multiple Choice

1. As a general rule, the legal life of a negotiable instrument does not begin until:

    a) it is negotiated by the payee to a third party.
    b) it is issued by the maker or drawer.
    c) it is signed by the maker or drawer.
    d) the maker or drawer issues it and receives consideration in return for his issuing it.
    e) none of the above.

2. The major difference between a blank indorsement and a qualified indorsement is that:

    a) once an instrument has a qualified indorsement, no subsequent purchaser could qualify as a holder in due course (HDC).
    b) a qualified indorsement contains the name of the indorsee--i.e., "pay to X."
    c) the qualified indorser promises to pay the instrument only if the maker (or drawer) does not pay at maturity and the holder of the instrument gets a judgment against the maker (or drawer) and the judgment is not paid by the maker (or drawer).
    d) none of the above.

3. A negotiation is defined by the UCC as "a transfer of an instrument in such form that:

    a) the transferee qualifies as a holder in due course of the instrument."
    b) the transferee qualifies as a holder of the instrument."
    c) the transferee has the legal ability to negotiate the instrument further."
    d) none of the above.

4. H is in lawful possession of a note payable to bearer, and he wishes to transfer it to X in payment of a debt he owes X. If X is willing to accept the note in payment,

    a) he will have to have H indorse the note in order to be sure that he (X) gets title to the note.
    b) he will have to have H indorse the note in order to be sure that he (X) qualifies as a holder of the note.

Chapter 19

    c) he will not have to have H indorse the note in order for him (X) to acquire title or qualify as an HDC, but he (X) would not be legally able to negotiate the note further without H's indorsement.
    d) a and b.
    e) none of the above.

5. Which of the following statements in regard to blank indorsements is/are true? A blank indorsement:

    a) converts an order instrument into a bearer instrument.
    b) imposes conditional liability on the indorser.
    c) can be converted into a special indorsement by act of the indorsee.
    d) all of the above.
    e) a and b.

6. Which of the following kinds of indorsers make certain warranties to subsequent holders?

    a) blank indorsers.
    b) special indorsers.
    c) qualified indorsers.
    d) all of the above.
    e) a and b.

7. In regard to restrictive indorsements, which of the following is/are true? Restrictive indorsements:

    a) give to the restrictive indorser a certain amount of protection which other indorsers do not have, in the event that the indorsee ignores or fails to act consistently with the provisions of the indorsement.
    b) can be made only by banks (and perhaps some other financial institutions) who acquire commercial paper in the bank collection process.
    c) are, by UCC definition, only those indorsements which indicate that the indorsement is being made solely for the purpose of permitting the indorsee to collect the instrument, at maturity, on behalf of the indorser.
    d) all of the above.
    e) a and b.

8. Which of the following kinds of banks are not given notice of, or otherwise affected by, restrictive indorsements?

    a) intermediary banks, and payor banks which are not the depositary banks.
    b) intermediary banks only.
    c) intermediary banks, and depositary banks.
    d) none of the above is correct.

9. A check is drawn by D in Austin, Texas on an Austin bank, and mailed by D to the payee, P, in Columbus, Ohio. P deposits the check in his account in a Columbus bank, which forwards it to the Austin bank via the First National Bank of Chicago. The Austin Bank then honors the check and charges D's account with it. In this situation:

Chapter 19

    a) the Columbus bank is the <u>payor</u> bank, since it cashed the check for P.
    b) the Columbus and Chicago banks are both <u>intermediary</u> banks, since neither of them is the drawee.
    c) the Columbus bank is the <u>depositary</u> bank, and the Austin bank the <u>payor</u> bank.
    d) none of the above.

10. If the "fictitious payee" rule is applicable to a given situation, the usual result is that:

    a) the drawer of a check, who had no actual intent that the designated payee really be given the proceeds of the check, <u>can recover</u> the amount of the check from the drawee bank.
    b) the drawer of a check can <u>not recover</u> the amount of the check from the drawee bank, even though he (drawer) did not actually intend that the designated payee ever to have the proceeds of the check.
    c) a dishonest employee who prepares a check on behalf of his employer, the drawer, (and thereby obtains money which he is not entitled to), is <u>permitted to keep</u> the money (i.e., he is not liable to his employer for the amount of the check).
    d) a and c.
    e) b and c.

11. An <u>assignment</u> is defined by Article 3 as a transfer of an instrument in such form that:

    a) transferee qualifies as HDC of the instrument.
    b) transferee qualifies as holder of the instrument.
    c) Article 3 does not define an assignment and the transferee's rights are governed by common law contract rules.
    d) none of the above.

12. A qualified indorsement is one whose wording indicates that the indorser is:

    a) not guaranteeing payment.
    b) limiting the amount the indorser will pay.
    c) agreeing to pay only when certain conditions are met.

Short Essay

1. Explain the distinguishing characteristics of blank, special, qualified, and restrictive indorsements, insofar as their <u>legal effects</u> are concerned.

2. P is the payee of a $500 check drawn on the X Bank, and he indorses it "For deposit in the Wheel and Deal Company account only, (s) P." B, a business associate of P, finds the check among some of his business papers and takes it to the Y Bank, where he asks that it be cashed. The Y bank does so, giving B̄ five $100 bills in exchange for it.

Chapter 19

a) If the money never reaches the Wheel and Deal Company, what are P's chances of recovering the $500 from the Y Bank (the depositary bank)? Explain.

b) If the money never reaches the Wheel and Deal Company, what are P's chances of recovering the $500 from the X Bank, the drawee bank? Explain. (Assume that the drawee bank, when it honored the check when it was presented for payment, did not know of the circumstances under which the check was cashed.)

Chapter 20

Commercial Paper/Holders in Due Course

True-False

1. It is not possible for a person to be a holder in due course (HDC) of a nonnegotiable instrument.

2. It is not possible for a person to be an HDC of an instrument unless he has given "value" for it.

3. A check is negotiated by P (payee) to H on January 5, with H promising to pay P $100 for it by the following January 25th. At this point--January 5--H has now given "value," as that term is defined by the UCC.

4. It is possible in some circumstances for a person to be an HDC even though he is clearly <u>not</u> a "holder" as that term is defined by the UCC.

5. A person who steals or finds a negotiable <u>bearer note</u> is a "holder" of such instrument, as that term is defined by the UCC.

6. A note is "payable to the bearer." The first holder, X, endorses it "Pay to Y, (signed X)" and delivers it to Y. In this situation, if the instrument got out of Y's possession <u>without</u> Y's endorsement, no subsequent taker would be a holder.

7. Under the UCC, a person cannot qualify as an HDC of an instrument if, at the time he acquired it, it was "incomplete" in any respect (that is, contained a blank--an unfilled blank--of any kind).

8. If a person receives a check that has, in fact, been <u>materially altered</u> since it was originally issued, such person may qualify as an HDC, nevertheless, if the alteration was not apparent in any way. (Assume no negligence on part of the taker.)

9. For the purposes of determining whether a holder of a check took it before it was "overdue," the UCC presumes that a check is overdue only after it has circulated more than <u>60 days.</u> (E.g., if check is dated and issued March 1, and holder requires it by May 1, he will be HDC assuming all other requirements are met.)

10. An HDC takes an instrument free of personal defenses, but subject to real defenses.

11. P has $500 in his checking account in Bank X. On October 1 he receives a $100 check (payable to him) which is drawn on an out-of-town bank, and on that same day he deposits it in his account. In the next week P draws checks on his account totalling $110, which were honored by the X Bank. At this point the X Bank <u>has given value</u> for the $100 check.

Chapter 20

12. When the question arises in a particular case whether the holder took the instrument in "good faith," the general test is whether the holder took the instrument honestly (rather than whether he exercised <u>reasonable care</u> in taking the instrument).

13. If a promissory note is due on August 1, a purchaser who acquires it within a reasonable time after August 1 may qualify as an HDC (assuming he meets the other HDC requirements).

14. If a person acquires an instrument when it is clearly overdue, he will <u>not</u> qualify as an HDC even if he made a diligent effort (before acquiring it) to determine whether a defense existed, and could find none.

15. If a third party acquires an instrument knowing at the time that the maker or drawer has a valid defense against the payee, it is still possible for the third party to qualify as an HDC as long as he (third party) was not in any way responsible for the existence of the defense. (i.e., as long as the defense did not grow out of any misconduct on the part of the third party).

16. A material alteration of an instrument does not necessarily prevent a subsequent holder from qualifying as an HDC.

17. As a general rule, a person who fails to qualify as an HDC of a negotiable instrument stands in no better position than an assignee of a nonnegotiable instrument.

18. A draft goes from drawer to P (payee), to X (1st indorsee), to Y (2nd indorsee), to H. X qualifies as an HDC, but Y and H do not. In such a situation, H has <u>all the rights of an HDC</u> since a prior owner (X) did qualify as an HDC.

19. X acquires an instrument, negotiates it to Y, who negotiates it to Z. Thereafter Z negotiates it back to X. In such a case, if X did not qualify as an HDC when he first acquired the instrument, X (upon reacquiring the instrument) will <u>not</u> be a "holder with the rights of an HDC" even if Y or Z qualified as an HDC.

Multiple Choice

1. M issues a bearer note to H, and thereafter T steals it from him. In such a case:

   a) T is a holder of the instrument.
   b) T has title to the instrument.

Chapter 20

    c) T is legally capable of transferring title to an innocent purchaser.
    d) a and b.
    e) a and c.

2. H is a holder of a negotiable instrument, but he fails to qualify as an HDC because he did not give value for it. In such a case,

    a) H is entitled to payment of the instrument at maturity, even though he is not an HDC, if the primary party has no defense.
    b) H is entitled to payment of the instrument at maturity even if the primary party possesses a personal defense, as long as H did not know of the existence of the defense when he acquired it.
    c) H is not entitled to payment of the instrument at maturity, regardless of whether or not the primary party has a defense.
    d) a and b.
    e) none of the above.

3. A check is drawn by D and issued to P. P negotiates the check to H, and thereafter the question arises whether or not H is a holder for value. In such a situation, H has given value if he:

    a) promises, in a letter, to pay P a specified sum of money (in exchange for the check) at a specified later date.
    b) took the instrument in payment for a past due debt owed him by P.
    c) gave P, in exchange for the check, either a negotiable or a non-negotiable instrument that is payable to the order of P.
    d) a and c.
    e) b and c.

4. D draws a check on the X Bank and issues it to P, who lives in another city. P deposits the check in his checking account at his bank, the Y Bank. The check is presented through banking channels to the X Bank, which refuses to honor it because of a stop payment order issued by D. The check is thus returned to the Y Bank. At this point, the Y Bank:

    a) usually has the contractual right to charge P's account with the amount of the check (in which case it will then return the check to P, its depositor).
    b) has clearly given value for the check, since it credited P's account with the amount of the check at the time it first acquired it.
    c) both of the above.
    d) none of the above.

5. As a general rule, a check presumably is overdue:

    a) 30 days after the date of its first negotiation.
    b) 60 days after its issue.
    c) 30 days after its issue.
    d) none of the above.

6. A time note is issued by M to P (payee), who negotiates it to A as a birthday present. A subsequently negotiates the note to B, who gives A

Chapter 20

value for it and who purchases it before it is overdue, and without knowledge of any defenses. Later, B renegotiates the note to A in full payment of a debt which B owed A. In such a case:

a) it appears that A was an HDC when he first acquired the note.
b) if A did not qualify as an HDC when he first acquired the note, he would--upon reacquiring it--be a holder "with all the rights of an HDC" if B qualified as an HDC.
c) if A did not qualify as an HDC when he first acquired the note, he would not--upon reacquiring it--have all the rights of an HDC for the reason that a reacquirer can not improve his position.
d) a and b.
e) a and c.

7. The payee of a negotiable note:

a) may qualify as an HDC even if a defense of some kind exists in favor of the maker, as long as the defense was not the result of any misconduct on the part of the payee and was not known to the payee when he acquired it.
b) may not, under the UCC, qualify as an HDC under any circumstances.
c) may, under some circumstances, qualify as an HDC--but only if the maker of the note possesses no defense against it.
d) may, under some circumstances, qualify as an HDC even if a defense exists in favor of the maker, and even if the defense arose out of some default or other misconduct on the part of the payee.
e) none of the above.

8. The purpose of the "inferable knowledge" test is to help courts determine whether a holder of an instrument:

a) actually knew a defense existed at the time he acquired the instrument.
b) had actual knowledge of facts from which he could reasonably infer that a defense existed at the time he acquired the instrument.
c) had actual knowledge of facts from which he could reasonably infer that the instrument was nonnegotiable in form.
d) failed to exercise due diligence in acquiring the instrument.
e) none of the above.

9. A major purpose of Article 3 of the UCC is to facilitate negotiation of commercial paper by:

a) spelling out the requirements that must be met by a purchaser in order to acquire the status of HDC.
b) identifying the specific kinds of defenses that are cut off after attaining HDC status.
c) establishing all the pleadings that are necessary to prosecute the HDC instrument.
d) a and b.
e) all of the above.

Chapter 20

10. A holder in due course is a holder who takes the instrument:

    a) for value.
    b) in good faith.
    c) without notice that it is overdue or has been dishonored or of any defense or claim to it on the part of any person.
    d) all of the above.
    e) a and c.

11. In the case of <u>Salter</u> v. <u>Vanotti</u> the issue to be determined was whether Salter qualified as a Holder in Due Course. The court determined that Salter failed to qualify on which of the following points:

    a) purchased for value.
    b) without notice.
    c) good faith.
    d) a and b.
    e) all of the above.

12. The "shelter provision" of Article 3 is designed to protect:

    a) HDC.
    b) ordinary holder.
    c) holder through a HDC.
    d) none of the above.

Short Essay

1. a) Indicate in what general type of situation a holder of a negotiable instrument will be able to obtain payment of the instrument even if he does <u>not</u> qualify as an HDC.
   b) Indicate in what general type of situation an HDC of a negotiable instrument will be able to obtain payment of the instrument even if the maker or drawer possesses some kind of defense.

2. The P Co. contracted to install storm windows on D's home for $1100. When the work was substantially commenced the president of the P Co. persuaded D to give him a check for the full purchase price. The check was payable to the order of the P Co. and was drawn on D's bank, the XYZ Bank.

   The next day the president of the P Co. had the check cashed at an out-of-town bank, the B Bank. The B Bank then put the check into the channels of collection, only to find that the drawee bank (XYZ Bank) refused to honor it because of a stop payment order issued by D as a result of the P Co.'s failure to complete the job. The check was thus returned to the B Bank, and the B Bank now sues D, drawer, to recover the amount of the check.

Chapter 20

In the action of the B Bank v. D, D admitted that the bank had given value for the instrument and had acquired it before it was overdue and without notice of the P Co.'s breach of contract, but D did claim that the B Bank was not an HDC because it took the check in bad faith. Most of D's claim of bad faith was based on testimony of several officers of other banks in the area that in their opinion the B Bank clearly was guilty of negligence in the transaction--that is, clearly failed to live up to acceptable commercial standards--by taking the instrument from the president of the P Co. without requiring identification, by permitting the president (with whom it had not done business before) to receive cash before the check had cleared the drawee bank, and by not having an officer of the B Bank approve the payment before it was made.

On the basis of the above facts only, do you think the B Bank probably failed to take the instrument in good faith? Explain.

Chapter 21

Commercial Paper/Defenses

True-False

1. The fact that an instrument is nonnegotiable does not, in and of itself, constitute a defense (i.e., the maker of a nonnegotiable note must pay the holder at maturity of he has no defense).

2. Real defenses can be successfully asserted against both ordinary holders and holders in due course (HDCs).

3. The drawer of a check issues it to the payee in payment for services to be rendered by him under a contract with the drawer, and thereafter the payee fails to perform those services. In such a case the drawer possesses only a "personal" defense.

4. Breach of contract is a universal or real defense.

5. Lack of failure of consideration can be raised as a defense against a holder and a HDC.

6. "Discharge in bankruptcy" is a real defense.

7. D buys goods from P and gives P a check in payment for them, and P negotiates it to H. If it turns out that the goods are defective, D may successfully assert that defense against H even if he is an HDC.

8. Fraud in the inducement occurs when a person knowingly signs a negotiable instrument after being induced to do so by intentional misrepresentation.

9. Nondelivery or conditional delivery is a good defense as to a HDC.

10. The defenses of intoxication, illegality, and fraud can be either personal or real defenses, depending upon the exact nature of each in a particular situation.

11. In some circumstances a person can have the rights of a HDC even though they have not met the requirements of being an HDC.

12. In most circumstances, "duress" is merely a personal defense.

13. A negotiable instrument executed by a minor is void.

14. If a person signs a negotiable instrument honestly believing that it is some other type of document or agreement (e.g., a lease), he is not liable to an HDC even if he was guilty of negligence in failing to determine the true nature of the instrument.

Chapter 21

15. If a note is materially altered after it leaves the hands of the maker, as a general rule a subsequent HDC is entitled to enforce the instrument according to its original tenor.

16. M issues a note that is subsequently altered. If the alteration is not a "material" one, any subsequent holder of the instrument is normally entitled to enforce it according to its original terms.

17. M issues a $200 note to P. Later it is altered to $500. A subsequent holder of this note who qualifies as an HDC is entitled to recover $200 from M at maturity.

18. In the above case, a subsequent holder of the note who did not qualify as an HDC is still entitled to recover $200 from M at maturity as long as he (the holder) did not know of the alteration, and had no reason to believe that it had been altered.

19. In the last few years, various state statutes have been enacted for the purpose of enlarging the rights of holders of certain credit instruments against the makers and drawers of such instruments which they (the makers and drawers) issued in payment for the purchase of consumer goods.

20. Under the "FTC Rule," the maker or drawer of a credit instrument which was issued in payment for the purchase of consumer goods may--as a general rule--assert against all subsequent purchasers of such instrument any defense which he (maker or drawer) may possess which grows out of a breach of contract (or some other misconduct) on the part of the seller of the goods.

Multiple Choice

1. The main advantage of being an HDC is that this status, as a general rule:

    a) cuts off personal defenses.
    b) cuts off real defenses.
    c) cuts off both types of defenses.
    d) none of the above.

2. Which of the following conditions or defenses will prevent an HDC from recovering against the maker of a bearer note, M?

    a) theft of the instrument from M.(Assume instrument was complete at time of theft.)
    b) breach of contract on the part of the payee.
    c) lack of consideration.
    d) a and b.
    e) none of the above.

Chapter 21

3. In August M issues a note to P, payable to the order of P, which is due the following December 1st. In early October P indorses it in blank, intending to negotiate it soon, but 2 days later M unexpectedly offers to pay it off. P accepts the money, but forgets to return the note to M. In November the note is stolen from P's home and is sold to H, who does not know of the theft. On December 1st H demands payment of the note from M. In this situation:

   a) M has no liability to H, even if he is an HDC, since he (M) actually paid the note once.
   b) M is liable to H if he is an HDC; otherwise not.
   c) the name of M's defense in this case is "nondelivery of an instrument."
   d) a and c.
   e) none of the above.

4. Which of the following defenses may generally be asserted by the maker of a note against an <u>ordinary</u> holder?

   a) fraud in the inducement ("ordinary fraud").
   b) fraud in the execution.
   c) breach of contract on the part of the payee.
   d) all of the above.
   e) a and c only.

5. Which of the following defenses may be successfully asserted by the maker of a note against an HDC?

   a) breach of contract on the part of the payee.
   b) unauthorized completion.
   c) material alteration (to the extent of alteration, only)
   d) nondelivery of a completed instrument.
   e) b and d.

6. A major purpose underlying passage of the "FTC Rule" was a desire on the part of the FTC (and others):

   a) to cut down on the use of personal checks by buyers of consumer goods.
   b) to help cut down on inflationary pressures by making it much more difficult for prospective purchasers of consumer goods to borrow money from banks in order to purchase such goods.
   c) cut down, as much as possible, situations in which a buyer of consumer goods would pay for such goods by giving a credit instrument to the seller of the goods, and, subsequently, be required to pay an HDC the full amount of the instrument even though he (the consumer buyer) received defective goods from the seller, or received goods that were not as warranted, or did not receive the purchased goods at all.
   d) all of the above are major purposes of the rule.

Chapter 21

7. A check is drawn in the amount of $1,000 and is later altered to read $7,000. (Assume that figures and writing are both changed.) For some reason or other, payment is stopped on the check by the drawer, so now H (holder) sues D (drawer) for the $7,000. In this case, assuming no negligence on part of drawer:

   a) if H is an HDC, he is entitled to recover the $7,000.
   b) if H is only an ordinary holder, and if the alteration is found to be fraudulent and material, he recovers nothing.
   c) neither of the above.
   d) a and b.

8. S sells a prize winning dog to B for $200, who gives his personal check to S in payment. S then negotiates the check to Fix-em-up Vets, Inc., in payment of veterinarian bills owed that company. B then learns that the dog had been stolen by S, and he stops payment on the check. If Fix-em-up Vets now sues B (drawer) on the check,

   a) B has no liability, because his defense in this case (illegality) is a real defense.
   b) B has no liability, because his defense in this case (fraud in the inducement) is a real defense.
   c) B has no liability, because his defense in this case (delivery of defective title) is a real defense.
   d) B _is_ liable, assuming Fix-em-up Vets is an HDC, for B's defense in this case is clearly not a real defense.
   e) none of the above.

Short Essay

1. Simply list four personal defenses, and four real defenses.

2. The XYZ Co. bought a used truck from Friendly Bob, a used car dealer, giving FB its $3,000 check in payment. FB deposited the XYZ check in his checking account in the B Bank. Thereafter FB drew several checks on its account in the B Bank, believing that the XYZ check was good. That check, however, was not good--i.e., it was dishonored by the XYZ Co.'s bank--and thereafter it was returned to the B Bank.

   The B Bank then charged FB's account with the amount of the check, $3,000, thereby creating an overdraft in FB's account. Later FB made several deposits in his account, and the B Bank was then able to properly charge his account with the $3,000 check. For some reason, however, this check was not returned by the B Bank to FB, as normally would have been done. Instead, the B Bank kept the check, perhaps by mistake, and later it indorsed the check to Sooper Dooper stores in partial payment of a claim that Sooper Dooper stores had against the B Bank.

   Sooper Dooper then presented the check to the drawer, XYZ Co., and demanded payment of it. When XYZ Co. refused, Sooper Dooper sued it on the check. In the case of Sooper Dooper v. XYZ Co., the XYZ Co. (drawer

Chapter 21

of the check) raised two defenses. First, it alleged that it had the defense of "fraud in the inducement" against Friendly Bob (the payee), claiming he misrepresented the truck. Secondly, it claimed the defense of "prior payment," in view of the fact that the B Bank actually was able to charge, and did charge, FB's account with the amount of the instrument.

Assuming that Sooper Dooper is a holder in due course of the check, rule on the validity of the XYZ Co.'s defenses. Explain your reasoning.

Chapter 22

Commercial Paper/Liability of the Parties

True-False

1. As a general rule a primary party is absolutely liable on an instrument, while a secondary party is conditionally liable on the instrument.

2. A is an agent of P, principal. P authorizes A to sign a note as maker in P's name (e.g., "P, by A, agent"). In fact, A simply signs the note in his own name. In such a case, assuming P's name appears nowhere on the instrument, he (P) can not be held liable on it by a subsequent holder, despite the fact that he actually did authorize the issuance of the note in the first place.

3. D draws a draft on X, payable to the order of P. P indorses the draft to H, who gives value for it. Soon thereafter, P--who happens to be a minor--disaffirms his indorsement and recovers the instrument from H. In such a situation, if H loses any money as a result of the disaffirmance, he can probably hold D liable on one of his (D's) "admissions" (or warranties).

4. If a drawee of an ordinary draft does accept it when it is presented to him, his liability on the instrument is very similar to that of a maker of a note.

5. H is holder of a time draft that matures "August 17, 1980." On April 1, 1979, H presents the draft to the drawee for his acceptance, and the drawee refuses to accept. In such a case the refusal is not a dishonor if the presentment for acceptance was optional, rather than required.

6. As a general rule, the unqualified indorser of a note is freed of his conditional (secondary) liability if the note is not "properly presented" for payment. ("Properly" means at the right time, right place, etc. as specified by the UCC.)

7. As a general rule, a late notice of dishonor frees an indorser of his conditional liability to the same extent as a late presentment for payment.

8. As a general rule, where a note is payable at a specified time at a designated bank, the failure of that bank either before or after the maturity date frees the maker of the note of liability to the holder to the extent that the maker suffered a financial loss as a result of the bank's failure.

9. The liability of makers of notes and indorsers of notes is similar in that-- as a general rule--a late presentment of the instrument for payment frees both such parties of liability on the instrument.

Chapter 22

10. A note is payable at the X Bank on August 1, 1980. H, the holder, does not present it to the bank until August 20, only to learn at that time that the bank failed August 10. In such a case, if the maker suffered a total loss of his funds in the bank as a result of its failure, he (maker) is entirely freed of liability to H.

11. Under some circumstances, an indorser of an instrument is a primary party.

12. In general, an indorser is freed of both his promissory and warranty liability if the holder of the instrument fails to make a proper presentment for payment (e.g., the holder does not present at all, or makes a late presentment).

13. D issues a draft to P, and the draft is not one of those where presentment for acceptance is mandatory. In such a case, P (or any subsequent holder) still has the right to make an optional presentment for acceptance, even if the draft was a demand instrument.

14. A check is issued by D to P on March . On March 9 P indorses it to X, and on March 15 X indorses it to H. On March 20 H presents it to the drawee bank, which dishonors it because of insufficient funds in D's account. In such a case, since H presented it for payment within seven days of the last indorsement, he (H) may now hold either of the prior indorsers liable on their indorsements.

15. Blank, special, and qualified indorsers all have conditional (promissory) liability and warranty liability.

16. A transferor of an instrument has warranty liability only if he receives consideration from his transferee. (E.g., if holder of instrument makes a gift of it to X, holder makes no warranties to X even if holder indorses it.)

17. When a holder of a bearer instrument negotiates it "by delivery only," any warranties which the holder/transferor makes extend only to his immediate transferee.

18. A person who negotiates a bearer instrument by "delivery only" has no conditional liability.

19. A promissory note is due January 10, 1981. Under the UCC, any presentment for payment after January 10 (assuming it is a regular business day) is a late presentment.

20. As a general rule, an accommodation indorser is not liable to the holder of the instrument in case of default unless he (the accommodation party) was given some consideration for his signing.

Chapter 22

Multiple Choice

1. P negotiates a <u>demand note</u>, by blank indorsement, to H. In order to hold P on his conditional liability in the event of a default by the maker, H must present the instrument for payment:

   a) within a reasonable time after the note was issued.
   b) within 30 days after the note was issued.
   c) within 7 days after P indorsed the note.
   d) within a reasonable time after P indorsed the note.
   e) none of the above.

2. A note is apparently signed by M, maker, and is payable to the order of P. P indorses the note to H, who is unable to obtain payment because M's signature is proved to be a forgery. In this case:

   a) P (indorser) is liable to H regardless of whether or not he (P) knew of the forgery when he negotiated the instrument to H (i.e., P warranted the instrument to be genuine).
   b) P is liable to H only if he knew, or should have known, of the forgery at the time he negotiated the instrument to H.
   c) if P has any liability to H, it would be on the "warranty of title" theory.
   d) a and b.
   e) none of the above.

3. A qualified (without recourse) indorser warrants--among other things--that:

   a) he will pay the instrument to any subsequent holder if such holder is not able to collect from the primary party at maturity.
   b) he has no knowledge that his title is defective.
   c) he has no knowledge of the existence of a defense.
   d) b and c.
   e) none of the above.

4. A person who negotiates a bearer instrument by "delivery only" (i.e., without indorsing it):

   a) incurs no conditional (promissory) liability to subsequent holders.
   b) incurs conditional liability, but only to his immediate transferee.
   c) makes the same warranties as unqualified indorsers, but they extend only to his immediate transferee.
   d) a and c.
   e) a, b, and c.

5. An accommodation party:

   a) is liable to a subsequent holder of the instrument only after the holder brings suit (and obtains judgment) against the accommodated party.
   b) ordinarily incurs both conditional and warranty liability to subsequent

Chapter 22

      holders.
- c) does not possess the "right of reimbursement" against the accommodated party (in the event that he--accommodation party--has to pay the holder of the instrument at maturity).
- d) a and b.
- e) a, b, and c.

6. Which of the following acts by the holder of an instrument constitutes the cancellation of that instrument?

   a) marking the instrument "paid".
   b) destroying the instrument, intentionally or unintentionally.
   c) striking out the name of a prior indorser.
   d) all of the above.
   e) a and b.

7. A note bearing three successive indorsements, A, B, and C, is purchased by H. In regard to such a situation, which of the following statements is/are true?

   a) If H released indorser A, this would probably also release indorsers B and C even if H expressly "reserves his rights" against B and C.
   b) If H released indorser A without "reserving his rights" against B and C, B and C would still probably be liable, as indorsers, to H if the note were dishonored.
   c) both of the above.
   d) none of the above.

8. P, payee of a note, indorses it to X, X indorses it to Y, and Y thereafter indorses it to P, the original owner. In such a situation,

   a) indorsers X and Y are freed of liability to P.
   b) if P should recirculate the note further, indorsers X and Y would be freed of liability to all subsequent purchasers.
   c) both of the above.
   d) none of the above.

9. All parties to commercial paper fall into which of the following categories:

   a) dominant parties, servient.
   b) primary parties, secondary parties.
   c) all of the above.
   d) none of the above.

10. The maker of a note is primarily liable on the instrument:

    a) even if the holder does not make demand on due date.
    b) but is discharged by the fact that the instrument is presented for payment late.
    c) is totally discharged after the statute of limitations has run.
    d) none of the above.

Chapter 22

Short Essay

1. List the five warranties made by an unqualified indorser of a negotiable instrument.

2. D draws a check on Drawee Bank on October 1 and issues it to P, payee, on that date. P indorses the instrument on October 10 to the X Company in payment for supplies purchased by P.

    The X Company indorses the check to the Y Company on November 4. The Y Company presents the check to Drawee Bank for payment on November 10, only to learn that the bank failed on November 5.

    a) The Y Company now seeks to hold D (drawer) on the instrument, and D claims that he is fully--or at least partially--discharged of liability because of the Y Company's late presentment. In this case, does D remain fully liable on the instrument, only partially liable, or does he have no liability at all? Explain fully.

    b) Suppose, in the basic fact-pattern initially presented, that the Y Company chooses to bring action against the indorsers, P and the X Company, rather than against D (perhaps because D's whereabouts after November 10 are completely unknown).

    Indiate what liability--if any--P and the X Company have to the Y Company. (Assume both indorsements were blank indorsements.)

Chapter 23

Commercial Paper/Checks and the Bank-Depositor Relationship

True-False

1. If a holder of a check presents it for payment to the drawee bank more than 30 days after it was issued, the drawer is not in any way, shape, or form discharged of liability if the drawee bank has remained solvent during the entire time period (i.e., the bank is solvent at the time of issue and remains solvent at the time of the actual presentment).

2. While checks are one type of commercial paper, they are the same as promissory notes and drafts.

3. C, a creditor of D, accepts a check drawn by D in payment of the debt, and he gives D a "paid in full" written receipt. Such a receipt is merely conditional (i.e., if the check is not honored by the drawee bank, D remains liable to C on the debt).

4. Once a check is certified, the drawer is thereby discharged even if he was the party who obtained the certification.

5. The certification of a check by the drawee bank is absolutely final (i.e., there are no circumstances in which the certification may be revoked).

6. Under the UCC, a drawee bank is not permitted to honor "stale" checks.

7. D has a checking account in the X Bank, and he dies on November 10. The X Bank officers learn of his death on November 12. In such a case, the X Bank has no right to honor checks drawn by D that are presented to it after November 12.

8. When a bank customer deposits cash and checks (of which he is the payee) in the bank's night depository safe, a bailor-bailee relationship between the customer and the bank is created.

9. On June 18 at 9 a.m. D gives a stop payment order via telephone to his bank, only to be told by the bank's cashier that it was the bank's policy that stop payment orders had to be in writing. At 2 p.m. D did sign a stop payment order at the bank, but the check in question (it was learned later) had in fact been honored by the bank at noon that same day. In such a case, the bank is not liable to D even if he suffered a loss as a result of the honoring of the instrument (i.e., the oral stop-payment order is ineffective).

Chapter 23

10. Many banks have clauses in their stop payment order forms which provide that the banks shall not be liable to the depositor in the event that they pay the check "through inadvertency or oversight." The courts of most states take the view that such a provision is <u>invalid</u> (i.e., if depositor can prove negligence, the provision does not free the bank).

11. Once a check is certified, a valid stop-payment order <u>cannot thereafter be issued</u> by the drawer, regardless of whether it was he (the drawer) who obtained the certification, or a subsequent holder who obtained the certification.

12. The possible liability of a drawer of a check is greater than that of a drawer of a draft in that the drawer of the check may have both civil <u>and criminal</u> liability in the event the check is dishonored because of insufficient funds (whereas the drawer's liability is civil, only).

13. D draws a check payable to the order of P, and thereafter issues a stop payment order to the drawee bank. If the bank, without legal excuse or justification, should thereafter ignore the stop payment order and pay the check when it is presented, the bank is--under the UCC--liable to D as a <u>matter of law</u> (i.e., the bank is not permitted to escape liability by proving that D suffered no loss as a result of its misconduct).

14. If a written stop payment order expires, and if the drawee bank <u>thereafter</u> honors the check without getting authorization of the drawer to do so, the bank is liable to the drawer for the amount of the check as <u>a matter of law</u> (i.e., the bank is liable even though it may have paid the instrument in good faith).

15. A check is apparently drawn by D, payable to the order of P, and is endorsed in blank by P to H. H obtains payment from the drawee bank, and the bank some time thereafter learns that the signature of D (drawer) is a forgery. In this case, the bank is ordinarily entitled to recover the amount of the check from H, even if H knew nothing of the forgery, for the reason that a person who surrenders a check to the drawee bank warrants that the signature of the drawer is genuine.

16. If a drawee bank honors a check apparently drawn by one of its depositors (D) and later learns that D's signature (through no neglect on his part) is a <u>forgery</u>, the bank must recredit D's account with the amount of the check even though it honored the instrument in good faith and without knowledge of the forgery.

17. In the above situation, after the bank learns of the forgery, it has the right to recover the amount of the check from the person who obtained payment of the check (i.e., the person who surrendered the check to the bank).

18. A check goes from D (drawer) to P, to X, and to H. At the time that H acquires the instrument it bears what appear to be the indorsements of P and X. H surrenders the instrument to the drawee bank and obtains pay-

Chapter 23

ment of it. If the bank later learns that the indorsement of P was forged, the bank may recover the amount of the check from H, the surrenderer, on a breach of warranty of title theory.

Multiple Choice

1. If a bank certifies a check, this means that:

   a) the bank is liable on the instrument to the party obtaining the certification, but not to any subsequent holders.
   b) the bank is liable on the instrument to the party obtaining the certification, and to all subsequent holders, unless the drawer stops payment on the check.
   c) any person who indorsed the instrument before, or after, the certification is discharged of liability.
   d) a and c.
   e) none of the above.

2. In regard to "stale" checks, indicate which of the following statements is/are true. (Assume no certification.)

   a) Such a check is defined as one that is presented to the drawee bank more than 30 days after its issue.
   b) The drawee bank is under no obligation to honor such a check, but may do so if it wishes.
   c) The drawee bank is prohibited by the UCC from honoring such a check.
   d) a and b.
   e) a and c.

3. In regard to stop payment orders, which of the following statements is/are true?

   a) Such an order may be issued either by the drawee or the payee of a check.
   b) Such an order, if disobeyed by the drawee bank, causes the bank to be liable to the drawer if he suffers a loss as a result of the wrongful payment, but not otherwise.
   c) Such an order, under the UCC, has no effect unless it is in writing.
   d) b and c.
   e) none of the above.

4. Once a check has been certified,

   a) the drawee bank must honor it even if it is clearly stale when presented for payment.
   b) the drawee bank cannot, under any circumstances, revoke its certification.
   c) the drawee bank must honor it--as a general rule--even if the drawer issued a stop payment order after the certification occurred.

Chapter 23

  d) all of the above.
  e) a and c.

5. A drawee bank honors 20 checks apparently drawn by D during the month o July, and returns the cancelled checks to him on August 2. Two of the checks are, in fact, forgeries. If D does not give the bank notice of these forgeries within 14 days,

  a) D has lost his right to require the bank to recredit his account with the amount of either check.
  b) D has lost his right to require the bank to recredit his account with the amount of the second forgery, only.
  c) D probably still possesses the right to require the bank to recredit his account with the amount of both checks (but not as to forged checks honored after August 16).
  d) none of the above.

6. A check goes from D to P to H. The drawee bank honors the check by paying H, and the bank then charges D's (drawer's) account. Later, it develops that the indorsement of P (payee) was a forgery. In this situation, normally:

  a) the bank must credit D's account with the amount of the check, even if it did not know the indorsement was forged, and even if it was not guilty of negligence of any kind.
  b) the bank may recover the amount of the check from H, even if he did not know of the forged indorsement, because by surrendering it H warranted he had title.
  c) the bank may recover the amount of the check from H if--and only if-- H knew of the forgery (or should have known of it).
  d) a and b.
  e) a and c.

7. When the holder of a check (H) surrenders it to the drawee bank for payment, and the drawee bank later learns that the signature of the drawer was forged,

  a) the bank cannot recover the amount of the check from H (assuming he did not know, and had no reason to know, of the forgery).
  b) the bank can recover the amount of the check from H, regardless of whether he did or did not know of the forgery.
  c) neither of the above.

8. A holder of a check who presents it for payment to the drawee bank warrants, among other things, that:

  a) the instrument has not been materially altered.
  b) he has no knowledge that the instrument has been materially altered.
  c) he has good title to the instrument.
  d) a and c.
  e) b and c.

271

Chapter 23

9. The rule that the drawee bank is liable to its depositor in the case of forgery does not apply if:

   a) the drawer was guilty of negligence.
   b) the instrument was materially altered.
   c) the drawer was guilty of negligence that substantially contributed to the forgery.
   d) a and b.
   e) b and c.

10. When a bank pays on an altered check and no negligence exists on the part of the drawer:

    a) the loss is borne by the bank.
    b) the loss is borne by the drawer because the bank can charge the drawer's account the full amount of the check.
    c) the bank is entitled to collect its loss from FDIC (Federal Deposit Insurance Company).
    d) the bank is entitled to recover that loss from the person who surrendered the instrument for payment.

Short Essay

1. The rules spelling out the liabilities and duties that exist between the drawer of a check and the drawee bank arise from four different sources. List those sources.

2. P contracted to paint the rooms in a duplex owned by D for $850. When the work was approximately one-half done, on September 1, D issued P a check for $850 drawn on the X Bank. On September 3 P negotiated the check to the Latex Company in partial payment for a paint bill he had owed it for some time.

   On September 5 D issued a stop payment order on the check after a dispute arose between him and P, during which P flatly refused to do any more of the work. On September 6 the Latex Company presented the check to the X Bank for payment, and the bank negligently honored it and charged D's account with the $850. When the bank refused to recredit D's account, he sued it to recover the amount of the check.

   At the trial of D vs. the X Bank, the bank admitted that its payment of the check was wrongful, but claimed that D suffered no loss if the Latex Company was an HDC of the check. When the bank offered to prove that the Latex Company was an HDC, the trial judge ruled that such proof was inadmissible for the reason that the bank was liable to D regardless of whether or not the Latex Company qualified as an HDC.

   Is the judge's ruling correct? Why or why not?

Chapter 24

Secured Transactions

True-False

1. A security agreement is an agreement by which the debtor conveys to the creditor an interest in specific personal property owned by the debtor.

2. A secured transaction has a dual purpose, that is, to give the creditor a specific interest in the debtors property and to establish a priority claim in and to the property.

3. As a general rule, if an unpaid seller of goods lawfully retakes possession of the goods, his interest is thereby perfected without the aid of Article 9 of the UCC.

4. A security agreement may only be created in tangible physical goods.

5. It is possible for one person to possess a valid security interest in an account receivable even though the "agreement" on which the interest is based is not in writing.

6. As a general rule, a financing statement alone can serve as an adequate substitute for a security agreement.

7. If a debtor and creditor enter into a security agreement which is never perfected, neither party is bound by the agreement.

8. In some situations a security interest is perfected the moment that the interest itself is created (i.e., without any subsequent action--such as filing--being taken by the creditor).

9. The most common method by which security interests are perfected is through the filing of a financing statement.

10. In some instances a creditor who claims a security interest in money is able to perfect his interest without taking possession of the money.

11. In general, the place where a financing statement must be filed in order to be valid depends upon the location of the collateral (as distinguished from the classification--or type--of the collateral).

12. A security interest in negotiable "documents of title" can be perfected only by the creditor's taking of possession of the documents.

13. To perfect a security interest in consumer goods, the financing statement in all cases must be filed in the county where the goods are located.

Chapter 24

14. One of the primary characteristics of the "floating lien" concept is the fact that a security agreement that creates a security interest in specific collateral of the debtor may also be drafted so as to convey to the creditor a security interest in property which the debtor may thereafter acquire.

15. Debtor gives creditor a security interest in specified goods, and later these goods are comingled with other goods so that their identity is lost. In such a case, the creditor's security interest is terminated.

16. The X Bank, in State A, makes a loan to a bridge construction firm, taking a security interest in the firm's equipment. The bank then files a financing statement in State A. If, one month later, the firm moves its equipment to State B, the X Bank has lost its perfection in regard to such equipment.

17. In general, perfected security interests in a merchant's inventory are lost in regard to goods which the merchant/debtor sells to a buyer who purchases in the ordinary course of business.

18. Under some circumstances a party who holds a perfected security interest in goods may lose that interest even if the debtor sells the goods to a buyer who does not buy in the ordinary course of business.

19. When chattel paper is sold to a third party on a "notification" basis, the buyer of the paper (the third party) collects payments directly from the debtor.

20. When the debtor is in default, the UCC permits the creditor to take possession of the collateral only after getting a court order permitting him to do so. (Assume that the contract itself does not prohibit the creditor from taking possession.)

21. Once personal property is affixed permanently to real estate and becomes a fixture, the security interest will cease to exist.

22. In the case of lumber that is used to build a house, any security interest is lost when it becomes a part of the building because it is not considered to be a fixture.

Multiple Choice

1. Under the UCC, a security interest can exist in

    a) all types of personal property, and in fixtures.
    b) tangible personal property, and in fixtures.
    c) all types of personal property (except money), and in fixtures.
    d) none of the above.

Chapter 24

2. A security interest in an <u>account receivable</u>:

   a) can exist if the account receivable is in the possession of the creditor, even if no written security agreement has been executed.
   b) can not exist, under the UCC, in any circumstances.
   c) can exist only if a written security agreement, signed by the debtor, has been entered into.
   d) none of the above.

3. The filing of a financing statement is a necessary step in accomplishing "perfection" of a security interest:

   a) in all cases.
   b) in all cases, with the exception of "purchase money security interests."
   c) in all cases, except situations in which the creditor has taken possession of the collateral.
   d) none of the above.

4. Perfection of a security interest is usually accomplished by the creditor's act of:

   a) taking possession of the collateral.
   b) filing a financing statement.
   c) filing the security agreement (or a copy of the agreement).
   d) none of the above.

5. In which of the following type(s) of property can a security interest <u>not</u> be obtained?

   a) raw materials in the hands of a manufacturer.
   b) consumer goods, if they are actually being used in the consumer's home.
   c) patents and copyrights.
   d) b and c.
   e) none of the above is correct (i.e., security interests can exist in <u>all</u> of the above types of property).

6. A major weakness of an <u>unperfected</u> security interest is the fact that such an interest:

   a) is of little or no use as against an innocent third party's claim to the property.
   b) may, under the UCC, be <u>set aside</u> by the debtor (i.e., legally rescinded or cancelled) until perfection actually occurs.
   c) <u>is void and of no effect</u> as between the debtor and creditor unless the creditor takes possession of the collateral.
   d) a and b are both major weaknesses.
   e) none of the above.

7. In regard to "purchase money" security interests, which of the following statements is/are true?

   a) Such an interest is normally perfected <u>by attachment</u>.

Chapter 24

  b) Such an interest--in general--is <u>invalid</u> as to claims of innocent third parties.
  c) Such an interest in some circumstances <u>has priority over</u> conflicting claims of innocent third parties.
  d) all of the above.
  e) a and b.

8. B buys a TV from R, retailer, and at that time B executes as security a conditional sales contract which is designated as a "purchase-money security agreement." R does not file any financing statement, or any other notice of the agreement.

   The day after the purchase B takes the TV to P, a pawnbroker, and pledges it (i.e., gives possession) to P as security for a $100 loan. Thereafter B defaults on both obligations, and R and P both claim priority for their respective interests in the TV. In such a case,

   a) P's claim has priority because of R's failure to file a financing statement.
   b) P's claim has priority because he took actual possession of the TV.
   c) P's claim has priority because he has the same status as a purchaser in the ordinary course of business (who, in this case, because the goods are consumer goods, prevails over R).
   d) R's claim has priority because his security interest was perfected--without the necessity of filing--on the day the sale was made since the TV is a consumer good, and R does not have the status of a purchaser in the ordinary course of business.
   e) none of the above.

Short Essay

1. Prior to the enactment of the UCC, there were several separate and distinct types of security devices that were in common use. List four of these.

2. M, a manufacturer, borrows $50,000 from a bank, and signs a security agreement covering all the equipment "now in the M plant, and any additional equipment installed hereafter." The agreement also provides that the equipment will also be security "for any future advances made to M." The bank immediately files a financing statement.

   Thereafter M buys a new piece of equipment for his plant, for which he pays cash and which is installed. Later M gets a $20,000 loan from X so that he can buy needed raw materials, and under the loan agreement it is expressly provided that the new piece of equipment will be security for the loan. X immediately files a financing statement covering this agreement. Six months later, at which time M still owes the bank $10,000, he goes back to it and borrows another $50,000. This loan agreement, a standard form supplied by the bank, also provides that it is secured by "any and all equipment now in borrower's plant." (The bank knows of the new equipment purchased by M, but is not aware of X's

Chapter 24

loan to M). While it was standard practice for the bank to file all of its loan agreements, it unexplainably <u>did</u> <u>not</u> <u>file</u> this second agreement.

Soon thereafter M suffered heavy losses, at which time he owes X $15,000 on the loan obtained from him, and $50,000 on the second loan from the bank. In regard to the new piece of machinery, is X's interest superior to that of the bank's? Explain.

Chapter 25

Bankruptcy

True-False

1. A writ of execution is directed at the debtor, while garnishment is directed at a third party who possesses money or property that belongs to the debtor.

2. Garnishment of wages is usually limited to 25 percent of the debtor's weekly take-home pay.

3. A writ of attachment can be obtained by a creditor only after a judgment has been rendered against the debtor.

4. A creditor who has participated in an assignment for the benefit of creditors cannot petition the debtor into bankruptcy.

5. Bankruptcy as a method of debt resolution originally applied only to commercial business failures.

6. A party who owes debts does not have to be insolvent to successfully petition himself into bankruptcy.

7. An involuntary bankruptcy proceeding is one that is initiated by government authorities.

8. The object of a liquidation proceeding is to sell the debtors assets, pay off creditors, and make arrangements to pay the balance of the debts in 7 years.

9. A farmer may be forced into involuntary bankruptcy when his debts exceed his fair market assets by $5,000.

10. Under the Bankruptcy Act, a person is insolvent if he fails to pay his debts in the ordinary course of business or is unable to pay his debts as they become due.

11. Under the new bankruptcy act a husband and wife may file a joint petition if both of them consent.

12. A permanent trustee is appointed by the debtor in order for the debtor's rights to be protected.

13. A trustee's duty includes opposing the debtor's discharge from its obligations when the trustee feels there are legal reasons why the debtor should not be discharged.

Chapter 25

14. A debtor is entitled to a jury trial, if he so requests, in either a voluntary or involuntary bankruptcy proceeding.

15. The judge of the Bankruptcy Court is not permitted to attend a creditors' meeting.

16. A debtor in bankruptcy will only be denied a discharge if the creditors prove an intent to defraud.

17. The debtor's exempt property is set out in state statutes only.

18. The debtor's exempt property may be selected at random between state and federal exemption statutes.

19. A debtor's transfer of property does not constitute a preference that can be set aside by the trustee in bankruptcy if the transfer was to a creditor who neither knew nor had reason to know the debtor was insolvent at the time.

20. A bankrupt cannot obtain a discharge of his debts if his assets are insufficient to fully pay all claims against him.

Multiple Choice

1. An individual debtor in bankruptcy may claim certain exemptions, but must:

    a) select state exemptions.
    b) select federal exemptions.
    c) select the most advantageous items from both state and federal.
    d) elect either state exemptions or federal exemptions.
    e) all of the above.

2. In the case of Mickelson v. Detlefsen the court decision points out:

    a) if a principle of state law conflicts with the purpose of the Bankruptcy Act, the state rule will be applied.
    b) if a principle of state law conflicts with the purpose of the Bankruptcy Act, the state rule will not be applied.
    c) state laws are not subordinate to the federal policies that inhere in the Bankruptcy Act.
    d) none of the above.

3. Which of the following parties can file a petition for voluntary bankruptcy?

    a) insolvent bank.
    b) solvent insurance company that owes debts.
    c) insolvent railroad.
    d) solvent manufacturing partnership that owes debts.
    e) solvent retail grocery corporation that owes debts.

Chapter 25

4. A secured creditor in a bankruptcy:

   a) may proceed directly against the property that is secured for his satisfaction.
   b) has no priority over unsecured creditors.
   c) must wait until the debtors assets are liquidated and then be paid in full.
   d) none of the above.

5. The creditors' first meeting is important because

   a) the trustee is usually elected at the meeting.
   b) the referee is usually appointed at the meeting.
   c) the debtor usually receives his discharge at the meeting.
   d) the petition for involuntary bankruptcy is usually filed at the meeting.

6. Which of the following are "nondischargable" debts:

   a) liability of a negligent tort.
   b) liability for property settlement in a divorce suit.
   c) obligation for a student loan if due and payable 7 years prior to filing of the petition.
   d) all of the above.
   e) none of the above.

7. Which of the following is a voidable transfer?

   a) fraudulent conveyance.
   b) sale of property by debtor to buyer who induced the sale by fraud.
   c) preference.
   d) all of the above.
   e) a and c, but not b.

8. Which of the following must be proved in order to establish that a particular transfer should be classified as a preference?

   a) Transfer enabled transferee to receive a greater percentage of his claim than similar creditors.
   b) Bankrupt debtor destroyed records relating to the transfer.
   c) Transferee concealed assets after receiving them.
   d) Transferee made a false statement about his financial condition prior to the transfer.

9. After payment of the costs and expenses of conducting the bankruptcy proceeding itself, which of the following claims has the highest priority?

   a) expenses of creditors in attempting to prevent debtor's discharge.
   b) taxes incurred within three years prior to bankruptcy petition.
   c) wages that do not exceed $2,000 per claimant and were earned within three months prior to bankruptcy petition.
   d) that portion of a wage claim exceeding $2,000 per claimant or earned more than three months prior to bankruptcy petition.

Chapter 25

10. Which of the following acts by a bankrupt debtor does not prevent his debts from being discharged?

   a) concealed assets with intent to defraud within twelve months prior to petition.
   b) received a discharge in another bankruptcy proceeding ten years prior to petition in this proceeding.
   c) refused to answer court's questions.
   d) failed to satisfactorily explain a loss of certain assets.

Short Essay

1. What is the basic premise underlying the power of the trustee in bankruptcy to set aside a preference?

2. Walter owned a dry cleaning business which had been extremely unprofitable. The fair market value of his assets was $10,000 and his debts totaled $15,000. Walter continued to try diligently to pay his debts and on June 15 sent $500 to Williams, a creditor who did not know or have reason to know of Walter's financial condition since he was one of the few creditors who had always been paid on time by Walter. On the same day Walter sent letters to two of his other creditors indicating that he would not be able to pay the $300 he owed each of them. On August 1, the two creditors who had received the letters plus one other creditor signed and filed a petition with the federal district court asking that Walter be declared bankrupt. Walter challenged the action and claimed that he could not be petitioned into involuntary bankruptcy under the circumstances. Is Walter correct? Explain.

Chapter 26

Agency/Nature, Creation, Duties, and Termination

True-False

1. Most people do not come into contact with the agency relationship in their everyday lives.

2. Although an agency relationship is often created by a legally enforceable employment contract, a legally binding contract is not essential.

3. It generally is required that an agent's authority be spelled out in writing (a power of attorney), although a few exceptions do exist.

4. A minor may serve as an agent, and the agreement making him an agent does not have to be supported by consideration.

5. The principal-agent relationship is a fiduciary one, which requires that each be entirely open with the other and not keep any information from the other that has any bearing on their arrangement.

6. If the principal's instructions to the agent are ambiguous and the agent has no opportunity to consult with the principal and obtain clarification, the agent is entitled to disregard the instructions entirely.

7. An agent may sometimes be under a duty to depart from his principal's legal and clear instructions.

8. When acting for his principal, an agent is normally expected to exercise the degree of care and skill that is normal under the circumstances, but he may sometimes be required to exercise more than an ordinary degree of care and skill.

9. An agent can compete with his principal without the principal's consent so long as no substantial economic harm is done to the principal.

10. In fulfilling his duty of loyalty to the principal, the agent must not only avoid actual conflicts of interest but also potential ones.

11. If the principal knows that the agent is continuing to make efforts to perform his assigned task, and if the principal does nothing, the agency relationship may continue to exist for a period of time longer than would otherwise be deemed reasonable.

12. An ordinary agency relationship can be terminated by either principal or agent without the other's consent, even if they have an enforceable contract between them and even if they had agreed that their relationship would be irrevocable.

Chapter 26

13. An agency coupled with an interest cannot be terminated by the principal without the agent's consent.

14. An agency coupled with an interest involves a situation in which the agent has an interest in the subject matter of the agency.

15. The death or bankruptcy of either the principal or agent automatically terminates the agency relationship.

16. Contracts that are made by an agent that is a minor are voidable.

17. An individual that has an interest against that of the principal can not act as his agent.

18. Ratification takes effect at the time of the ratification and cannot relate back to the time the unauthorized act was performed.

19. A person in a position of trust and confidence is generally referred to as a fiduciary.

20. An agent is allowed to make secret profits from his relationship as an agent.

Multiple Choice

1. Principal hires an agent to sell a piece of property for no less than $50,000, with agent to receive a 6% commission. Without principal's knowledge, which of the following is permitted?

   a) The agent sells the property to his wife for $50,000 and is now entitled to the 6% commission.
   b) The agent discovers land values in the area are decreasing rapidly and, not having an opportunity to consult with the principal, sells the property for $49,000. The agent is entitled to the 6% commission.
   c) The agent tells his principal that he is unable to find a purchaser for more than $50,000. Principal gives agent permission to sell for that price not knowing that agent is also representing the buyer. Agent can still collect 6% commission.
   d) While trying to sell principal's property, agent rents the house on the property to someone. Agent is entitled to keep the rent plus his 6% commission upon selling the property for $60,000, more than principal thought the property would sell for.

2. X was purchasing agent for Z. X purchased goods for Z from O, who paid X a commission of $500 without Z's knowledge.

   a) Since X breached his duty of loyalty to Z, O is entitled to a return of the $500.
   b) Z is entitled to recover the $500 from X, and X forfeits his right to compensation from Z for the services rendered in making the purchase.

Chapter 26

  c) X must return the $500 to O, and X forfeits his right to receive compensation from Z for his services in the transaction.
  d) X breached his duty of loyalty to Z and, therefore, X forfeits the right to compensation for his services, but he may keep the $500 since it was paid by a third party and not by his principal.

3. An agent owes a duty of loyalty to his principal

  a) which is breached if the agent acts in a negligent manner.
  b) and, if this duty is violated, the agent is liable only for losses incurred by the principal as a result.
  c) but this duty prohibits an agent from making a secret profit while representing the principal only if the interests of the principal are actually affected adversely.
  d) because the agent occupies a fiduciary relationship with the principal.

4. Creation of the agency relationship does not require

  a) consideration.
  b) contractual capacity on the part of the agent.
  c) agreement between principal and agent.
  d) consent of the agent.
  e) a and c.
  f) a and b.

5. The fact that an agent is a minor

  a) is totally irrelevant.
  b) is not important with regard to the question of the principal's liability on a transaction made by the minor with a third party.
  c) is irrelevant to the question of whether the principal and agent have a binding employment contract with each other.
  d) all of the above.
  e) b and c, but not a.

6. Under which of the following circumstances is the agent required to strictly follow the principal's instructions?

  a) where the instructions are legal and clear.
  b) where the instructions are clear but illegal.
  c) where the instructions are legal but ambiguous.
  d) where the instructions are legal and clear but a sudden emergency arises, there is no opportunity to consult with the principal, and following the original instructions would not be in the principal's best interests.
  e) a and c.
  f) a and d.

7. An agent owes which of the following duties to the principal.

  a) obedience.
  b) to act with reasonable care.

Chapter 26

    c) duty to notify.
    d) all of the above.
    e) b and c.

8. An agent, employed to perform only one specific business transaction is:

    a) special agent.
    b) implied agent.
    c) independent contractor.
    e) general agent.

Short Essay

1. Briefly explain why the contractual capacity of the agent is immaterial with regard to the principal's liability on transactions made by the agent with third parties.

2. Sam was hired by Crystal Glass Works, Inc. as a sales agent. His job was selling, for a commission, glassware manufactured by Crystal. These sales were usually made to retailers. Several months later, while still working for Crystal, Sam was given an opportunity to buy the business of a wholesale glass distributorship that sold several brands of glassware to retailers. Sam bought the distributorship but kept his position as sales agent for Crystal. He said nothing to Crystal about it. After three months Sam had made $5,000 profit from the distributorship. At this time Crystal owed Sam $2,000 in commissions he had earned. The company then discovered the facts about his other business. As a result, Crystal terminated his position as a sales agent and refused to pay the commission. Discuss all the legal consequences of these facts.

Chapter 27

Agency/Liability of the Parties

True-False

1. Both express and implied authority are types of actual authority.

2. A salesperson in possession of his principal's samples ordinarily has no implied authority to sell them.

3. A salesclerk in a retail store ordinarily has implied authority to sell the goods in the store and collect payment or grant credit.

4. A salesperson in a retail store can usually collect payment for goods he sells but cannot be given express authority to accept payment from the customer for prior credit purchases.

5. The manager of a retail store does not, under any circumstances, have authority to hire an electrician to rewire the building at a substantial cost.

6. An agent's implied authority can expand in emergency situations if he is unable to consult with his principal and if he acts reasonably.

7. The essence of the concept of apparent authority is the misleading of reasonably acting third parties by the action or inaction of the principal.

8. The concepts of implied and apparent authority are mutually exclusive--there can be no overlapping between the two.

9. When an agent's actual authority is terminated by the principal, his apparent authority is terminated as well.

10. When the principal terminates his agent's actual authority, he can effectively terminate the agent's apparent authority merely by placing a notice of termination in a newspaper of general circulation.

11. The viewpoint of the third party with whom the agent deals is more important than the viewpoint of the agent in determining whether apparent authority existed.

12. An unauthorized act ratified by the principal is treated by the courts in the same manner as if it had been actually authorized from the beginning.

13. An undisclosed principal cannot ratify his agent's unauthorized transaction with a third party.

Chapter 27

14. Ratification can be accurately described as "after-the-fact authorization."

15. In the case of <u>Wing</u> v. <u>Lederer</u> (involving the tree surgeon), the court held that a part-time yardman cannot be given authority to hire a tree surgeon to perform work of a substantial nature.

16. Notice to an agent is treated as notice to the principal whenever the agent and the third party giving notice are not conspiring to defraud the principal.

17. If the principal is dead at the time the agent purports to contract in the principal's behalf, the agent is liable only if he knows of the principal's death and the third party's ignorance of it.

18. An agent, acting in behalf of an undisclosed principal, agrees to perform personal services for a third party. If the principal reveals himself after the contract is made, he can hold the third party to the contract.

19. The employer is generally liable for the torts of his servant or independent contractor committed in the scope of their employment.

20. A master's liability under the doctrine of respondeat superior is based upon his own fault rather than that of his servant.

Multiple Choice

1. An agent cannot obligate his principal in a contract with a third party

    a) unless the principal had agreed to pay consideration for the agent's services.
    b) if the agent acted without authority.
    c) if the principal had been declared insane by a court prior to the making of the contract.
    d) if the agent is a minor.

2. An agent is liable to a third party with whom he deals

    a) whenever the agent exceeds his authority.
    b) whenever the agent acts in behalf of a nonexistent principal.
    c) whenever the agent acts in behalf of a principal who did not have contractual capacity at the time of the transaction.
    d) only if the agent expressly assumes liability and thus becomes a party to the contract.

3. When an agent acts within the scope of his authority for an undisclosed principal,

    a) the agent is usually not liable to the third party with whom he deals if sufficient information is disclosed which would enable the

Chapter 27

      third party to inquire further and ascertain the existence and identity of the principal.
- b) the agent is liable to the third party, but not vice-versa.
- c) the agent and principal are both liable to the third party, but the third party must make an election as to which one he wants to hold responsible.
- d) the agent is liable to the third party, but only until the third party learns of the existence and identity of the principal.

4. Which of the following has no relation to the concept of implied authority?

- a) incidental acts.
- b) nondelegable duty.
- c) customary.
- d) emergency.

5. Which of the following has no relation to the concept of apparent authority?

- a) notice to third parties.
- b) misleading of third party.
- c) agent exceeding actual authority.
- d) respondeat superior.

6. Which of the following has no relation to the concept of ratification?

- a) unauthorized act.
- b) undisclosed principal.
- c) entire transaction.
- d) same formalities as for authorization.

7. When the principal chooses to ratify the unauthorized act of his agent,

- a) some courts hold that the third party has no choice and must honor the transaction.
- b) some courts hold that the third party can withdraw from the transaction if the principal has waited beyond a reasonable time to ratify.
- c) some courts, taking a view which is becoming the most common one, allow the principal to ratify only if the third party has not yet indicated he wishes to withdraw from the transaction.
- d) all of the above.
- e) a and b, but not c.

8. In which of the following situations is the agent not personally liable?

- a) Agent exceeds authority.
- b) Agent breaches duty of loyalty.
- c) Agent does not disclose principal's identity.
- d) Agent's unauthorized act is ratified by the principal.
- e) All of the above.
- f) None of the above.

Chapter 27

9. Which of the following bears a relation to the concept of vicarious liability for the torts of one's subordinate?

   a) superior's control over method by which subordinate accomplishes the task.
   b) scope of employment.
   c) negligent entrustment.
   d) all of the above.
   e) a and b, but not c.
   f) b and c, but not a.

10. In which of the following situations is an employer liable for the tort of his independent contractor?

    a) Independent contractor, without negligence, harms a third party while doing blasting for employer.
    b) Independent contractor causes harm to a motorist because of negligently repairing street for city.
    c) Independent contractor, without negligence, harms a third party while hauling sulfuric acid for employer.
    d) all of the above.
    e) a and c, but not b.

11. In the case of Industrial Molded Plastic Products, Inc. v. J. Gross and Son, Inc. the issue(s) involved dealt with:

    a) the limit of the agents authority.
    b) express authority.
    c) implied authority.
    d) apparent authority.
    e) a and d.

12. When the agent is acting for the principal, the agent ordinarily incurs no personal responsibility when they:

    a) act in a proper fashion.
    b) breach their duty.
    c) exceed their authority.
    d) assume liability.
    e) all of the above.

Short Essay

1. Pat was a paving contractor and Albert was employed as his foreman and superintendent. Pat was attempting to procure a contract with Smith who had a large road construction contract. Albert, secretly, bid the job and procured it for himself, thereupon leaving Pat's employment. Albert completed the work for Smith and made a profit of $5,000. Pat brought suit against Albert to account for the profits he made on the contract with Smith. May Pat recover?

Chapter 28

Forms of Business Organizations

True-False

1. Anyone who does business without creating an organization is a sole proprietor.

2. Limited liability is the key characteristic of the limited partnership.

3. In a limited partnership, there must be two or more general partners and at least one limited partner.

4. A limited partner is only an investor and thus cannot perform any services for the limited partnership.

5. Unlike an ordinary partnership, a limited partnership can be created only by following certain formalities required by statute.

6. In a limited partnership, a general partner is treated by the law the same as a partner in an ordinary partnership.

7. A limited partner who participates in management of the business is liable to business creditors as if he were a general partner.

8. The joint stock company is a fairly recent innovation and is becoming increasingly popular as a form of business organization.

9. Shareholders in a joint stock company are liable for business debts as if they were partners, but they are usually not treated as agents of one another as partners are.

10. In a business trust, legal ownership and management of business property are in the hands of beneficiaries.

11. The term "syndicate" generally refers to a limited partnership, since the participants are investors.

12. A joint venture is a partnership created for a limited purpose or duration.

13. Depending on the type of business, there usually will be a specific form of organization that <u>must</u> be used for a particular business.

14. The form of the organization used to conduct a business is always solely determinative of the issue of owner's liability.

15. A corporation possesses a greater degree of continuity than a partnership.

Chapter 28

16. Expansion of the business and the resulting need for additional capital is perhaps the most common reason for changing from a sole proprietorship or partnership to a corporation.

17. A partnership is not subject to double taxation.

18. The degree of control over the business that is exercised by a partner is always greater than that exercised by a shareholder in a corporation.

19. A sole proprietorship is generally formed and the business is established when the legal formalities are completed.

20. A corporation does not offer limited liability to the shareholders.

Multiple Choice

1. In which of the following forms of business organization does a single individual usually have the most control over business decisions?

   a) partnership.
   b) joint stock company.
   c) sole proprietorship.
   d) limited partnership.
   e) corporation.

2. As a general rule, the law shields which of the following individuals from personal liability for business debts?

   a) partner.
   b) general partner.
   c) sole proprietor.
   d) shareholder in a corporation.

3. Which of the following is not characteristic of a limited partnership?

   a) limited liability for limited partners.
   b) loss of limited liability status for a limited partner who takes part in management.
   c) general partners are just like partners in an ordinary partnership.
   d) created by agreement, with no required formalities.

4. Which of the following is not characteristic of a joint venture?

   a) a type of partnership.
   b) limited liability.
   c) treated under the law virtually the same as a partnership.
   d) implied authority of a participant more restricted than in ordinary partnership.

291

Chapter 28

5. Which of the following is characteristic of the limited liability concept?

   a) established by law and cannot be varied by agreement with business creditors.
   b) applies to shareholders in a corporation and general partners in a limited partnership.
   c) only exists where created by statute or by agreement of business creditors.
   d) applies to shareholders in a corporation regardless of any agreement they might make.

6. Which of the following has nothing to do with the degree of control exercised by an individual owner of an interest in a business?

   a) the number of owners.
   b) the size of the individual's interest.
   c) indebtedness of the business.
   d) use of centralized management.
   e) Subchapter S.

7. An organization will be taxed as a corporation if it has which of the following characteristics?

   a) continuity of life and free transferability of interests.
   b) limited liability.
   c) centralization of management.
   d) b and c.
   e) all of the above.

8. "Subchapter S Corporations" are taxed in a manner:

   a) that is designed to discourage their formation.
   b) similar to that of a partnership.
   c) that is considered "double taxation."
   d) that is higher than an ordinary corporation.

Short Essay

1. Explain how debt can limit the control of owners over their business.

2. X, Y, and Z formed a business organization in which Z made all management decisions. It was agreed that the death, bankruptcy, or resignation of any of them would not dissolve or otherwise interrupt the business. It was also agreed that any of them could sell his interest to an outsider without getting the consent of the other two. X, Y, and Z were all potentially liable for business debts because they were not given limited liability by any statute. How would this organization be classified for federal income tax purposes? Explain.

Chapter 29

Partnerships/Nature, Formation, and Property

True-False

1. The law of partnerships originated with the Uniform Partnership Act in 1914.

2. A minor can be a partner, but his maximum possible liability to business creditors is the amount of his investment in the business.

3. Under the traditional view a corporation could not be a partner, but this rule has been changed in about half the states in recent years.

4. To be a partnership, an association must engage in a "business," which excludes professional associations of doctors, lawyers, and the like.

5. An association formed for the furtherance of the separate economic interests of its members is not a partnership.

6. An association formed primarily for some purpose other than profit-making is not a partnership.

7. The traditional common law approach was to treat a partnership simply as an aggregation of individuals, rather than as a separate and single legal entity.

8. As a general rule, a partnership can be created only by a written contract called the "articles of partnership."

9. Fictitious name statutes, which exist in most states, prohibit a partnership from doing business under a name other than the name of one or more of the partners.

10. Where parties have not been explicit in declaring their intentions as to whether or not they are forming a partnership, the most important factors to be considered in deciding whether they are partners are joint control of the business and joint ownership of business property.

11. The payment by a tenant to his landlord of a share of the profits made by the tenant in his business does not create a presumption that the two are partners, but it also does not mean that they cannot possibly be partners.

12. Joint ownership of property is inconsistent with any conclusion except that the owners are partners.

13. Joint ownership of property plus the sharing of income from the property creates a strong inference that the owners are partners.

Chapter 29

14. If one of the owners of a business delegates his management powers to one of the other owners, the former can no longer be considered a partner because of his relinquishment of control.

15. It is not essential that a partnership own any property at all--it may operate by simply "borrowing" necessary items of property from individual partners.

16. If "legal title" to an item of property is in the name of an individual partner, this fact conclusively establishes that the item is not partnership property.

17. The fact that an item of property has been purchased with partnership funds is viewed by the courts as very weak evidence on the question of whether the item is partnership property.

18. The fact that an item of property has been used in the business of the partnership is viewed by the courts as very weak evidence on the question of whether the item is partnership property.

19. If an item of property is carried in the partnership books as an asset of the firm, this strongly tends to indicate that it is partnership property, and the inference is even stronger if an unpaid balance on the property is carried in the records as a partnership liability.

20. The fact that taxes on a piece of property have been paid by the partnership tends to support a conclusion that it is partnership property.

Multiple Choice

1. Which of the following would most strongly indicate the existence of a partnership.

    a) A hires B. B is to receive in addition to $1,000 a month, 15% of the net profits.
    b) A and B own a truck farm as tenants in common.
    c) A loans B $100,000 with B to pay back the loan at 10% of B's profits each and every month.
    d) A and B buy an existing business including the goodwill and agree to share profits from the sale of goods during the next year.

2. Under the Uniform Partnership Act,

    a) an association of persons will be a partnership only if they have executed a written partnership agreement and filed it with the Secretary of State.
    b) a new partner admitted to an existing partnership has no liability whatever for partnership obligations arising prior to his admission.
    c) an association of persons will be a partnership only if it carries on a business with a profit motive.

294

Chapter 29

    d) a partnership is not recognized as a legal entity for the purpose of property ownership.

3. The sharing of profits generated by a business

    a) ordinarily raises a presumption that a partnership exists, as is also true of the sharing of gross revenues.
    b) will be in the same ratio as the amounts of capital contributed to the business by each participant, unless they have agreed otherwise.
    c) does not raise a presumption of partnership if the profits are paid as consideration for the purchase of property.
    d) raises a presumption of partnership only if the parties have also agreed to share losses.

4. Which of the following is not descriptive of a partnership?

    a) a voluntary association.
    b) members are co-owners.
    c) formed to carry on a business.
    d) creature of statute.

5. Which of the following shows recognition of the aggregate theory of the nature of the partnership?

    a) UPA definition of a partnership.
    b) Liability for partner's act while conducting partnership business is placed first on the partnership itself.
    c) concept of partnership property.
    d) A partnership can sue and be sued in its own name in most states.

6. The UPA

    a) sets forth many formalities that must be met to form a partnership.
    b) does not require a legally enforceable contract for creation of a partnership.
    c) requires registration of a fictitious name used for a partnership.
    d) all of the above.
    e) b and c, but not a.

7. In which of the following situations does profit sharing create a presumption that partnership was created?

    a) profits received by a creditor in payment of a debt.
    b) profits shared, but no express agreement as to sharing of losses.
    c) profits received by a lender as interest on a loan.
    d) profits paid as royalty for a trademark license.

8. The phrase "tenants in partnership"

    a) describes the status of individual partners with respect to their individual property being used in the partnership business.

Chapter 29

    b) describes those who rent property from a partnership.
    c) describes the status of individual partners with respect to partnership property.
    d) none of the above.

9. "Legal title" to property

    a) is irrelevant in determining whether the property belongs to the partnership or to individual partners.
    b) refers to the name in which the property is held.
    c) is conclusive on the issue of whether an item is partnership property.
    d) is the only factor a court will consider in deciding whether an item is partnership property.

10. Partnership property

    a) includes funds generated by the business operations of the partnership.
    b) includes funds paid into the partnership by individual partners and used by the partnership as working capital, unless such payments were clearly loans to the partnership.
    c) includes property purchased with partnership funds, unless the evidence clearly indicates otherwise.
    d) all of the above.
    e) a and c, but not b.

11. In the case of *Grissum* v. *Reesman* the plaintiff asked the court to declare that she and her brother had been partners. The issue involved was whether a partnership existed. The court determined which of the following to be the controlling factor(s) in the determination that a partnership existed:

    a) sharing of profits.
    b) joint control of the business.
    c) joint ownership and control of capital or property.
    d) a and c.
    e) all of the above.

12. Which of the following factors might influence a court's decision that an item is partnership property:

    a) partnership funds were used to repair the property owned by an individual partner.
    b) property taxes have been paid by the partnership.
    c) income generated by the property is paid to the partnership.
    d) all of the above.

Short Essay

1. Explain what part the UPA plays today in governing partnerships.

Chapter 29

2. Warnecke, Vance, Jordan, and Powell conduct a wholesale produce business as partners. One of the refrigerated produce trucks the partnership uses was owned by Vance before the partnership was formed, and the certificate of title remains in his name. The articles of partnership say nothing about the truck, and the partners have made no oral agreement regarding its status. One of Vance's personal creditors is now seeking to seize the truck to satisfy a judgment against Vance. Vance tries to prevent seizure by showing that the truck is really partnership property. What types of evidence might be helpful in making this determination in court?

Chapter 30

Partnerships/Operating the Business

True-False

1. Regardless of what the partnership agreement says, each partner has an equal right to possess partnership property for partnership purposes.

2. Each partner owns a part of the partnership property in proportion to his interest in the partnership.

3. Even though a partner owns a proportionate part of the partnership property, he cannot sell his part to someone else without consent of the other partners.

4. Unless it has been agreed otherwise, differences among partners regarding management of the business are usually settled by majority vote.

5. Unless previously agreed otherwise, the articles of partnership are amendable only by unanimous vote.

6. Where the partnership agreement does not express the specific division of profits to be made, the division is based on the relative amount of each partner's capital contribution.

7. If the partners have not agreed on how losses are to be divided, the division will be in the same proportion as profits.

8. Except for a partner in charge of winding up, partners are not entitled to compensation for services they render to the partnership unless there has been an agreement for such compensation.

9. A partner is entitled to reimbursement from the partnership only for expenses incurred while acting under the express authority of the other partners.

10. A partner may not engage in another business besides that of the partnership unless he obtains the consent of the other partners.

11. A partnership is liable for the tort or crime of an individual partner only where the wrongful act is within the ordinary course of partnership business and proof of criminal intent is not required for conviction.

12. A partnership cannot be held liable under the doctrine of apparent authority because a partnership is not a human being and thus cannot mislead a third party.

13. Under the traditional definition, a partnership of accountants is a nontrading partnership.

14. Courts have usually held that a partner in a trading partnership generally has implied authority to borrow money, but a partner in a nontrading one does not.

15. In modern times most courts have abolished the distinction between trading and nontrading partnerships.

16. A partner can ordinarily hire an employee to work for the partnership only if the partner was given express authority to do so.

17. Unanimous consent of the partners is required to make an assignment for the benefit of creditors.

18. A newly admitted partner can be held liable for partnership obligations that arose before his admission, but only to the extent of his interest in the partnership.

19. An assignee of a partner's interest in the partnership is entitled to that partner's share of profits and surplus and nothing else.

20. A partner's assignment of his interest to an outsider does not dissolve the partnership.

Multiple Choice

1. With respect to partnership property,

    a) all partners have an equal right to use the property for partnership purposes.
    b) all partners have an equal right to use the property for partnership or personal purposes.
    c) a partner's right to use such property passes to his heirs upon his death.
    d) a partner's right to use such property does not pass to his heirs when he dies, but may be reached by his personal creditors.

2. A, B, and C form a partnership for the purpose of conducting a TV repair business. If there is no agreement to the contrary,

    a) each partner must have made a capital contribution to receive profits.
    b) profits will be shared in the same ratio as capital contributions.
    c) if A makes a loan, A is entitled to interest.
    d) B gets sick and A assumes B's duties. A is entitled to be compensated, as otherwise the partnership would have to hire someone to fill in for B.

3. A partner

    a) is not entitled to compensation even though he performs more services

Chapter 30

in the partnership than other partners, except where the services are related to the winding up of partnership affairs and except where the partnership agreement provides otherwise.
b) is not entitled to interest on his capital contribution or on loans made to the partnership, unless agreed otherwise.
c) has implied authority to submit partnership controversies to arbitration.
d) in a trading partnership usually does not have implied authority to borrow money in behalf of the partnership.

4. Which of the following is not true regarding management of a partnership?

   a) Differences are usually settled by a majority vote.
   b) Amendment of the articles of partnership can be accomplished by majority vote unless previously agreed otherwise.
   c) Unless previously agreed otherwise, admission of a new partner requires a unanimous vote.
   d) Management powers can be delegated to a "managing partner" by either express or implied agreement.

5. Which of the following best describes the relationship between partners?

   a) competitive.
   b) arms-length.
   c) neutral.
   d) trust.
   e) indifferent.

6. An accounting

   a) is a legal proceeding in which all partnership records are formally produced and all balances computed under court supervision.
   b) can usually be demanded by a partner only when the partnership is being dissolved.
   c) can be demanded without dissolution of the partnership if the demanding partner has been wrongfully excluded by the other partners from the partnership business or partnership property.
   d) all of the above.
   e) a and c, but not b.

7. Clark, a partner in an electrical contracting business, struck Williams in the face without justification. The act occurred in the ordinary course of partnership business.

   a) The partnership will be liable for the crime of assault and battery only if conviction of that criminal offense does not require proof of criminal intent.
   b) The partnership cannot be held liable for a tort or crime of this type.
   c) Clark will be liable for the crime of assault and battery only if conviction of that criminal offense does not require proof of criminal intent.

Chapter 30

   d) all of the above.
   e) a and c, but not b.

8. Which of the following has no relation to a partner's implied authority to act for the partnership?

   a) customary.
   b) trading and nontrading.
   c) charging order.
   d) hiring employees.

9. In the law of partnerships, arbitration and confession of judgment have something in common. Which of the following best describes the relationship between the two?

   a) not impliedly authorized.
   b) absolutely unauthorized without express agreement by all partners.
   c) cannot be provided for in articles of partnership.
   d) requires express authorization, which can be given by majority vote.

10. Which of the following best describes an assignment by a partner to a nonpartner of the partner's interest in the partnership?

    a) same as a charging order.
    b) dissolves the partnership.
    c) gives management rights to assignee.
    d) gives assignee no rights in partnership property.

Short Essay

1. What is the difference between a partner's interest in the partnership and his rights in partnership property?

2. Thompson is a partner in a company that makes blueprints. His capital contribution was $10,000; the capital contributed by the other two partners was $5,000 each. The articles of partnership provided that these contributions would be repaid to partners on June 1, 1981. Thompson also loaned the partnership $5,000, which was to be repaid on April 1, 1981. Nothing was said about interest on the loan. During 1981 the partnership made a $40,000 profit, and Thompson worked many more hours than his partners. On Dec. 31, 1981, what is Thompson entitled to receive from the partnership, assuming that he has received no payments of any kind during 1981?

Chapter 31

Partnership/Termination

True-False

1. Regardless of the terms of the articles of partnership, dissolution of a partnership can occur at any time by agreement of all the partners.

2. Regardless of the terms of the articles of partnership, dissolution of a partnership can occur at any time by the withdrawal, death, or bankruptcy of a single partner.

3. The partnership does not dissolve automatically when a partner becomes insane.

4. The partnership automatically dissolves when a partner commits fraud in dealing with partnership property.

5. Any partner can obtain a court decree ordering dissolution of the partnership when it becomes evident that the business is unprofitable and will probably not be profitable in the future.

6. After dissolution none of the partners has authority to engage in any transaction in behalf of the partnership.

7. If the partners have chosen one of them to act as "winding up partner" after dissolution, third parties who are notified of this fact can bind the partnership only by dealing with the designated partner.

8. If a transaction in the ordinary course of partnership business is made by a partner who did not know that the partnership had been dissolved by the death of another partner, the partnership is liable on that transaction even if it was not appropriate for winding up partnership affairs.

9. A third party, whether a past creditor of the partnership or not, cannot hold the partnership liable on an unauthorized transaction made after dissolution, if the third party had actual knowledge of the dissolution at the time of the transaction.

10. A postdissolution transaction entered into by a bankrupt partner will bind the partnership only if the transaction is appropriate for winding up partnership affairs.

11. Dissolution in and of itself can greatly alter the existing liabilities of the partnership and the individual partners.

Chapter 31

12. The order in which claims against the partnership must be paid after dissolution is not important if partnership assets are sufficient to pay all of them in full.

13. After dissolution of the partnership, loans to the partnership from individual partners must be repaid before partners' capital contributions are returned.

14. After the partnership is dissolved, claims of outside creditors must not be paid until loans to the partnership from individual partners are repaid.

15. If partnership assets are insufficient to pay its debts, the assets of individual partners can be used for this purpose only if the partners did not agree otherwise in the articles of partnership.

16. A partner's individual creditors may reach his personal assets only insofar as these assets are not needed to pay the debts of the dissolved partnership.

17. Dissolution of a partnership does not necessarily mean that the business itself will be liquidated.

18. Where dissolution has been caused by the rightful withdrawal of a partner, and the other partners continue the business, the value of partnership goodwill is included in determining the value of the withdrawing partner's interest.

19. After dissolution, the value of partnership assets is determined by their book value because this is the most objective and certain figure available.

20. Where settlement between a rightfully withdrawing partner and those continuing the business is not made immediately, the withdrawing partner is entitled not only to the value of his interest in the partnership but also to interest on that amount or his proportionate share of partnership profits earned since dissolution.

21. A partnership may be dissolved upon the expiration of a specified period of time.

22. Where partnership agreements make no provision for a definite duration or undertaking, the partnership is commonly called a partnership at will.

23. Upon dissolution, the authority of individual partners to act in behalf of the partnership usually ceases, except for acts necessary to complete unfinished transactions or those necessary for winding up partnership affairs.

24. Dissolution of a partnership in and of itself does not alter the existing liabilities of the partnership or individual partners.

Chapter 31

Multiple Choice

1. The death of a partner

   a) automatically dissolves the partnership, unless the original partnership agreement had provided otherwise.
   b) automatically dissolves the partnership, but if the surviving partners continue the business, the deceased partner's spouse or representative automatically becomes a member of the new partnership.
   c) automatically dissolves the partnership and the business must be liquidated rather than continued.
   d) automatically dissolves the partnership.

2. Which of the following does not automatically cause dissolution of the partnership?

   a) death of a partner.
   b) bankruptcy of a partner.
   c) serious misconduct by a partner.
   d) withdrawal of a partner from the partnership.

3. Which of the following does automatically cause dissolution of the partnership?

   a) insanity of a partner.
   b) prolonged illness of a partner.
   c) serious neglect of partnership affairs by a partner.
   d) bankruptcy of either the partnership or an individual partner.
   e) unprofitability of the business.

4. Regarding dissolution of a partnership by court decree:

   a) one of the grounds for such a decree is the insanity of a partner, but only if there has already been a formal declaration of insanity by a court in a sanity hearing.
   b) such a decree may be sought only by a partner and not by a partnership creditor.
   c) such a decree may be sought by a partnership creditor in the same circumstances as it may be sought by a partner.
   d) a decree of dissolution may be sought by a partner's personal creditor who has gotten a charging order on that partner's interest in the partnership, if the partnership is "at will" when the charging order is obtained.
   e) none of the above.

5. Which of the following is most accurately descriptive of the type of transaction that a partner is authorized to make in behalf of the partnership after dissolution?

   a) appropriate for winding up partnership affairs.

b) in the ordinary course of the partnership business.
c) necessary to make the partnership's operations profitable for that year.
d) must be made by a partner specifically designated as "liquidating partner" or "winding up partner."

6. In which of the following situations can <u>knowledge</u> of dissolution have a relation to the question of whether a partnership is liable on a particular transaction?

   a) The transaction was not in the ordinary course of partnership business, was not customary, and would not have been binding on the partnership even if there had been no dissolution.
   b) The transaction entered into by a partner after dissolution was in the ordinary course of partnership business but was not appropriate for winding up partnership affairs.
   c) A postdissolution transaction is entered into by a partner who is personally bankrupt.
   d) all of the above.
   e) none of the above.

7. Which of the following has nothing to do with the winding up of partnership affairs?

   a) financial position of individual partners.
   b) articles of partnership.
   c) the way that dissolution came about.
   d) all of the above (that is, neither a, b, or c has anything to do with winding up).
   e) none of the above (that is, a, b, and c all have something to do with winding up).

8. Which of the following statements is true regarding distribution of partnership and individual partners' assets after dissolution?

   a) If any assets of individual partners are needed for partnership debts, this means that the partners are not going to receive any profits in the distribution.
   b) An individual partner's creditor can reach partnership assets after the partnership's outside creditors have been fully paid.
   c) The order of priority for payment of claims against the partnership is important only where partnership assets are insufficient to pay the partnership's outside creditors.
   d) all of the above.
   e) a and c, but not b.

9. Which of the following statements is false regarding the winding up process?

   a) Where the business itself is to be continued, the winding up process consists primarily of bookkeeping entries and the purchase of continuing partners of the interests of withdrawing partners.

Chapter 31

    b) A partner who has wrongfully caused dissolution has no right to exercise any control over the winding up process.
    c) Since only one partner can control the winding up process, the partners must appoint one of their group as a winding up partner, or else the court will appoint a receiver.
    d) The winding up process is more likely to include liquidation of the business when that business has been unprofitable than when it has been profitable.

10. When the business itself is to be continued after dissolution of the partnership,

    a) the continuing partners can postpone settlement with a wrongfully withdrawing partner without the latter's consent, but only until expiration of the agreed term or undertaking.
    b) the continuing partners can postpone settlement with a withdrawing partner without the latter's consent, regardless of whether he rightfully or wrongfully caused the dissolution, but only until expiration of the agreed term or undertaking.
    c) a postponement in settling with either a rightfully or wrongfully withdrawing partner entitles him to compensation for the delay.
    d) a postponement in settling with a rightfully withdrawing partner entitles him to receive interest, and nothing more, as compensation for the delay.

Short Essay

1. Explain why a partner's insanity results in dissolution of the partnership only if a court decree orders dissolution, rather than automatically causing dissolution.

2. Tom, Jerry, and Bob operated a barbershop as a partnership. Although the business had been profitable, each wanted to go his separate way, so they agreed on dissolution. All partnership assets were sold, and the proceeds were sufficient to fully pay off partnership debts and partners' capital contributions. No loans had been made to the partnership by individual partners. After these distributions, $18,000 remained. Bob had been unable to pay all his personal creditors on time. One of these creditors sued Bob and obtained a court judgment against him for $10,000. The creditor claimed that he was entitled to be paid this $10,000 out of the $18,000 remaining from partnership assets. Is the creditor correct? How much, if any, can he claim? Explain.

Chapter 32

Corporations/Nature and Formation

True-False

1. During the first few decades after the Revolutionary War, corporations in the United States were formed only by special acts of state legislatures.

2. The famous overseas trading companies chartered by the English government in the sixteenth and seventeenth centuries, such as Hudson's Bay Company, became the models for our present-day business corporations.

3. The federal government can charter a corporation for all the same purposes for which a state government can charter corporations.

4. As a "person," a corporation enjoys many, but not all, of the constitutional rights and privileges enjoyed by individual citizens.

5. As a general rule, shareholders of a corporation, but not officers or directors, enjoy freedom from personal liability for corporate debts.

6. A parent corporation and its partly-owned subsidiary are considered separate legal entities, but a parent and its wholly-owned subsidiary are not.

7. If it so chooses, a Subchapter S corporation pays no federal income tax.

8. A Subchapter S corporation, if it so chooses, is taxed under federal income tax laws in the same manner as a partnership.

9. When a corporation has only one shareholder, courts always consider the corporation and the shareholder as a single entity rather than as two separate entities.

10. A foreign corporation is one that has been incorporated in another country.

11. In most states today persons can form corporations for the purpose of engaging in the practice of a profession.

12. A public corporation is one whose shares are bought and sold publicly.

13. After actual incorporation, a promoter may still be liable on a pre-incorporation contract that he had made in behalf of the proposed corporation, on the ground that he was acting as an agent for a non-existent principal.

14. When two or more promoters are involved in the creation of a corporation, they are viewed as being engaged in a joint venture prior to incorporation,

Chapter 32

but they do not owe fiduciary duties to each other since they are not actual partners.

15. Since a promoter is the person who conceives and develops the idea behind formation of the corporation, he is entitled to compensation for his idea and effort by being allowed to make whatever profit he can from the promotional scheme without any duty of disclosure to those who invest in the enterprise.

16. Incorporators are those who technically apply to the state for incorporation, and they need not have any interest in the business enterprise itself.

17. Both the articles of incorporation and the bylaws are usually filed with a state official such as the secretary of state.

18. The validity of a de jure corporation's existence can be challenged only by the state, but the validity of a de facto corporation's existence can be challenged by either the state or by another interested party.

19. State securities agencies, as well as the SEC, generally have authority to pass judgment on the merits of a particular issue of stock and forbid its issuance.

20. To be a private offering, and thus exempt from the registration requirements of federal securities laws, there simply has to be some type of limitation, however minor, placed on the class of persons to whom the shares are offered.

21. A corporation could be defined as an artificial being with a legally recognized identity of its own.

22. A corporation can be both a citizen of the state where it is incorporated and where it has its principal place of business if it is a different state.

Multiple Choice

1. Which of the following is not descriptive of corporations?

    a) usually formed today under "general incorporation" statutes.
    b) can sue and be sued.
    c) each one must be created by a special legislative enactment.
    d) can own property and make contracts in its own name.

2. Which of the following is a result of the basic rule that a corporation has an identity separate from the identities of those who own and manage it?

    a) Incorporators are not required to have an interest in the enterprise.
    b) double taxation.

Chapter 32

    c) Promoters are treated prior to incorporation as participants in a joint venture.
    d) The state can challenge the validity of a de facto corporation's existence.

3. Which of the following is not true regarding the historical background of corporations?

    a) Substantial utilization of the corporation for commercial purposes occurred under ancient Roman law.
    b) The overseas trading companies chartered by the English government in the sixteenth and seventeenth centuries were given substantial governmental powers.
    c) The concept of the corporation as an artificial person with a separate identity developed under canon law.
    d) The "concession theory" was developed under English law.

4. A corporation does not enjoy which of the following constitutional rights and privileges?

    a) to be secure from unreasonable searches and seizures.
    b) not to be deprived of life, liberty, or property without due process of law.
    c) against self incrimination.
    d) not to be denied equal protection of the laws.
    e) not to be subjected to double jeopardy.

5. A subsidiary corporation

    a) is one the stock of which is all or mostly owned by another corporation.
    b) and its parent are normally viewed as a single entity.
    c) and its parent cannot be treated as a single entity because they are separately incorporated, even if their records and advertising intermingle and confuse their identities.
    d) and its parent will be treated as a single entity if anyone serves on the boards of directors of both corporations, because this is an interlocking directorate.

6. Which of the following is not required for qualification as a Subchapter S corporation?

    a) only one class of stock.
    b) written consent by all shareholders filed with IRS.
    c) assets of less than one million dollars.
    d) fifteen or fewer shareholders.
    e) all shareholders are individuals or estates.

7. A court will "pierce the corporate veil"

    a) whenever the corporation is family-owned.
    b) whenever the corporation qualifies as a Subchapter S corporation.

Chapter 32

    c) whenever the corporation's assets are insufficient to meet its business obligations.
    d) all of the above.
    e) none of the above.

8. Which of the following best describes corporate promoters?

    a) agent for a nonexistent principal.
    b) shady character out to make a fast buck.
    c) incorporator.
    d) motivating force behind the creation of the corporation.
    e) officer.

9. The formation of a corporation requires

    a) filing of articles of incorporation and issuance of certificate of incorporation.
    b) registration of securities with SEC.
    c) perfect compliance with statutory formalities.
    d) issuance of bonds.

10. Registration of securities under federal law

    a) has the purpose of discouraging securities issuances.
    b) has the purpose of preventing misconduct by requiring full disclosure of information relevant to the issuance.
    c) is not required if the issuing corporation is a newly formed company.
    d) is required for issuances offered for sale in interstate commerce or through the mails, unless an exemption applies, but failure to register when required is punishable only by a civil suit and not by a criminal prosecution.

Short Essay

1. What is the essential focus of a court's inquiry when faced with the question of whether an issuance of securities is a public or private offering?

2. Centron Corporation was formed by three brothers, Sam, Mack, and Joe Willie, for engaging in the business of constructing commercial structures such as office buildings, retail stores, and the like. The three brothers were the only shareholders and were also the officers and directors of the corporation. The initial working capital of the corporation was obtained by the sale of 99 shares of $10 par value stock to the three brothers in equal portions. All other assets used in the business, including equipment, business office, and additional cash, were loaned by the brothers to the corporation. No official directors' or shareholders' meetings were ever held. The corporation maintained a bank account in its own name, and some of its bills were paid from this account,

Chapter 32

but many of its bills were paid by the brothers from their personal bank accounts. After doing business for over a year, Centron Corporation was sued by Winston Co. for breach of a construction contract. Winston Co. prevailed and obtained a judgment for $100,000. Since the assets actually owned by Centron amounted only to a few hundred dollars, Winston asked the court to "pierce the corporate veil" and hold the three brothers personally liable for payment of the judgment. Will the court do so? Explain.

Chapter 33

Corporations/Corporate Powers and Management

True-False

1. A corporation has implied power to lend money without interest to customers.

2. Corporations are prohibited from making contributions to charities unless it is directly related to the business interest of the corporation.

3. Under the ultra vires doctrine, which is still as important as it ever was, a corporation is empowered to act only insofar as is necessary to further the purposes for which it was organized.

4. In a majority of states today, ultra vires has been abolished as a contractual defense, but shareholders may sue for an injunction to prevent performance of an ultra vires contract if performance has not yet occurred.

5. During his term of office, a director can be removed without cause only if the shareholders expressly reserved this power when the director was elected.

6. In different states the bylaws are initially adopted by either the incorporators, the directors, or the shareholders.

7. When the board of directors is given authority by statute or by the articles of incorporation to adopt or amend the bylaws, the shareholders cannot override the board's actions pursuant to such authority.

8. Shareholders as such are not agents of the corporation.

9. The notice to shareholders of a special shareholders' meeting must state the purpose or purposes for which the meeting is being called, but the business transacted at the meeting does not have to be limited to the purposes set forth in the notice.

10. Cumulative voting applies only to the election of directors.

11. A proxy creates an agency relationship.

12. Cumulative voting guarantees minority shareholder representation on the board of directors.

13. All states require that the board of directors have at least three members.

Chapter 33

14. Today there is a growing tendency to have some of the positions on the board of directors filled by disinterested outsiders.

15. If a board of directors is "classified," its members serve staggered terms.

16. A director as such is not an agent of the corporation.

17. As a general rule, directors can vote by proxy in the same manner as shareholders.

18. Unless expressly required, notice of regular board meetings does not have to be given to individual directors.

19. An "executive committee" is a committee of shareholders chosen to present the views of all shareholders to the board of directors.

20. In recent years a few states have enacted statutes allowing the shareholders of close corporations to manage the enterprise without a board of directors.

21. In most states a director is prohibited from serving as an officer of the corporation.

22. Most states, as a general rule, prohibit the same person from serving as president and secretary simultaneously.

23. A close corporation is generally listed only on the New York Stock Exchange

24. Corporations are prohibited from entering into partnership.

25. Corporations in general are highly regulated and rarely can do all the things an individual in business can do.

Multiple Choice

1. Which of the following actions are generally within the implied power of a corporation today?

    a) make charitable contributions.
    b) lend corporate funds to a completely unrelated company without interest or other value received in return.
    c) make campaign contributions.
    d) all of the above.
    e) none of the above.

2. Today, as a general rule, which of the following legal consequences can result from the making of an ultra vires contract?

    a) contract is void.
    b) contract is valid and there are no other legal consequences.

Chapter 33

    c) shareholders acting in behalf of corporation can sue responsible directors and officers for damages.
    d) suit by the state for damages.
    e) none of the above.

3. Which of the following actions are generally within the power of shareholders to perform?

    a) remove a director during his term of office without cause.
    b) dictate details of daily corporate operation.
    c) approval of sale of corporate assets not in the regular course of corporate business.
    d) all of the above.
    e) a and c, but not b.

4. Which of the following is not a method of concentrating shareholder voting power?

    a) cumulative voting.
    b) voting by unanimous written consent.
    c) use of proxies.
    d) voting trust.
    e) shareholder agreement.

5. Shareholders' meetings

    a) have been replaced in recent years by written consent as the most common method for shareholder action.
    b) must be held at least three times a year under the law of most states.
    c) must be held in the state of incorporation.
    d) are either manual or special.

6. Action by shareholders

    a) can be taken at a shareholders' meeting only if a quorum is present.
    b) can be taken at an annual shareholders' meeting only if the action relates to the purpose of the meeting that had been stated in the notice of meeting.
    c) can be taken at a shareholders' meeting only if votes are counted by impartial "tellers."
    d) all of the above.
    e) a and b, but not c.

7. Which of the following are required by statute in a majority of states as qualifications for serving on a board of directors?

    a) minimum age.
    b) resident of state of incorporation.
    c) own shares in the corporation.
    d) all of the above.
    e) none of the above.

Chapter 33

8. Which of the following is descriptive of a director?

   a) agent of the corporation.
   b) agent of shareholders.
   c) cannot bind the corporation by action as an individual.
   d) viewed by law as being engaged in a joint venture with other directors.

9. Which of the following is false with regard to the board of directors' exercise of its functions?

   a) In almost all states a director cannot vote by proxy at a board meeting.
   b) In most states the board meeting is the only way for the board to take any official action.
   c) A quorum must be present before action can validly be taken at a board meeting.
   d) State laws generally do not require that notice of regular board meetings be given to directors.

10. The board of directors

    a) cannot delegate any of its powers.
    b) can delegate power to officers, but not to corporate employees who are not officers.
    c) can delegate power to an executive committee to make ordinary decisions but not unusual ones such as filling a vacancy on the board.
    d) can usually take action only by a greater-than-majority vote, such as two-thirds.

11. Corporate powers are derived from which of the following:

    a) statutory, express, actual.
    b) implied, express, actual.
    c) statutory, implied, actual.
    d) statutory, implied, express.

12. Most states usually provide that a quorum is present when:

    a) all directors are present.
    b) one-half the directors and 2 corporate officers are present.
    c) a majority of the authorized number of directors are present.
    d) none of the above.

Short Essay

1. Explain why directors are not agents of the corporation or of the shareholders who elect them.

2. Burbank Corporation has 100,000 shares of stock outstanding. Five

Chapter 33

director positions are up for election at its annual meeting. Cumulative voting is in effect. Carlson owns 40,000 shares. He has nominated his own slate of candidates for the five positions. Carlson would like to elect a majority of the board, or if not a majority, as many of his candidates as possible. Can he elect a majority by using cumulative voting? If not, how many can he elect? Explain.

Chapter 34

Corporations/Rights and Liabilities of Shareholders and Managers

True-False

1. All shares of stock carry voting rights in the form of one vote per share.

2. Dividends cannot be paid out of the original capital investment in the corporation.

3. A person who owns stock that is "preferred" as to dividends has a guarantee that he will receive annual dividends in the stated amount.

4. When a dividend preference is "cumulative," it means that if dividends are not paid in any year in the amount of the preference, they accumulate and must be paid in a future year before any dividend is paid to common shareholders.

5. A preemptive right is one requiring that each shareholder must be given an opportunity to purchase the number of newly issued shares that will maintain his proportionate interest in the corporation.

6. All shares of stock carry some form of preemptive right.

7. Restrictions on transferability of shares are valid if they take the form of an option to purchase within a reasonable time period, but such restrictions are much less important in close corporations than in others.

8. A shareholder's right to inspect corporate records, if such right exists, includes the right to copy these records.

9. A stock subscription is a contract to purchase shares of stock.

10. The "par value" of shares may or may not bear any relation to their market value.

11. Watered stock is stock which is sold upon its original issuance at a price below its par, stated, or market value.

12. A shareholder is always liable for the return of an illegal dividend if he knew of the illegality when receiving the payment.

13. In most states a director's right to inspect corporate records is absolute and unqualified.

14. A corporation is never permitted to indemnify a director for his legal expenses incurred in connection with a lawsuit if that director had

Chapter 34

actually committed a wrongful act that led to the lawsuit.

15. The "business judgment rule" means that a corporate manager is required to exercise his best judgment in running the corporation and can be held liable for damages to the corporation if he makes an honest, non-negligent decision that turned out to be wrong.

16. Directors and officers are deemed to be fiduciaries of the corporation, but lesser corporate managers are not.

17. Under the "line of business" test, a corporate manager cannot take personal advantage of a business opportunity that is closely associated with the corporation's line of business unless the corporation rejects or is unable to exploit the opportunity.

18. A corporate director cannot personally make a contract with the corporation he serves.

19. Controlling shareholders, but not minority shareholders, have fiduciary duties to the corporation that are similar to the duties owed by directors and officers.

20. SEC Rule 10(b)-5 prohibits the use of material inside information only by officers, directors, or ten percent owners of stock.

21. The significance of preemptive rights diminishes if a corporation's stock is closely held.

22. Shares of stock are recognized by law as items of real property.

23. Restrictions of transferability must be included in the articles and bylaws and does not have to be shown on the stock certificate.

24. A shareholder only has access to corporate records after proving that they will do so at any reasonable time or times, for any proper purpose.

Multiple Choice

1. Which of the following has no relation to dividends?

    a) insolvency.
    b) surplus.
    c) watered stock.
    d) preference.

2. Which of the following statements regarding preferred shares of stock is true?

    a) cannot be participating, but can be cumulative.
    b) cannot be both participating and cumulative.

Chapter 34

    c) presumed to be participating if not made expressly nonparticipating.
    d) can be preferred as to dividends, distribution of assets upon liquidation, or both.

3. Existing shareholders have preemptive rights in connection with which of the following sales of shares by the corporation?

    a) sale of treasury stock by the corporation.
    b) sale of newly issued shares by the corporation in return for services rendered to the corporation.
    c) sale of newly issued shares by the corporation in return for property transferred to corporation.
    d) all of the above.
    e) none of the above.

4. Restrictions on the transferability of shares

    a) are more important in the case of close corporations than in corporations having widely dispersed ownership of its shares.
    b) must be stated on the stock certificate to bind a purchaser of the stock who is unaware of the restriction.
    c) generally take the form of options to purchase.
    d) all of the above.
    e) a and c, but not b.

5. Shares of stock cannot lawfully be issued

    a) for more than the par value.
    b) in return for services that are merely promised rather than already performed.
    c) for more than the stated value.
    d) for more than the market value.
    e) in return for property.

6. Which of the following are not basic rights of a director?

    a) recognition as a director by his associates.
    b) voting at a directors' meeting.
    c) inspection of corporate records.
    d) compensation for services as a director.

7. Which of the following is a violation of a director's duty of diligence?

    a) inadequate supervision of an inept subordinate.
    b) failure to exercise the kind of care that an ordinarily prudent person would exercise in a similar position and under similar circumstances.
    c) repeated and unexcused absence from board meetings.
    d) unquestioning reliance on obviously unreasonable advice of an expert.
    e) all of the above.
    f) only a and c.

Chapter 34

8. Which of the following has the least relation to the duty of loyalty owed by a director or officer?

   a) confidential information.
   b) restriction on transferability of shares.
   c) corporate funds.
   d) corporate opportunity.

9. Even though an activity that violates federal securities laws will frequently also be a breach of fiduciary duty under state common law, the federal laws are nevertheless very important because they

   a) provide for enforcement by a federal agency, the SEC.
   b) provide for penalties that may not have existed at common law.
   c) define some types of duties with greater precision than existed at common law.
   d) all of the above.
   e) a and c, but not b.

10. Which of the following is true with regard to short-swing profits?

    a) absolutely forbidden.
    b) absolutely forbidden for directors.
    c) must be turned over to corporation if made by owner of ten percent or more of any type of shares issued by the corporation.
    d) must be turned over to corporation only if the profits resulted from use of material inside information.

11. Courts have not recognized preemptive rights in all circumstances. Which of the following are situations in which such rights have been held not to exist.

    a) sale of new stock.
    b) issuance of shares for patent rights.
    c) issuance of shares for compensation to recruit new executives.
    d) a and b.
    e) b and c.

12. In the case of Francis v. United Jersey Bank the issue involved was:

    a) did a corporate director aid the officers of the corporation in "looting" the funds?
    b) did a corporate director act negligently in the role by allowing the "looting" to continue?
    c) is a "figurehead" director liable for acts done by the officers?
    d) all of the above.

Chapter 34

Short Essay

1. Explain the rationale behind the corporate opportunity rule.

2. The managers of Cornwall Corporation wanted the company to acquire Quasi Corp., a smaller firm producing a line of products somewhat related to Cornwall's product line. A merger plan was adopted by Cornwall's board of directors and approved by its shareholders. The plan was also approved by Quasi's directors and shareholders. According to the plan, Cornwall would issue its own shares to Quasi shareholders who would, in turn, transfer their shares of Quasi to Cornwall. Quasi shareholders received one share of Cornwall for three shares of Quasi. In order to carry out the plan, however, the shareholders of Cornwall had to authorize the issuance of additional Cornwall shares, since there were not enough authorized but unissued Cornwall shares in existence to accomplish the plan. At the shareholders' meeting where the question of authorizing the issuance was being voted on, McArthur, a Cornwall shareholder, claimed that all existing Cornwall shareholders would have preemptive rights with respect to the new shares. Cornwall's articles of incorporation said nothing about preemptive rights. Is the shareholder correct in claiming that preemptive rights exist? Explain.

Chapter 35

Corporations/Merger, Consolidation, and Termination

True-False

1. Although a technical distinction is made between a merger and a consolidation, there is little practical difference between the two.

2. A merger is something that the "acquired" firm itself will never initiate, that is, no firm ever seeks to be acquired.

3. The vote required for approval of a merger or consolidation by each company's shareholders varies among the states from a simple majority to four-fifths of the outstanding shares.

4. In a majority of states the merger of parent and subsidiary corporations can be accomplished without shareholder approval, but only if the parent owns 90 or 95 percent of the subsidiary's shares.

5. Prior to being changed by statute, the common law rule was that a merger required the unanimous approval of the shareholders of each corporation.

6. The appraisal right is a dissenting shareholder's right to require that the assets of his corporation be appraised before the corporation is bought out by another company.

7. The same practical results as a statutory merger or consolidation can be achieved by an asset or stock acquisition.

8. In an asset acquisition, the acquiring company usually does not have to obtain shareholder approval.

9. The acquired company must obtain shareholder approval before selling all or most of its assets.

10. A corporation automatically dissolves when it sells all of its assets.

11. Control of a corporation can never be obtained by acquisition of less than 50 percent of its assets.

12. A tender offer is simply a publicly advertised offer to purchase shares from shareholders of a "target" company.

13. A "sale of control" is the sale of a corporation's controlling shares at a price that exceeds their market value.

14. A party who makes a tender offer cannot place a limit on the number of shares to be purchased, but must take all shares made available in

Chapter 35

response to the tender offer.

15. A party making a tender offer cannot make it conditional upon it being accepted by the holders of a sufficiently large number of shares to give the offeror control.

16. The board of directors does not have the power to dissolve the corporation.

17. The shareholder vote required for voluntary dissolution is generally the same as for a merger or consolidation.

18. A court will dissolve a corporation at the request of a single shareholder if it finds that the corporation is being so grossly mismanaged that its assets are actually being wasted.

19. A total absence of corporate activity does not automatically cause dissolution, but it does give the state a basis for obtaining court-ordered dissolution.

20. After dissolution of a corporation, a receiver will always be appointed by a court for the purpose of winding up corporate affairs.

Multiple Choice

1. Which of the following might be a reason for a merger?

    a) acquisition of technological know-how.
    b) diversification.
    c) growth for growth's sake, without increased efficiency, but with possibly greater personal rewards for managers.
    d) all of the above.
    e) a and b, but not c.

2. Regarding the procedures for a formal merger or consolidation,

    a) the process is usually begun by the board of directors.
    b) shareholder approval is generally not necessary.
    c) the most common requirement for shareholder approval is a simple majority vote.
    d) none of the above.
    e) a and c.

3. The shareholder vote required to approve a merger

    a) is not less than two-thirds in any state.
    b) was unanimous at common law, but today it is two-thirds in every state.
    c) is as high as four-fifths of the outstanding shares in some states.
    d) is a simple majority in all states.

Chapter 35

4. The appraisal right

   a) came into existence as a result of the change from a requirement of unanimous to less-than-unanimous shareholder approval of a merger.
   b) was created out of concern for fairness to those shareholders who voted against a merger that was approved.
   c) gives shareholders who voted against a merger that was approved the right to sell their shares back to the corporation for cash.
   d) all of the above.
   e) none of the above.

5. Which of the following is not true with regard to an acquisition by one corporation of all the assets of another corporation?

   a) has the same practical effect as a statutory merger.
   b) the purchase can be made only with cash.
   c) shareholders of acquired company must give approval.
   d) the acquired company does not automatically dissolve.

6. Which of the following is not true with regard to an acquisition by one corporation of a controlling portion of the stock of another corporation?

   a) is a useful method for acquiring control over another corporation when the managers of the target company are opposed to the takeover.
   b) acquiring company cannot deal directly with target company's shareholders, but must deal with that company's directors.
   c) can sometimes be accomplished by a tender offer.
   d) after control is obtained, acquiring company might operate acquired company as a subsidiary.

7. Which of the following has the least relation to a combination of two corporations?

   a) antitrust laws.
   b) federal and state securities laws.
   c) ultra vires.
   d) tender offer.
   e) appraisal right.

8. Which of the following has the greatest relation to a combination of two corporations?

   a) deadlock.
   b) piercing the corporate veil.
   c) promoters.
   d) two-thirds vote of shareholders.
   e) cumulative voting.

9. Dissolution of a corporation

   a) can never be accomplished by the incorporators.

Chapter 35

   b) can be accomplished by vote of the shareholders, the required vote varying among the states in the same manner as for mergers.
   c) can in some circumstances be accomplished by the board of directors.
   d) can be ordered by the state only in the case of a deadlock.

10. In which of the following situations does the state not have power to file a court action seeking dissolution of a corporation?

   a) Corporation has performed ultra vires acts.
   b) Corporation has abandoned its business.
   c) Corporation has violated state antitrust laws.
   d) Corporation has been unprofitable.
   e) Corporation misrepresented material facts in obtaining certificate of incorporation.

Short Essay

1. What is a "sale of control," and how is it viewed by the courts?

2. Corporation X was to be merged with Corporation Y. Jones, a shareholder of X, voted against the merger, but it was approved by the required vote of both X's and Y's shareholders. Jones did nothing at the time, but several months after the merger actually took place, he decided that he no longer wanted to be a shareholder in the merged company. He asserted his appraisal right, claiming that the corporation should pay him the fair value of his shares. Does Jones have this right? Explain.

Chapter 36

Real Property

True-False

1. Minerals in the ground are considered to be real property, but if the owner removes them and then sells them separately, it is a sale of personal property.

2. Naturally growing vegetation on the land is generally treated as real property, but cultivated vegetation on the land is generally treated as personal property.

3. The law concerning air rights is merely a theoretical novelty, and has no practical economic significance today.

4. In some states oil and gas in the ground are not treated like other minerals with respect to ownership.

5. An item that once was personal property but has become real property because it is not a fixture can never again acquire the status of personal property.

6. Under no circumstances can an item be a fixture unless it is firmly and permanently attached to the land or to a building.

7. An item attached to real property by a landlord is more likely to be a fixture than is an item attached by a tenant.

8. A life estate is basically the equivalent of a fee simple estate for one's lifetime.

9. One of the most common limitations on a fee simple defeasible is one that relates to the use that is to be made of the land.

10. A tenancy for years is a leasehold created for a stated period of time.

11. An easement is described as "in gross" if it is created specifically for use in connection with another tract of land.

12. There is no distinction between an assignee of a leasehold and a sublessee.

13. A joint tenancy is characterized by the "right of survivorship," but a tenancy in common is not.

14. An open listing is an arrangement between an owner of real property and a broker, whereby the broker is entitled to a commission only if he is the first one to procure a buyer who is ready, willing, and able to buy at the stated selling price.

Chapter 36

15. An abstract is a compilation of the official records relating to a particular parcel of land.

16. A special warranty deed is a sufficient performance of the seller's obligations under the sale contract unless that contract specifically required a general warranty deed.

17. A quitclaim deed is one that purports to convey title but contains no warranties.

18. Consideration is not a requirement for a valid deed.

19. Metes and bounds descriptions in deed are more commonly employed in rural areas than in urban areas.

20. To acquire title by adverse possession, the possessor must actually live on the property for the period of time prescribed by statute.

21. Land includes not only the earth's surface but also everything above and beneath it.

22. Mineral interests may never be severed from surface rights.

23. A life tenant may lease the mineral interests in the property and may further extract and sell them as long as they live on the land.

24. A life tenant has no duty to pay taxes on the property as his tenancy is only temporary.

25. An oil and gas lease is not truly a lease because there is no conveyance of a possessory interest in the real property.

Multiple Choice

1. Which of the following is not classified as real property?

    a) air space above the land.
    b) naturally growing trees on the land.
    c) fixtures.
    d) coal that has been removed from the ground.
    e) shingles on the roof of a house.

2. Which of the following is important in determining whether an item is a fixture?

    a) intent.
    b) whether item can be removed from a building without damage to the building.
    c) purpose for which item was made.
    d) local custom.

Chapter 36

    e) all of the above.
    f) a and b only.

3. Which of the following is a possessory interest in real property?

    a) lien.
    b) life estate.
    c) easement.
    d) profit.
    e) license.

4. Which of the following is a nonpossessory interest in real property?

    a) leasehold.
    b) periodic tenancy.
    c) tenancy at will.
    d) easement appurtenant.
    e) fee simple defeasible.

5. A life tenant cannot do which of the following things in connection with the land he occupies?

    a) conduct a business on it.
    b) rent it to someone else.
    c) drill a new oil well on it.
    d) cut timber for the purpose of sale, where the land was already being used for this purpose when the life tenant became a life tenant.
    e) take coal from an existing mine.

6. Which of the following has the least relation to concurrent ownership of real property?

    a) partition.
    b) open and notorious.
    c) right of survivorship.
    d) presumption of tenancy in common.
    e) joint tenancy.

7. Which of the following arrangements between a landowner and a broker for the purpose of selling the owner's land is most advantageous to the broker?

    a) exclusive agency.
    b) open listing.
    c) bargain and sale.
    d) exclusive right to sell.

8. Which of the following is generally required for a valid deed?

    a) consideration.
    b) acknowledgment.
    c) written.

Chapter 36

    d) recorded.
    e) all of the above except a.

9. Which of the following is true with regard to "recording"?

    a) An unrecorded deed is void between grantor and grantee.
    b) A grantee qualifies as a BFP only if he records his own deed.
    c) Recording statutes apply only to the sale of a fee simple interest, not to easements or mortgages.
    d) An unrecorded deed is void with respect to a subsequent good faith purchaser for value.

10. Which of the following is not a requirement for acquisition of title by adverse possession?

    a) good faith of possessor.
    b) reasonably continuous possession.
    c) hostile possession.
    d) open and notorious possession.
    e) physical control of land by possessor.

11. In a sales transaction of land the seller will receive:

    a) only the natural vegetation on the property.
    b) the cultivated and natural vegetation always.
    c) the cultivated vegetation, a natural vegetation has no value.
    d) none of the above.

12. In the case of *Cook v. Beerman* the issue established by the court was:

    a) whether the irrigation equipment was included in the sale.
    b) the admissibility of parol evidence in a contract for the sale of land.
    c) whether the pump and motor were fixtures or items of personalty.
    d) whether the contract was ambiguous.

Short Essay

1. What is a real estate "closing" (or "settlement")? Explain what happens at a closing.

2. Thompson owned a tract of land. He sold the land to Williams, who did not record his deed. Before Williams took possession of the land, Thompson fraudulently executed a mortgage on the land to secure a loan he received from Colby. If Thompson defaults on the loan, can Colby enforce his mortgage against Williams's land? Explain. Does it matter whether Colby recorded his mortgage? Explain.

Chapter 37

Personal Property

True-False

1. An important exception to the "all-or-nothing" concept of personal property ownership is a lease.

2. Unlike real property, personal property cannot be jointly owned by two or more persons.

3. A gift of personal property is made only if the donor intends to transfer ownership, not merely possession or the right to use the property.

4. A retention by the donor of even partial control over the item claimed to have been given usually prevents the gift from being effective.

5. Delivery of an item of personal property to the donee's agent is not a sufficient delivery to constitute a valid gift.

6. Assuming that the donor intends to make a gift of personal property, no formal delivery is necessary if the property is already in possession of the donee.

7. If it is impractical or inconvenient to deliver actual physical possession of an item of personal property because of its size or location, the requirement of delivery for making a gift is entirely dispensed with.

8. A gift cannot be made of <u>intangible</u> personal property because there is no way to accomplish physical delivery.

9. In the case of a joint tenancy bank account (that is, with a right of survivorship) in the names of X and Y, created with funds belonging to X, there is a presumption that X intended to make a gift to Y of those funds remaining when X dies.

10. The phrase "joint account," used to describe a bank account, may or may not mean that the account is a true joint tenancy.

11. A majority of courts have relaxed the delivery requirement for making a gift in the case of a joint tenancy bank account.

12. A gift inter vivos is made between two living persons; a gift causa mortis is not.

13. A gift causa mortis is automatically revoked if the donee dies before the donor.

Chapter 37

14. A gift causa mortis is automatically revoked if the donor does not die from the current illness or peril.

15. The only way to make a valid gift conditional on the donor's death without an immediate transfer of possession is by executing a formal "will."

16. If property has been abandoned, ownership is acquired by the first person who takes possession of it with an intent to become the owner, even if that person is a trespasser on the premises where he finds the property.

17. As a general rule, the finder of lost property automatically becomes the rightful owner, whereas the owner of the premises where the property is discovered automatically becomes the owner of mislaid property.

18. When one person permanently affixes something to another's personal property without the latter's consent, ownership of the resulting product goes to the owner of the "principal" item.

19. A confusion of goods occurring by agreement of the owners of the goods causes them to be tenants in common of the resulting mass.

20. If a confusion of goods is caused by the deliberately wrongful conduct of a party who had owned some of the goods, he automatically loses ownership of the goods that had been his.

Multiple Choice

1. Which of the following is an exception to the "all-or-nothing" concept of personal property ownership?

    a) bailment.
    b) security interest.
    c) lease.
    d) easement.
    e) profit.

2. For there to be a valid gift of personal property the donor must have an intent to transfer ownership. This means that

    a) there is no gift if the donor's intent is to transfer mere possession.
    b) a gift cannot be made if the property is subject to a security interest.
    c) a tenant in common cannot make a gift to someone of his undivided interest in the property.
    d) transfer of possession creates a very strong presumption of intent to transfer ownership.

3. Which of the following has no relation to the requirement that there be a delivery of possession for a valid gift to be made?

331

Chapter 37

   a) accession.
   b) control.
   c) constructive.
   d) symbolic.

4. In which of the following situations is there not a sufficient delivery of possession to be a valid gift?

   a) delivery of keys to a car.
   b) delivery to donor's agent.
   c) delivery to donee's agent.
   d) delivery of savings account book.

5. X deposits $5,000 of his money in a joint tenancy bank account in the name of X and Y. The money is still in the account when X dies.

   a) In most states Y will not get the money because X did not give up complete control over it during his lifetime and thus there was no gift.
   b) As a general rule, the money will go to X's heirs, not Y.
   c) The law presumes that X intended to make a gift to Y and this presumption cannot be rebutted.
   d) A majority of courts have relaxed the delivery requirement for a valid gift in this type of case.

6. A difference between gifts inter vivos and gifts causa mortis is that

   a) a gift inter vivos is automatically revoked by the donor's death.
   b) a gift causa mortis is not a gift between two living persons.
   c) a gift causa mortis is automatically revoked if the donee dies before the donor.
   d) a gift inter vivos is automatically revoked if the donor does not die from his current illness or peril.

7. W's diamond ring is discovered by X on Y's premises. Which of the following parties is the owner of the ring immediately after its discovery?

   a) X, if the ring was lost.
   b) W, regardless of whether the ring was lost or mislaid.
   c) Y, if the ring was mislaid.
   d) a and c.

8. Ownership of which of the following types of personal property can be acquired by "occupation"?

   a) wild animals.
   b) abandoned property.
   c) wild birds and fish.
   d) all of the above.
   e) a and c, but not b.

9. Which of the following has the least relation to the concept of accession?

Chapter 37

    a) tenancy in common.
    b) addition.
    c) change of identity.
    d) increase in value.
    e) good faith.

10. Which of the following has the greatest relation to the concept of confusion of goods?

    a) delivery of possession.
    b) identifying which is the "principal item."
    c) tenancy in common.
    d) increase in value.

Short Essay

1. What types of personal property can be the subject of a gift made by constructive delivery?

2. Carla owned several rubies, emeralds, and other precious stones that she kept in a small locked jewelry box in her dresser drawer. She wished to give the stones to her friend Sandra. Carla took Sandra to the room where she kept the stones, opened the dresser drawer, and showed her the jewelry box containing them. Carla told Sandra, "The stones in the box are yours." Leaving the stones where they were, Carla shut the drawer and then gave Sandra the key that would open the jewelry box. Sandra left, taking the key with her. Several weeks later Carla died, the stones still being located in the jewelry box in her dresser drawer. Sandra claimed that Carla had made a gift of the stones to her, but Carla's heirs claimed that there had not been a valid gift and therefore the stones belonged to them. Who is correct? Explain.

Chapter 38

Wills, Trusts, and Estates

True-False

1. A will transforms a person's wishes about the disposition of his or her property into a valid, legal instrument.

2. A minor may make a valid will to dispose of his property.

3. With regard to the disposition of the testator's property, real estate is bequeathed, money passing under the will is devised, and all other property is disposed of by a legacy.

4. When a will is published it is printed in the newspaper after the testator's death.

5. Formalities in the preparation of a will are not often strictly observed as the courts usually regard the intent of the testator/testatrix to be the controlling factor.

6. It is not essential for a will to state it revokes any and all prior wills, as the will with the most current date will supersede all other wills.

7. A will cannot operate to transfer property until the testator/testatrix dies.

8. A will may be revoked only by the testator's express written direction.

9. A holographic will is purely statutory in nature, it must be made in compliance with the appropriate state law.

10. A nuncupative will is an oral will and is valid only during the testator's last illness or in contemplation or fear of death.

11. Under the state laws of intestacy, real property will descend and personal property is distributed.

12. The law of Dower and Curtesy is still effective in most of the states today.

13. As a general rule property descends to the children and lineal descendants to the exclusion of parents, or brothers and sisters.

14. An estate will ascend only if there are no surviving descendants or spouse.

Chapter 38

15. Relatives by marriage may claim an interest in the estate only if there are no living blood relatives.

16. Life insurance proceeds are subject to the administration of the estate.

17. A sole proprietor's business cannot continue to operate unless it is provided for by will.

18. A trust established and effective during the life of the settlor is known as an inter vivos trust.

19. A testamentary trust becomes effective as soon as the testator signs the trust instrument.

20. Trust law recognizes two types of property ownership, legal and equitable.

Multiple Choice

1. The term testamentary capacity includes which of the following:

   a) ownership of property.
   b) minimum age.
   c) mental capacity.
   d) b and c.
   e) all of the above.

2. Generally when a will is written it must contain the following requirements:

   a) testator/testatrix signature.
   b) signature of a witness.
   c) signed paragraph that will was published.
   d) all of the above.
   e) a and c.

3. The main function of a will is to provide for the disposal of property, but it can:

   a) provide for the appointment of the executor.
   b) cancel all previous wills.
   c) cancel the clause making the spouse the beneficiary.
   d) a and b.
   e) all of the above.

4. To establish a trust the settlor must:

   a) transfer legal ownership of property to trustee.
   b) name a beneficiary of the trust.
   c) write a will.
   d) a and b.
   e) all of the above.

Chapter 38

5. It is a general requirement that an express private trust be:

   a) established in writing.
   b) if oral, subsequently proved by a writing.
   c) a formal instrument detailing the property and beneficiary.
   d) a and c.
   e) a and b.

6. In a living trust the <u>res</u> may be which of the following properties:

   a) future interests.
   b) proceeds from life insurance on settlors life.
   c) nonproducing mineral interests.
   d) rental income on unfinished apartments.

7. In the event a trustee dies or declines to serve or is removed for cause the:

   a) court will declare the trust invalid and the property will revert to the settlor.
   b) court will let the beneficiary pick a new trustee.
   c) court will manage the trust.
   d) court is required to appoint an attorney to be the trustee.
   e) none of the above.

8. A trustee is charged by law to:

   a) make every effort to carry out the purpose of the trust.
   b) act with care and prudence and exercise his best judgment at <u>all</u> times.
   c) exercise an <u>extraordinary</u> degree of loyalty to the beneficiary.
   d) all of the above.

9. A spendthrift trust protects the:

   a) beneficiary from his creditors.
   b) beneficiaries' rights to receive principal and income.
   c) income and principal of the trust at all times.
   d) none of the above.

10. A settlor may revoke a trust at any time if:

    a) the trust <u>res</u> is not profitable.
    b) the beneficiary is abusing the income.
    c) the settlor merely changes his mind.
    d) they have specifically reserved that power.

Short Essay

1. M died intestate with an estate valued at near $1 Million. His heirs are as follows: X, his son; Y, a legally adopted cousin; Z, his aunt's

Chapter 38

illegitimate daughter; S, a half-brother of A's mother; and three children of another half-brother of A's mother.

a) Under the general rules of intestacy, who will take what share?

b) If his son X predeceased A, what would the distribution be?

Chapter 39

Bailments

True-False

1. A bailment probably is not created when a customer hangs his coat on a coatrack at a restaurant.

2. Leaving a car at a parking lot is generally held to constitute a bailment only if the car owner is required to leave the car keys with the parking lot compay.

3. A nonowner cannot be a bailor.

4. Since a transfer of possession is required for there to be a bailment, intangible personal property cannot be the subject of a bailment.

5. The contract creating a bailment must be express, not implied, but it does not have to be in writing.

6. A so-called "bailment with the option to purchase" is not really a bailment at all.

7. Most bailments fall in the mutual benefit category.

8. A bailee may or may not have the right to use the bailed property, depending on the terms of the bailment contract and the general purpose of the bailment.

9. As a general rule, a bailee has the duty to exercise reasonable care to protect the property in his possession.

10. Characterization of a bailment as being one of mutual benefit or as being for the sole benefit of the bailor or bailee is irrelevant to the question of the degree of care that must be exercised by the bailee in handling the bailed property.

11. A provision in a bailment contract purporting to relieve the bailee from liability for any damage to the bailed property that might result from his negligence is frequently held by the courts to be contrary to public policy and unenforceable.

12. A bailee is liable to the bailor for damage to the bailed property only if the damage was caused by the bailee's negligence, even if he was using the property in an unauthorized manner at the time of the accident.

13. The bailee's duty to use reasonable care in handling the bailed property is based on principles of tort law, while his duty to return the property to the bailor is based on principles of contract law.

Chapter 39

14. In cases where a bailee rents an item from a bailor who is in the business of renting such items, the modern trend is for courts to hold the bailor to an implied warranty that the item is fit for its intended purposes.

15. In connection with a bailor's liability for supplying a bailee with a defective item that causes harm to the bailee, there is no practical difference between the negligence and warranty theories of liability.

16. A common carrier is one who furnishes transportation facilities to the general public and who is liable for damage to the bailor's goods only if it is shown that the carrier was negligent.

17. A common carrier in interstate commerce is permitted by federal law to limit its liability for loss or damage to the bailed property.

18. The liability of a public warehouseman is generally the same as that of an ordinary bailee rather than that of a common carrier.

19. There is no distinction between an ordinary bailee and a public warehouseman.

20. The taking of articles of personal property to a hotel room by a guest does not create a bailment relationship between the guest and the hotel.

Multiple Choice

1. Which of the following creates a bailment?

    a) renting an automobile.
    b) owner leaving car at parking lot and keeping the keys.
    c) customer hangs coat on a coatrack in a restaurant.
    d) guest taking a suitcase into a hotel room.

2. Which of the following items of property cannot be the subject of a bailment?

    a) shares of corporate stock.
    b) residential house and lot.
    c) airplane.
    d) boat.

3. In which of the following bailments is the bailee generally not required to return the identical goods to the bailor.

    a) bailment of technologically complex goods such as electronic equipment.
    b) bailment of grain or other fungible goods.
    c) bailment of goods that rapidly fluctuate in value.
    d) bailment for sole benefit of bailor.

Chapter 39

4. Which of the following are examples of a mutual benefit bailment?

   a) paying for parking space, parking car, and leaving keys with parking lot attendant.
   b) leaving television at repair shop for service.
   c) leaving coat with checkroom attendant at a restaurant.
   d) renting a power saw.
   e) all of the above.
   f) a and c only.

5. A bailee's right to use the bailed property

   a) does not exist.
   b) depends on the express terms of the bailment contract.
   c) usually does not exist if the contract is for storage.
   d) depends on the general purpose of the bailment if there is no express contract.
   e) none of the above.
   f) all of the above except a.

6. Jones leaves his car at Sam's garage for repairs. When Jones returns to pick up the car, it has been repaired but it also has acquired a huge dent in the right rear fender.

   a) Sam's garage is liable for the damage regardless of whether the garage was negligent.
   b) It is presumed that Sam's garage was negligent.
   c) Sam's garage is liable for the damage only if the garage was negligent.
   d) a and b, but not c.
   e) b and c, but not a.

7. Which of the following has no relation to the liability of a bailor in an ordinary bailment?

   a) knowledge of defect in bailed property.
   b) negligence.
   c) act of the shipper.
   d) warranty.
   e) reasonable care.

8. In which of the following situations is a common carrier most likely to be held liable for damage to the bailed property?

   a) damage caused by act of God.
   b) damage caused by unavoidable accident.
   c) damage caused by act of the shipper.
   d) damage caused by act of public authorities.
   e) damage caused by the inherent nature of the goods.

9. Which of the following ways is a public warehouseman distinguishable from an ordinary bailee?

Chapter 39

    a) Public warehouseman is strictly liable for damage to bailed goods.
    b) Public warehouseman has the same liability for damage to bailed goods as does a common carrier.
    c) Public warehouseman issues document of title for bailed goods.
    d) Public warehouseman is liable for damage to bailed goods only if he intentionally caused the damage.

Short Essay

1. What is the rationale for the rule that a bailee is presumed to have been negligent if the bailed property is lost or destroyed?

2. Thompson delivered 100 head of cattle to the Short Line Railroad for shipment from Tulsa, Oklahoma to Omaha, Nebraska. While en route, 35 of the cattle died of brucellosis. When the shipment arrived at Omaha, the dead cattle were examined by a veterinarian who indicated that the animals had been diseased before shipment from Tulsa and that the railroad car in which they were carried was the kind normally used for shipping cattle. Thompson, however, claimed that the Short Line was liable to him for the value of the dead cattle because of its status as a common carrier, which makes it absolutely liable for such a loss. Is Thompson correct? Explain.

ANSWERS

Chapter 1

True-False

1. F 2. T 3. T 4. F 5. T 6. F 7. T 8. T 9. T
10. F 11. F 12. F 13. F 14. F 15. F

Multiple Choice

1. b 2. d 3. c 4. e 5. d 6. a 7. c 8. d

Short Essay

1. a. Equity courts arose primarily because the remedies which the courts of law could grant were limited. Courts of law could only grant judgments for damages (i.e., in cases where the plaintiff wanted money), and judgments in which the ownership of real or personal property was decided.

   b. i. Injunction -- an order of a court ordering the defendant to refrain from a certain activity, or to perform a specified act.
      ii. Decree of specific performance -- an order of a court ordering the defendant to live up to the terms of a contract.
      iii. Rescission -- an order of a court cancelling a contract (upon proof that legal grounds exist for doing so).

2. Normally the suit would have to be filed in an Indiana state court having jurisdiction of Y's residence. Suit could not be commenced in a federal court in Indiana on diversity grounds because less than $10,000 is involved. And suit could not be brought in a Pennsylvania state court having jurisdiction of Y's land because this is a _personal action_ -- that is, Y's land in Pennsylvania is _not_ the subject of the action.

Chapter 2

True-False

1. T 2. T 3. F 4. T 5. F 6. F 7. F 8. T 9. F 10. F 11. T 12. F 13. T 14. T 15. F 16. T 17. T

Multiple Choice

1. e 2. d 3. b 4. a 5. e 6. a 7. c 8. e 9. a 10. a

Short Essay

1. The court <u>overruled</u> the separate but equal doctrine. The reason why this case, <u>unlike</u> some earlier ones, "directly presented" the question as to whether the doctrine should be continued is because in this case the facilities afforded (in the states involved here) were equal or substantially equal to those afforded whites. Thus, for the first time in the educational arena, the court had to decide whether segregation <u>alone</u> violated the equal protection clause. The court said it did.

2. Administrative agencies do make law if they are given rule-making authority -- as is often the case. Such agencies make law by promulgating their rules and regulations pursuant to the authority granted by the statute by which they are created.

3. a) Most torts violate the rights of individuals, but do not constitute wrongs against the state -- that is, do not violate criminal law.

   b) While a breach of contract is a wrong, it is not a tort. A breach of contract violates a duty one person owes to another by virtue of an agreement having been entered into between the parties. That is, each contracting party owes certain duties to the other, but not to society in general. A tort, on the other hand, is the violation by one person of another person's rights which spring not from contract, but from general obligations that are inherently owed to all members of society.

Chapter 3

True-False

1. T 2. T 3. F 4. F 5. T 6. F 7. F 8. F 9. T 10. F
11. F 12. F 13. F 14. T 15. F 16. T 17. T 18. T

Multiple Choice

1. d 2. b 3. a 4. e 5. c 6. d 7. a 8. b 9. d 10. c
11. c 12. c

Short Essay

1. Express contracts are those in which the intentions and obligations of the parties are spelled out--usually but not necessarily in writing--in detail. In implied contracts, on the other hand, the intentions and obligations of the parties have to be "guessed at" to some extent, depending on the parties' conduct and the circumstances within which the conduct took place. Quasi-contracts are fictitious contracts imposed by courts only to prevent unjust enrichment. The actual intentions of the parties in such an instance are not material.

2. While no true contract existed between X and the school district--that is, no express or implied contract--X can recover on the quasi-contract theory. Where the school district had a clear legal obligation to provide transportation and did not do so, the district would be unjustly enriched if X were not allowed recovery of the $175.

Chapter 4

True-False

1. T 2. T 3. T 4. F 5. T 6. T 7. F 8. T 9. F 10. T
11. F 12. T 13. F 14. F 15. T 16. T 17. F 18. T 19. T
20. T

Multiple Choice

1. b 2. a 3. b 4. b 5. c 6. d 7. e 8. a 9. d 10. b

Short Essay

1. Prior to adoption of the UCC there were some instances where a sales contract had apparently been made between two companies, and, later, one of the parties sought to get out of the contract by showing that the terms appearing on its acceptance were at least slightly different from the terms appearing in the form used by the other company. Because some courts ruled in such circumstances that a sales contract was never formed, but rather there was only an offer and a counter-offer, the drafters of the UCC decided that if the basic terms of the contract were agreed to, minor variations in the forms should not be allowed to defeat the entire agreement.

2. a) A contract does not exist, based on the Lucier case in the text. Rather, there was an offer and a counter-offer, since the terms were not identical.

   b) There is still no contract. A decision by an offeree to accept an offer has no significance until it is in some way communicated to the offeror.

Chapter 5

True-False

1. F 2. T 3. T 4. T 5. T 6. F 7. F 8. T 9. T 10. T
11. T 12. F 13. F 14. T 15. F 16. T 17. T 18. F 19. T
20. T

Multiple Choice

1. a 2. d 3. b 4. b 5. a 6. d 7. a 8. c 9. a 10. c

Short Essay

1. The doctrine of promissory estoppel is the idea that, in certain circumstances, a person who makes a promise ought to be liable on it even if the promisee did not give consideration in return. The doctrine is applicable to the situation in which a promisor makes a promise in circumstances in which he knows or ought to know will cause the promisee to perform an act or embark on a course of action, significant in nature, and where in reliance on the promise the promisee does so react. The purpose of the doctrine is to let the promisee (if he has acted reasonably) recover from the promisor even though his conduct (the promisee's) did not constitute consideration. In most general terms, then, the doctrine is applied to <u>prevent injustice</u> to the promisee.

2. The Seller Company is wrong. This is a valid <u>requirements contract</u>; i.e., consideration is present. The consideration given by the Buyer Company, the moment the contract was made, was the implied promise that <u>if</u> it needed any chicken pluckers, it would not buy them from anyone other than the Seller Company. This constitutes the waiver of a legal right, which is consideration. (The fact that it was possible that the Buyer Company would not have any need for any pluckers is thus immaterial.)

Chapter 6

True-False

1. T   2. F   3. T   4. T   5. T   6. T   7. F   8. F   9. F   10. F
11. T   12. F   13. T   14. F   15. T   16. F   17. T   18. F   19. T
20. F

Multiple Choice

1. c   1. a   3. e   4. e   5. c   6. b   7. b   8. d   9. b   10. a

Short Essay

1. Jennifer is liable on the contract. Jennifer ratified the contract by continuing to pay after reaching majority age of 18.

2. Convicted felons while imprisoned are civilly dead, and any contract they enter into is void. Therefore, Ruby's contracts will be set aside. Ruby was still incarcerated even while she was free as her time was tolled until she was returned to serve her prison time.

Chapter 7

True-False

1. F 2. T 3. T 4. F 5. T 6. T 7. T 8. F 9. F 10. T
11. T 12. T 13. T 14. T 15. T 16. T 17. T 18. F 19. T
20. F 21. F

Multiple Choice

1. c 2. e 3. a 4. c 5. e 6. d 7. a 8. b 9. d 10. a

Short Essay

1. Wiley would be able to recover a judgment for his kit but not for his advice. In order to dispense legal advice Wiley must be licensed by the State Bar Association and this is a regulatory license.

   This is also an example of a severable contract as a portion of the contract is enforceable and a portion is not.

   Wiley, would probably find it difficult to explain his breach of ethics of practicing law without a license to the State Bar Association also. (Strange case, but true.)

Chapter 8

True-False

1. T 2. T 3. F 4. T 5. F 6. T 7. F 8. F 9. F 10. F
11. T 12. T 13. F 14. F 15. T 16. F 17. F 18. T 19. F
20. T

Multiple Choice

1. b 2. a 3. c 4. c 5. b 6. c 7. a 8. d 9. e 10. b

Short Essay

1. Reality of consent does not exist if fraud, innocent misrepresentation, mistake of fact (in some instances), or duress is present when the contract was formed. Fraud is the <u>intentional</u> misleading of one person by another; innocent misrepresentation is a statement <u>thought to be true</u> but which in fact is false and misleads the other party. Mistake of fact is grounds for avoiding a contract if the mistake is mutual or unilateral (one-sided only), if the other party was aware or should have been aware of the mistake when the contract was made and did not correct the mistaken party. Duress is conduct, unlawful in nature, which produces such fear in a contracting party that it prevents him from exercising his true will--that is, it "forces" him to consent to an agreement against his will.

2. a) S's contention that his statement was <u>dealer's puffing</u> is wrong. A statement as to the net profit of a company during a given year is a statement of fact; that is, a statement in regard to a fact.

   b) In the given circumstances, S is probably not guilty of fraud. While S might have liability to the government for having signed a return that is incorrect, he may very well <u>not</u> be guilty of fraud insofar as B is concerned in view of the fact that he honestly and reasonably thought his statement was true. The essence of fraud is the making of a statement known to be false. (Here, then, S is probably guilty of an innocent misrepresentation only.)

Chapter 9

True-False

1. T 2. F 3. F 4. T 5. F 6. T 7. F 8. T 9. T 10. F
11. T 12. F 13. F 14. F 15. T 16. T 17. F 18. F 19. T
20. F

Multiple Choice

1. d 2. b 3. c 4. c 5. a 6. a 7. e 8. a 9. a 10. b

Short Essay

1. The following kinds of oral contracts are usually held to be enforceable, even though in general they are required to be in writing.

    a) Contracts calling for the sale of land, where the buyer has taken possession, made part payment, and has substantially improved the land.

    b) Promises to pay the debts of other persons, if the promisor has received a benefit as a result of the creditor's reliance on the promise.

    c) A promise to pay the debt of another, if the promise is conditioned upon the creditor's release of the original debtor, and if the release does occur.

2. Y's defense is not good. Since it was possible, within a year from the time the oral contract was made, that X would have ceased operating his business in Cheyenne, the contract could have been fully performed within a year from the time it was made. It does not, therefore, fall within the Statute of Frauds and Y is thus liable on his oral promise.

Chapter 10

True-False

1. F   2. F   3. F   4. T   5. F   6. T   7. T   8. T   9. T   10. F
11. T   12. T   13. F   14. F   15. F   16. T   17. F   18. T   19. T
20. T

Multiple Choice

1. a   2. d   3. b   4. e   5. d   6. b   7. b   8. c   9. b   10. b

Short Essay

1. Since the insurance company had assumed the risk and based the issuance of the policy on Stein, they are not liable. The assignment to Crashem would be a completely different risk and the law will not require that they take that risk.

2. Dazzler is entitled to the payment of the proceeds under the theory of third party donee beneficiary. Even though Dazzler gave no consideration and was not in privity or a party to the contract he is the only proper party to enforce the insurance contract.

Chapter 11

True-False

1. T   2. T   3. F   4. T   5. F   6. T   7. T   8. F   9. T   10. T
11. T   12. T   13. F   14. T   15. T   16. F   17. F   18. F   19. F
20. T   21. T   22. T   23. F

Multiple Choice

1. c   2. b   3. e   4. c   5. c   6. e   7. e   8. a   9. d   10. e
11. c   12. c

Short Essay

1. At first blush it appears subsequent illegality would be the appropriate defense, but, the illegal act would be to sell wine, not make cask's for dispersing it. Secondly, the defense of Frustration of Purpose seems to be applicable in this situation. Frustration of Purpose will not apply in this area because the purpose of only one party is involved, Roller. The adoption of a general rule that contracts are discharged whenever the purposes of one party cannot be attained would cast uncertainty on the enforceability of all contracts. Skilled would prevail.

Chapter 12

True-False

1. F 2. F 3. T 4. T 5. T 6. F 7. T 8. T 9. F 10. F
11. F 12. F 13. T 14. T 15. T 16. F 17. F

Multiple Choice

1. a 2. c 3. e 4. a 5. e 6. b 7. d 8. a 9. a 10. a

Short Essay

1. The test is whether the "predominant factor" in the transaction is a sale of goods or performance of a service. In other words, what is the essential thrust or purpose of the contract? Is the purchaser primarily contracting for a service, with goods only incidentally involved (like a paint job on a car)? Or is he primarily contracting for goods, with service only incidentally involved (like a room air conditioner plus installation).

2. George did not regularly buy or sell cars as a business, so he probably did not "deal" in them. He also did not act through an intermediary who was a merchant. Thus he would be a merchant only if "by his occupation, he held himself out as having knowledge or skill peculiar to the goods or practices involved in the transaction." As an automobile mechanic he did not hold himself out as having knowledge or skill peculiar to sales of automobiles (practices), but a good argument can be made that he did hold himself out as having knowledge or skill peculiar to automobiles themselves (the goods).

Chapter 13

True-False

1. T 2. F 3. T 4. T 5. F 6. T 7. T 8. T 9. F 10. T
11. T 12. F 13. F 14. T 15. T 16. F 17. T 18. F 19. T
20. F

Multiple Choice

1. a 2. a 3. d 4. d 5. a 6. b 7. c 8. b 9. d 10. c

Short Essay

1. Course of performance essentially refers to the conduct of the seller and buyer while performing the particular contract in dispute. Course of dealing refers to the conduct of seller and buyer in previous transactions between them. Usage of trade refers to a well-established custom in a particular trade or industry. Evidence of any of these can be used by a court for the purpose of contract interpretation--in other words, as aids to assist the court in ascertaining the intent of the parties.

2. a) Since this is a sale of goods, the UCC would apply. Under 2-207, an offeree's communication which indicates a definite intent to accept will be an acceptance even though it states terms different from or additional to those contained in the offer. By saying "Accept your order," Chamberlain obviously fulfills this requirement.
   A qualification to the above rule exists, however. Such a communication is not an acceptance if it is expressly conditional on the offeror's consent to the changes or additions. Here, there was a conditional acceptance ("subject to the following terms and conditions") but it was not "expressly conditional on the offeror's consent" to the new terms. Courts have so held under facts such as these. Therefore, there would be an acceptance.

   b) Even though Havlicek didn't expressly agree to these terms, both parties are apparently merchants, and the terms would become part of the contract unless they materially alter the contract. The courts have held that an arbitration clause does materially alter the contract, so it would not be included. Unless an exclusion of warranties is a well established custom in such a transaction (and it probably is not), it would seem to sufficiently affect the buyer's rights so as to be material.

Chapter 14

True-False

1. T 2. T 3. F 4. T 5. F 6. F 7. T 8. F 9. T 10. F
11. F 12. T 13. T 14. T 15. F 16. T 17. T 18. F 19. T
20. T

Multiple Choice

1. b 2. d 3. b 4. d 5. c 6. d 7. c 8. b 9. b 10. b

Short Essay

1. The purpose of the rule is to facilitate the free flow of trade by relieving ordinary customers from the necessity of inquiring into the status of the merchant's title.

2. X's creditors will have to prove either of two things: (1) the sale was not made for "fair consideration" and, since X was insolvent at the time, the sale was a fraud on X's creditors; or (2) X's principal business was selling goods from inventory, that the sale was of a major portion of his inventory, and that the notice requirements for bulk sales were not complied with.

Chapter 15

True-False

1. T 2. T 3. F 4. F 5. T 6. T 7. T 8. F 9. T 10. T
11. F 12. F 13. T 14. F 15. F 16. T 17. T 18. T 19. T
20. F

Multiple Choice

1. d 2. b 3. a 4. c 5. e 6. a 7. b 8. c 9. c 10. d

Short Essay

1. A seller who wishes to avoid liability on any type of express warranty obviously should not do anything that creates one. But as a practical matter this course of action may be rather difficult to carry out. The seller will have to avoid using samples or models that establish a standard of quality, avoid making statements or promises about the goods, and avoid giving any description of the goods. Any seller who is so concerned with escaping liability for product defects will probably not make many sales.

    As an alternative the seller can include in the contract an express statement that completely disavows warranty liability or that limits the type or amount of such liability. If the warranty itself has actually become part of the contract, however, an attempt to disclaim liability will usually not be effective. Sec. 2-316(1) states that a disclaimer will be disregarded if it is inconsistent with the words or conduct that created the express warranty. Suppose that an express warranty has been created by some statement of the seller, by the use of a sample, or by the seller's description of the goods. The seller's disclaimer in the contract--"these goods are sold without warranties," or other words to that effect--is almost always inconsistent with the words or conduct that created the warranty. In sum, it is extremely difficult for a seller to disclaim an express warranty, assuming that it has been created and has become part of the contract.

2. He should expressly disclaim such liability. Although the disclaimer does not have to be in writing, it of course should be. And, if in writing, the disclaimer must be conspicuous. The disclaimer must use the word "merchantability" or else it must use other very explicit words like "as is" or "with all faults."

Chapter 16

True-False

1. F 2. T 3. T 4. T 5. T 6. F 7. F 8. F 9. F 10. T
11. T 12. T 13. F 14. T 15. T 16. T 17. F 18. T 19. F
20. T

Multiple Choice

1. d 2. c 3. b 4. a 5. d 6. d 7. d 8. c 9. d 10. c
11. a 12. d

Short Essay

1. <u>First</u>, an acceptance can be revoked only if the nonconformity substantially impairs the value to the buyer of the delivery or commercial unit in question. <u>Second</u>, where the buyer knew of the nonconformity when accepting, he can revoke the acceptance only if it was made on the reasonable assumption that the nonconformity would be cured, but it has not been. Where the buyer did not know of the nonconformity when accepting, he can revoke only if the acceptance had been made because of the difficulty of discovering the nonconformity at an earlier time or because of the seller's assurances that there were no defects. <u>Third</u>, revocation of acceptance must occur within a reasonable time after the buyer discovers the basis for it and before any substantial change occurs in the condition of the goods (other than by their own defects).

2. No. Since Winston was a merchant, Bailey had no agent or place of business in Winston's area, and the goods were perishable, Winston was under a duty to try to resell them for Bailey's account.

Chapter 17

True-False

1. F 2. T 3. T 4. F 5. T 6. F 7. F 8. T 9. T 10. F
11. F 12. T 13. T 14. F 15. F 16. T 17. T 18. T 19. T
20. F 21. F 22. F 23. T 24. F 25. T

Multiple Choice

1. a 2. d 3. c 4. d 5. e 6. c 7. d 8. d 9. d 10. a

Short Essay

1. a) Checks, drafts, and trade acceptances all contain orders to pay money (as distinguished from promises to pay money).

   b) Checks, drafts, and trade acceptances differ in these respects: Checks must be drawn on banks, and must be payable on demand. Drafts (other than checks) are often drawn on persons other than banks, and, additionally, are often time instruments. Trade acceptances are almost always drawn on purchasers of goods rather than on banks, and--like other drafts--are usually time instruments. Additionally, trade acceptances always require an acceptance by the drawee, whereas checks are never "accepted" in the strict sense of the term.

2. Based on the decision of the Darden case, the estate's claim that C is not an accommodation party is incorrect. C is an accommodation maker for the reason that such a party is defined as anyone "who signs an instrument for the purpose of lending his credit to another party to the instrument." The fact that C may possibly have gained a benefit by signing the note is immaterial.

Chapter 18

True-False

1. T   2. T   3. T   4. F   5. F   6. F   7. T   8. T   9. F   10. T
11. T 12. T 13. T 14. F 15. T 16. T 17. T 18. T 19. T
20. F 21. F 22. F 23. T 24. T 25. F

Multiple Choice

1. e   2. e   3. a   4. a   5. a   6. b   7. c   8. a   9. e   10. c

Short Essay

1. There are no circumstances in which an instrument can be subject to another agreement and still be negotiable. The UCC (Sec. 3-105) provides, in part, that "a promise or order is <u>not unconditional</u>" if it states that it is "subject to or governed by" any other agreement.

2. The note is nonnegotiable because a) it is not payable to the order of P; b) it is not payable at a definite time; and c) it is payable out of a fund, and therefore conditional.

Chapter 19

True-False

1. T 2. T 3. F 4. F 5. T 6. F 7. T 8. F 9. T 10. F
11. F 12. T 13. T 14. T 15. F 16. F 17. F 18. F 19. T
20. T 21. T 22. T 23. F 24. F 25. T

Multiple Choice

1. b 2. d 3. b 4. e 5. d 6. d 7. a 8. a 9. c 10. b
11. c 12. b

Short Essay

1. A <u>blank indorsement</u> transfers title to the indorsee, and, additionally, it imposes both conditional and warranty liability on the indorser. It also converts the instrument into a bearer instrument. The same is true of a <u>special indorsement</u>, except that the instrument remains an order instrument. A <u>qualified indorsement</u> transfers title to the indorsee, and, like the other indorsements, imposes warranty liability on the indorser. Unlike the other indorsements, however, it does not impose conditional liability on the indorsers. A <u>restrictive indorsement</u> also transfers title in most cases, and also, in most cases, imposes warranty and conditional liability upon the indorser. However, unlike the other indorsements, most restrictive indorsements reserve certain rights to the indorser if the terms of the indorsement are disregarded by subsequent parties, and if this causes a loss to the indorser.

2. a) The chances of P recovering from the Y Bank, the depositary bank, are good. (See the <u>Quantum</u> case in book.) The Y Bank, the restrictive indorsee, had the duty to do only one thing with the proceeds of the check--deposit them in the Wheel and Deal Company's account. It is thus liable to the indorser for its failure to live up to this duty.

   b) P cannot hold the X Bank, the drawee, liable. The UCC (Sec. 3-206(2)) permits a payor bank which is not the depositary bank to <u>disregard any restrictive</u> indorsement (except that of the payor bank's immediate transferor). In this case the exception is not applicable, since the restrictive indorsement was made by the first holder of the instrument, rather than by the bank that transferred the check to the X Bank.

Chapter 20

True-False

1. T 2. T 3. F 4. F 5. T 6. T 7. F 8. T 9. F 10. T
11. F 12. T 13. F 14. T 15. F 16. T 17. T 18. T 19. T

Multiple Choice

1. e 2. a 3. b 4. a 5. c 6. c 7. a 8. b 9. d 10. c
11. e 12. c

Short Essay

1. a) An ordinary holder of an instrument may enforce payment of it if the maker (or drawer) has no defense against the instrument.

   b) An HDC may enforce payment against the maker (or drawer) as long as the defense that exists is "personal" only. It is only where the defense is "real" that the HDC is unable to get a judgment.

2. On the basis of the given facts only, it is probable that B Bank did take the check in good faith. The testimony of D's witnesses indicate that the B Bank may have clearly been guilty of negligence in accepting the check, but that proof--alone--is not proof of bad faith. From the facts it appears that the B Bank took the check honestly--particularly since there is no evidence that the B Bank had knowledge that the P Co. had a past record of failing to live up to its contracts--and thus probably took it in good faith.

Chapter 21

True-False

1. T   2. T   3. T   4. F   5. F   6. T   7. F   8. T   9. T   10. T
11. T   12. T   13. F   14. F   15. T   16. T   17. T   18. F   19. F
20. T

Multiple Choice

1. a   2. e   3. b   4. d   5. c   6. c   7. b   8. a

Short Essay

1. Some of the most common personal defenses are breach of contract on the part of the payee; other types of failure of consideration; unauthorized completion; fraud in the inducement; and some types of illegality. Some of the most common real defenses are forgery, material alteration (to the extent of the alteration), fraud in the execution, illegality (if of such degree that entire contract is void), and discharge in bankruptcy.

2. The XYZ Co.'s defense of fraud in the inducement is clearly not good. That defense is only a personal defense, which would not be assertable against an HDC such as Sooper Dooper. And, on the basis of Lamson v. Commercial Credit Corp., the XYZ Co.'s defense of "payment" would not be good, either. If Friendly Bob, the indorser, were being sued on his indorsement, he would have the defense of "prior payment" available, since his account was charged by the B Bank. But that defense is Friendly Bob's only, and hence the XYZ Co., the defendant, can not take advantage of the defense. Thus the XYZ Co. is liable to Sooper Dooper.

Chapter 22

True-False

1. T   2. T   3. T   4. T   5. F   6. T   7. T   8. F   9. F   10. T
11. F   12. F   13. F   14. F   15. F   16. T   17. T   18. T   19. T
20. F

Multiple Choice

1. d   2. a   3. c   4. d   5. b   6. a   7. d   8. a   9. b   10. a

Short Essay

1. An unqualified indorser warrants that (1) he has good title to the instrument; (2) all signatures are genuine or authorized; (3) there is no material alteration; (4) no defense of any party is good against him; and (5) he has no knowledge of any insolvency proceeding against the maker or acceptor (or against the drawer of an unaccepted instrument).

2. a) Because the instrument was presented late (i.e., more than 30 days after issue), and because the drawee bank failed after that time but before the actual presentment, D (drawer) need only give a written assignment of funds--in the amount of the check--to the Y Company. The Y Company may then seek to enforce this assignment against the Drawee Bank. (E.g., if the bank pays out 60¢ on the dollar, the Y Company will receive 60% of the amount of the check only.) Thus D is partially discharged of liability--i.e., he is discharged to the extent of 40% of the check. (Sec. 3-502(1)(b))

   b) The first indorser, P, is entirely freed of conditional liability since the Y Company did not present the check within 7 days of his indorsement. The second indorser, the X Company, is presumably fully liable since the Y Company did present the check within 7 days of its indorsement. (NOTE: In the opinion of the authors, the second indorser can not avail itself of the partial discharge--or possible discharge--of the drawer, based on Sec. 3-606(1)(a).)

Chapter 23

True-False

1. T 2. F 3. T 4. F 5. F 6. F 7. F 8. T 9. F 10. T
11. T 12. T 13. F 14. F 15. F 16. T 17. F 18. T

Multiple Choice

1. e 2. b 3. b 4. e 5. c 6. d 7. a 8. d 9. c 10. d

Short Essay

1. The rules that govern the relationship between the drawer of a check and the drawee bank arise from Article 3 of the HCC: from rules applicable to creditors and debtors; from rules based on the principal-agency relationship, and from Article 4 of the UCC.

2. The judge's ruling is incorrect. When a bank disobeys a stop payment order it is liable to the drawer only for the loss he suffers as a result. In this case, since D's defense against P (his reason for stopping payment) was merely a personal defense, the Latex Company--if an HDC--was entitled to payment from D ultimately in any event. In other words, even if the bank had obeyed the stop payment order, the Latex Company would have been able to recover the full amount of the check from D in a subsequent suit. Hence the bank's wrongful act did not cause a loss to D.

Chapter 24

True-False

1. T 2. T 3. T 4. F 5. T 6. F 7. F 8. T 9. T 10. F
11. F 12. T 13. T 14. T 15. F 16. F 17. T 18. T 19. T
20. F 21. F 22. T

Multiple Choice

1. a 2. a 3. d 4. b 5. e 6. a 7. d 8. d

Short Essay

1. Prior to the UCC, the most common security devices were the conditional sale, chattel mortgage, pledge, and trust receipt.

2. Despite the fact that the bank did not file a financing statement or other notice in regard to its second loan to M, its interest in the new piece of machinery in M's plant <u>has priority over</u> X's interest. This is so because of the after-acquired <u>property clause</u> and the "future advances" clause that were contained in the first agreement with the bank. As a result of the coupling of these two clauses, the interest acquired by the bank in the machinery as a result of its second loan <u>dates back to the time of the perfection of its first interest</u>. It is therefore fully protected by virtue of the first agreement, and hence it is immaterial that no filing of its second security agreement was ever made.

Chapter 25

True-False

1. T 2. T 3. F 4. T 5. T 6. T 7. F 8. F 9. F 10. F
11. T 12. F 13. T 14. F 15. T 16. F 17. F 18. F 19. T 20. F

Multiple Choice

1. d 2. b 3. e 4. a 5. a 6. e 7. d 8. a 9. c 10. b

Short Essay

1. One of the objects of bankruptcy is to discharge the bankrupt's debts fairly among all unsecured creditors, and a preference enables one creditor to receive a greater percentage of his claim than other creditors.

2. Walter may or may not be correct. Even though Walter owes over $1,000 and the petition was signed by three creditors having claims totaling more than $500, Walter can be petitioned into involuntary bankruptcy only if he had committed an act of bankruptcy. The payment to Williams, although occurring within four months of the petition, was not a preference because Williams neither knew nor had reason to know of Walter's insolvency. The letters to the other two creditors admitted an inability to pay debts but did not admit a willingness to be declared a bankrupt, so they would not be acts of bankruptcy. The only way that an act of bankruptcy can be shown is for the petitioning creditors to prove that Walter intended to defraud his creditors in making the payment to Williams (that is, that it was a fraudulent conveyance). The facts presented are insufficient to permit a determination as to such intent.

Chapter 26

True-False

1. F 2. T 3. F 4. T 5. T 6. F 7. T 8. T 9. F 10. T
11. T 12. T 13. T 14. T 15. F 16. F 17. T 18. F 19. T
20. F

Multiple Choice

1. b 2. b 3. d 4. f 5. b 6. a 7. d 8. a

Short Essay

1. The reason is that it is the principal's contract, not the agent's. If the agent acts with authority, it is the same as if the principal had personally dealt with the third party. The agent is only a conduit through which the principal transacts business.

2. By competing with the principal (Crystal) without its consent, Sam breached his duty of loyalty. He forfeits the right to be compensated for his services, so he cannot get the $2,000 from Crystal. He also can be compelled to turn over his $5,000 profit to Crystal and is responsible to Crystal for any damages it suffered as a result of his actions.

Chapter 27

True-False

1. T   2. T   3. F   4. F   5. F   6. T   7. T   8. F   9. F   10. F
11. T   12. T   13. T   14. T   15. F   16. F   17. F   18. F   19. F
20. F

Multiple Choice

1. c   2. b   3. c   4. b   5. d   6. b   7. d   8. d   9. e   10. d
11. e   12. a

Short Essay

1. Yes. A confidential relationship exists between every principal and agent, which requires utmost good faith of the agent as to the business affairs of the principal that are within the scope of the employment. When an agent places himself in a position where his personal interests conflict with his principal, he breaches his duty of loyalty. If his breach results in damages to the principal, the agent is required to account for his secret profits to the principal.

Chapter 28

True-False

1. T 2. T 3. F 4. F 5. T 6. T 7. T 8. F 9. T 10. F
11. F 12. T 13. F 14. F 15. T 16. T 17. T 18. F 19. F
20. F

Multiple Choice

1. c 2. d 3. d 4. b 5. c 6. e 7. e 8. b

Short Essay

1. Few lenders will allow their capital to be used in a business without retaining a certain amount of control over how it is used. Thus a creditor may impose various conditions in the loan agreement and will almost certainly acquire a lien on business assets that will limit or exhaust the credit of the enterprise.

2. It would be classified as a corporation for federal income tax purposes because it has a majority (3 out of 4) of the key corporate characteristics: continuity of life, centralization of management, and free transferability of interests. (It does not have the limited liability characteristic.)

Chapter 29

True-False

1. F 2. T 3. T 4. F 5. T 6. T 7. T 8. F 9. F 10. F
11. T 12. F 13. F 14. F 15. T 16. F 17. F 18. T 19. T
20. T

Multiple Choice

1. d 2. c 3. c 4. d 5. a 6. b 7. b 8. c 9. b 10. d
11. e 12. d

Short Essay

1. The UPA sets forth the basic requirements an association must meet to be a partnership, but it does not require any particular formalities for creation of a partnership. And while the UPA governs many aspects of the operation of a partnership, it is intended primarily to fill in the gaps of the partnership agreement. Many UPA rules are applicable only if the partners do not agree otherwise--the rules that can not be altered by the partners are mainly those aimed at protecting outsiders.

2. a) Partnership accounting records: Do they show the truck as a company asset? Do they show that partnership funds have been used to improve, repair, or maintain the truck? (Not very persuasive, though, because this might just indicate payment by partnership for use of truck.) Do they show that property taxes on the truck were paid by the partnership? (May not be any more persuasive than repair, etc.)
   b) Type of use: Did partners allow Vance to use truck for any personal reasons? (This might indicate that truck is still Vance's.)
   c) Income: Did truck generate any income apart from partnership business (such as rental or nonproduce hauling)? If so, who received the income?

Chapter 30

True-False

1. F 2. F 3. F 4. T 5. T 6. F 7. T 8. T 9. F 10. F
11. F 12. F 13. T 14. T 15. F 16. F 17. T 18. T 19. T
20. T

Multiple Choice

1. a 2. c 3. a 4. b 5. d 6. d 7. a 8. c 9. b 10. d

Short Essay

1. His interest in the partnership is his proportionate share of business profits and surplus. This can be assigned to a nonpartner or reached by his personal creditors. His only right in partnership property is the equal right with other partners to possess it for partnership purposes. This right cannot be assigned or reached by his personal creditors.

2. Regardless of the amount of his capital contribution, Thompson would be entitled to only one-third of the profits ($13,333.33), unless agreed otherwise. Thompson is entitled to no compensation for the extra hours he worked, unless the other partners so agreed. He is entitled to receive his $10,000 capital contribution, but he gets interest on that amount only since June 1, the agreed date for repayment. Thompson is entitled to repayment of the $5,000 loan plus interest from the date of the loan (not just from the agreed date for repayment).

Chapter 31

True-False

1. T   2. T   3. T   4. F   5. T   6. F   7. T   8. T   9. T   10. F
11. F   12. T   13. T   14. F   15. F   16. F   17. T   18. T   19. F
20. T   21. T   22. T   23. T   24. T

Multiple Choice

1. d   2. c   3. d   4. d   5. a   6. b   7. e   8. a   9. c   10. a

Short Essay

1. A person's mental competency is inherently subject to doubt and dispute. Even if a partner has been officially declared insane in a separate sanity hearing, there can be a dispute as to whether he is still insane or how long he might remain in such a condition.

2. Bob's creditor is only partially correct. After a partner's personal assets are exhausted, the only thing relating to the partnership that the creditor can reach is the partner's <u>interest in the partnership</u>. Assuming no agreement to the contrary, Bob's interest would be an equal share--$6,000. Thus, the creditor can claim $6,000 of the $18,000. The remaining $4,000 of the creditor's claim continues as an unpaid judgment against Bob.

Chapter 32

True-False

1. T   2. T   3. F   4. T   5. F   6. F   7. T   8. T   9. F   10. F
11. T   12. F   13. T   14. F   15. F   16. T   17. F   18. F   19. F
20. F   21. T   22. T

Multiple Choice

1. c   2. b   3. a   4. c   5. a   6. c   7. e   8. d   9. a   10. b

Short Essay

1. The focus of the inquiry is whether those persons to whom the securities were offered were in such a position as to have access to the same kind of information that would be disclosed by registration and therefore do not need the protection given by registration.

2. The court probably will do so. First, an initial working capital of $990 would hardly be deemed by a reasonable person to be sufficient to meet the reasonably expectable obligations of a corporation engaged in the commercial construction business, where buildings costing hundreds of thousands (or several million, even) of dollars are commonplace. The formation of Centron has the appearance of a scheme the sole purpose of which is to evade legitimate obligations. Second, the brothers themselves largely ignored the separateness of the corporation's identity from their own. These two factors together (inadequate working capital initially and confusion of corporate identity) are sufficient to justify piercing the corporate veil and holding the brothers personally liable.

Chapter 33

True-False

1. T 2. F 3. F 4. T 5. T 6. T 7. F 8. T 9. F 10. T
11. T 12. F 13. F 14. T 15. T 16. T 17. F 18. T 19. F
20. T 21. F 22. T 23. F 24. F 25. F

Multiple Choice

1. a 2. c 3. c 4. b 5. d 6. a 7. e 8. c 9. b 10. c
11. d 12. c

Short Essay

1. There are two reasons for this. First, directors' powers are conferred by the <u>state</u> rather than by the shareholders. Second, directors do not have <u>individual</u> power to bind the corporation, as agents do; they can only act <u>as a body</u>.

2. Carlson cannot elect a majority, but using cumulative voting he can elect two directors. There will be 500,000 total votes (100,000 shares X 5 directors to be elected). Carlson will have 200,000 votes (40,000 shares X 5). If he casts 100,000 votes each for two of his candidates, they will be elected. The owner(s) of the other 60,000 shares will have 300,000 votes and will be able to elect three directors.

Chapter 34

True-False

1. F 2. T 3. F 4. T 5. T 6. F 7. F 8. T 9. F 10. T
11. F 12. T 13. T 14. F 15. F 16. F 17. T 18. F 19. T
20. F 21. F 22. F 23. F 24. F

Multiple Choice

1. c 2. d 3. e 4. d 5. b 6. d 7. e 8. b 9. d 10. c
11. e 12. b

Short Essay

1. Since a director or other manager is in a fiduciary relationship with the corporation, he should not be allowed to consider his own interests above those of the corporation. Also, since a corporation can act only through flesh and blood individuals, the corporation could not be profitable if the individuals in charge of the corporation personally exploit all business opportunities.

2. The claim that preemptive rights exist is **not** correct. Courts have not recognized preemptive rights in the case of new stock issues for a noncash consideration. Preemptive rights would thus not apply to a "stock swap" such as this.

Chapter 35

True-False

1. T 2. F 3. T 4. T 5. T 6. F 7. T 8. T 9. T 10. F
11. F 12. T 13. T 14. F 15. F 16. T 17. T 18. T 19. T
20. F

Multiple Choice

1. d 2. a 3. c 4. d 5. b 6. b 7. c 8. d 9. b 10. d

Short Essay

1. A sale of control is the sale by one or more shareholders of a controlling interest in the corporation at a price above the market value of the shares. According to some courts, this is a breach of the fiduciary duty owed by controlling shareholders to minority shareholders, because the power to control the corporation is a corporate asset and rightfully belongs to the corporation rather than to those who possess the power at a given time. In a majority of states, however, the courts do not regard a sale of control as a breach of duty by controlling shareholders unless the sale is made to corporate looters or the sale is accomplished by sale of a directorship or office.

2. Jones has lost the appraisal right by his inaction. State laws generally require a dissenting shareholder to formally object before or at the meeting where the merger is voted on and demand payment within a relatively short time (10 days in the Model Act) after the merger is approved.

Chapter 36

True-False

1. T 2. T 3. F 4. T 5. F 6. F 7. T 8. F 9. T 10. T
11. F 12. F 13. T 14. T 15. T 16. T 17. F 18. T 19. T
20. T 22. F 23. F 24. F 25. T

Multiple Choice

1. d 2. e 3. b 4. d 5. c 6. b 7. d 8. c 9. d 10. a
11. d 12. c

Short Essay

1. The closing or settlement is the procedure for actual transfer of ownership from seller to buyer. It may take the form of a meeting attended by the seller and buyer as well as other interested parties such as their attorneys, the broker, and a representative of the mortgagee. At the meeting the seller signs and delivers to the buyer a deed that transfers the ownership; and the buyer or the mortgagee pays the purchase price. It is also common for the mortgage to be executed at the closing and for other incidental financial matters to be settled (such as apportionment of prepaid taxes and insurance).

   The closing may occur in a different manner, however, by the use of an escrow agent. This is a disinterested third party to whom the seller has delivered the deed and to whom the buyer has made payment. This party's instructions generally are to close the deal by delivering the deed to the buyer and the payment to the seller on receipt of the required evidence of good title.

2. If Colby had no knowledge of the earlier sale to Williams, Colby qualifies as a BFP (good faith purchaser for value). The deed from Thompson to Williams, being unrecorded, is void with regard to Colby (a later BFP). Therefore, Williams's ownership is subject to Colby's mortgage. In most states, the BFP does not have to record <u>his</u> <u>own</u> deed in order to prevail over a prior unrecorded deed.

Chapter 37

True-False

1. F   2. F   3. T   4. T   5. F   6. T   7. F   8. F   9. T   10. T
11. T   12. F   13. T   14. T   15. T   16. F   17. F   18. T   19. T
20. F

Multiple Choice

1. b   2. a   3. a   4. b   5. d   6. c   7. b   8. d   9. a   10. c

Short Essay

1. The types of personal property that can be given by constructive delivery are (a) items that are either too large or too distantly located to be physically delivered as a practical matter and (b) intangible property.

2. There was not a valid gift to Sandra. Constructive delivery, as was attempted here, is a sufficient form of delivery only when actual physical delivery of the item being given is impractical or inconvenient. This does not seem to be the case here--there appears to be no good reason why Carla did not deliver the stones themselves. Furthermore, Carla retained control over the stones. Even if she gave away the only key, she still had a substantial degree of control over them.

Chapter 38

True-False

1. T 2. F 3. F 4. F 5. F 6. F 7. T 8. F 9. T 10. T
11. T 12. F 13. T 14. T 15. F 16. F 17. T 18. T 19. F
20. T

Multiple Choice

1. d 2. e 3. e 4. d 5. c 6. c 7. e 8. d 9. b 10. d

Short Essay

1. An intestate's estate is divided among the lineal heirs. Since X is the only living lineal, or descending heir, X will receive the entire estate.

2. In the event that X predeceased A, there is now no descending lineal heir, and, by the law of intestate succession, the ascendency application will be made. The estate would be divided as follows:
Y - First Cousin, even though adopted, as adoptive children may inherit by and through the adoptive parent.
Z - First Cousin, even though illegitimate, she is the daughter of A's aunt and is entitled to inherit through her mother.
First Cousin, even though of the half-blood, takes equally with cousins of the whole blood.
First Cousin - The three living children of the half-brother (deceased) are entitled to share equally.
Therefore, the estate would be divided equally six ways among the six cousins.

Chapter 39

True-False

1. T   2. T   3. F   4. F   5. F   6. F   7. T   8. T   9. T   10. F
11. T   12. F   13. T   14. T   15. F   16. F   17. T   18. T   19. F
20. T

Multiple Choice

1. a   2. b   3. b   4. e   5. f   6. e   7. c   8. b   9. c

Short Essay

1. Oftentimes the bailor <u>cannot</u> find out exactly what caused the loss or damage. The bailee, having been in possession of the property at the time of the loss or damage, is much more likely to know and be able to explain what really happened. Therefore, it makes more sense to place the burden of explanation on him.

2. Thompson is not correct. It is true that a common carrier is absolutely liable for loss of or damage to the bailed property, regardless of any proof of negligence. But there are exceptions to this liability. One of these exceptions applies to this case: a common carrier is not liable for loss or damage if it was the result of the <u>inherent nature of the goods themselves</u>.